Father Mississippi

THIS OLD REFUGEE, HELPLESS AND ALONE, SEEMS A SYMBOLIC FIGURE
TYPIFYING THE MISERY OF THOUSANDS WHO LIVE BEHIND
THE LEVEES IN THE LOWER MISSISSIPPI VALLEY

Father Mississippi

by

L y l e   S a x o n

PELICAN PUBLISHING COMPANY
Gretna 2006

The word "Pelican" and the depiction of a pelican are
trademarks of Pelican Publishing Company, Inc., and
are registered in the U.S. Patent and Trademark Office.

Printed in the United States of America
Published by Pelican Publishing Company, Inc.
1000 Burmaster Street, Gretna, Louisiana 70053

INTRODUCTION

This book is not a history of the Mississippi River in the strict sense of the word, although I have outlined the discovery, the exploration, and the settlement of the valley. A great many learned men have written weighty tomes dealing with the various phases of the Mississippi, but this volume is like a scrap-book in which I have collected men's thoughts, my own thoughts, and the thoughts and experiences of other men. These incidents seem to me informative, or amusing, or terrible, or tragic, or fantastic; but they are all a part of the living pageant which moved down the great river through the changing years.

Here you will find jottings from old diaries written by men and women who came down the river a century or more ago. In every instance where it was possible I have let these men and women speak for themselves. So here you will meet La Salle, Father Hennepin, Henri de Tonty, and the rest, and you will read their narratives, uncolored by comments of mine; you will read the hitherto unpublished memoir of a woman pioneer who came down the river in 1810; you will read the journal of a flatboatman of 1817; you will meet heroes and gamblers, heroines and murderesses —men and women who lived beside the Mississippi and whose adventures gave color to the times in which they lived.

Only twice do I speak directly to you: in the beginning and in the end of this volume. At first, I try to let you see into the life of a Louisiana plantation as I remembered it; at the end, because I wanted to try to picture for you the horror of the floods of 1927.

Many people have given me assistance. The publications of the Louisiana, Mississippi, and Kentucky historical societies have been of great help; and I wish particularly to thank Mr. Henry P. Dart, editor of the Louisiana Historical Society Quarterly, for permission to use the diary of J. G. Flugels, and the records of the case of Molly Glass, the murderess. Other references will be found in the bibliography at the end of the volume.

I wish to thank Mrs. Cammie Garrett Henry of Melrose plantation for the use of her library and for permission to read scrap-books pertaining to the Mississippi which she has been compiling for thirty years. I wish to thank Miss Gwen Bristow of the staff of "The New Orleans Times-Picayune" for her work in compiling data from current newspapers and magazines. And I am most grateful to Miss Mercedes Garig of the Louisiana State University for suggestions and assistance in collecting source material.

But, perhaps most of all, I want to thank members of the United States Coast Guard Service, officers and sailors alike, who took me with them into the flooded areas in May and June, 1927.

The three episodes, "Down on the Levee," "Acadians in the Flood," and "And the Waters Receded," have been printed in "The Century Magazine," and I wish to thank the editor of "The Century" for permission to reprint them here.

L. S.

CONTENTS

Part One

PLANTATION

Part Two

IN THE BEGINNING

Part Three

"I HEAR THE TREAD OF THE PIONEERS"

ILLUSTRATIONS

This old refugee, helpless and alone, seems a symbolic figure typifying the misery of thousands who live behind the levees in the Lower Mississippi Valley . .

Frontispiece

Part One

PLANTATION

And a river went out of Eden to water the garden; and from thence it was parted, and became into four heads.

—Genesis, II, 10

A leaf for hand in hand;
You natural persons old and young!
You on the Mississippi and on all the branches and bayous
of the Mississippi!
You friendly boatmen and mechanics! you
roughs!
You twain! and all processions moving along
the streets!
I wish to infuse myself among you till I see it common for
you to walk hand in hand.

—Walt Whitman

Oh, wuzn't dat a awful flood,
De wust yo' evah see?
It drowned de churches an' buildin's,
But, thank Gawd, it spared yo' an' me!

—Negro Spiritual

Chapter I

A CHILD LOOKS AT THE RIVER

OUTSIDE the plantation-house the world is saturate with moonlight. The trees of the long avenue are fountains, dripping streamers of Spanish moss into the dark pools formed by their shadows. Down the walk from the white-columned house comes a man leading a small boy by the hand. Slowly they go through the pale night—figures in a dream.

The man says: "I am going to show you something that you will never forget as long as you live."

"Never forget as long as you live . . . as long as you live. . . ." It is like a song. The boy says it to himself, over and over—"You'll never forget as long as you live . . . never forget . . ."

"Never forget what, sir?"

The man does not answer. The two go slowly down the avenue, the boy making two steps to the man's stride. They pass through moonlight into shadow, back into moonlight again. Fireflies flicker like falling stars. The man opens a gate and they pass through. They cross a dusty road. Before them rises a high, grass-grown wall of earth, very steep—the levee. They climb up. An old white cow with a tinkly bell moves along the slope, munching the grass. . . . "Something you'll never forget as long as you live. . . ." What can it be? For to the boy this is all familiar ground.

As they go up, the boy counts his steps: fifty-one, fifty-two, fifty-three . . . a few more steps and he will be able

3

to look over the levee-top. He knows what he will see—
he has seen it many times before: a long downward slope,
grass-grown like the one they have climbed, then a wide
sand-bar with a fringe of willow-trees, and beyond it, far
off, the silver river rushing past in the moonlight.

But as they reach the top, he draws in his breath in
astonishment. At his very feet stretches a great sea! There
is no familiar downward slope, there is no sand-bar, there
is no fringe of willows. The water has covered them all.
The tops of black trees are visible upon the opposite shore.
All other landmarks are gone.

The boy cannot speak. He gasps instead. The man lifts
him in strong arms and swings the child to his shoulder.

Out there in the vast stretch of water a steamboat is
nosing its way upstream. *Puff-puff!* A pause. *Puff-puff!*
. . . *Puff-puff!* Pause. *Puff-puff!* The red and green lights
on the twin smokestacks are bright against the sky; a plume
of black smoke trails out behind the boat. There are lights
in the cabin. Some one is lighting a torch forward. At first
only a spark, then a yellow flare, which is reflected in the
moving water. In the rushing water there are floating objects: trees with branches reaching up into the air, like
arms of drowning men.

The steamboat moves forward under full steam, but it
makes slow progress against the roaring current. As the
man and the boy stand watching the river and the boat, a
streak of fire mounts the sky. From the landing at the
plantation opposite, a mile away, a rocket has been sent up.
It curves its fiery course upward, bursts into a shower of
yellow and blue stars, fades, and vanishes. The folks over
there are signaling the steamboat. Slowly the boat turns her
nose about and makes her panting way toward the landing.
A puff of white steam rises, disappears. The steam has gone

AN AVENUE OF LIVE-OAK TREES

Photo by Earl Norman, Natchez

completely before the boy hears the whistle sound, deep and mellow.

The man turns away from the river and gazes back over the land: "Look!"

From the levee-top the man and the boy gaze downward. There, a quarter of a mile away, at the end of the avenue of moss-draped trees, stands the plantation-house bathed in moonlight. There are lights in the windows, and from the open door a stream of warm lamplight floods the gallery and pours out into the flower garden. The house, its lofty roof level with their feet, is below them; the fields of sugar-cane, billowing in the moonlight, are below them. But on the other side of the levee the river laps at their feet.

Without understanding why, the boy is afraid. His arm tightens around the neck of the man. He tries to ask a question: "Where is my river?" He means the river that he remembers, the peaceful river of other times, flowing between the willows. The man does not understand: "Why, here is the river. We're standing at the very edge of it."

No, this can never be the same river. It must be another one. "What has happened to my river?" the boy asks.

The man laughs, but there is little merriment in his laugh: "This is the same river that is always here—old Father Mississippi!"

Father Mississippi!

Father Mississippi . . . You'll never forget as long as you live . . . as long as you live. . . .

Chapter II

PLANTATION LIFE—AND A WEDDING

I REMEMBER the plantation. . . . Yea, Lord! Oh, how
well do I remember the plantation. I lived there in summer,
but in winter I had to go to school in town. Not that I liked
school less, but I loved the plantation more. It was like
heaven, I thought, a perfect place.

I would linger on, well into the month of September,
dreading the return to school, until at last came the stern
summons that I could evade no longer. Then there were
tears, reproaches; but finally I became reconciled, told every
one a sad farewell, and was bundled aboard the mail-boat.

No place on this planet could be half as fascinating as the
plantation that I remember so well. It was a glamorous
place, and even now, looking back across the years, I cannot
see it stripped of its romantic quality. The house was large,
white, and cool-looking. There were faded green window-
blinds. A wide gallery stretched across the front of the
building. Big red brick chimneys rose at the end of the
gables. Vines grew riotously over everything. The house
was set in a flower garden, and beyond the white palings
of the fence there was a six-acre "front yard" in which
sheep were kept, in order that the grass might always be
smooth and short. On each side of the yard the sugar-cane
fields stretched out to infinity. An avenue of pecan-trees led
from the flower garden a quarter of a mile to the front
gate. Before the gate was the road, then the levee, and beyond—the Mississippi River.

6

In ordinary times the levee presented a high green wall, a man-made mountain upon which cows and horses grazed. But in the spring, when the high water came, the river stood at the very top of the embankment, and from the front gallery of the plantation-house we could see the Mississippi River steamboats passing by, high in the air.

The river brought everything to us, and took everything away. All our supplies for the house came from the steamboats; and in the fall the cotton and sugar were loaded aboard and carried to New Orleans. The river was our one means of transportation—except for horses and carriages, of course—and the river and things pertaining to it furnished the topic for nearly all of our conversation.

Like nearly all Louisiana country houses, the plantation-house was large and rambling. An "L" extended behind the main building, and the brick kitchen was some distance from the house, perhaps the distance of half a city square. This was a precautionary measure, for all plantation people lived in dread of fire. Fire was the greatest of all calamities. Children were forbidden to touch matches or lighted lamps.

To the children the kitchen was a place of great charm, for here the negroes held full sway; and it was here that we received many a sweet-cake or a "taste" of icing, or cuite—sugar-house candy—between meals.

"Aunt" Rhody was the cook. She was very old-fashioned, very fat, very black. She preferred cooking in an open fire-place, and surely no food ever tasted half so good as that which came from the old brick kitchen. The fireplace was set up in the north wall and was fully six feet wide. The hearth was built up two feet or more from the brick floor, and upon the hearth the fire burned, roaring up the chimney; or sometimes a bed of embers glowed in the twilight. The big cook-stove stood at one side of the chimney, and it was upon the stove that soup or gumbo was made; and at the back of the stove there simmered a large iron pot of "dog dinner." This phrase "dog dinner" is one of my earliest recollections, for there were many hunting dogs on the plantation, and the "dinner" was for them, cooked especially every day: cornbread, meat, vegetables, cooked together and "served" to the dogs in individual tin plates at three o'clock every afternoon. The dogs were pointers and setters, beautiful animals, very gentle with children. Some of the dogs had pedigrees much longer than ours, I remember; and there was one strain that had been in Louisiana ever since the first of our family had come pioneering into the State in 1740. I cannot vouch for the truth of this dog pedigree, but so the legend went—and now there is no one alive to tell me whether this was true or merely a story told to children.

At any rate, there was great respect for fine dogs, and a real camaraderie existed between the dogs and the children. We knew all about the puppies: the father, the mother, the grandmother, and so on. We carried it further and spoke of the "aunts" and "uncles" of the dogs. And, of course, they were all cousins!

This love for dogs, by the way, is very characteristic of plantation people. There was one family—our neighbors in the country—that had lived in the same old red brick house since 1808, and had never, in all those years, had a rug or carpet on the floor in any of the rooms; for the old planter, the grandfather of the old folks of my day, had wanted his hunting dogs in the house, and they slept in a semicircle around the open fireplace in winter—and, since dogs and carpets did not agree, they had no carpets.

So, we all had dogs, and all the dogs had "dog dinners." The phrase was a household joke with us; anything cluttered up, or mixed up generally, was spoken of as "dog dinners." A problem in long-division, for example, that wandered around and did not "come out" was called by this term; or a handbag carelessly packed—anything.

Aunt Rhody prepared the dinner for the dogs, as she prepared dinner for the white folks, with efficiency and despatch, and woe to any of the children who "meddled" with the pots simmering on the back of the stove! We were forbidden the kitchen—sometimes put out, squalling; but it was our own private feud and never came to the ears of the older people. Negroes are wonderfully kind in their treatment of children, I think; for certain it is, had Aunt Rhody complained, the children's kitchen-paradise would have been closed to them forever. But Aunt Rhody never carried tales, although she had threatened to from time to time.

It seems to me I can hear yet: "What's in that pot, please, Aunt Rhody?" And her invariable reply, "Larows to catch meddlers!" The phrase has puzzled me all my life; and I've never known a negro who could, or would, explain it. "Dat's what I heah de ole folks say," they reply when you question them. It is possible that they mean "Lay-lows to catch meddlers," for a "lay-low" is a ghost or wicked spirit that lurks in graveyards; but I am not sure.

Although the impressions from childhood are but broken and disconnected pictures, it seems to me that to this day I can see and hear and even smell the plantation. There was the wide hall through the center of the house, for example— a long, bare expanse of shining floor, with a few rocking chairs and small tables making islands here and there. The stairs went up at one side. Doors opened into the parlor, the "spare room," and two bedrooms opposite. The hall ended at the dining-room at the back of the house, double doors leading in; and opposite in the dining-room more double doors leading to the back gallery. Everything was left open, in order that the air might circulate freely; and always a cool breeze blew through the hall, tinkling the crystals in the chandelier. Fully twenty feet wide that hall must have been, and nearly twice as long. Between the parlor door and the door which led into the spare room stood a mammoth mahogany sofa, very deep and soft, as the black haircloth had worn out long since and it was covered with some old hand-woven cloth. The sofa sagged in places, and the springs were broken, but it was the favorite place to sit, or to lie, reading some of the big illustrated books that were in the plantation library. My pleasure in the sofa, however, was spoiled entirely by a chance remark that I heard once—that many of the members of the family had been "laid out" on it after death. My quick fancy did the rest; I saw them all—cold, pale women, covered with white veils; tall, dark men with drooping black mustaches—lying there, crossed hands holding white cape jasmine flowers!

Above the sofa hung a portrait of a slender young woman with dark ringlets, some long-departed great-aunt. I would dream of her lying dead on the sofa—and so real became this dream that I would wake, crying out in the night. And the strange part of it all was this: I could never bring myself to confide my fears to any one. Night after night I would dream of her, until the sofa became a thing of horror. At twilight I would run through the hall toward the lighted dining-room, afraid to turn my head for fear that she would be lying there, covered with white flowers.

On the stair landing there was another portrait that I disliked, but it held none of the fear that the other held for me. The portrait on the stairs was that of a very cross-looking old gentleman in military uniform, holding a sword. He seemed ready to pounce down upon us children as we went up to bed by flickering candlelight; but once past him, we were safe, or so we reasoned.

These terrors came only with twilight, for by day the house was a friendly place. White curtains fluttered in the breeze, and sunlight came in through the bowed green shutters, making a striped pattern on the floor—a pattern broken by other shadows of swaying vines. In the hall my aunts sat—elderly ladies—or so I thought them—wearing white dresses with many little ruffles. Their hands were filled always with sewing or fancy-work. Negro servants would come in (*plop! plop!* of bare feet) carrying trays with tinkling cups. The elderly ladies in white would lay aside their sewing and smile, saying: "Thank the Lord for coffee!"

All my childhood seems centered in that hall . . . looking out toward the river.

The parlor was on the north side of the house, a cool, dark room used only on state occasions. I thought of the parlor as a place of horror, and I suppose it was. The Lord knows what atrocities lurked in that dim room! I do remember one rug, fearful and grand, upon which an enormous dog— a sort of cross between a mastiff and a St. Bernard—was rescuing a fat child from a watery grave. It was hooked by hand, they told me, by my grandmother's sister, who had married a Yankee and lived in Salem, Massachusetts. I never hear of Massachusetts now that I do not think of that rug. Probably this is the reason why I have never been there!

I remember a wedding that took place in that parlor when I was perhaps six years old. It was some cousin of my uncle's wife—one of the many vague "relations" of the family. There was hubbub and excitement. The brick kitchen was like a madhouse, with Aunt Rhody screaming raucous directions to half a dozen half-grown black girls who were helping her. They scurried around like crayfish, falling over each other in their excitement. Cakes were being baked before the open fire in iron pots that were called "spiders." Half a dozen turkeys had been roasted and were reposing on big blue platters, all in a row; for there was to be supper served in the dining-room after the ceremony. At intervals Aunt Rhody would leave the fire and go to the door, squinting with her weather eye toward the sky. "An' sho' rain's a-comin'!" she declared, although the sun was shining and the sky was filled with fleecy white clouds.

Rain presented a real problem to Aunt Rhody, for the kitchen was some distance from the house, as I have said, and the food must be carried in and out. And rain it did! In torrents! What a commotion! What excitement! What lamentations arose! Black girls in faded dresses ran back and forth, to and from the big house. They went in couples, one carrying a smoking dish, the other carrying an umbrella. Aunt Rhody screeched advice and admonition after them. The girls enjoyed it, and played tricks upon each other, while Aunt Rhody wailed and threatened by turns.

"Yo'-all quit dat! Quit dat, Ah say! Gawd knows, Ah'm goin' tuh smash yo' down!"

The climax came when Cindy, a half-grown girl, ran so fast that her companion could not keep the dish covered with the umbrella, although she pursued Cindy wildly down the brick-paved path. The walk was slippery from the rain, and half way to the house Cindy lost her footing and fell to her knees—and a big chocolate cake landed upside down in a bed of wet white clover. This proved too much for Aunt Rhody, and she descended upon the luckless Cindy then and there, rushing forth into the slanting rain and

A WHITE-COLUMNED PLANTATION HOUSE

grabbing the girl by her woolly hair, while she belabored her with a dishpan.

Such shrieks arose that one of my uncles came out of the dining-room doorway, and, seeing the tableau, burst into laughter and turned to call several other men to come and witness the spectacle. Aunt Rhody released Cindy, who was bawling and howling, more from fear than from pain, and retreated to the kitchen, muttering that "Mister Paul's got little to do to come shamin' me befo' company!" The dogs ate the abandoned chocolate cake—and everybody lived happily ever after.

Everybody except me. Aunt Rhody put me bodily from the kitchen, and, upon reaching the big house, one of my aunts discovered that I was wet from the rain, and I was sent upstairs to get into dry clothes. This proved a diversion, for in the room opposite the children's room the bride was being dressed—and the door was open. I peeped in.

The bride stood before a mirror. It was just beginning to grow dark. Beside her, two negro girls stood holding lighted candles so her toilet could be completed. Half a dozen ladies were gathered around her, patting her here and there. The bride's skirts billowed out to enormous dimensions and her waist was a marvel of slimness. Upon the four-post bed was a cloud of white—the wedding veil. I heard a shocked voice exclaim: "What, only three petticoats!" Then the door slammed.

I changed my clothes hastily and went downstairs again.

Of the wedding ceremony itself I remember nothing, but I do remember that the bride dragged countless yards of white lace train behind her as she came down the stairs, leaning on my uncle's arm. The bridegroom met her at the foot of the staircase. He was a very tall man, with a drooping black mustache. The minister stood in the parlor—now lighted by many candles, which were reflected in the mirror over the mantel. The ceremony was performed in the very center of the rug, with the fat child and the rescuing dog ruthlessly trampled underfoot!

It seemed to me that hundreds of people were there—probably there were only fifty or sixty. At any rate, there were twenty horses tied to the hitching-rack just beyond the flower garden, and thirteen buggies and surreys and phaëtons out at the stables, for I counted them.

A good many of the guests were, I believe, relatives. Half a dozen were guests in the house. Everybody called everybody else "cousin." The ladies gathered around the bride, kissing her, laughing and crying by turns; but the bridegroom was carried off to the dining-room shortly after the ceremony. There the men stood in a semicircle, drinking whisky and soda, and clapping the bridegroom on the back. "Well, a bird can't fly with one wing," they would say, refilling their glasses from the decanters, which glittered with reflected light from the lamps and candles.

In the parlor a fat old lady, dressed in black lace, was weeping copiously and kissing the bride. She clasped the bride around her wasp-like waist and cried: "Oh, would that this day had never come!" which, even as a child, I thought ridiculous, and communicated this opinion to my cousin Kitty, a little girl of my own age. But Kitty, very prim and prudish in her white dress and pink ribbons, merely said "Sh! Sh!" which hurt my feelings. So I went back to the dining-room again and dodged about among the long black legs of the gentlemen. They were toasting the bride, and stood holding glasses high. It was very dramatic, I thought.

Just then the ladies descended upon them, swishing in with

much rustling of starched petticoats; I was surrounded by a billowing sea of lace and ruffles—and I fled.

The children were not allowed at the table for the wedding supper, but we gobbled down our food in the pantry and rushed back to the door of the dining-room in order to hear the flowery speeches that the gentlemen made when they toasted the bride with champagne. I would give an eye-tooth to have a record of all that was said—for today it would be very funny, indeed, although in the early nineties, in Louisiana, those fine flowers of rhetoric were considered indispensable. But I can remember one phrase—and only lately it dawned upon me how funny the whole speech must have been: ". . . and the sunlight fades from the western sky like the rosy blush from a fair maiden's cheek!"

Then the ladies clapped their hands, the gentlemen cried "Hurray!" and the old country doctor who had made the speech bowed right and left and kissed the bride's hand.

"A gentleman of the old school!" some one exclaimed.

This led to a discussion of the old-time Southern gentleman, and one iconoclast brought disgrace upon himself by declaring that "The old-time Southern gentleman won't lie and he won't steal—but everything else will he do!"

Whereupon the men: "Ah, come now . . ." or "Oh, I say, that's a bit too much . . ." and so on, while the ladies cried: "Oh, for shame!" and "How can you say such things!" and fanned themselves rapidly with their tiny fans, which fluttered like so many indignant butterflies.

Then the bride went upstairs to put on her traveling dress, and the bridegroom was left at the table surrounded with men, who smoked huge black cigars or rolled cigarettes. Alone, the men slouched down in their chairs, or turned the chairs sideways, facing the end of the table. They even sang a little, I remember, but the song I have wholly forgotten.

While they were still at table, in the candlelight, the sound of a steamboat's whistle came, full and clear, from the river.

Every one sprang up, filled with excitement. The ladies ran shrieking up the stairs to hurry the bride's toilet, and the men gathered the bridal luggage together and went out upon the veranda. The rain had stopped falling and the moon was shining. At intervals, down the avenue which led to the front gate, torches of fat-pine were burning, making a lurid light and much black smoke. The negroes were lined up on each side of the walk in the flower garden, garbed in their Sunday best, ranged there for a glimpse of the bride and bridegroom. The coachmen had brought the carriages and surreys around to the flower garden gate, and many of the men went out to the hitching-rack and mounted their horses. Two of them went galloping down the avenue to the river, to tell the steamboat captain that the wedding party was on the way.

And, finally, the party did get under way, after many kisses and embraces. The negroes cheered as the couple appeared at the top of the steps which led down to the garden walk. A shower of rice was thrown after them as they ran down the walk toward the waiting carriage. There were cries from the women, exclamations from the men. Cigars were cast aside by the gentlemen who accompanied ladies— cigars which were eagerly grabbed up by the negro men who stood about in the "audience."

Gayly the whole party went down the walk, and the ladies and gentlemen climbed into the carriages—except those dashing bachelors who rode their steeds. And the whole cavalcade went down the avenue toward the road and the levee. I rode behind one of the men on horseback, clutching him about his middle, my nose pressed between his shoulder

A PLANTATION PARLOR

blades. He cried out: "Hold tight, sonny!" and we were off at what I thought to be the speed of lightning. All my attention was centered in holding on, and in keeping myself from bumping against the back of his saddle as the horse galloped. When I got my wits together, we were already riding up the side of the levee—over a ramp built for the carriages and wagons which hauled our supplies from the steamboat landing.

And then, before my wide eyes, the river came into sight. But how different the landing appeared! Torches were burning at intervals. A dozen flambeaux were held by negro men who moved about on the bank. The steamboat, which was tied up near the bank, was filled with men and women from other plantations near-by, for everybody knew everybody in those days, it seemed. They all crowded the decks to shower congratulations upon the bride and bridegroom. The captain was serving wine on the deck. Every uplifted hand held a glass.

The guests from our plantation got out of the carriages, stepping into the mud, the ladies ruining their slippers with many a cry of affected excitement. Dresses were held up, but white petticoats dragged through the puddles. Finally, every one was on board except the negroes, who waited on the bank waving their torches.

A toast was proposed. Some one responded. Then came the cry "All ashore!" and the guests ran back across the gangplank to the landing again. In the water the lights were reflected, and the gay colors of the ladies' dresses were repeated in the rippling water as they crossed the plank, illumined by the dancing flames.

There were many messages shouted. The fat lady in black lace ran back for one last embrace and one last explosion of tears, and was finally dragged back to land again

by her husband. The gangplank was raised. Roustabouts on
the deck rolled their eyes and showed flashing white teeth.
Negroes on shore called out good-bys to the negroes on the
deck. The boat began to puff; the wheel at the stern began
to revolve. The strip of water between the bank and the
boat widened. The boat moved out into the current. As it
receded, those on the bank began to sing in chorus:

> I saw the boat go round the bend—
> Good-by, my lover, good-by!
> All loaded down with gentlemen—
> Good-by, my lover, good-by!

Voices rose high and clear. The moon shone down on the
rippling water. Willow-trees along the bank rustled in the
breeze and the torches flickered. One negro's torch burned
out and he tossed it, sizzling, into the river.

The steamboat was in mid-current now, the twin lights
on the smokestacks red and green against the deep blue of
the night sky. From the upper deck we could still see the
bride, waving a white scarf.

There was a sudden hush, and there came to us, distinctly, the ship's bell; the pilot was signaling the engineer
full speed ahead.

Chapter III

WINTER time on the plantation. Frosty nights and sunny days, crisp and cool. Wood smoke rises from cabin chimneys, and upon the wide hearths are blazing fires of pine knots. At twilight the smell of wood smoke mingles with the smell of sizzling bacon. The fields are brown, and brown men toil in the furrows, "gettin' ready for spring." The sugar-cane has all been cut and carried to the sugar-house. Grinding time is over, and the sugar in barrels and hogsheads has been carried aboard the steamboats and shipped away down the river.

The pecan-trees are bare of leaves, and the branches make a curious pattern against the sky; but the live-oaks are as green as ever, and palms and Spanish-daggers in the garden seem doubly green against bare tree trunks. The banana-trees will survive the winter, unless there is an unusually heavy frost; their large leaves are ragged, though, and flap in the wind. Red winter roses are blooming in the flower garden.

Inside the plantation-house the children are cracking pecans for pralines that Aunt Rhody has promised to make for us; we sit around the table in the dining-room, each armed with a nutcracker. There are two blue bowls on the red table-cloth: one bowl for the nut meats, one for the shells, for we have been told not to "make a mess." The log fire burns with a steady glow. Reflections of the fire shine in a dozen goblets on the sideboard. While we are busy with the nuts, "Uncle" Isaac comes in, staggering under the weight of three large logs, which he adds to the fire. The flames dart up the chimney, and we children move our chairs farther away from the blaze as the heat burns our faces. We listen for imaginary howling of wind in the chimney and we hope that there will be snow. I can remember only one snow flurry; but it set the whole plantation wild with excitement. I was very small, but I was carried out into the yard and given a handful of snow, in order that I should remember the strange phenomenon. Why, it even snowed in New Orleans that year. Everybody stopped work and threw snowballs!

When we have cracked and shelled enough pecans, the little girls go into their bedroom to play with their dolls, and I wander out upon the front gallery. It is cold, but my coat is warm. I hang over the railing, watching the negroes at work in the fields. They sing as they work behind the plows. A group of women and girls with hoes are working together in another part of the field.

I can hear their cries, at intervals, clear in the frosty air, as they shout back and forth to one another.

And then, suddenly, comes another sound—an unfamiliar sound, mellow and sweet. Music from beyond the levee.

With one accord the negroes throw down their hoes. Negro men leave their plows standing in the furrows. A great cry rises:

"It's de calliope!"

The cry is repeated over and over: "Calliope! Calliope!"

There is a mad dash for the levee. Men and women, half-grown boys and girls—they run through the furrows like mad things, screaming out in joy. Astonished mules, left behind at the plows, turn their heads and watch the black folks run.

My little cousins come scampering out of the house, their black nurse with them. "Calliope!" they all scream.

The little girls, the nurse, and I run down the long avenue of bare trees. We are panting, breathless, but we scream "Calliope!" at intervals.

And the magic music continues. Why, I even recognize the tune—"Daisy Belle."

> Daisy, Daisy, give me your answer true;
> I'm half crazy, all for the love of you!
> It won't be a stylish marriage,
> We can't afford a carriage—
> But you'll look sweet, upon the seat
> Of a bicycle built for two!

We scramble up the levee, falling down, tearing the knees of our stockings. Many black folks are ahead of us, standing on the levee-top.

Breathless we stand and look down the long slope, look past the batture, the sand-bar, beyond to the steamboat-landing; and there, tied up at our own wharf, is a show-boat. A grand, gay-looking boat with a large red sign, "French's New Sensation," painted along the side.

We can see the "calliope," or steam-piano, and we can see the man who is playing upon it! The music continues— waltzes, popular tunes unfamiliar to us. We all shout and applaud when the musician pauses.

"What is it? What is it?"—I want to know, for I have never seen one before. My little cousins are amazed at my stupidity.

"Why, it's the Floatin' Palace!" they answer, grandly, smoothing down their dresses. "Everybody knows that!"

"Sho' do! Everybody know dat!" says the nurse.

I am crushed under the weight of my ignorance, but rally bravely: "But what is it? Tell me!"

"Lawzee, dere'll be a big show on bo'd tonight," the black woman assures me. "De whole plantation'll be dar!"

Her assertion proved to be true enough, for luckless indeed was the white person or negro who could not scrape up, beg, borrow, or steal enough to get on board for the show-boat's one-night stand at the plantation landing. And not our plantation alone, for those across the river came too, in rowboats, and the news circulated up and down the river; people who lived ten miles away came driving up in buggies and surreys. It was quite exciting.

The interior was like a small theater, with the usual fittings—a stage, stage boxes, a parquet, a gallery. It was probably tawdry and small enough, but we thought it magnificent. The white people sat downstairs; the negroes filled the balcony. We applauded everything, indiscriminately.

There was a short play—a melodrama called, I remember, "Triss; or, Beyond the Rockies." The first act was laid in "Granny Grimes's Barroom." The heroine flaunted about, sat on tables, and shot pistols. There were many gallant rescues and fine speeches. There was a dastardly murder, and the villain said "Ha!" when he escaped after killing our heroine's father and another victim. The heroine, after a few shrieks, made a vow that she would track down the murderers; whereupon the innocent hero said: "But there is no clue!" Then the heroine, snatching up something from the floor, turned to him and cried: "Oh, yes, there is! This handkerchief!" And the curtain fell upon our rapturous applause.

The rest of the play is dim in my mind, but there were "specialties" by members of the cast, between the acts, and a sort of vaudeville performance afterward in which the

actors displayed their disdain for human limitations by per-
forming any number of tricks. Our *Triss* of the play came
out in tights and stood against a wooden screen, and the
hero threw knives and hatchets at her, outlining her body;
Granny Grimes sang a sad song, illustrated with lantern
slides; the villain balanced a lighted candle on his forehead
and juggled Indian clubs. Our cup of bliss ran over.

Afterward we all trooped up the levee in the frosty night.
From the levee-top we looked back down the long slope
and across the batture, to the "Floatin' Palace" as she lay
snug at the landing. It had been too much. We children could
hardly bear the joy of it.

I woke at dawn, dressed myself, and ran to the levee
before breakfast. But the landing was empty. A few pieces
of paper blew about; there were marks on the willow-trees
where the ropes had been tied, and many footprints in the
sand. But the show-boat was gone.

Desolate, I went home to breakfast.

Chapter IV

PEOPLE who do not know about life on a plantation often make the mistake of thinking the planter's life is one of rest and lassitude. "Oh," they say, "how I envy you the peace and quiet of your life on the old plantation!" If they only knew!

For we lived on excitement there. Our world was shut off to itself, it is true. But picture to yourself a little community comprising four thousand acres of land, peopled with six or eight white folks and three hundred and sixty negroes; and in this world as many feuds, excitements, heart-burnings, fights, accidents, as in any part of any city. More, probably. Or at least it seemed so, because we knew of all the things that went on, and we lived in a state of constant upheaval. Yet, to an outsider, perhaps, our lives did appear tranquil, for when we had company unpleasant things were barred from the conversation.

At any rate, the children led an exciting life. Each of the children had his "body servant." This was merely a figure of speech, of course, but it was a custom that remained from days before the Civil War, when children of planters were each given a slave at the time of their christening, and it became the duty of this slave to keep watch over the white child in later life. I was devoted to little black Lawrence, who was supposed to take care of me. He was, perhaps, three years older than I. And he taught

A FAN SUSPENDED FROM THE CEILING OVER THE DINING-ROOM TABLE

me all that he knew about life—and that was plenty! The amount of misinformation that I received from him was truly appalling; but the good outweighed the bad by far.

It was Lawrence who taught me to swim—in the Mississippi River; although this was strictly forbidden, and rightly enough, too, for the river is a dangerous place for a mature swimmer, to say nothing of a child. But it was to the river that we would go, riding our ponies to some distant sand-bar. There we would undress and wade in, and there we would remain for hours, flopping around in the shallow water near the bank.

Once I fell into a deep hole and was nearly drowned, but Lawrence pulled me out, literally by the hair of the head. Lord, how it hurt! But I laughed when I saw Lawrence's terrified face and rolling eyes. "Don't tell yo' maw! Don't tell yo' maw! Promise yo' won' tell yo' maw!" He kept crying this phrase over and over. And I promised, of course.

However, some one did tell—probably some white person riding along the levee-top—and after that I was forbidden to go swimming in the river. Lawrence and I argued it out. Well, I had given my promise about the river, but how about the bayou? Well, I wasn't sure . . . but finally he convinced me that the promise did not include this delightful place. So, together we went to swim in the black water of the sluggish stream which ran through a strip of woodland some two miles from the house. There were black water snakes in it, and alligators too, probably, although I do not remember seeing them there, and the stream was choked with purple water hyacinths and half covered with green scum. But there we swam to our hearts' content every afternoon throughout the summer.

It was from Lawrence that I learned my first superstitions: about the bad luck that followed seeing the new moon

through the trees, or falling down on Monday, or putting
a hat on the bed, or not answering when a jaybird spoke to
you. For jaybirds were in league with the devil—every one
knew that—and on Friday they go to hell and bring a grain
of sand to old Mister Satan. When all the mountains and
hills on earth are leveled flat by the sand-carrying of the
jaybirds, then Judgment day will be here, and then—watch
out, everybody! I believed .it implicitly, and when a jaybird would flaunt his blue wings over the bayou and give
his raucous call, both Lawrence and I would respond:
"Good mawnin', suh!" or "Good evenin', suh," according
to the hour of the day. Otherwise, the bird would report
our incivility direct to the devil on Friday.

In addition to his supervision of my early education,
Lawrence had another and more arduous job. His was the
task of pulling the big fan which hung suspended over the
dining-room table, and his services were required at meal-
times. It seems to me that I can see him yet, a little black,
sleepy-looking boy, standing or sitting beside the fireplace,
pulling the cord that moved the fan back and forth.

In those days every one had such fans over dining tables,
but nowadays they have disappeared entirely, and in old
plantation-houses only the hooks remain in the ceiling where
once the fans swayed to and fro. These fans were modeled
after the punkahs of India, or so they told me. A wire
frame hung down from two hooks; sometimes the fan
itself was made of white paper cut into strips, but oftener
it was made of white cloth, embroidered with a "design"
by some of the ladies of the family. In one house that I
remember the fan was made of sheet iron and was painted
with a snow scene! Ours, however, like everything else in
that plantation-house, was very plain and very simple. It was
made of white linen, stiff with starch. It hung down over the

center of the long table, possibly three feet above the cloth. When properly manipulated it gave a gentle breeze and kept away flies and mosquitoes, and made dining a pleasure rather than a contest. But woe betide the unlucky family if the fan was operated by unskilled or clumsy hands. If it moved too slowly, the flies came anyway, and if it moved too rapidly it blew things about. This stiff breeze did not matter so much in the daytime, but at night it was disastrous, for it caused the candles to flicker wildly, or put them out altogether.

Sometimes in the evening, Lawrence, tired out from a day's "care" of me, would fall asleep at his post. The fan would move more and more slowly and would finally come to rest altogether—usually directly above a lighted candle, which terrified the family and caused my uncle to shout at Lawrence. The little negro would awaken suddenly and give a violent jerk to the cord; then the candles would go out in the gust of wind that swept the table, and we would be left in darkness.

There is no light softer or more lovely than candlelight, and we preferred it to the brighter glow of an oil lamp. The supper table was lighted with three candles burning under hurricane shades—or *"cylindres,"* as we called them, having borrowed the word from the creoles. Fully three feet high were these clear glass shades, and in an ordinary breeze they prevented the candles flickering. In the daytime two of these candle shades adorned the ends of the dining-room mantelpiece and the third one stood on the sideboard. (There had been four of them in the dining-room originally, but one had been broken before my day.) In the parlor there were two more of these shades; but those in the parlor were engraved with bunches of grapes and had been a wedding present to somebody or other in the eighteen-thirties. For this reason they were highly prized and seldom used. But those in the dining-room saw service every day, and frequently, after supper, my uncle would carry one to the front gallery, where he would sit reading "The Pica-yune," the New Orleans morning newspaper, by candle-light.

All Louisiana people live upon their verandas—and we call them galleries. It is here that we read or gossip; it is here that we entertain callers. It was upon the gallery of the plantation-house that we children got our lessons—for there were lessons even in this heavenly place; but, oddly enough, I did not mind them. It was so pleasant outdoors. The birds made their nests in trees near-by, especially the mocking-bird, for mocking-birds seem to enjoy human companionship. I could never understand this friendliness on their part, for it brought disaster to them almost always. The cats caught the birds, or climbed the trees and got the young. There was a constant warfare going on.

We could tell when there were young birds in the nests, because the mother bird would begin her attacks upon the cats. Let but one of the cats come sauntering out into the garden, and with a flashing of wings the mother bird would be down upon its back, pecking at its uplifted eyes. Then the children would begin an investigation—and sure enough, near-by, in a small tree, or in a hedge, we would hear the cheeping of young birds, or we would see them, their yellow bills gaping for worms. Many a tear did the children shed over the cats and the mocking-birds; but the birds never learned their lesson, and year after year they would build their nests quite close to us.

There were many other birds, the scarlet cardinal and the little yellow warblers that Louisianians called "pops"— probably a corruption of "pape," meaning the Pope; for the creoles and Cajans' were fond of church dignitaries, and many of the Louisiana birds are named in their honor. In the swamps back of the plantation were white and blue herons, and often we would see them, winging their way home from the river just after sunset. Once in a long while we would see a pelican—but this was a rare occasion, for we were too far up the river, and pelicans prefer the waters nearer the Gulf of Mexico. Nevertheless, we had great interest in the pelican, for he was the bird upon the state seal —and the seal was reproduced upon the cover of our Louisiana history book.

We were surrounded by animal life; there were birds in every thicket, and every stream was full of fish. The negroes caught catfish in the river. They considered this fish a rare delicacy; but the white people did not care for it, although I have tasted it and found it good. In the summer the negroes would have "fish-fries" on the river-bank—and jolly affairs they were, too, although usually a fight ensued, and occasionally some one was killed. Because of these fights the children of the plantation were never allowed to go to a fish-fry, although I always wanted to go; and I was perhaps fifteen years old before I got a chance to attend one. But it was worth waiting for.

However, I was allowed to go down into the "quarters" or the "street" where the negroes lived, some distance back of the big house. The cabins were old and had been built back in slave times, at the same time that the large house was built. They were nearly all alike—small, box-like houses of two rooms, with a chimney rising at one end; they were whitewashed, and each one had a small yard. The theory was that each negro family could have a vegetable patch behind its house; but, as a matter of fact, only one or two of the families made a pretense of such a prosaic thing as making a garden. It.was too much trouble—although I remember that my uncle offered garden seeds or plants from his own garden, year after year. Many of the cabins had flower beds, however, usually filled with sunflowers and cannas and ribbongrass and red lilies. Before some of the cabins grew the beautiful and fragrant cape jasmine, sometimes called the gardenia. They grow luxuriantly in Louisiana, great hardy shrubs with shining dark leaves. In early summer they are covered with white, wax-like blossoms, their thick, fleshy petals heavy with perfume.

Honeysuckle vines covered the crooked fences, and here and there a magnolia-tree grew. But before most of the cabins the earth was bare and clean-swept, and scraggly chinaberry-trees grew beside the houses. It was in the shadow of these thick-leaved trees that the women washed their clothes, singing over the washtubs and indulging in jokes and much repartee.

The last house in the "street" belonged to "Aunt" Julia, the oldest woman on the plantation. She had been born a slave, and her mother had come from Africa. Aunt Julia professed herself a healer, and knew the secrets of curing fevers by mysterious brews of herbs. The other negroes admired and feared her, although a gentler old black woman never lived. She had been a house servant in her younger days and had learned "white folks' ways." Accordingly, her cabin was the neatest and cleanest of the lot, and her quilts were admired extravagantly. Aunt Julia was very black, very old, very withered. She wore a bright-colored *tignon* around her head, and a black straw hat on top of that. Even in the house she wore that hat. I never remember seeing her when she didn't have it on. Too old to work with the other servants in the big house, Aunt Julia had charge of the children of the field laborers, and kept "school" in her cabin while the parents were at work. She ruled the children with a rod of iron—or, as a matter of fact, with a peach-tree switch. The little girls she taught to make quilts and to sew; the older boys worked in her garden—and the bed and the floor were always covered with sleeping babies and dogs, for many of the children brought their curs with them.

There were twenty-five or thirty little negroes at Aunt Julia's cabin every day; many of them were babies, but the older girls were taught to cook, and the boys worked outdoors. The old woman would move about among the children, the gold hoops glittering in her ears, the peach-tree switch in her hand. The switch was more a symbol than a means of punishment, but the very sight of it brought about perfect behavior. And upon occasion Aunt Julia had been known to use it thoroughly and efficiently.

Upon the whitewashed wall of her cabin hung a "pattern quilt," its gay red and blue and green and yellow patchwork making a bright spot in the room. The old woman was very proud of this masterpiece, for it represented her ability as a maker of coverlets. The old negro women made these pattern quilts in the same spirit that our grandmothers made samplers—a proof of their skill with the needle. In a pattern quilt are included all the varying patterns of patch-work that the woman knows, and the blocks are put to-gether with strips of turkey-red calico. I am not sure that turkey-red is essential, but it was the favorite color. If you were interested, Aunt Julia would point out the different squares with her peach-tree switch and would tell you the names of them: the "steamboat" pattern, the "lone-star," the "going to Jerusalem," the "chicken-foot." The chicken-foot design was a favorite, for it was based upon the impression of a fowl's track in mud, and it was an intricate and pretty pattern. There were many others, but I have forgotten them.

There remains in my mind a very definite picture of the interior of that cabin, with the little black children grouped around, busy at their tasks. The sun shining in through the back door made an oblong blotch of light upon the white-scrubbed boards of the floor; the sunlight would illumine the pattern quilt, making the colors glow; it would shine into the wide fireplace, in which cold ashes were piled and where the old hand-made andirons stood askew. But the hearth was reddened with brick dust, and everything was sweet and clean. The old four-post bed in the corner—a gift from "ole Miss" to Aunt Julia, many years ago—was a marvel of cleanliness, and the hand-made white coverlet had been woven by Aunt Julia herself upon a loom still in her possession—a loom which was not used nowadays because "store-bought" cloth was the style.

"But ef yo' grampa wuz alive," she would say, "Ah'd be a-weavin' fo' him. Lawzee, ole Mistah Jacob would nevah, nevah weah dem sto'-bought clothes! Not 'im! He wo' de Attakapas cottonade dat Ah make 'im, till de day he die. . . . An' he wuz buried in it, too!"

The weaving of Attakapas cottonade seems to be a lost art today, and it is rather a pity, for the blue and white material which our grandfathers wore in summer was pretty, bright-colored stuff, and, as Aunt Julia often said, "Dere ain't no wear-out to it!"

These discussions were usually broken off short, because the watchful eye of the old woman would discover that some small black girl was "sewin' dis-a-way an' dat-a-way," instead of making the fine seam that was Aunt Julia's law. She would snatch the offending cloth from the little kinky-

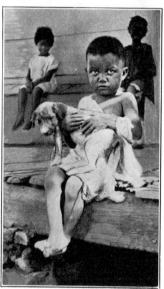

PLANTATION TYPES

headed girl's hand with a shout: "Fo' Gawd! What kine er way to do is dat!" A pause, then: "Um! Umph! But yo' is a lazy chile!" Then the girl would burst into loud weeping and lamentation, fearing the switch; but usually Aunt Julia would relent and smile. The thing always ended, though, with the little girl's ripping out the seam and beginning all over again.

Old "Uncle" John Nash made baskets when he was not confined to his chair with rheumatism. He and Aunt Julia were great friends, and he would come often and sit on the edge of her gallery in the shadow of the gourd vine, discussing heaven with her. They were both very much preoccupied with God and His angels and discussed them with a frankness that was both startling and convincing. Once, I remember, Aunt Julia proclaimed that she intended to "piece a quilt for my Jesus" when she got to heaven; and when Uncle John said: "Lawzee! W'at He want wid one o' yo' ole quilts?" she became indignant and said: "Ah speck He kin wrap up in it in de cool o' de day!"

Yes, heaven was very close to Aunt Julia and to Uncle John. They spoke of it as "across de rivah." They meant the river Jordan, but I thought that they meant the Mississippi.

Chapter V

THE MAIL-BOAT

MANY river steamboats passed the plantation, boats both large and small—although to me they all appeared enormous. There was the *T. P. Leathers,* the *Natchez,* the *America* and many others. These boats passed on the way to New Orleans. When we went to Baton Rouge, however, where my grandfather lived, we took the *Julian Poydras* or the *Cleon*—for these were the mail-boats, and one of them passed the plantation every day.

I suppose the boats were small and not particularly impressive, but I remember them as enchanted castles—no, much better than that, for there was nothing in all the fairy tales so romantic or so exciting as the mail-boat.

We would wait at the steamboat-landing for the *Cleon,* my uncle and I, for frequently he took me with him on his errands to town. The boat would appear around a bend; the whistle would sound, deep and mellow, never sharp. I would experience a spinal thrill. I breathed with difficulty. The boat would come nearer, men on the decks would be seen: negro roustabouts lolling about on cotton bales or hogsheads of sugar; the men in the pilot-house; the captain, wearing a cap, walking out on the upper deck.

Captain Mossop was the owner of the *Cleon*—and I considered his little girl the luckiest child on earth; for she could ride upon the boat every day, if she wished, and frequently she did. She was very grand, always in a white dress, floppy hat and fluttering blue ribbons. She was older than I was, and I thought her very beautiful. She would recline in a deck-chair, and negro servants would bring her tall glasses of lemonade in which red cherries floated. Delicious!

Even today I can remember the very taste of that steamboat lemonade. It was superbly different; nothing on shore ever tasted half so good or half so sweet. But then everything pertaining to a steamboat was of exquisite charm to me.

We would go aboard, up the gangplank, climb the stairs to the upper deck, and there, in the shadow, we would sip lemonade—rather, I sipped lemonade, while my uncle had whisky and soda with the captain. Sometimes there were small cakes, each one with half a pecan imbedded on top of the pink icing.

There was a bar where the men congregated. I was too small to be allowed inside, but I would peep, hoping, waiting for the day when I should be old enough to put on long trousers and be admitted into that delightful place where the men sat about, or stood at the bar, while a negro man in a white coat dispensed the drinks. I would listen to the mysterious man-talk, most of it unintelligible to me, about crops and the stages of the river, how the gauge read at Baton Rouge or Bayou Sara; or what "The Picayune" had to say about the high water; or about the price of cotton— a hundred different things.

On one occasion I was sent to Baton Rouge alone, and was put in special charge of the captain. Good Lord, what an experience! I remember every detail. In the first place, the captain let me sit in his room while he took his bath—and such luxury I never imagined in our austere life on the plantation. He had a valet, a negro man, very sleek and black, a "soft-spoken negro" who said "Yassuh!" and little else. First a round tub was placed on the floor of the stateroom, then an array of bath-towels, soap, a bottle of alcohol. The captain came in and seated himself in a chair, while the negro boy unlaced his boots and took them off. I sat enthralled while the toilet was completed. The captain got into the tub and the negro scrubbed him with a brush, dried him, then stepped off a few feet and fanned him dry with the folded towel. Then the captain stretched out in one of the bunks, and the negro boy rubbed him down with alcohol. The captain, though well past middle age, was a man of fine, robust physique. The toilet was performed with a total lack of self-consciousness; it appeared that the captain never knew of, or ignored totally, the presence of the small boy who sat by looking on at this rite with round eyes.

I tell all this because I think that this captain was characteristic of the river-boat captains of that time. He was immaculately clean, and his clothes were changed completely every day; underwear, shirt, and suit. His underwear was of sheer linen; his suit was of heavy white linen. This bath was a daily occurrence, called "getting ready for the evening." Afterward he sat on deck and had a mint julep, a tall drink in a glass filled with tinkling ice, with whisky, and with sprigs of mint rising above the frosted glass. Because I was his guest and "almost a man"—eight years old probably—I was allowed a sip from his glass, and liked it! When I grew old enough to wear long trousers, the captain assured me, I could have all the mint juleps I wanted. From that day forth I lived for that proud moment. Not that I wanted the julep especially, for secretly I preferred the lemonade, but because long trousers were the symbol of emancipation.

THE "J. M. WHITE"

This is considered one of the finest steamboats ever known on the Mississippi

In those days I regarded "growing up" as a definite thing. I should put on long trousers and become a man. "When I get big" was a sort of refrain; it ran through all my thoughts and through my conversation: "When I get big, I shall be a steamboat captain . . ." or "When I get big and have a plantation of my own . . ."

All the river boats were noted for the excellent food served on board, and it was upon the *Cleon* that I first had a dinner served in courses: a cocktail, a relish, soup, fish, entrée, meat-course, dessert, ice-cream, coffee! At the plantation the food was placed upon the table all at once, and we passed it around—the theory being that the negroes were better out of the dining-room than standing around worrying us. Only the little negro boy whose duty it was to pull the fan above the table remained, and at intervals a woman-servant, barefoot, would come in *plop, plop!* with a plate of hot biscuits or with the water-pitcher.

Not so on the steamboats. Here all was "style," that thing spoken of sneeringly at home, for democracy was our watchword and snobbishness the one unforgivable sin; but on a steamboat my uncle would abandon himself to the fine linen, the silver, the finger-bowls, and would enjoy it.

Early in life—on one of my first trips—I disgraced myself. The shame of it still haunts me. I had been taught to be frank, to be unpretentious, not to "show off." At table I found a long line of forks, spoons and knives beside my plate at the captain's table. I decided that there must be some mistake, and so, gathering them all together in my hand, I summoned a waiter and handed them to him. "I need only one knife and one fork," I said. "You can take all these away." A roar of laughter went up from the table. I was humiliated beyond measure. But my uncle, I remember, did not scold me. And when he told my mother about it afterward, he was rather pleased, I think. But this did not lessen my humiliation.

But the wonderful things that were served on board those boats! Gumbo and fried chicken and ice-cream every day. And fish cooked with white wine sauce. . . .

Steamboats were places where men held full sway and women were guests—just the reverse from the plantation, where the women-folks had the supervision of all things pertaining to house management. The captain had full charge, of course, and the servants were all negro men. The cook was a shining black man with wonderful white teeth: he wore a tall, starched cook's cap; and the waiters wore spotless white. They were tremendously good-natured and waited on all of us, even the children, hand and foot.

I reveled in this man's-world, and longed for the time to come when I should be truly a part of it. The captain, in my eyes, was the most fortunate man on earth, finer than a planter, finer than any other man in the world. He was like a king, master of a floating palace, with many men to do his bidding.

In the afternoons we would sit outside and watch the roustabouts lying about the lower deck; they would sprawl on cotton bales or on hogsheads of sugar. They would assume the most fantastic positions, and would sleep with the full afternoon sun beating down upon them. But when a landing was reached and the gangplank lowered before some wharf, they would spring up with electric vitality and would carry bundles and bales ashore, singing as they went. Usually there was a "singing nigger" that led them. These singing negroes were of great value, and the captain usually managed to have one aboard, for it was a well-known fact that the men worked ten times better when there was a leader for the singing. There were dozens of songs:

Oh, I got forty dollars an' I got it fo' to spen';
If de wimmin don't wan't it, gonna give it to de men!

And there was another, called "Jus' de same!" which I
have heard all my life aboard the river steamboats. It is a
song of philosophy, relative to the white, the mulatto, and
the black man. There are dozens of verses. Here are a few
of them :

White gal smell like Castile soap;
Yellow gal tries to do de same.
Black gal smell like a ole billy-goat,
But she git dere jus' de same!

Then came the chorus, swelling out over the river, sweet
and clear :

Down de river, charmin' Betsy,
Down de river, Miz Collee!
Ef I don't see you-all no' mo',
May de good Lawd 'member me!

There were many other verses, some of them funny, many
of them filthy. Most of them I have forgotten, but one remains forever in my mind, so characteristic is it of the
black man's ability to see humor even in his own misery :

White man live in a big brick house;
Yellow man try to do de same.
Nigger lay up in de county jail,
But it's a brick house, jus' de same!

I can see them yet, strutting, throwing dice, dancing on
the decks, while the twilight gathered and the boat nosed its
way downstream. The sun would set with glowing rose and
gold in the sky. The twilight settled down and the colors
faded out of things. The levee and the line of trees along
the bank turned from brilliant green to soft gray. The night

came down and the lanterns on the steamboat were reflected in the water. There were no electric lights on board,
and the lamplight fell softly; the boat became mysterious,
full of strange shadows. When a landing was reached the
gangplank was lowered and the men would run ashore with
their lanterns, which they would put down at intervals to
light the way into the sheds where the stores were carried.
From far off, as we approached these landings, we could see
a lantern at the edge of the wharf, reflecting itself in the
rippling water. . . .

Then, after the brief landing, when the mate would shout
and curse at the negroes—or the captain would shout orders
from the deck overhead—the boat would get under way
again and continue down the broad river. The eastern sky
would grow brighter, and then the moon would untangle
itself from the trees on the bank and rise, round and silver,
above the horizon, making a bright path on the water.

And then, ahead of us, we would see the lights of Baton
Rouge, shining bright. . . . I would sigh, for the trip was
nearly over, and before me lay town, and my grandfather's
house . . . and school tomorrow morning.

Captain Mossop and his family lived in Bayou Sara, some
thirty miles above Baton Rouge. Bayou Sara and St. Francisville were really one town, but Bayou Sara lay at the
foot of the hill, behind the levee, while St. Francisville was
high above, beyond the reach of the high water. Nearly
every year that the water rose very high the levee would
break at Bayou Sara, so the people in that town had got
used to the idea and didn't make a great fuss about it. It
was something so usual that they did not seem to mind
particularly.

The Mossops lived in the parsonage of the Methodist church, some five squares back from the river. The church was empty, for there was no resident preacher. The Mossops were river people and always set a sort of example for calmness in the face of disaster. One year—I think it was 1897—the water was unusually high, and as usual the levee began to slough off at Bayou Sara. The Mossops had been expecting such a calamity, and had made ample preparations. The church was much higher than the parsonage, so they moved their household possessions there. One went up a flight of stairs, eight or nine steps, into the vestibule, then into the church proper. It was not a large building, but rather impressive—all white, with green trimmings. Before the door grew rose-bushes, covered with red roses. The town was quiet and peaceful; cows roamed along the streets, and dogs slept in the shade under the sheds before the stores on the river-front . . . a great peace seemed to hang over everything. But beyond the levee the Mississippi River was rising higher and higher every day; the wise ones said it was impossible for the levee to withstand the pressure, and predicted that the break would occur near a small bayou which, in low-water time, emptied into the river. They were quite right, for it was there that the levee did break—and when the break came, the Mossops moved into the Methodist church: beds and bedding, cook-stove, chairs, sewing-machine, and all the necessary things. In addition to these things they brought their dogs, cats, and chickens.

The church was rather high, and inside there were two balconies, one on either side. On one of these balconies Mrs. Mossop and her daughter arranged their beds and furniture The chickens were given the opposite balcony, roosts were built for them, and all made secure. Captain Mossop had his box-spring and mattress put across the tops of the pews in the church, as he was sure the water would not rise that high.

The levee broke in the middle of the night, and the Mossops left home and went to the church. The water rose more than a foot an hour in the town. By morning the water was twelve feet deep, and was high in the church, almost to the tops of the pews.

It was an odd sight; there lay the captain upon his bed, with the water lapping at its very edge, while high on the balcony his wife and daughter were sleeping, as snug as you please, with their cat and dog. In the morning the sunlight streamed in through the stained-glass windows—blue, yellow, and red—and the roosters began crowing. Some of them tried to fly down from the balcony and fell into the water, from which they had to be rescued by the negro servants. The dog, however, was highly pleased with the whole affair and swam about in the church among the pews. The cat sat on the railing of the balcony in the sunshine, washing herself. And the cook, a negro woman, made a fire in the wood-burning cook-stove and cooked eggs and made coffee for breakfast.

The water did not recede and the Mossops lived in the Methodist church for a month. They became so used to it that they did not seem to mind in the least. Every day the *Cleon* would arrive with the mail, and Captain Mossop would remain overnight with his family. Meals were cooked aboard the boat, and the wife and daughter would go aboard and eat supper, or supper would be sent to them in a rowboat.

The daughter had a skiff all her own and a negro boy to row her around. Every day she would go out into the streets of Bayou Sara, to call upon friends. Many people were living in the upper stories of houses, while below stairs the water rippled. Some plank walks had been built upon stilts, and the stores on the river-front were open and transacting business. The water was level with the tops of the counters, and the clerks ran about on them, taking down foodstuffs from the shelves. Men would row up to the door in skiffs, and then get out, directly upon the counters. Within a week it seemed as though the stores had always been that way. Nobody seemed to mind in the least.

At any rate, the Mossops didn't mind. The daughter enjoyed it thoroughly, rowing about, going downtown shopping, coming back, leaving her boat at the foot of the hill, and climbing up to visit, perhaps, some girl friend who lived in St. Francisville, above the high-water line.

Surely there was no stranger sight anywhere than the church, with the water rippling about the tops of the high pew backs, and with the little girl coming in at the double door in a rowboat and rowing up the aisle; while above her, on a balcony, her mother sat, placidly reading or sewing, and opposite the chickens pecked about at their food, or quarreled, or made love, as though they had been in a barnyard.

The one regret of the Mossops was for their garden, for the water killed all the rose-bushes and other flowers, and ruined the fig- and peach-trees. The great flowering pink crêpe myrtles, however, did not seem to mind the water, but rose out of it, covered with the feathery pink blossoms, all summer long.

Chapter VI

CREVASSE

THERE was a time of feverish activity on the plantation; the river was lapping at the top of the levee. Men in Louisiana, men in Mississippi, men in Arkansas were worried, sleepless. The levees were holding, the levees must hold; it was inconceivable that they should break. All labor in the fields had stopped and all the negroes were working on the levee, strengthening the weak places, building it higher—"topping," they called it.

All day long and far into the night the men toiled. From the gallery of the big house we could see lanterns bobbing along the levee-top. No longer were cows and horses permitted to roam upon the grass-grown slope; no longer did men ride horses upon the high ridge. Instead, the white men took turns acting as levee-guards. Every foot before the plantation was guarded; and where our line of guards ended, the guards of the plantations adjoining took up the work.

Long lines of negroes with wheelbarrows passed. There was a great hole in the sugar-cane field south of the house, near the road; it was from this hole that the earth was taken to build the levees higher. Far into the night we could hear the negroes singing or "hallooing" to each other. They made a game of the hard work and did not seem to mind the heavily loaded barrows of earth which they trundled up the steep slope of the levee. Boards had been laid, end to end,

44

Photo by Marshall Gray, U. S. Engineers' Corps, 1927

SAND BAGS PILED UPON THE CREST OF THE LEVEE AS AN ADDITIONAL PRECAUTION AGAINST OVERFLOW

so the barrows would roll easily, and so the slope of the levee would not be worn away.

The white men were haggard, unshaven, worried. Meals were served at odd hours to the guards. There were strange men, wearing mud-stained clothes, at every meal. The coffee-pot rarely left the stove nowadays; and it was no unusual sight to see a negro man riding on horseback, carrying a coffee-pot in one hand, while a string of tin cups jangled over his shoulder. He was taking hot coffee to the men on the levee.

The women at the plantation-house were worried too. The men of the family were insisting that the women go aboard a steamboat and remain in the town of Baton Rouge until the water receded; but the women would not hear of it. "What? Leave everything that we have in the world? The idea! And what would you do without us?"

They tried to make a joke of it, but even the children knew the difference between this kind of jest and the other kind. This was something else altogether, like whistling in the dark to keep up your courage when you passed a grave-yard at night.

The negroes, however, did not seem disturbed at all. They played about as usual, and laughter rose in the evenings from the plantation "street" as it did in other times. But at intervals all day long the colored women would pass through the "front yard" carrying dinner buckets to the black men who labored on the levees. In ordinary times passing through the "front yard" was forbidden; but this was an unusual time. Everything was different.

"The highest water in the history of the river. . . . The levee is bound to break somewhere. . . . It's bound to . . . and if it doesn't, the water will be running over the top. . . ." Nothing else was discussed. Nothing else mattered. The children had no lessons. We were forbidden to go outside of the front yard. And we must be within calling distance always. We promised this.

All day long in the burning sun the men toiled, building up the levee, putting in "cribbing" in the weak places, and "topping" the whole levee as far as eye could reach north and south. "Topping" consisted of building a sort of wooden fence on the river side of the levee-top. Posts were driven three feet into the earth of the levee and a board fence put against them; and against this "topping" were piled "sandbags"—gunnysacks filled with earth. Already the water was pounding against this "topping," and the waves from passing steamboats washed over the top and trickled down among the clover and grass on the land side of the levee.

The crest of the flood would reach us within a day or two; if we could withstand that, we were safe. "We'll pull through the next few days someway or other." Phrases like this were repeated over and over, as though to give us strength.

A dozen flat-bottomed rowboats lay in the dust of the plantation "street," each boat tied securely to a fence post. "So, if the worst comes to the worst. . . ." Negro women went back and forth, filling the boats with water. One of my uncles made an inspection of the boats every day.

"Hey, Mattie! Your boat's as dry as a cinder. Fill it up with water right now. You heard me! And don't let me catch it dry again."

"How come you-all white folks wants them boats full er water, Mister Paul?"

"Now listen, Mattie—I've explained this over and over. You must understand it. If the levee breaks—and it may break, you know—your dry boat will leak and sink. But these boats that are filled with water will save your lives.

That dry boat of yours wouldn't keep you afloat half an hour. If the levee breaks, you are to turn your boat upside down at once and let the water out of it, then put into it what you want to save—and when the water rises, get into it yourself!"

"Yassuh. . . . Mister Paul!" A pause, and then: "Dat ole levee ain't a-gwine to break, Mister Paul!"

"All right, Mattie, but you do as I tell you!"

And, grumbling, the black girl would fill pail after pail with water from the well and pour it into the boat—grumbling at the white man's "foolishness," only half realizing that his anxiety was for the lives of the negroes, not for his boats.

Night. The grown folks were seated around the dining-room table. The three candles burned under their glass shades, but little black Lawrence had been sent to bed, and the children had been excused from the table. I had climbed up on a chair in order to look on the top shelf of the big bookcase which stood against the wall opposite the fireplace. I stood fingering the books, only half listening to what was said by the others:

". . . but, after all, my dear, we might as well face the fact that every minute may be our last one here. I'd feel safer if you and Mary joined the rest of the family in Baton Rouge."

It was my uncle's voice, very quiet, very earnest. My mother, resting her elbow on the table-cloth and shading her eyes from the candlelight, did not answer for a moment. Then she said: "I'd rather stay. I know that Mary feels the same way about it. We're not in actual danger. There's always the levee. And I would be miserable in town. I would feel that I had deserted when you needed me most. Mary and I can at least see that you are comfortable. . . . And besides, I want to stay."

My uncle leaned over and patted my mother on the shoulder. "If that's the way you feel . . ." he said. Then he broke off, only half persuaded. "But what about . . . ?" and he made a gesture toward the hall. They had both forgotten that I was still in the dining-room. But I knew that they were speaking of me.

I got down from the chair and came up to the table, standing beside my Uncle Paul's chair. "Why do you want us to go away?"

My feelings were hurt. It seemed terrible to think of being sent away from the plantation, although I realized that there was some unknown danger. . . . I could not realize the actual horror of a crevasse.

My uncle put his arm around my shoulder.

"Sonny," he said, "you've got to remember that you're only a little boy. Something might happen to you. A crevasse is no place for women and children . . ."

My throat tightened, but I fought down the desire to cry. If I cried, I should give proof to his words that I was a child. Then I would surely have been sent away. My cousin Kitty and her sister had been sent down on the mail-boat to Baton Rouge days ago. There were only my two uncles, my mother, and one aunt left on the plantation. I fought down the tears and said, shakily: "I don't want to go. I want to stay here. I'm not afraid."

"But if the levee breaks . . ."

"Hush, Paul; don't say such things!" This from my mother.

"I can swim!" I blurted it out.

They both laughed, and this broke the tension. My uncle

Photo by Ewing, Baton Rouge

CREVASSE!—A SCENE NEAR MOREAUVILLE, LOUISIANA, MAY, 1927

rose from the table and pushed back his chair: "Well, for the present then . . . unless things get worse."

My mother kissed him. "We'll stay," she said. And she began to gather up the dishes from the table-cloth. "I told Aunt Rhody to go home," she said in explanation. "Mary and I will clear up tonight."

There was a little more talk, about coffee at midnight and again at three o'clock in the morning. "Better send over two large pots, and get Uncle Isaac to keep up the fire in the stove all night. We may need something."

I listened no longer. I was very glad that we were to stay on the plantation, high water or no high water.

But, just the same, it was a strange sight—those lines of toiling negroes and white men. Cries resounded through the dark as the lanterns went bobbing about on the levee. My mother sat on the gallery for a long time, watching the bobbing lanterns. She didn't talk to me as usual, or tell me stories. She just sat there staring into the dark.

The lamplight made a golden path across the gallery and down the walk; the white pickets of the fence around the flower garden were seen dimly. We sat in silence, listening to the shouts from the levee, watching the flashing lights. After a while some one built a bonfire just outside the front gate, in order that there should be light on the levee just before the big house. I had never seen a fire there before, and it changed the familiar landscape. The big trees were black against the red glow; we could see men passing and repassing between us and the fire. I asked permission to go down to the front gate and watch, but my mother refused. "It's no place for us," she said; "we'd only be in the way."

Once during the night I was awakened by a hoarse shouting. I looked out of the window and saw a man running down the walk. He was calling for my Uncle Paul: "A bad sand boil just below the landing. Those damned crawfish!"

I knew all about crawfish boring holes in the levee, and of the danger of the resulting "boils" that began near the base of the levee on the land side. Unless they were attended to at once, the levee would be undermined.

The door from my room was open, and in the room across the hall I could see my uncle pulling on his boots. My mother stood at the door, holding a steaming cup of coffee in her hand, but my uncle waved it aside and rushed, bareheaded, from the house. I could hear him shouting out instructions to men outside. The voices moved away, the words became indistinct. I slept again.

The next day dragged through somehow. All day long my mother and my aunt worked in the kitchen with Aunt Rhody, making hundreds of sandwiches and gallons of coffee. The door of the smoke-house stood open, and from time to time one of the half-grown black girls would emerge carrying a shoulder of meat or a ham. When the bread was all gone, big boxes of soda crackers were opened and sandwiches made of these. I was allowed to help the black girls carry the tin trays of sandwiches down to the front gate. But on my second trip my uncle spied me and ordered me sternly back to the house. "Don't leave your mother for one minute," he said. Then, smiling in the midst of his admonition, he said: "You see, old fellow, we're having a lot of trouble, and you only hinder us if we have you on our minds as well as the levees!"

Things were worse in the afternoon. My uncle went down into the negro quarters and rounded up all of the able-bodied negro women. They followed him down to the levee. I knew that they were going down to help fill sandbags.

There were other sand boils now, and water was seeping through into the big road just at one end of the front yard.

Nobody came to supper. I ate alone, at one end of the long table, gulping down my eggs and milk and biscuits, in order that I might go back to the front gallery and watch the levee workers.

The negro women had finished their work and had gone back to the quarters. I could hear them laughing in the dark. My Aunt Mary stood in the back door looking out into the darkness. "How I envy their light-heartedness!" she said. My mother, filling an oil lamp just outside the dining-room door, replied with a question: "Do you suppose that they don't understand the danger, or is it merely that they don't care?"

Old Uncle Isaac, bowed and bent with age, came in to ask if the "white ladies" wanted anything. Mr. Paul had sent him. My mother told him to go upstairs and bring down a certain small leather trunk that stood in her bedroom. "We can pack the silver in that," she said to my aunt.

While they were putting in the knives and forks and other things—there were not many—my Uncle Paul came into the dining-room, and, dropping down at one end of the table, rested his head upon his hand. My mother stopped her packing and brought him food, but he was too tired to eat. He sat sipping black coffee. Uncle Isaac stood in the door-way looking at him. Uncle Isaac had taken care of my Uncle Paul when he was a little boy—just as little black Lawrence took care of me—and there was a deep bond between the two men.

"Yo' sho' Gawd oughta take some res'," he said to the white man.

My uncle shook his head: "I can't. I'm too worried about the levee." Suddenly he paused, smiled, and the lines of worry smoothed out of his face. "Why aren't you worried, Isaac?" he asked. "Nothing seems to bother you."

The old negro shuffled his feet, grinned, and replied: "Well, to tell yo' de trufe, Mister Paul, I figgers dis way: 'Tain't no use in both of us worryin' ovah de same thing!"

For the first time that day I saw my uncle's face relax. He roared with laughter. "That's the situation in a nutshell," he said.

Outside in the darkness we could hear the cries of negro men as they drove the horses and mules into the front yard. They were putting them there tonight because they would be nearer the levee in case of overflow.

Everything seemed strange. Nothing was in its accustomed place. My mother and I slept in the guest-room, downstairs, that night. Outside our door stood three trunks, packed with our clothes and a few possessions. I tossed about in the big four-post bed, looking up at the tufted blue silk of the tester, for my mother had forgotten to draw the mosquito bar. A big white moth came and flew about the candle flame. I watched it drowsily. Outside I could still hear the shouts of men at intervals, and the creaking of the heavily loaded wheelbarrows. And I could hear the cows in the yard lowing—uneasy, because they were in an unaccustomed place. It all seemed strange and unreal; but finally all the noise blended itself into one murmuring, it seemed. And I slept.

"Crevasse! Crevasse!"

Shouts in the night. Hoarse cries. "Crevasse! Crevasse!"

There was a candle burning. My mother was helping me put on my shoes. I dragged on my clothes as best I could. My mother was fully dressed, all in black, beside me, urging me to hurry.

We went into the hall. In the doorway my aunt stood, looking out. She held a bundle in her arms. A negro man was standing on the sofa, lifting down the portrait that hung above it—the same portrait of my great-aunt that had terrified me as a small boy. He placed it beside the trunks and ran half way up the staircase in order to get the other portrait that hung there. In the lamplight I could see that there was a pale square on the wall where the portrait had hung. It had been hanging there for many years.

My Uncle Paul and a strange man came dashing up the front steps. "Hurry! Hurry!" they cried. "The water will be here any minute now!" We ran out together through the flower garden, leaving the front doors open behind us. My uncle and the other man were carrying a trunk between them. The negro man had the two portraits. Other negroes were lifting the trunks for us. We ran down the avenue under the arching trees. The moon was shining, clear and bright. Aunt Rhody emerged from the darkness, carrying a lighted lantern. "Ah'm goin' tuh stay wid you, Mis' Mary," she said. Under her arm she was carrying a white rooster.

We ran. And as we hurried, I was conscious of a new sound, a dull roaring, deep and terrible. The sound of the crevasse.

Half way down the avenue I cried out in dismay. There were many black snakes crossing the roadway . . . streams of water, as big around as my arm, writhing through the dust . . . already the crevasse water was upon us. We quickened our pace. The negroes were panting as they ran. All around us from the dark came cries and shouts, and the stamping of animals.

"Look out!"

We stopped and turned to one side of the avenue, for through the front gate a stream of horses and mules was passing. The men were driving the animals out to the levee. One of the negroes set down his burden and put his shoulder against the white pickets of the front fence. There was a rending sound and the picket fell away. We crawled through into the road. Behind us we heard the men knocking off another picket so the trunks could be passed through.

There was no water in the road, but the ditches were level full. We waded knee deep in crossing them. Then the slope of the levee rose before us, and we began to climb up. My Uncle Paul was there, helping us. The men had abandoned the work on the levee—all useless now. Wheelbarrows of earth stood abandoned on the slope. Spades and shovels lay scattered about. The moon made everything clear. The levee was full of moving men.

At the top of the levee we stopped. We had reached our destination. The water outside lapped at the very top, rushing against the sandbags that were piled there. The levee-top was muddy and tramped by many feet.

We were breathless, exhausted. I saw my mother sitting on a trunk, her hand pressed to her side. My Aunt Mary was beside her, her arm about her shoulder. My Uncle Paul was taking count of us.

"Is every one here?" Then, a moment later, "Have we forgotten anything?"

The negroes were driving the animals up on the levee. The mules and horses were excited, running about, kicking. The cows were lowing. We were in danger of being trampled underfoot at any moment. At the foot of the levee, far below us in the road, a negro man on horseback was riding up and down, shouting. The frightened horses were trying to leave the levee and go down into the road again; he rode back and forth, driving them back upon the slope. The animals were all around us now. We barricaded ourselves as best we could behind trunks and bundles. A negro man armed with a stick stood on guard, to keep the animals from stamping us to death.

"I think that you'll be safe enough here." It was my Uncle Paul speaking. "I'm going back to the quarters to see if everybody got out safely."

My mother tried to stop him: "Paul! You'll be drowned. The water must be waist deep back there!" But he only waved his arm and smiled: "I'll be all right! I must go." And he rode down the slope of the levee. We watched him. The horse stopped at the wide ditch at the bottom, snorting, throwing up its head before the water which was now covering the road. But my uncle struck the horse's neck with his hand, and the horse jumped over the ditch and went splashing across the road. We saw him disappear down the avenue which led to the house. My aunt buried her face in her hands.

Aunt Rhody was making inquiries of the other negro women grouped around us concerning the safety of different people in the quarters. She was counting her nieces and nephews and cousins: "Wha's Leafy? Wha's Jeems? Wha's Queen? Wha's Dicey?"

Every moment it seemed that the roaring of the crevasse grew louder as the opening increased in size and the mad torrent of muddy water went sweeping over the fields. In the moonlight we could see the water in the road plainly now, and the fields showed water between the rows of sugar-cane. But the plantation-house stood there as serenely as ever, the lights in the hall burning bright. It seemed impossible that the water could rise high enough to enter the house, so secure and safe it seemed standing there, with the wide front door open and the light streaming out into the trees. But from the levee-top we could see the water, far back in the field. The whole plantation would be under before morning.

Around us the animals bellowed and snorted. They made futile dashes down the slope to the edge of the road, then came rushing back. Negro men moved about, trying to quiet them, fearing that some would be killed or would fall into the deep ditch. Near us stood Uncle Isaac, armed with a stick, driving off the animals when they came too close.

My aunt and my mother were frantic with anxiety for my uncle's safety. It seemed hours before he came into sight again, still on horseback; but the horse was more than knee deep in water now, and my uncle was wet through, for both he and the horse had fallen into some deep ditch which was hidden below the rising water. Behind him on the horse was the old negro woman, Aunt Julia. She was crying and moaning as he helped her up the levee. She had lost all her treasures—her pattern quilt, her "buryin' clothes," everything. These things had been put into Mattie's boat— but Mattie had allowed her boat to dry out—and it had sunk. Aunt Julia had barely escaped with her life.

The other negroes, my uncle reported, were all safe and would remain in their boats until morning. Some of them were already making their way toward the levee as the water increased in depth. But there was a strong current running from the crevasse and it made the passage difficult.

"The supports under the back of the house are beginning to go," he concluded.

"That means that the house will go?" My aunt asked. He nodded: "I'm afraid so."

He rode away from us, down the levee toward the crevasse. We tried to comfort Aunt Julia, but she only moaned and cried for her lost possessions.

It seemed a long time before my uncle came riding back, with the news that the levee was caving rapidly, and that we must move farther along in order to be safe. "For with the river rushing at this rate," he said, "there's no telling how wide the break will be."

Accordingly, we began a sorry pilgrimage along the levee-top, moving farther away from the house at every step. The negroes moved with us, slowly, carrying their bundles and baskets with them. Many of them had saved their dogs, and we went forward like a broken army in retreat.

Our dogs were with us, worried, frightened. They remained close at heel, whimpering at intervals.

And behind us the cattle came, moving slowly, held in check by the negroes. The cows never ceased lowing.

After we had gone five hundred yards or more along the levee-top we stopped again. Our possessions were put down, and we took inventory again. The portrait of my great-aunt lay on the levee slope at our feet. The familiar face, its dark, tragic eyes staring upward, seemed strangely unreal in the moonlight.

Just as we paused, the cattle and mules began to stampede. We were swept under a rush of bodies, almost trampled upon, almost forced in the rushing water just below us on the river side. I saw a terrified mule come down upon me, and threw up my arm for protection; he shied off and went blundering down the slope, but the mule behind him crashed into the portrait that was lying on the grass. I saw the forefoot of the animal go through the painted face, and when he pulled it out again there was only a gaping hole, with the white clover showing through, and the gold frame glinting in the moonlight.

It was perhaps an hour later that I heard my mother

cry out, and following the direction of her gaze I saw that the lights in the plantation-house had gone out; the water had risen high enough to extinguish the lamps on the marble-topped table in the hall.

Slowly the long night passed. The first gray showed in the eastern sky. When the moonlight had faded, we sat disconsolately watching the water rise higher and higher on the land side of the levee. It was more than half way up now, and the river outside the levee had fallen two feet or more as the current rushed through the crevasse.

We watched the sun rise round and red over the ruined fields. And in its first rays we saw that the plantation-house was askew; the whole building slanted down sharply to one side; one of the chimneys had fallen. The water was almost at the top of the front door. The flower garden and the shrubs had disappeared. Only the trees remained, standing with water half way up their trunks, each tree making a fan-shaped ripple in the current. Between us and the ruined house was an unbroken stretch of muddy water.

The river had taken the land again. The plantation of my childhood no longer existed.

Part Two

IN THE BEGINNING

Chapter VII

BEFORE THE WHITE MEN CAME

WHEN you were a child you played the wishing game, probably. Nearly all children play it. You wish for a million dollars, or to be a policeman, or a prize-fighter, or queen of the fairies, according to your age or sex or state of mind. Very early in life I found myself wishing that I could turn back the clock of the years and live again in the old days of the Mississippi Valley.

This, I suppose, was because I heard so much about the old days. De Soto, La Salle, and the other explorers took their places beside Robinson Crusoe and Santa Claus. It was as easy to believe in one as it was to believe in the other; so I believed in them all. Iberville and Bienville were as familiar as *Br'er Rabbit* and *Br'er Coon,* and negro folk stories and Indian legends were as familiar as *Little Red Riding Hood* and *Cinderella.* But I think that I liked the stories best which dealt with the Mississippi and the land lying along its banks.

As a very small boy I remember a group of men who came to make an examination of Indian mounds near my home. The man in charge was a professor from some university. He had an assistant, and six negroes with shovels made the excavations. These excavations were rather disappointing, for the pottery brought to light was broken into fragments, and the bones of long-dead Indians were so brittle that they crumbled at a touch.

But it was from these men that I heard something that set my imagination aflame. They spoke among themselves of the probable age of these mounds. It seemed as though they spoke of eternity.

And the idea of antiquity fascinates me today, just as it charmed my fancy then. How I wish that I could turn back the clock and see with my own eyes that great valley as it appeared hundreds, thousands of years ago!

A vast wilderness, a land stretching away to the north, the east, the west. Gigantic forests; animals strange and terrible. Huge prehistoric beasts prowling among trees and through tangled vines. And always the Mississippi River coming down through the center of the valley as it comes now. But it was, probably, a very different river from the one we see today; for it spread out its width then, and the lowlands were a network of streams and lakes in times of low water, and joined the mighty river in one huge, slow-moving stream as the water rose in the spring.

It would appear that in prehistoric times great glaciers moved down from the north and cut a wide, deep valley through the upper reaches of the river. And through this valley came frequent floods. For ages these floods brought sand and soil and silt into the stream, which widened as the water rose, and which narrowed again as the water receded. So much drift has been brought down that the main channel has been crowded from the center of the valley toward one of the precipitous banks on either side, while the remainder of what formerly constituted the river bed is now a low tableland, with a gradual ascent toward the hills.

Some geologists tell us that, at one time in the past, the Mississippi River ended at bluffs where the city of Baton Rouge, Louisiana, stands today, and that the great fertile lowlands which lie between that point and the Gulf of Mexico have been added gradually, year by year. But how slowly these lands are built up!

Mark Twain points out in his "Life on the Mississippi" that this statement of geologists gives us the exact age of this—the newest part of North America—and that exact age, he says, is one hundred and twenty thousand years! Call it new, if you like!

It is useless for me—with unscientific mind—to try to tell you just when these strange prehistoric beasts prowled about in the Mississippi Valley, beasts which dined delicately upon the fronds of maidenhair fern twenty-five feet high; but such beasts were there. And men were there before them. Or, rather, some primitive type of man was there.

In 1898, Professor George E. Beyer, of Tulane University, New Orleans, made an investigation and study of Indian mounds in Louisiana. In this investigation many interesting things were brought to light. But perhaps the most startling information contained in his report (Publications of the Louisiana Historical Society, Vol. XI, part 2) has to do with an accidental discovery. In sinking a shaft for a salt mine at Avery's Island in southwest Louisiana, the mine caved in and made a great fissure in the earth. Several strata were exposed, and bones of prehistoric animals were found embedded ten feet below the surface of the ground. But of even greater interest was the fact that eighteen feet below the surface, and below the strata containing the bones of animals, were found articles which were clearly the handiwork of man. The things were of small importance in themselves, only small mats of woven basketry, which had been preserved in salt deposits; but the fact that they lay in deeper layers than the bones of the now extinct animals gives proof that there were men alive in the Mississippi Valley even then.

"The remains of extinct mammalians, such as Mastodon, Elephas, Mylodon, Equus and others, have been found embedded in strata from eight to ten feet above the drifts," Mr. Beyer writes, "and no matter at what computation of age you may arrive, the fact remains nevertheless that man existed in lower Louisiana prior even to the embedding in the soil of these gigantic Pachyderms."

Bones of extinct animals have been found in many parts of the valley. In 1811 a great earthquake destroyed the town of New Madrid, Missouri, and played havoc with the Mississippi River generally. In a large opening in the earth at New Madrid, bones of an animal were seen, "bones so large that those who saw were afraid." Now Missouri and Louisiana are not near each other, so it seems likely that these fantastic beasts were numerous in the valley.

But, after all, we know very little of these animals and men that lived beside the Mississippi before the coming of the white man. Our real history begins with the coming of de Soto. But we can deduce some things of the country's past from the statements made by the early explorers. We know, for example, that there were Indian trails or "traces" —long, clear-cut roads which ran through the wilderness. And the Indian trails usually followed the paths made by roving animals.

The buffalo—and the country was full of buffalo, both east and west of the Mississippi—were sagacious beasts, and could be depended upon to find the shortest route between two given points. If the path curved, it was for some good reason: a swamp, or dangerous ground, or a depression too deep to be crossed without danger. The Indians

INDIAN MOUNDS PROVED ISLANDS OF REFUGE

Near Greenville, Mississippi, during the floods of 1927

followed the old buffalo roads. Such a road was the old "Natchez Trace," or part of it, at least, some of which is in use today.

The early explorers spoke of these roads "worn deep in the earth," and they spoke frequently of the Indian mounds which dotted the country. A great deal has been written about these mounds, but even today they remain a baffling mystery. Some were burial mounds; that much is certain, for excavations have brought many skeletons to light—skeletons buried in orderly rows, side by side. In some mounds the bones have been found in disorder and buried in ashes, seeming to point to burning at the stake; but this is a conjecture. Some writers believe that these mounds were the scenes of human sacrifice, a part of the sun worship.

De Soto's men speak of finding a chief's house upon one of these mounds, a house with a palisade, while the village of huts lay at the foot of the mound. It is probable that many of the mounds were fortifications. But there are many which seem to serve no purpose, unless as a place of refuge from high water which inundated the valley.

Certain it is that Indians took refuge upon these mounds in time of inundation by the Mississippi. Certain geologists point to the ridges of earth which connected these mounds in some localities. They believe that these elevated runways were used as a means of communication when a tribe was living above the waters which covered the surrounding country. Other writers take issue with this statement, saying that many of the mounds, especially those in the State of Missouri, are above the reach of flood.

But whether the mound-builders made these round and rectangular embankments as refuges from inundation, or whether they served some other purpose, it is certain that in later times the mounds have proved a sanctuary to Indian and white man alike, and to animals, driven from lowlands by encroaching water.

They proved a sanctuary to hundreds of men—and hundreds of animals—in the flood of 1927.

Negroes and white men fled to the mounds in Mississippi, Arkansas, and Louisiana during the overflow of this year, and in some remote places the mounds housed as strange a gathering as the celebrated collection in Noah's Ark.

With high water from broken levees all about, and with no high land anywhere near-by, domestic and wild animals clung to these mounds as their only escape from certain death. I do not believe that I shall ever forget the strange scene I witnessed as I went close by one of these artificial mountains of earth with members of the Coast Guard rescue squad.

Extending but two or three feet above the surface of the rushing water, the mound rose—a wooded island not more than twenty-five feet long—crowded with animals. There were cows and mules, standing near the edge, looking out toward the rescue boats. Chickens were at the water's edge. 'Coons and opossums filled the trees, and knotted snakes hung from the branches in close proximity to the smaller animals. Crouched upon the ground were wildcats, their tails lashing, their teeth bared. But they made no move to attack the other animals around them, nor did they attempt to escape when the rescue boat came near. They held their ground because they could retreat no farther, terrified equally of man and of water. A black and white cat—some child's pet—stood between the forepaws of an antlered buck. A doe and two spotted fawns cowered behind the larger deer. The grass seemed alive with field mice and wood rats, and there were small black and white animals unfamiliar to me and to the sailors in the boat with me.

We came close to the mound in the motor-boat, looking for men or women who might have taken refuge there; but the animals were alone. Our boat was small; there was no way to save any of them. The domestic animals came close to the water, as though asking help. The wild animals did not move, but stood watching us with wide eyes. Our boat drifted with the current—farther, farther away. The tops of half-submerged trees came between the mound and the boat. We went on. The animals were left to their fate.

Similar scenes must have taken place upon these old Indian mounds since time immemorial; but we can only guess at the tragedies which the Mississippi brought to man and animal, before the coming of the first white man.

Chapter VIII

THE NAME "MISSISSIPPI"

In the writings of the early explorers of the continent of North America the great river which flows through the central valley is spoken of by various names. But from the very beginning, it may be noted that the Algonquin Indians called the stream "Mech-e-se-be," meaning Great Waters, or Father of Waters. Other Indian tribes, lower in the valley, had other names for the stream.

The first appearance of a great river on a map of the New World was on a chart sent to Charles V, in 1520, by Cortez. A forked stream is indicated as entering the Gulf of Mexico somewhere near the point where the Mississippi enters the Gulf. This river is called "Rio del Spiritu Sancto" (River of the Holy Ghost). As far as we know, the maker of the map indicated the river on hearsay—for there were stories afloat of mighty streams and mighty monsters, cities of gold, cities of jewels, of man-eating trees, nations of pygmies, and of men like gods. What was one great river, more or less?

Cabiza de Vaca had strange tales to tell, but he did not name the broad stream that he found on his way to Mexico from Florida in 1528. De Vaca was sailing along the Gulf coast, and he tells that he encountered a fresh water outflow at a point about longitude 90 degrees. This was many years before de Soto came afoot across the continent and crossed the great river which he called "Rio Grande." Shortly after,

68

THE MISSISSIPPI RIVER NEAR NATCHEZ

It was somewhere near this point that DeSoto and his men first looked upon the great river.

he died and was buried in the stream. Garcillasso, who wrote an account of de Soto, called the river "Chucagua," and declares that the Indians called it so; but this, it may be noted, was one of the early names for the Ohio River. Other early writers designated the Mississippi as "Tamalisieu," as "Tapatu," and as "Mico."

De Soto left no maps. A map of Florida by Ortelius, in 1580, shows the first interior course of the Mississippi, and here he calls it by its earlier name, "Rio del Spiritu Sancto." Other old maps show the river designated by such names as "Chucaquax," "Canaveral," and "Rio de Flores." It was not until 1661 that the Algonquin name "Mischipi" was given to the stream, and this spelling appears on a map by Peñalosa, governor of New Mexico, who went in that year to visit the Quivera Indians. Now, as Peñalosa heard this name from the Arkansas Indians, who were not of Algonquin stock, it appears that among the Indians themselves the whole watercourse was called by this name in pre-pioneer days. The pronunciation is indicated as "Mee-chee-see-bee."

In Vol. 51 of the Jesuit Relations, edited by Thwaits, Allouez, the Jesuit missionary, is credited with using the word "Mississippi" for the first time by priest or pioneer. This was before the discovery by Marquette, but for thirty years there had been indications in the Jesuit letters of a great river flowing south or southwest, its sources not far from the Great Lakes.

"Palisado" and "Escondido" were later Spanish designations, the first referring to the trees seen floating in the stream near its mouth, and the latter name from the fact that numerous bayous, cut-offs, and wanderings of channel made the river difficult to follow.

"St. Louis" was the original French name for the Mississippi. Joliet called the river "Baude." La Salle first called the Mississippi "Colbert," for the great French statesman. Every explorer, it seems, called the river by his particular designation. But the name Mississippi continued to be used. The Indians called it so, and so it remained. The bottom lands near the mouth of the river were called by the Indians "Mis-ku-tuk." This means "meadow people," or a place of meadows and grass.

And as "Mississippi" we know it today—for after having been called by various and sundry terms, it resumes the original name, which comes so easily to the lips, and which, in its very sound, seems to give us a picture of the mighty river, rushing ever onward toward the Mexican Gulf.

Chapter IX

HERNANDO DE SOTO discovered the Mississippi River in 1541.

You may find this simple statement in any child's history of the United States. But the expedition of de Soto was far from a simple thing. It was said in Spain, when the fleet set sail, that this was the most lavish fleet ever sent to the New World. The historian Garcillasso relates hundreds of incidents of de Soto's expedition—two large volumes, in fact. And many other historians have written of it. But the discovery of the Mississippi—the fact that makes de Soto an important figure to us—was merely an accident in a search for gold. To de Soto and his men the Mississippi was only another river to cross—and a large and swift river at that. And it is quite certain that none of these men foresaw the importance of their discovery. They were in search of treasure, and of new worlds to conquer. They had been lured into the wilderness, like many adventurers before and after them, by a bright dream. And they traveled hopefully in search of golden cities. The muddy Mississippi stood between them and this dream—a vision which had begun to fade before they reached the river's bank and saw the stream glittering before them in the sun.

De Soto had been one of the lieutenants of Pizarro in the conquest of Peru, and he had returned to his native Spain to enjoy his riches. He was married to a beautiful woman and he loved her very much, it is said. And she sailed with him from Spain when he left for America. De Soto's expedition was fitted up at his own expense and nothing had been spared to provide for his men in all their needs. Six hundred picked men he had with him, and hundreds of horses. The men wore armor and carried swords and cross-bows. A group of musicians accompanied the party, and the army was imposing as the armor glinted in the sun, and the colors of pennants and flags shone bright.

The fleet arrived in Cuba in due time (1538), and here were assembled the notables of the island to pay homage to de Soto and his bride. The welcome, it is said, lasted for three months, "with banquets, balls, masquerades, bull-fights, and games, with prizes of gold and silver for the gallants, as if celebrating in anticipation the triumphs of conquest."

The Doña Isabella, the bride of de Soto, was left in Cuba, and the six hundred men and the hundreds of horses, with all their paraphernalia, set sail for the coast of Florida, arriving near Tampa Bay in 1539. Here they left the ships and marched inland—an army with banners flying, marching into the wilderness.

The rest of the story is one of the cruelest and most terrible in the history of the New World. One becomes sated with horror in reading of it. The Indians opposed their progress from the beginning, and fighting began almost immediately. One sickens to read of Indian villages set ablaze, of men killed and tortured, or women ravished, then killed. Six hundred strong men were there—and these were brutal times. And the Indians were equal to the Spanish in cruelty.

One has but to read the story of Juan Ortiz to realize that. Ortiz had come to Florida with an earlier expedition and had been captured by Indians. For three years he had lived among them, tortured, goaded beyond endurance. At every Indian feast day he was brought out—a boy of nineteen—and tortured for the Indians' pleasure. His account of his suffering is almost past belief. He managed to escape and joined de Soto's party. They had found him naked in the wilderness, his body covered with burns and lacerations —mute testimony for the story he told.

His story, told to the six hundred men in armor, inflamed them further. From that time they gave no quarter to the Indians. The story of the expedition becomes a record of cruelty unequaled elsewhere. Men were crucified, head down; women were raped and men disemboweled, while villages aflame threw their lurid light into the dark wilderness. Children were thrown high into the air and fell quivering to the ground, pierced by many arrows. A gentle form of punishment was that of cutting off both hands of a captured Indian and setting him free in the forest.

Nor were the Indians slow to learn refinements of torture from the Spanish, to which they added their own cruder forms. Battle succeeded battle; more villages blazed, more men lay dead. The Spanish pressed on, traversing the territory now known as Florida, Georgia, Alabama, Mississippi, Arkansas, and Louisiana. The Altamaha, Ogeechee, Coosa, Mississippi, White, and Ouachita rivers were discovered in the order named.

The nearest approach to the golden cities for which they sought was found at Cofachiqui, which Indian legend locates somewhere in Barnwell County, South Carolina. Here the Spanish encountered a gentler, kindlier tribe of Indians than they had met heretofore. This tribe was governed by an Indian princess, who, when she heard of the approach of the white men, came out to meet them. An account of the meeting, taken from original sources, is incorporated in Grace King's excellent history of Hernando de Soto called "De Soto in the Land of the Floridas."

The Spanish forces were waiting upon a river bank when the princess came to meet them. "Only a few moments later the Spaniards saw two large canoes hastily made ready," Miss King writes. "A canopy was raised over one of them. Then a litter approached the bank, borne upon the shoulders of four warriors; a young squaw, evidently the princess, descended from it and seated herself in the canoe that had the awning. Eight Indian women followed, taking the paddles; the men went in the other canoe. The women rowed the princess across the river, and when she stepped out of the canoe, they followed, walking up the bank after her."

She received de Soto graciously—Juan Ortiz acting as interpreter—and gave him the freedom of her village. She begged, however, that he would take only half the corn from her granary, as her people must be fed; and pestilence, she said, had weakened the tribe. The eyes of the Spaniards glittered as they observed the string of large pearls around her throat. And when de Soto asked her about them, she took them off and presented them to him. In return, he gave her a ring from his finger, a gold ring, set with a ruby. It must have been a pretty ceremony, there in the wilderness —the Indian princess and her women, and de Soto and his men in armor. But the generosity of the princess and her submissiveness did not save the treasure-houses of the tribe. Finding that the princess had only polished copper—not gold—and no silver, de Soto asked her if there were jewels or precious stones. She led him to the burial house of the tribe. He took with him thirty of his officers.

"The usual burial room of the Indian temples was presented to them," Miss King continues. "Around the four sides on benches were ranged the burial chests of the tribe —chests of wood or great baskets of plaited osier. The Spaniards lifted the covers; all were filled to the top with pearls, large and small, fine and coarse, pure and discolored, quantities upon quantities of them. And here and there over the floor lay heaps of the finest skins, dressed with the fur on, and dyed, hardly less valuable in European markets than the pearls. It seemed there were no less than thousands of bushels of pearls in the temple, and while de Soto was looking around, the officers of the treasury began quickly to weigh them in their scales, which they had brought along. When he saw what they were doing, he told them that the army could not be hampered and burdened by heavy loads of pearls; that his intention was to take only two arrobas of them (fifty pounds) to show their quality and purity; as for the quantity, he said that would have to be described in writing. The treasury officers implored him to let them take what they had weighed, which they said could not be missed from what was left. He consented to that, and dipping into the pearls, he gave his two joined hands full to each cavalier to make rosaries of, he said, to say prayers for their sins on. So they left the temple elated, but also ardent to see the other one, which the princess said was larger and richer than this."

The treasure-houses were looted before de Soto and his men went on their way, but their loot was lost in the battle of Mauvilla—a fierce battle in which de Soto lost heavily of both men and horses.

Inflamed with anger, made mad by their losses, the Spaniards now entered into further excesses of carnage. A battle with Chickasaws at an Indian fort left two thousand dead Indians in the field—if one can believe the accounts left us by those who accompanied the party. This was not battle;

it was wholesale slaughter, for the Indians were penned up in the fort like cattle, and the naked, writhing mass was powerless before the swords of the armed and armored men. The number of Spaniards lost is not stated, but fifteen men died in camp during the first days of the march onward.

Through swamp and morass they went, encountering Indians, killing them, or burning villages and taking the corn from the granaries as the terrified Indians fled to the woods. At last they came to the banks of a great river—and the Mississippi lay before them. Authorities disagree as to the exact spot of the discovery. Some believe that the Spaniards approached the river somewhere near the bluffs of Natchez, Mississippi; others believe that it was near the mouth of Red River. Still others write that it was thirty miles below the spot where Memphis, Tennessee, now stands.

On Sunday, May 8, 1541, according to Ranjel, who accompanied the expedition, and who wrote of it afterward, the Spaniards "reached the Indian village of Quisquis, but finding little maize there, they moved on to the shore of a great river." The "Gentleman of Elvas," a Portuguese, who was a member of the party, writes as follows:

He [de Soto] went to see the river and found that near unto it was a great store of timber to make barges and good situation of ground to encamp in. Presently he removed himself thither. They made houses and pitched camp in a plain field a crossbow-shot from the river. And thither was gathered all the maize of the towns which they had lately passed. They began presently, to cut and hew down timber and to saw planks for barges. The Indians came presently down to the river. They leaped on shore and declared to the Governor that they were subjects of a great lord whose name was Aquixo, who was lord of many towns and governed many people on the other side of the river, and came to tell him on his behalf that the next day he, with all his

LAKE ITASKA, MINNESOTA, THE SOURCE OF THE MISSISSIPPI

men would come to see what it would please him to command him.

The next day, with speed, the cacique came with two hundred canoes full of Indians with their bows and arrows, painted, and with great plumes of white feathers and many other colors, with shields in their hands wherewith they defended the rowers on both sides; and the men of war stood from the head to the stern with their bows and arrows in their hands. The canoe wherein the cacique was has a tilt over the stern, and he sat under the tilt and so were other canoes of the principal Indians. And from under the tilt where the chief man sat, he governed and commanded the other people.

All joined together and came within a stone's cast of the shore. Then the cacique said to the Governor, which walked along the river's side with others that waited on him, that he was coming thither to visit, to honor and obey him, because he knew he was the greatest and mightiest lord on the earth; therefore he would see what he would command him to do. The Governor yielded his thanks and requested him to come on shore that they might the better communicate together. And without any answer to that point, he sent him three canoes, wherein were great store of fish and loaves made of the substance of prunes like bricks. After he had received all he thanked him and prayed him again to come on shore. And because the cacique's purpose was to see if with dissimulation he might do some hurt, when they saw that the Governor and his men were in readiness they began to go from the shore; and with a great cry the crossbowmen which were ready, shot at them and slew five or six of them. They retired with great order. None did leave his oar, though the next to him were slain, and, shielding themselves, they went farther off. Afterwards they came many times and landed, and when any of us came toward them fled into their canoes; which were very pleasant to behold, for they were very great and well made, and had their tilts, plumes, and flags and, with the multitudes of people that were in them, they seemed to be a fair army of galleys.

In thirty days space while the Governor remained there, they

made four barges; in three of which he commanded twelve
horsemen to enter, in each of them four. In the morning, three
hours before day, men which he trusted would land in despite
of the Indians and make sure the passage or die, and some footmen, being crossbow-men, went with them, and rowers to set
them on the other side. And in the other barge he commanded
John de Guzman to pass with the footmen, which was made
captain in stead of Francisco Maldonado. And because the
stream was swift, they went a quarter of a league up the river
along the bank and, crossing over, fell down with the stream
and landed right over against the camp. Two stones' cast
before they came to land, the horsemen went out of the barges
on horseback to a sandy plot of very hard and clear ground
where all of them landed without any resistance. As soon as
those that passed first were on land on the other side, the
barges returned to the place where the Governor was; and
within two hours after sun rising all the people went over.

The river was almost half a league broad. If a man stood
still on the other side it could not be discerned whether he was
a man or no. The river was of great depth and of a strong
current. The water was always muddy. There came down the
river continually many trees and timber, which the force of the
water and stream brought down. There was a great store of fish
in it of sundry sorts, and most of it differing from the fresh
water fish of Spain.

So much for the description by an "eye witness." Those
of us who have stood upon the river bank in the State of
Mississippi know what difficulties this crossing must have
entailed. For the river is indeed swift and deep, and in times
of high water—clearly stated, in that trees and bushes were
floating down the river—there are eddies and "boils" in the
river which play havoc with small boats. The Indians in their
light canoes must have been expert river men in that they
were able to "retire in great order."

It must have been something to see! De Soto and his men
in their armor, there under the moss-draped trees beside the

Mississippi, and the many canoes of painted Indians, bedecked with feathers: men like brightly painted toys, set down in the wilderness, beside the rushing river.

On the other side of the stream the Spaniards stopped only long enough to break up the boats in order to save the nails and fastenings. Then they resumed their march.

All summer the company marched through a country inhabited only by fierce and hostile Indians. Three years before, when they set sail from Spain, they were six hundred strong, and, as we have seen, they had more than two hundred horses. But now the company had been reduced to less than half its strength, and more than half of the horses had been killed. Their clothes had worn out, and they were now clothed in skins. They were broken, exhausted. They wanted to return, yet they marched farther and farther into the wilderness. The golden cities were as remote as ever—and the men had begun to doubt if such treasures existed at all.

Winter came on, and the party went into camp in the western part of what is now the State of Arkansas. It was here that de Soto was compelled to give up his search for the Eldorado, and in the spring he determined to retrace his steps to the great river. The backward march cheered the men. For return, to them, signified Cuba, and beyond Cuba was Spain. The company marched south, entered Louisiana, and reached the shore of the Mississippi again. De Soto and his men began building two small vessels to send to Cuba with the news of his expedition. He had decided to plant a settlement on the banks of the river; and to effect a beginning, he had taken over an Indian village which could be easily defended from hostile tribes.

But here de Soto became ill. For months he had been suffering from some illness, though he kept bravely on; now he became worse. The malady baffled those around

him. None of the simple remedies that the men knew benefited him. Whatever his sickness was, he saw that the end
was near. He called officers to his bedside and gave them
instructions. The soldiers were brought before him in squads
of twenty, and he said good-by to them all.

When the priest who had followed him through his wanderings told him that his hour approached, he said: "I submit without a murmur to the will of God." And so died
Hernando de Soto, in the forty-second year of his age,
May 21, 1542.

His death was a calamity. His was the only spirit that
could hold the hostile Indians in check. The Spaniards had
impressed upon the Indians that their leader was a god and
could not die. Now, with his death, they were afraid that
the Indians would become bolder and would attack them at
once.

Accordingly, they tried to conceal his death from the
savages who were all about them. He was buried at night,
in an excavation that the Indians themselves had made—a
place where earth had been taken to build one of the Indian
mounds, it is said. The soldiers were ordered by Luis de
Moscoso, de Soto's successor, to tell the Indians that their
leader was better; and in order to keep up this deception
the soldiers were bidden to hide their grief under gay, care-
less faces, and to say that they were happy that their commander was recovering. Accordingly, the soldiers played
games, riding their horses over and over the new-made
grave, in order that the Indians might not see the fresh
earth. But the Indians were suspicious. It was noted that
they passed and repassed the pits from which earth had been
taken, whispering together, and "motioning with their
chins."

The Spaniards were afraid that the Indians would dig up

the body and wreak their vengeance upon it. And so it was decided to remove the body to a safer place. The Mississippi River offered sanctuary. Two nights later the body was disinterred and taken into midstream. Here de Soto was laid finally to rest in the mighty river which he had discovered.

Accounts of the burial differ. Some historians say that the body was wrapped in cloth, weighted with sand, and dropped noiselessly overboard. Another historian declares that a tree was cut down, a place in the trunk hollowed out; de Soto's body was placed within the tree-trunk and the opening closed; the tree-trunk was then dropped into the river, where "it sank from view." The latter, while a much better story, sounds improbable, as it is quite certain that the tree-trunk would have floated in the stream—and there were no stones with which to weight it down. Nevertheless, all authorities agree that de Soto was buried at midnight, or near midnight, in the Mississippi.

The exact spot where this dramatic burial service took place is not known, and it is possible that, with the shifting of the river, the place in its channel where the body of de Soto settled in the ooze may be dry land today.

As soon as their chief was buried, the followers of de Soto turned their thoughts to escaping from the land which had brought only misery to them. They abandoned the idea of sending ships to Cuba, and decided to strike out overland for Mexico. But so many obstacles stood in the way of such a journey that, after a time, they retraced their steps to the Mississippi, and summoning all their sinking energies, built enough rough vessels to embark all that remained.

In these boats they set out, pursued by hundreds of Indians in canoes. The Spaniards had no weapons and no ammunition. They had used their guns and swords to make fastenings for the ships. Many of the men, and some of the few remaining horses, were killed by arrows. Many more lives were lost before they reached the mouth of the river. At last a remnant of the miserable party reached a Spanish fort in Mexico, and later embarked for Cuba.

The river was left to the Indians again. The cruelties of the Spaniards were remembered in Indian legends. Men died, men were born, and Time's pageant rolled on. One hundred and twenty years passed before another white man looked upon the Mississippi.

Chapter X

EXPLORATION

It seems strange to us today that such a long period of time elapsed between de Soto's discovery of the Mississippi and the second coming of white men to the shores of the river. But it must be remembered that the continent of North America was a vast and trackless wilderness, and no man could say how great it was. The wilderness swallowed up men and they were seen no more. Or those remnants of parties that had penetrated far into the forests brought back such tales of horror and fear that brave men paused before entering this vast labyrinth.

Nevertheless, as early as 1634, French missionary priests penetrating the interior westward from Canada, in order to preach the gospel and make converts to Christianity, heard rumors of a great river which ran through regions toward the farther west. And in 1665, Father Allouez brought back the first authentic account of it. He wrote that he had seen the river with his own eyes, and it extended away across the continent, and that no man could say where the stream led.

Father Marquette, a Canadian priest, and Joliet, a merchant, left Quebec in 1673, penetrated the Wisconsin River and entered the Mississippi. They are the first white men who made an exploration of the Mississippi, so far as we know. They floated down the Mississippi as far as the mouth of the Arkansas River. Satisfied that the river led southward to the sea, they returned—a long and tedious journey up the great stream.

It was not until 1678 that La Salle made his expedition down the Mississippi. La Salle reached the Mississippi by way of Lake Michigan and the Illinois River. In the Illinois country he encountered difficulties and dangers. Iroquois messengers had incited the Indians against him, and his own men threatened his life. He erected a fort on the Illinois River in 1680 and, in sadness, called it "Crèvecœur"— Broken Heart. Leaving his men there, he walked back through the snow to Quebec to secure supplies. In his absence the men mutinied and destroyed the fort. But La Salle was dauntless; nothing could turn him away from his purpose. Accordingly, a year later, with men and supplies, his boats were ready for the voyage. He went down the Illinois River and entered the Mississippi on the sixth of February, 1682. He made short stops at the mouths of the Missouri and Ohio rivers, but the first landing of importance was at Chickasaw Bluffs, near the present location of Memphis, Tennessee. Here a log fort was built and called Fort Prudhomme—so called in jest, for Prudhomme was the carpenter who accompanied the expedition, and at the Chickasaw Bluffs settlement he had wandered away from the party and become lost. It was here that La Salle took formal possession of the territory for France.

The party continued down the river, passing the spot where the luckless de Soto had been buried in the muddy water. And it would appear that, although more than a century and a quarter had passed, de Soto's expedition was remembered still by the Indian tribes along the lower river —for it was here that the hostilities of the Indians increased to such an extent that it was difficult for La Salle and his men to proceed on their way.

At last the mouth of the Mississippi was reached—a vast and trackless swamp, filled with flowing streams and small islands, and with marsh grass and canes growing high everywhere. Here, within sight of the Gulf of Mexico, La Salle erected a cross on April 9, 1682, and in the name of Louis XIV, King of France, he took possession of the river and all its tributaries, and of all the land drained by it—although he had no idea of the vast sweep of territory that this included. It was all for his country, he declared, and in taking formal possession he called the river "Saint Louis" and the land "Louisiana."

La Salle's plan, from the beginning, had been to open up the river for trade and navigation; his plans were limitless. His dream included forts all along the river, and settlements at all the forts. He had been accompanied on his first expedition by de Tonty. And Father Hennepin, who had been sent on a separate exploration, ascended the river as far as the Falls of St. Anthony, which he named in honor of St. Anthony of Padua. And here it may be said that La Salle's fort of the Broken Heart—somewhere near the present site of Peoria, Illinois—was the first attempt made to colonize the Mississippi Valley. For this reason it is important in the history of the river.

After his discovery of the mouth of the Mississippi, and his realization of the tremendous territory that the river commanded, La Salle returned to France to make his report to the king. He was royally received, and his glowing tales of new empire so fired the imagination of Louis XIV that he was ready to help with money and men in taking possession of the territory. It was proposed that colonies be sent over to build the forts and make the settlements. The settlements were to extend from Canada to the Gulf. La Salle, of course, was to have charge of the new expedition.

Accordingly, he set sail from France with four ships. But after months of sailing, and after reaching the Mexican Gulf, the mouth of the Mississippi eluded him. The ships sailed on and on, past the low-lying land and countless sandbars at the river's mouth, and the expedition landed somewhere near the present site of Matagorda, Texas. The colony failed to prosper. And all the high hopes came to nothing. La Salle started overland to Canada and on the way was murdered by some of his own men.

Nevertheless, La Salle had blazed the way. And from that time the French began to come down the river from Canada—slowly, of course, but they came. And they penetrated farther and farther into the wilderness.

Fortunately for those of us interested in the early history of the Mississippi, nearly all of the explorers left reports of their travels and experiences: Robert Cavelier de La Salle, Henri de Tonty, Father Louis Hennepin, Iberville, Bienville —all of these left long memoirs and some of them kept diaries. When one begins to examine the sources of history in the Mississippi Valley, one is confronted with such a mass of material that it is hard to choose; but it seems only fair to let some of the explorers speak for themselves. Accordingly, in this chapter, it is my intention to let La Salle tell you his impression of the lower Mississippi and of his ceremony in taking possession of the land for his king; Tonty shall tell something of the Indian tribes encountered; Father Hennepin will give his eyperiences when kidnapped by Indians, and will tell you of the murder of La Salle. These brief excerpts are taken from among the vast number of documents collected by B. F. French in his "Historical Recollections" and published in 1846. In so far as I know, the seven volumes have never been reprinted and, in consequence, the work is difficult to find nowadays.

La Salle writes in the third person, as this is part of his report to the king of France. It is probable that he dictated the report to La Métairie, the notary who accompanied the party, but La Salle's signature appears at the end of the document, as well as the signatures of the other leaders of the expedition, including Henri de Tonty. After describing the gradual descent of the river, he tells of passing the village of the Oumas (the present city of Baton Rouge) in the fog, and landing farther downstream:

On the 3d of April, at about 10 o'clock in the morning, we saw among the canes thirteen or fourteen canoes. M. de la Salle landed, with several of his people. Footprints were seen, and also savages, a little lower down, who were fishing, and who fled precipitately as soon as they discovered us. Others of our party then went ashore on the borders of a marsh formed by the inundation of the river. M. de la Salle sent two Frenchmen, and then two savages, to reconnoitre, who reported that there was a village not far off, but that the whole of this marsh, covered with canes, must be crossed to reach it; that they had been assailed with a shower of arrows by the inhabitants of the town, who had not dared to engage with them in the marsh, but who had then withdrawn, although neither the French nor the savages with them had fired, on account of the orders they had received not to act unless in pressing danger. Presently we heard a drum beat in the village, and the cries and howlings with which these barbarians are accustomed to make attacks. We waited three or four hours, and, as we could not encamp in this marsh, and seeing no one, and no longer hearing anything, we embarked.

An hour afterwards, we came to the village of Maheouala, lately destroyed, and containing dead bodies and marks of blood. Two leagues below this place we encamped. We continued our voyage till the 6th, when we discovered three channels by which the River Colbert [Mississippi] discharges itself into the sea. We landed on the bank of the most western channel, about three leagues from its mouth. On the 7th, M. de la Salle went to reconnoitre the shores of the neighboring sea, and M. de Tonty likewise examined the great middle channel. They found these two outlets beautiful, large, and deep. On the 8th, we reascended the river, a little above its confluence with the sea, to find a dry place, beyond the reach of inundations. The elevation of the North Pole was here about 27°. Here we prepared a column and a cross, and to the said column were affixed the arms of France, with this inscription:

"LOUIS LE GRAND, ROI DE FRANCE ET DE NAVARRE, RÈGNE; LE NEUVIÈME AVRIL, 1682."

The whole party, under arms, chanted the *Te Deum,* the *Exaudiat,* the *Domine salvum fac Regem;* and then, after a salute of fire-arms and cries of *Vive le Roi,* the column was erected by M. de la Salle, who, standing near it, said, with a loud voice, in French:—"In the name of the most high, mighty, invincible, and victorious Prince, Louis the Great, by the Grace of God King of France and of Navarre, Fourteenth of that name, this ninth day of April, one thousand six hundred and eighty-two, I, in virtue of the commission of his Majesty which I hold in my hand, and which may be seen by all whom it may concern, have taken, and do now take, in the name of his Majesty and of his successors to the crown, possession of this country of Louisiana, the seas, harbors, ports, bays, adjacent straits; and all the nations, people, provinces, cities, towns, villages, mines, minerals, fisheries, streams, and rivers, comprised in the extent of said Louisiana, from the mouth of the great river St. Louis, on the eastern side, otherwise called Ohio, Alighin, Sipore, or Chukagona, and this with the consent of the Chaouanons, Chikachas, and other people dwelling therein, with whom we have made alliance; as also along the River Colbert, or Mississippi, and rivers which discharge themselves therein, from its source beyond the country of the Kious or Nadouessious, and this with their consent, and with the consent of the Motantees, Illinois, Mesigameas, Natches, Koroas, which are the most considerable nations dwelling therein, with whom also we have made alliance, either by ourselves or by others in our behalf; as far as its mouth at the sea, or Gulf of Mexico, about the 27th degree of the elevation of the North Pole, and also to the mouth of the River of Palms; upon the assurance which we have received from all these nations, that we are the first Europeans who have descended or ascended the said River Colbert; hereby protesting against all those who may in future undertake to invade any or all of these countries, people or lands, above described, to the prejudice of the right of his Majesty, acquired by the consent of the nations herein named. Of which, and of all that can be needed, I hereby take to witness those who hear me, and demand an act of the Notary, as required by law."

To which the whole assembly responded with shouts of *Vive le Roi,* and with salutes of fire-arms.

In Tonty's memoir, we find him at Fort Prudhomme, mentioned in an earlier scene. And here we have an excellent picture of the Indians along the Mississippi as they appeared to the first white men who came that way:

Continuing our voyage about sixty leagues, we came to a place which was named Fort Prudhomme, because one of our men lost himself there when out hunting, and was nine days without food. As they were looking for him they fell in with two Chikasas savages, whose village was three days' journey inland. They have 2,000 warriors, the greatest number of whom have *flat heads,* which is considered a beauty among them, the women taking pains to flatten the heads of their children, by means of a cushion which they put on the forehead and bind with a band, which they also fasten to the cradle, and thus make their heads take this form. When they grow up their faces are as big as a large soup plate. All the nations on the sea-coast have the same custom.

M. de la Salle sent back one of them with presents to his village, so that, if they had taken Prudhomme, they might send him back, but we found him on the tenth day, and as the Chikasas did not return, we continued our route as far as the village of Cappa, fifty leagues off. We arrived there in foggy weather, and as we heard the sound of the tambour we crossed over to the other side of the river, where, in less than half an hour, we made a fort. The savages having been informed that we were coming down the river, came in their canoes to look for us. We made them land, and sent two Frenchmen as hostages to their village; the chief visited us with the calumet, and we went to the savages. They regaled us with the best they had, and after having danced the calumet to M. de la Salle, they conducted us to their village of Toyengan, eight leagues from Cappa. They received us there in the same manner, and from thence they went with us to Toriman, two leagues further on, where we met with the same reception. It must be here remarked that these villages, the first of which is Osotonoy, are six leagues to the right descending the river, and are commonly called Akancas [Arkansas]. The first three villages are situated on the great river [Mississippi]. M. de la Salle erected the arms of the King there; they have cabins made with the bark of cedar; they have no other worship than the adoration of all sorts of animals. Their country is very beautiful, having abundance of peach, plum and apple trees, and vines flourish there; buffaloes, deer, stags, bears, turkeys, are very numerous. They have even domestic fowls. They have very little snow during the winter, and the ice is not thicker than a dollar. They gave us guides to conduct us to their allies, the Taencas, six leagues distant.

The first day we began to see and to kill alligators, which are numerous and from 15 to 20 feet long. When we arrived opposite to the village of the Taencas, M. de la Salle desired me to go to it and inform the chief of his arrival. I went with our guides, and we had to carry a bark canoe for ten *arpens,* and to launch it on a small lake in which their village was placed. I was surprised to find their cabins made of mud and covered with cane mats. The cabin of the chief was 40 feet square, the wall 10 feet high, a foot thick, and the roof, which was of a dome shape, about 15 feet high. I was not less surprised when, on entering, I saw the chief seated on a camp bed, with three of his wives at his side, surrounded by more than 60 old men, clothed in large white cloaks, which are made by the women out of the bark of the mulberry tree, and are tolerably well worked. The women were clothed in the same manner; and every time the chief spoke to them, before answering him, they howled and cried out several times, *"O-o-o-o-o-o!"* to show their respect for him, for their chiefs are held in as much consideration as our kings. No one drinks out of the chief's cup, nor eats out of his plate, and no one passes before him; when he walks they clean the path before him. When he dies they sacrifice his youngest wife, his house-steward [*maître d'hôtel*], and a hundred men, to accompany him into the other world. They have a form of worship and adore the sun. There is a temple opposite the house of the chief, and similar to it, except that three eagles are placed on this temple, who look towards the rising sun. The temple is surrounded with strong mud walls, in which are fixed spikes, on which they place the heads of their enemies whom they sacrifice to the sun. At the door of the temple is a block of wood, on which is a great shell [*vignot*], and plaited round with the hair of their enemies in a plait as thick as an arm, and about 20 fathoms [*toises*] long. The inside of the temple is naked; there is an altar in the middle, and at the foot of the altar three logs of wood are placed on end, and a fire is kept up day and night by two old priests [*jongleurs*], who are the directors [*maîtres*] of their worship. These old men showed me a small cabinet within the wall, made of mats of cane. Desiring to see what was inside, the old men prevented me, giving me to understand that their God was there. But I have since learnt that it is the place where they keep their treasure, such as fine pearls which they fish up in the neighborhood, and European merchandise. At the last quarter of the moon all the cabins make an offering of a dish of the best food they have, which is placed at the door of the temple. The old men take care to carry it away, and to make a good feast of it with their families. Every spring they make a clearing, which they name "the field of the spirit," when all the men work to the sound of the tambour. In the autumn the Indian corn is harvested with much ceremony, and stored in magazines until the moon of June in the following year, when all the village assemble, and invite their neighbors to eat it. They do not leave the ground until they have eaten it all, making great rejoicings the whole time. This is all I learnt of this nation. The three villages below have the same customs.

Father Louis Hennepin, the Catholic priest accompanying La Salle on his explorations, had a most amazing experience, which he tells as though it were nothing out of the
ordinary. Kidnapped by Indians and held a prisoner for
months on end, adopted "as a son" by the chief of the tribe,
and "submitted to many indignities to his person," the priest
comes through triumphant and lives to tell his tale. This ex-
cerpt is part of a long chronicle which is so interesting that
I wish it were possible to quote it in full, as it gives such
an extraordinarily simple and vivid account of the hardships
of those men who came first to the shores of the Mississippi.
At the beginning of this quotation we find him not far from
the mouth of the river:

It is observable, that during the whole course of our sailing,
God protected us against the crocodiles, which are very numerous in that river, especially towards the mouth. They looked
dreadful, and would have attacked us, had we not been very
careful to avoid them.

Our canoe being loaded with three men only and our provisions, did not draw three inches water, and therefore we
could row very near the shore, and avoid the current of the
river. The next day, April 2nd, we saw, towards break of day,
a great smoke not far from us, and soon after discovered four
savage women loaded with wood, marching as fast as they
could to get to their village before us. But some buzzards coming
near us, one of my men could not forbear to shoot at them,
which so frightened the women that they left their wood, and
ran away to their village, where they arrived before us. The
savages having heard the noise, were in as great fear as their
wives, and left their village upon our approach. But I landing,
immediately advanced alone with the calumet of peace, whereupon they returned, and received us with all the respect and
civility imaginable. We made them some small presents to show
our gratitude, and left that place April the 4th, and rowed with
such diligence that we arrived the same day at Koroa. I was

surprised to see their Indian corn, which was left very green, grown already to maturity; but I have learned since that their corn is ripe sixty days after it is sown. They have three or four crops of Indian corn in a year, having no other winter than some rain. They have all sorts of trees we have in Europe, and many others unknown to us. There are the finest cedars in the world, and another tree from which drops a most fragrant gum, which in my opinion exceeds our best perfumes. The cotton trees are of a prodigious height; the savages made them hollow with fire to make their pirogues of them. We saw some of them, all of a piece, above one hundred feet long. They told us, "That to the westward are some beasts who carry men upon their backs," and showed us the hoof and part of the leg of one, which was certainly the hoof of a horse; and surely horses are not utterly unknown in northern America; for near the cape named by us St. Anthony, we saw a horse and some other beasts painted upon the rock with red colors, by the savages. But whereas we had been told that the Spaniards of New Mexico lived not above forty leagues from them, and supplied them with European commodities, we found nothing among them that might be suspected to come from thence, unless it be some little pieces of glass strung upon a thread, with which the women adorn their heads. We left the habitations of the Akansas, the 4th of April, and during sixty leagues saw no savage. Our provisions being spent, we had nothing to live upon but the game we killed, or the fish we could catch. On the 12th, as my two men were boiling a buzzard, and myself refitting our canoe on the bank of the river, I perceived on a sudden, about two o'clock in the afternoon, no less than fifty canoes made of bark, manned with one hundred and twenty savages stark naked, coming down the river with an extraordinary swiftness, to surprise the Miamis and Illinois, their enemies.

We threw away the broth which was preparing, and getting aboard as fast as we could, made towards them, crying out in the Iroquois and Algonquin languages, "Comrades, we are men of wooden canoes"; for so they call those that sail in great vessels. This had no effect, for they understood not what we said; so that surrounding us immediately, they began to let fly their arrows at us, till the eldest amongst them perceiving that I had a calumet of peace in my hand, came up to us and prevented our being murdered by their warriors.

They presently jumped out of their canoes, some upon land, others into the water; surrounding us on all sides with shrieks and outcries that were indeed terrifying. It was to no purpose to resist, being but three to so great a number. One of them snatched the pipe of peace out of my hand. We presented them with some small pieces of martinico tobacco, and made signs to them with our oars upon the sand, that the Miamis, their enemies, whom they were in search of, had passed the river, and were gone to join the Illinois.

Being then out of all hopes of surprising their enemies, three or four of the eldest of them laid their hands on my head, and began to weep bitterly, accompanying their tears with such mournful accents as can hardly be expressed; while I, with a sorry handkerchief I had left, made shift to dry up their tears; however, to very little purpose; for refusing to smoke in our calumet, they thereby gave us to understand that their design was still to murder us; and one hundred of their leaders coming up to us, made us to understand by signs, that their warriors were resolved upon our death. This obliged me to apply myself to their chiefs, and presented them with six hatchets, fifteen knives and some pieces of tobacco; after which, bending my neck and pointing to a hatchet, I signified to them, by that submission, that we threw ourselves on their mercy.

The present had the good effect to soften some of them, who, according to their custom, gave us some beavers' flesh to eat, themselves putting the three first bits in our mouths, having first blown upon it, because it was hot; after this they set their platter before us, made of the bark of a tree, leaving us at liberty to feed after our own fashion. These civilities did not hinder us from passing the night away very uneasily, because in the evening, before they went to sleep, they had returned us our calumet of peace. The two canoemen resolved to sell their lives as dear as they could, and to defend themselves like men to the last, in case they should attack us. For my part I told them, I resolved to suffer myself to be slain without the least resistance, in imitation of our Saviour. However, we watched all night by turns, that we might not be surprised in our sleep.

The next morning early, one of their captains who had been for killing us, came and demanded my pipe of peace; it being delivered to him, he filled it with tobacco, and made the rest who had been for putting us to death to smoke in it; then he made signs that we must go along with them into their country, to which they were then returning. This proposal was very welcome to us, and we rowed in their company for nineteen days together, sometimes north, and sometimes northeast, according to the best observations we could make by our compass; so that after these barbarians had forced us to follow them, we made more than two hundred and fifty leagues up the river Mississippi, and we were got about one hundred and fifty leagues up the same, above that of the Illinois, when we were first taken by them. One of the nineteen days of our most tiresome voyage, a captain called Aquipaguetin, who afterwards adopted me for his son, had killed a large fat deer, to which he invited the chief captains of the warriors. After the repast, the savages, with their hair anointed with oil of bears, and stuck all over with red and white feathers, and their heads covered with the down of birds, began to dance with their hands upon their hips, and striking their feet with great force against the ground. During the dance, one of the sons of the master of the ceremonies made them all smoke in the pipe of war, himself shedding abundance of tears. The father in the meanwhile laying his hands on our heads, and lifting up his eyes to heaven, bathed himself in tears. As for us, as far as we could judge, all this grimace boded us no good; and indeed, we afterwards understood that he meant nothing less than our destruction by it. But finding the opposition he was like to meet from the other chiefs, who were of a contrary opinion, he was content to suffer us to re-embark, resolving, however, to make use of some other stratagem to get into his own hands, by little and little, the rest of our things; not daring to take them from us openly by force, for fear of the rest of his own nation; by which it plainly appears, that he was a crafty designing knave. His son was killed by the Miamis, and finding he could not revenge himself on that nation, he vented his passion upon us. Having thus traveled nineteen days in our canoe by water, we came within six leagues of the falls of St. Anthony, where they held an assembly to consult what they should do with us. At last they separated and gave us to three of their chiefs, instead of three of their sons which had been killed in the war; then they seized our canoe and took away all our equipage; our canoe they pulled to pieces; their own they hid among the alders, so that though we might have gone conveniently enough quite up into their country by water, yet we were obliged by their conduct to travel no less than sixty leagues afoot.

Our ordinary marches were from break of day till ten at night; and when we met with any rivers, we swam them, themselves (who for the most part are of an extraordinary size) carrying our clothes and equipage on their heads. We never eat but once in twenty-four hours and then nothing but a few scraps of meat dried in smoke, after their fashion, which they afforded us with abundance of regret.

I was so weak that I often lay down, resolving rather to die than follow these savages any farther, who traveled at a rate so extraordinary, as far surpasses the strength of any European. However, to hasten us, they sometimes set fire to the dry grass in the meadows through which we passed, so that our choice was, march or burn. When we had thus traveled sixty leagues afoot, and undergone all the fatigues of hunger, thirst, and cold, besides a thousand outrages daily done to our persons; as soon as we approached their habitations, which are situated in morasses inaccessible to their enemies, they thought it a proper time to divide the merchandize they had taken from us. Here they were like to fall out and cut one another's throats about the roll of Martinico tobacco, which might still weigh about fifty pounds. Then arose a high dispute about the distribution they were to make of our persons. At last, Aquipaguetin, as head of the party, carried it; who turning towards me, presented me his calumet of peace to smoke in, receiving from me at the same time that which we had brought, and then adopted me for his son, in the room of him he had lost in the war.

Photo by Harvey, New Orleans

AT THE MOUTH OF THE MISSISSIPPI

Two other captains did the same by the two canoemen. This separation was very grievous to us, though somewhat allayed by the satisfaction we had to find our lives were safe. Picard, being sensible of the uncertain condition his life was in among so barbarous a people, took me aside to confess him. I should have been overjoyed to have seen Ako so well disposed. Being thus parted, the savages led us away, each to his own village.

I came to Aquipaguetin's habitation in the month of May, 1680. The next day he showed me to six or seven of his wives, telling them that they were to esteem me as one of their sons, and ordered those about him to give me the title that was due to the rank which I was to hold amongst my new kindred.

I spent three months very ill in this place among the Issati and Nadovessians. My new father gave me nothing to eat but a few wild oats five or six times a week, and the roes of dried fish. He sent me into a neighboring isle with his wives, children, and servants, where I digged, with a pickaxe and shovel I had recovered from those that robbed us. Here we planted tobacco, and some European pulse which I brought from thence, and were highly prized by Aquipaguetin.

During my stay among them, there arrived four savages in embassy, who said they were come above five hundred leagues from the west, and had been four moons upon the way. They assured us there was no such place as the strait of Anian, and that they had marched without resting except to sleep, or kill game for their subsistence, and had not seen or passed over any great lake; by which phrase they always mean the sea.

They further informed us that the nation of the Assenipoulaes, who lie northeast from the Issati, was not above six or seven days' journey from us; that none of the nations within their knowledge, who lie to the west or northwest of them, had any great lake about their countries, which were very large, but only rivers, which, coming from the north, run across the countries of their neighboring nations which border on their confines on the side of the great lake, which in their language is the same as sea. They further assured us that there were

very few forests in the countries through which they passed
on their way hither, insomuch that now and then they were
so put to it for fuel that they were forced to make fires of
bulls' dung to boil their victuals. All these circumstances make
it appear that there is no such place as the straits of Anian,
as we usually see them set down in maps. And whatever efforts
have been made for many years past by the English and Dutch,
the two nations of the world who are the greatest navigators,
to find out a passage to China and Japan through the frozen
sea, they have not yet been able to effect it. But, by the help
of my discovery, and the assistance of God, I doubt not but a
passage may still be found, and that an easy one too. For
example: one may be transported into the Pacific sea by rivers
which are large and capable of carrying great vessels, and
from thence it is easy to go to China and Japan without crossing the equinoctial line; and in all probability Japan is on the
same continent as America.

Towards the end of July, the Sieur de Luth, accompanied
with five men, arrived in our camp from Canada; and because
I had some knowledge of the language of the Issati, he desired
that I, with Picard and Ako, might accompany him to the
villages of those people. I was very willing to undertake it,
especially when I understood that they had not received the
sacraments in the whole two years and a half that they had
been out upon their voyage. We arrived at the villages of the
Issati the 14th of August, and having exchanged our commodities we returned to the camp. Towards the end of September we let them understand, that to procure them iron and
other merchandises which was useful for them, it was convenient that we should return to Canada; and that at a certain
time when we should agree upon between us, they should
come half the way with their furs, and we the other half with
our European commodities. Upon this they held a great council, and consented to our return. Ouasicoude, their chief captain, gave us some bushels of wild oats for our subsistence on
the way, having first regaled us in the best manner he could.
These oats are better and more wholesome than rice. Then,
with a pencil, he marked down on a sheet of paper which I

had left, the course we were to keep for four hundred leagues together.

We put ourselves into two canoes, being eight Europeans of us in all. We fell down the river of St. Francis into the Mississippi, and thence went up the river Wisconsin, navigable for large vessels above one hundred leagues; then we carried our canoes overland half a league. Thus having made more than four hundred leagues by water since our departure from the country of the Issati, we arrived at last at the great bay of the Puans, where we found many Canadians, who were come hither to trade; they having some wine with them, I administered the sacrament and preached. After two days' stay, we departed; and after one hundred leagues' rowing, having coasted along the great bay of Puans, we arrived at Missilimakinak, where we were forced to winter.

Father Hennepin accompanied La Salle on his last expedition, in which the party failed to find the mouth of the Mississippi and landed upon the coast of Texas. He tells of the hardships of the party, and the great bravery and fortitude of La Salle. After describing the quarrels among the men, and the treachery of some of them, Father Hennepin tells of La Salle's setting out overland for Canada with a small detachment of his followers:

M. de la Salle set out from the fort the 7th of January, 1687; and having crossed the river Salbonnière and Hiens, with divers others which were mightily swollen by the rains, they came into a fine country for hunting, where his people refreshed themselves after their tiresome travel, with excellent good cheer for several days together. He had sent out M. Moranger his nephew, his lackey Saget, and seven or eight of his men to a certain place where Nika, his huntsman aforementioned, had laid up a stock of wild bulls' flesh, that they might get it smoked and dried to carry along with them, and so not be obliged to halt so frequently to hunt for provisions.

With all his prudence, he could not discover the conspiracy of some of his people to kill his nephew; for they resolved upon it, and put it in execution, all of a sudden, on the 17th of March, wounding him in the head with a hatchet. They slew likewise the lackey and poor Nika, who had provided for them by his hunting, with great toil and danger. Moranger languished under his wound for two hours, forgiving his murderers, and embracing them frequently. But these wretches, not content with this bloody fact, resolved not to stick here, but contrived how to kill their master too, for they feared he would justly punish them for their crime. M. de la Salle was two leagues from the place where Moranger was killed, and being concerned at his nephew's tarrying so long (for they had been gone two or three days), was afraid they were surprised by the savages; whereupon he desired Father Anastasius to accompany him in looking after his nephew, and took two savages along with him. Upon the way, he entertained the father with a pious discourse of divine Providence, which had preserved him in the many dangers he had undergone during twenty years' abode in America; when all of a sudden Father Anastasius observed that he fell into a deep sorrow, of which he himself could give no account. He grew mighty unquiet and full of trouble, a temper he was never seen in before.

When they were got about two leagues, he found his lackey's bloody cravat, and perceived two eagles (a common bird in those parts) hovering over his head; and at the same time, spied his people by the water side. He went to them and inquired for his nephew; they made him little answer, but pointed to the place where he lay. Father Anastasius and he kept going on by the river side, till at last they came to the fatal place, where two of the villains lay hid in the grass; one on one side, and one on the other, with their pieces cocked. The first presented at him, but missed fire; the other fired at the same time, and shot him in the head, of which he died an hour after, March 19th, 1687.

Father Anastasius seeing him fall a little way from him, with his face all bloody, ran to him, took him up in his arms and wept over him, exhorting him as well as he could, in this conjecture to die a good Christian. The unfortunate gentleman had just time enough to confess part of his life to him, who gave him absolution, and soon after died. In his last moments he performed, as far as he was capable, whatsoever was proper for one in his condition, pressing the father's hand at everything he said to him, especially when he admonished him to forgive his enemies. In the mean while, the murderers, struck with horror at what they had committed, began to beat their breasts, and detest their rashness. Anastasius would not stir from the place, till he buried the body as decently as he could, and placed a cross over his grave.

Thus fell the Sieur de la Salle, a man of considerable merit; constant in adversities, intrepid, generous, courteous, ingenious, learned, and capable of everything. He had formerly been of the Society of Jesus, for ten or eleven years, and quitted the order with consent of his superiors. He once showed me a letter, written at Rome, by the general of the order, testifying that the Sieur de la Salle had behaved himself prudently in everything, without giving the least occasion to be suspected guilty of a venial sin. He had the ill hap to be massacred by his own servants, in the vigor of his age. The pious design he was upon, in relation to the conversion of those ignorant nations, seems to have deserved a better fate. But as God's ways are not our ways, we must submit to Divine Providence, without troubling ourselves about a vain inquiry into the secrets of God Almighty.

And so we end the story of La Salle, one of the most tragic, perhaps, in the history of America.

Chapter XI

IBERVILLE AND BIENVILLE

In 1697, d'Iberville was sent over from France to colonize Louisiana. He succeeded in finding the mouth of the river, which had eluded La Salle, and made explorations. He, like La Salle, saw the great possibilities that the river offered, but he did not believe that the time was ripe for its colonization. Instead, he founded his colony on the Bay of Biloxi, near the present location of Ocean Springs, Mississippi. In 1699, d'Iberville was made Governor General of Louisiana and brought more colonists over from France. Settlers along the Atlantic coast had heard of the fertile lands of Louisiana, and a few stragglers appeared from the east, some by sea and some by land.

In 1702, d'Iberville died and his brother Bienville was left in command. He moved his headquarters to Mobile. This was not far from the old Indian village of Mauvilla, where de Soto's men had fought their most terrible battle —and again it would appear that the Indians held their old hatred for the whites. For here the Indian hostilities were so great that the colony dwindled. In 1712, the Louisiana colony was turned over to Crozat. The entire population, scattered from Mobile, through the vicinity of what is now New Orleans, and up the Mississippi as far as the present city of Natchez, Mississippi, numbered only 324 men.

It was in 1715 that Louisiana was brought to the notice of all Europe by the notorious "Mississippi Bubble." This was a monumental scheme by John Law, which was started to help the depleted condition of the French treasury. "The Company of the West" was formed in France, and under the leadership of Law a great many emigrants were sent to Louisiana to colonize the country. John Law was a man far ahead of his time. He was America's first "booster." Nowadays he would be spoken of as a man of vision—and nowadays his scheme would succeed, probably. Law and his followers pictured Louisiana as a paradise on earth; according to their stories, it was a land of milk and honey. There were gold and silver mines; one had but to offer the Indians trifling presents, and the Indians would pour gold and precious stones at the donor's feet. Fortunes awaited every one. Europeans believed his stories, and the ships were crowded—so crowded and so inadequately provisioned that many of the emigrants never lived to reach Louisiana.

A constant stream of men poured into the colony. Many of them died at Dauphin Island, in the Gulf of Mexico—dying of starvation, of fever, and, one may almost say, of disappointment. For though Louisiana was a fertile country, it was still wilderness, and there were no mines, no jewels, no friendly Indians to give presents to the white men.

In 1715, Natchitoches was founded on Red River, and three years later Bienville founded the city of New Orleans. The phrase "the city of New Orleans" is used advisedly, for from the beginning, Bienville spoke of this settlement in the wilderness as a city. Bienville had chosen the site of his city some years before, but had waited until a favorable time before making the attempt to clear any land.

The spot he chose was one slightly higher than the swamps which lay north and south of it, and the reason for his choice lay in this: the site—or so it seemed to him

—commanded the entire Mississippi River. It was not too far from the river's mouth, yet far enough inland to escape the worst of the tropical hurricanes of the Mexican Gulf. For years before the white men came the site of New Orleans had been a portage for Indians. Here, by leaving the river and dragging a canoe a mile inland, one was able to reach the navigable stream, the Bayou St. John. By traversing this bayou one could reach Lake Pontchartrain, which connected with Lake Borgne, and finally with the Gulf of Mexico. This "back door" to the city was of untold advantage; it furnished a safer, shorter route to the Gulf coast and the settlements there—for the mouth of the Mississippi was a dangerous place. The river's mouth was filled with driftwood and sand-bars. The river divided in half a dozen streams before it reached the deeper water of the Gulf. As it had not been thoroughly explored for deep water, ships ran aground frequently and there had been many disasters there. Bayou St. John provided a way to the proposed city which was comparatively safe. Bienville foresaw that the great river would be of vast importance in later years—it was becoming more important every year—and he realized that France must have a strong foothold near the river's mouth.

In February, 1718, then, when John Law's first shipload of men, money, and provisions came to Louisiana, Bienville seized his opportunity for founding the city that had been in his mind for so long. Laborers cleared the wilderness between Bayou St. John and the Mississippi, and the streets were laid out. There was even a ceremony of breaking ground for a church. Rude huts were built, ditches were dug to drain the low spots. A small levee was thrown up along the river front to protect the "city" from the yearly overflow of the river. It was all as crude and simple as possible, but when the ship returned to France and told of the city in the wilderness, the minds of the French were fired with ambition to see this new world. Law's followers pictured it as a land of tropical luxury—where, living in a sort of splendor rivaling the Arabian Nights stories, men lived in close proximity to beautiful bronze-colored women, and were waited upon by Nubian slaves. Louisiana became the toast of the Paris *cafés*. The "city" which had been christened in honor of the regent, the Duke of Orleans, became a byword. Such extravagant tales were told that they seem absurd to us today. Placards, with a fantastic drawing of an Indian giving a white man lumps of gold in exchange for a small knife, were displayed in the streets.

There was a rush to invest in Louisiana real estate. The descriptions sounded as though the land were paradise, and the prices were astonishingly cheap. Hundreds, thousands of men invested all they had in Louisiana land. And why, one may ask, should not the land be cheap? For it was a wilderness extending away in all directions as far as the imagination could reach. But the Frenchmen in the Paris *cafés* did not know this when they sold their holdings in France and fared forth to the land of promise. Law and his followers realized that there must be cheap labor in the colony, and accordingly the French jails were emptied of their criminals, and these men were brought in shiploads to Louisiana to labor and die under the tropic sun.

The inevitable happened. Shipload after shipload of men arrived at Dauphin Island or Biloxi and were left to starve there. There was no food, no shelter. Men died and rotted, unburied. Men went insane. Shiploads of "brute negroes" intended as slaves for the colonists arrived and met the same fate. White men and black perished together or fell prey to malaria or contagious disease.

This was one of the first great disasters of the Mississippi Valley.

But some men survived and even prospered. Lands along the river, above and below New Orleans, were sold and granted out as plantations. Shiploads of negro slaves brought from Santo Domingo or other West Indian islands were sold in New Orleans—usually on credit. Fort Rosalie was built (1716) near the present site of Natchez, Mississippi. Its purpose was to protect the lower river from encroachments from above, just as the fort at Natchitoches was built to protect the country from Spaniards that came overland from Mexico.

John Law's "Mississippi Bubble" burst, and in its bursting many lives were lost and hundreds of men lost the savings of a lifetime. But some prospered. Those who managed to reach New Orleans or the fertile lands near-by, and who managed to secure enough negro slaves to till the soil after the land was cleared, succeeded. The influx of new blood into the colony gave impetus to New Orleans, and with the definite establishment of a settlement in the lower valley we see the French firmly rooted in Louisiana. And above, on the upper reaches of the river, we find their settlements growing and prospering, while at the same time, on the Atlantic seaboard, the English colonies were growing in both population and wealth, and their pioneers were already pushing beyond mountain barriers which separated them from Louisiana.

Chapter XII

NEW ORLEANS

It was the Chevalier Le Blond de la Tour, the engineer in charge of Bienville's colony, who surveyed New Orleans and laid out the streets; and the old section of the city remains today as it was when first hewn out of the forest. That is, the street names remain the same except in one or two instances; but the city itself was almost totally destroyed by fire in 1788, and was rebuilt under the Spanish *régime* in New Orleans; consequently, the part of the modern city of New Orleans known as the old French quarter is really the Spanish city that rose from the ashes of that great fire. Of the first town of wooden houses, nothing remains.

Perhaps it is just as well, for despite all the fine talk of the early colonists, the "city" must have been rather a poor place. A visitor, coming six years after its founding, describes it as a "wild and desolate spot, with about one hundred huts." Nevertheless, these huts were comfortable enough, for even today there are houses in the country not far from New Orleans which were built at that time, and they are not bad houses today, so far as comfort goes.

The houses were, for the greater part, of a single story, and were constructed of cypress logs. Some of them were the usual log house of the pioneer, but another type was more popular. This type of house was constructed of a framework of cypress logs, with walls made of clay and

Spanish moss, mixed and daubed into place by hand. Two hundred years after their construction, the finger marks of the builders can still be plainly seen. Chimneys were made in the same way. Later, when bricks were made in the colony, the houses were constructed with a framework of cypress, with the interstices filled with brick, and the whole daubed over with a sort of cement or plaster.

In many parts of Louisiana today one may find examples of the early eighteenth century plantation-house, Louisiana's contribution to American architecture—large, comfortable dwellings, the lower floor set flush with the ground and built of brick; the upper floor, which contains the sleeping-rooms, made of wood, or of a wooden frame filled with mud and moss. Wide porches extend across the façade, porches paved with brick downstairs, and having round or square columns of brick or masonry; while the posts of the second-floor porch are much smaller, and are made of taper-ing cypress logs. The stairs to the second floor are built upon the front porch—an outdoor apartment much in use in semi-tropical Louisiana, which Louisianians call the "gallery."

But it is doubtful if any house of this type existed in New Orleans for ten years or more after the founding of the little city in the wilderness. Instead, we find cottages of one story, made of cypress, mud, and moss, and set in gardens. The gardens were surrounded by high, hand-hewn cypress fences of tall pickets, pointed on top. Very early in the history of New Orleans we hear of these fences being white-washed. Within the fences were set out hedges of wild orange trees, as added protection, for the thick foliage and sharp thorns proved a barrier to chance prowlers by night. With the high pointed pickets, and with the further protection of hedges of thorny orange trees, the houses could be left open at night for coolness, which was very necessary in midsummer in New Orleans. Only four houses were built on each square of ground, in the beginning.

The squares were not very large, and each one was surrounded by a deep drainage ditch. The year that New Orleans was founded, the river rose and inundated the streets; the ditches filled to overflowing, and each square became a small island. To this day there is a creole word, *"islet,"* which signifies a city square. The sidewalks between the ditches and the picket fences were known as *"banquettes"* —another creole word, which is still in use today.

As for the streets themselves, their names give a clear indication of the spirit of the founders. The town centered around the Place d'Armes, now called Jackson Square. The square faced the river, and on the opposite side, also facing the river, the first rude log church was built—a simple structure, but it sufficed the needs of the colony.

As for the street names: Old Levee Street was the title given the tree-shaded walk that led along the river bank, where a small embankment had been raised to keep back the flood-waters of the Mississippi. It was upon this embankment that the men of the colony congregated in the evenings for social intercourse and gossip of the day. The next street parallel was called Chartres, for the Duc de Chartres, a title of the Orleans family; Royal Street came next, a sort of "Main Street," where the merchants kept their shops; then Bourbon Street, from the royal Bourbon family of France; then Dauphine Street, from dauphin, the eldest son of the king of France, but possibly after the dauphin's wife, for as *rue* is feminine, the name for euphony's sake became feminine too; Burgundy Street was named from one of the royal titles or from one of the provinces of France; Bienville Street was named after Governor Bienville, whose home stood on that street near the river; Conti Street was named for the prince of Conti, illegitimate son of Louis XIV; St. Louis Street after the patron saint of France; Toulouse Street after the Comte de Toulouse, and Dumaine Street after Duc du Maine, both illegitimate sons of Louis XIV by Madame de Montespan; St. Peter, St. Ann, St. Philip streets, after favorite saint baptismal names of the Orleans family. Barracks Street designated the street where the royal barracks were located, near the levee. Hospital Street, obviously, because the hospital was located there. The main cross street, a little wider than the others, was called Orleans Street, after the regent, Duc d'Orléans. It was the center of the original city, and began just back of the Place d'Armes.

One could walk through every street of the city in two hours' time or thereabouts; for the squares were small, and the streets themselves only fifty French feet wide. In 1726, eight years after the colony was founded, the population numbered only 880, of whom sixty-five were servants and 129 slaves. There were only ten horses in the settlement. It must be remembered, though, that most of the richer men lived upon their plantations and were not included in this census. In the community there were many planters who had as many slaves as all those numbered within the limits of the city.

In 1720 the India Company issued a proclamation informing the inhabitants of Louisiana that they might obtain from the stores of Mobile, Pensacola, and Dauphin Island all the merchandise and provisions necessary to their wants. In case the colonists should make it a condition of their purchase that the provisions and merchandise be delivered at New Orleans, they were to pay, in addition, a premium of 5 per cent., at Natchez 10 per cent., at the Yazoo River

13 per cent., and at the Missouri and Illinois settlements 50 per cent. It was made obligatory on the colonists to send their produce to New Orleans, to Mobile, or to Ship Island, where the company would purchase it. The next year it was decreed that all merchandise brought over from France by the India Company should be sold in New Orleans at a 50 per cent. profit, and at Natchez and Yazoo and higher points in the river at a 70 per cent. profit. Another proclamation stated that negro slaves brought to the colony should be sold in New Orleans at 600 livres (about $120) on three years' credit, and payable in yearly instalments. When two terms became due, and the owner could not pay for his slaves, the slaves were to be sold again at public auction, in order that the India Company might be reimbursed for its loss. If the slave did not bring enough at auction to repay the company, the debtor was liable for a term of imprisonment.

Now we find a steady stream of colonists pouring into the colony, and this time not the riffraff of the Paris streets. Sturdy peasants came, merchants, armorers, candle-makers, wig-makers, and the wives of the colonists accompanied them. For his concessions in lower Arkansas, John Law sent over a shipload of thrifty, hard-working Germans—and incomparable colonial stock they proved. They soon became dissatisfied in Arkansas and came back down the Mississippi to the vicinity of New Orleans, where they settled. "Des Allemands," a small village not far from New Orleans, is a reminder of them to this day. It seems odd that they were so soon absorbed into the French world in which they found themselves. Even the German names changed. And some of the most puzzling names in the city of New Orleans to-day may be traced back to these German settlers—German names which are spelled nowadays as they were pronounced by the French of an earlier day: Dubbs becomes Toups; Zeringer becomes Zeringue, Jake Schneider becomes Schexnayder. Some of the names of prominent creole families of today may be traced back to those hardy German pioneers.

In 1722 Bienville succeeded in having the seat of colonial government transferred to New Orleans. Under the supervision of de la Tour the city began to take shape; barracks were built, and the government-house and other official quarters were constructed. But just as the town was assuming the appearance of civilization, a great hurricane came blowing up from the Mexican Gulf. For five days the tempest raged and all the new buildings were demolished. New Orleans was destroyed almost completely, and the colonists had to begin all over again. Added to their troubles, an epidemic broke out in the settlement. Many died. Bienville became ill and his life was despaired of, but finally he recovered. The colonists buried their dead and began again. And a second city rose from the *débris* left behind by the storm.

Many strange types found their way into the colony— nobles exiled from home; younger sons of rich houses, in search of adventure; adventurers, and even a few adventuresses. But there were few enough women, except those who came as wives. Even the women from the French houses of correction who had arrived in the colony were speedily married off and became good citizens.

It was at this time that Bienville wrote in a letter to France: "Send me wives for my Canadians; they are running the woods after Indian girls!"

But the wives did not arrive for some years to come. That is, a large group of women designed as wives for the colonists. It is true, however, that several high-born women came over to join their husbands or their lovers who had

ST. PETER'S STREET, NEW ORLEANS, AS IT APPEARS TODAY

gone before to prepare the way. More than one high-bred girl, dragging the heritage of her illustrious name behind her, came to a home in the new colony. And it is recorded that these wives found New Orleans much to their taste. It is true that the houses were plain, but the slaves did all the work, and the high-born lady had only to nod and her bidding was done. The negroes were excellent servants, fine cooks, quick to learn to please. And Louisiana abounded in good things to eat. Wine was plentiful in the colony, and brandy was second in popularity. The earliest invoices on record show great shipments of liquor. Usually, when a woman came over to join her husband, or to marry her *fiancé,* she brought with her the household furnishings, the silver, the glass, the china. Furniture, too, came over in some of the early shipments; and we have one description of a New Orleans cottage so rich in its equipment that it seems almost incredible. We are told that crystal chandeliers holding candles swung from rough rafters, and that the floors were carpeted with fine furs "lying so close together that the boards could not be seen." And across the carpet of fur came the wife of the colonist, "dressed in the style of the French court," and offering hospitality so simple and so complete that the writer forgot for a moment that he was not in Paris itself!

"In fact," the writer continues, "there is a song in the streets that declares New Orleans to be a little Paris, and beyond that it is impossible to go!"

And yet another writer, of approximately the same time, tells us that New Orleans is a wild and desolate place, filled with ruffians and naked savages. Of course, it is all in the point of view. Possibly both of the writers were right. New Orleans was a strange mixture of savagery and civilization, of elegance and brutality.

Chapter XIII

A CAT LOOKS AT A KING

IF those writers and musicians who consider composing an American opera would turn their attention to the Mississippi Valley, they would find a wealth of material at hand. For the early history of the valley is replete with amazing and amusing incidents. For example, there is that extraordinary affair—the visit of a band of Illinois Indians to the court of Louis XV. Various historians have mentioned it and given brief accounts of it; but only within the last year or two new material has come to light which gives a real picture of this visit.

At the French court there had been great interest in Louisiana; stories were afloat of fabulous creatures inhabiting the wilderness—of beautiful Indian girls, of men of superb physique. Courtiers, *blasé* and effete, became interested in the tales of barbaric splendor—just as men of supercivilized and decadent epochs always turn to the primitive, hoping for a new sensation. The Duc d'Orléans had said many times that he was excessively curious to see these red-skinned Americans of whom French colonists spoke so much. And his gay and frivolous court was no less curious. Accordingly, the commander of the French fort in the Illinois country conceived the brilliant idea of transporting a group of Indians to Paris, where, dressed in their war paint and feathers, they should pay tribute to the king. He induced twelve warriors and some women to accompany him.

Naturally, the Indians were timorous. The ocean was unknown to them, and even the lower river was full of terrors. They believed that fabulous monsters lived near the mouth of the Mississippi, ready to pounce upon the traveler. But the commander managed to quiet their fears, both by lies and by extravagant promises. The ocean was pictured as only a "big salt lake"—and beyond this lake lay France, a land of flowing fountains and golden streets, of glittering crystal, of gorgeously bedecked women, and of men like gods. At last—to cut the story short—the Indians consented to go.

First came the voyage in canoes down the Mississippi. Many days were spent in this fashion; but here the territory was more or less familiar to the Indians. When New Orleans was reached, the first act of this American *opéra bouffe* began. Here, in the little village of log houses set behind picket fences, a motley crew was living—French gentlemen, soldiers, a sprinkling of priests, and a large number of the roughest of the rough, the riffraff of the French jails and prisons, men who had come to America to escape spending the rest of their lives behind bars. But all of them, gentlemen, priests, ruffians, and honest peasants, gathered together to give the Indians a rousing welcome.

Historians, at this point, begin to gossip a little. It is said that a very beautiful Indian princess, who accompanied the expedition, was the mistress of the French commander of the Illinois fort. Be that as it may, the princess was there, bedecked with feathers and gay-colored blankets. And she was the center of attraction. Even a *bona fide* Indian prince of the Illinois was given second place among the men of New Orleans. The prince was dignified and handsome, a magnificent savage, it is said, six feet tall and admirably proportioned; but the princess was small and delicately formed, and she had a roving eye. She was the toast of the town, so to speak, for the duration of her visit.

Now, among the members of the party which accompanied the Indians was one Sergeant Dubois, a fine, virile man. And it is said that the Indian princess turned her coy glance upon him—when the commander was not looking. All this was plainly seen by the men of New Orleans, and the welcome became rather a ribald affair. There was feasting, drinking, and—as one historian says briefly—"jokes." One can imagine those jokes! And no doubt Sergeant Dubois enjoyed them as much as any one. As for the Indians—well, the drinking, the feasting, the smoking of the pipe of peace, and the presents given them made them sure that the trip would be a grand success.

And it was. After several days of drinking and "jokes," the Indians were taken aboard a vessel and the voyage began. Five months they were on the water! Doubtless the Indians believed that their time had come. And it is probable that they wished that they had never undertaken this trip to the home of the great French lord across the "great salt lake."

But at last France was sighted, and some time in November, 1725, the party arrived in Paris. And from Paris they were conducted to Versailles.

Versailles! Here, in a setting which represented the acme of French elegance and French artificiality, the Indians were received in state. The naked and painted Indians came to court. It is true that the braves were draped in blankets, "for the cause of decency," and the women were clothed for the occasion. But in that gay court the Indians appeared minus blankets more than once!

Let me quote a little from the contemporary report in the

Journal Historique sur les Matières du Temps, of January 19, 1726:

While the court was at Fontainebleau, there landed on the French coast a young American prince coming from Louisiana on one of the vessels of the Company of the Indies; it is said that he has a little principality situated near the river which we call St. Louis, but which the natives call Mississippi. Two Jesuits, an interpreter, and some servants accompanied him when he arrived in Paris at the beginning of November. He is a young man of about 30 years of age, dressed much like Orientals, in a long robe and with slit shoes, but instead of a turban, he wears a cap ornamented with feathers which fall on his shoulders.

On the 16th of November, while the Duke of Orleans was in Paris, the American prince, when introduced to him, saluted him with all the ceremony which nature, aided by instructions received from his conductors, had taught him. The Duke of Orleans put some questions to the foreign prince on the extent of his possessions and how many men he could put on foot to defend his country against the invasion of neighbors. The prince replied through his interpreter, that his country, though limited by rivers which surrounded it, was large enough to content a prince who had only desired the necessary; that as to the number of his subjects, he could at least gather under his orders 16,000 in a short space of time. The Duke of Orleans, who was then about to leave for Fontainebleau, ordered the officers of the house to show the prince all those things in the Palais Royal which might satisfy his curiosity and to be careful to treat him well, with all those who accompanied him. Thus ended the audience.

They had been brought to France by the Chevalier de Bourgmont and Father de Beaubois, the Jesuit missionary, who served as interpreter. After the Indians had been shown the palaces, the gardens, the fountains, the machine of Marly, and so on, they were introduced to the Duke of Bourbon, and there they asked to meet the king himself.

The king received them in state; gifts were presented to the Indians, and in return the Indians presented gifts to the king.

Formalities ended, the fun began. The Indians were the sensation of the day. The French women of the court, bored perhaps, or merely perverse in their interest, took charge of "the American prince" and the ladies who accompanied him. Surrounded by painted beauties—rouged and sprinkled liberally with black "beauty spots"—it seems no wonder that the prince lost his head. What if he only grunted when spoken to? The French women were equal to that. Here was a superb specimen of primitive man . . . and there is a universal language in smiles, beckonings, inclinations of the head. There are stories afloat of Indian braves divested of their blankets and feathers for the amusement of the gay ladies of the court. And we can only surmise the bursts of laughter that were heard through closed doors!

As may be supposed, the Indians had the time of their lives. In return for the hospitality extended, they gave an entertainment themselves. To the amazement of every one, the Indians hunted deer and roped horses in the Bois de Boulogne, and gave a sort of wild west show at Versailles which astounded the court. The king ordered that clothes be given them, and accordingly the braves appeared in knee breeches and flowered coats; their cocked hats were "lined with gold." And as for the women, they were laced into corsets, and were given French dresses of the latest mode. They appeared in public dragging flowing trains behind them, and wearing their hair piled high and powdered. They laid aside their crude paint for rouge and "beauty spots." They were altogether grand!

One night at the Italian opera, however, they stripped themselves of their clothes and entertained the court by

Indian dancing—with much beating of drums and whooping. Men and women, it is recorded, appeared almost in "a state of nature." It is no wonder that the French were captivated.

The Indians were petted and spoiled, as though they had been truly the children of royalty. Every whim, no matter how ridiculous, was granted. For a brief time they were the sensation of Paris.

We have no record of the feeling of the French commander during this time, nor the reaction of Father de Beaubois, but we do find that Sergeant Dubois profited by the stay in France. And the second act of this Indian drama reaches its climax in the Notre Dame de Paris—for here in the dim cathedral, surrounded by guttering candles, and admired by the entire court, the Indian princess was formally baptized at the marble font. She threw aside her heathen gods and embraced Christianity. She embraced, also, Sergeant Dubois—and was married to him, with great pomp and ceremony, directly after the baptism.

In laughter it all began, and in laughter it continued. Sergeant Dubois was raised in rank to captain—for, as the king remarked, a mere sergeant was not grand enough for a real Indian princess. And to Captain Dubois came another honor: he was made commander of the Illinois. For the former commander had decided to remain in France, and announced then and there that he had selected a rich widow for his mate and was ready to marry and settle down!

Captain Dubois and his Indian bride were loaded down with presents—silks, satins, jewels, good things to eat. Some of the gifts were very gorgeous, it is said. Even the king sent a present, though what it was the contemporary journalist fails to tell us. To make the occasion complete—

the baptism and the wedding—the Indians were given "fitting costumes." The men appeared in their court dress, while the women were even more magnificent than before, with their spangled trains dragging after them, and their powdered hair, piled high and crowned with roses. But it must be confessed that most of the Indian women refused the high-heeled slippers of the French belles, and came to church barefoot.

This was a gay pageant which amused all of Paris. Great crowds gathered in the streets, and there was much laughter. The populace cheered when the Indians appeared in carriages in the streets. The court tittered, and the Indians grunted—all except the princess, or Madame Dubois, as we must call her now. She had assumed all the airs and graces of the court. She even wore shoes.

Wearing their fine clothes, and loaded down with gifts, the Indians embarked for Louisiana. The voyage was long and tedious, but New Orleans was reached at last. Here a welcome was given that exceeded even the celebration that marked their first visit. It is probable, too, that the Indians enjoyed this welcome more than the joys of Paris—for they were back in their native country once more, and they had received more presents than they had anticipated.

A fine party was given in New Orleans. There was more feasting, more merrymaking—and more "jokes," doubtless. But Captain Dubois carried the thing through with dignity, as befitting his new office as commander of the Illinois district. And if his coy bride cast doves' glances at any of the gay young blades of New Orleans, we have no record of it.

At last the canoes were made ready and the voyage up the Mississippi was begun. This time the commander of New Orleans gave the Indians an escort of soldiers to accompany them. Special rowers were given for the canoes, and a great crowd congregated on the levee when the party departed for the Illinois country.

They were warmly welcomed by the Indian tribe. For in their absence—a whole year had passed—the Indians had thought their chief dead. His triumphal return was the signal for more celebrations.

Dubois took charge of the fort, and he and his bride went to housekeeping. Everything was as it should be, and the wilderness quieted down again—for a time.

And now we come to the final act in the drama. And if this act is without humor, it is not without a fine irony.

For a time all went well. Dubois and his Indian princess reigned in state. Crops were good, and affairs at the settlement prospered. But as time went on, the Indian princess became restless. It is recorded that she visited her tribe more than Dubois liked, and frequently she stayed away from the fort for weeks on end. But he was a kind husband and looked upon his wife's comings and goings with a sleepy eye.

At last, one day, Madame Dubois helped her tribe surprise the fort. The whole garrison was massacred. Captain Dubois, her husband, was scalped. There was great carnage, much bloodshed. And the last picture of our Indian princess shows her stripping herself of her trailing French dress, her corsets, her religion—all at once. With one loud yell she tossed aside her crucifix and embraced again her heathen gods. Naked and happy, she returned to the wilderness.

And I for one hope that she lived happily ever after!

Part Three

"I HEAR THE TREAD OF PIONEERS"

Chapter XIV

By the end of the year 1721 there were six thousand people in Louisiana.

The French had made a settlement at the Indian village of Istrouma (or Itu-ooma), which stood on a high bluff overlooking the Mississippi, approximately one hundred and twenty miles above New Orleans. Both Iberville and Bienville had looked upon this high land with appraising eye, for it was the first land above the river's mouth that was beyond all danger of inundation. This location had been considered as a possible site for the principal city of the province, but Bienville had decided upon New Orleans because it was nearer the Gulf: and one hundred and thirty miles upstream was a long and laborious journey in those days.

But the location of Istrouma was ideal, and accordingly the French made a settlement there. They called the settlement Baton Rouge, for, when the first explorers had sailed up the Mississippi, a blasted cypress-tree stood out against the sky at the top of the bluff. This cypress was the subject of some debate among early historians. Some contended that it was merely a blasted tree; others said that it was a totem pole, marking the boundary between the hunting-grounds of two Indian tribes. But, totem pole or blasted tree, it became "Baton Rouge" to the French—and it is called so to-day. It is now the capital of the State of Louisiana and one of the oldest cities in the lower valley.

Opposite Baton Rouge, a few miles farther up the river, another settlement called Pointe Coupée was founded; in the vicinity was rich and fertile land, lying between the Mississippi and the Atchafalaya rivers, near the spot where the Red River empties into the Mississippi. Once it had been a delta; enclosed behind levees, it made a farming country as rich as any in the world. Bayou Goula, between Baton Rouge and New Orleans, was another settlement, and there were other villages at Yazoo, Black River, Pascagoula, and as far north on the Mississippi River as Illinois. In 1721 we see the great river beginning to assume its status as the main artery of travel in the west.

All these settlements sent their produce down the river to New Orleans; every day, almost, a flatboat or a large canoe would arrive at the New Orleans levee. The earliest settlers found the Indian canoe best suited to their needs, and used it for this reason, as well as for the reason that it was the only type of boat available. Indians along the lower river used *pirogues,* and the French settlers soon learned to use them too. This was a type of canoe made by the simple expedient of hollowing out a cypress log, pointing it at the bow, and squaring it off at the stern. Navigating a *pirogue* was a ticklish undertaking and required deft and delicate manipulation; for these round-bottomed boats were almost unbelievably unsteady, and the slightest movement turned them bottom-side up and left the passengers struggling in the water. Paddling a *pirogue* was rather like riding a bicycle; balance, at first, was difficult to maintain, but once the art of perfect balance was acquired, the actual propelling of the craft was easy enough. *Pirogues* were of nearly all sizes—the size determined only by the size of the log chosen for use. Some were small and held only one passenger; even the weight of one man made the gunwales of the little boat almost level with the surface of the water. Yet the French settlers soon learned to use them so skilfully that they could brave even the dangerous eddies and currents of the Mississippi.

Large, hand-hewn *pirogues* carried passengers and freight. Often a section in the center was used as a container for liquids or semi-liquids. Early in the history of New Orleans, one reads of "as much honey as a *pirogue* will hold" or "a *pirogue* of lard." And these unsteady boats, high-piled with skins, carried cargoes which seem incredible to us today.

As may be supposed, accidents were numerous. One reads of a *pirogue,* loaded high with skins, turning over as often as four times in one day. And it took a sturdy swimmer to stand such punishment—for, once dumped out into the water, the skins must be taken off before the boat could be righted again, then replaced after the boat was in its accustomed position. And last—and perhaps most difficult— the passenger must climb in over the stern and take his seat again in the bottom of the *pirogue.* If you have never tried to do this, you can have only a slight idea of the extreme difficulty of the undertaking.

Flatboats developed from rough rafts of logs. These rafts were built in order to float produce down the river; but as time passed, the colonists found it better to build a sturdier craft. Accordingly they constructed large, flat-bottomed boats of raft construction, slightly deeper amidships than at bow or stern. These flatboats varied in size according to the load they were designed to carry, and were propelled downstream by large wooden sweeps, or oars. The river was full of snags and sand-bars, and the current was swift and treacherous. Many of these flatboats went to pieces after striking submerged logs. Hardly a single trip was made in those early days without the flatboat running aground.

The current of the river was so strong that it was almost impossible to take these heavy boats back upstream. A few were towed up, painfully, laboriously, with a towline to the bank, or propelled with poles and oars. But the process was so tedious and so expensive that it was found cheaper to sell the boats at New Orleans, or to break them up and sell the timber, and then make the return trip upstream by means of canoe or *pirogue*. In many instances the trip upstream—or, rather, up toward the higher reaches of the river—was made on foot or on horseback, using the old Indian trails and paths through the forest. And as the years passed, these trails became more and more plainly marked. But overland trips were dangerous undertakings. There were hostile Indians and wild animals. Hundreds of men were swallowed up in the wilderness without leaving a trace.

The town of Kaskaskia is the oldest permanent settlement on the Mississippi River. It was founded in 1693 or thereabouts (some historians place its founding as early as 1686). It is on the east bank of the river, about eighty miles south of the present city of St. Louis. It was founded by Gravier, who founded also, it is said, the town of Cahokia, opposite and a little south of St. Louis and Peoria, Illinois. Fort Chartres, Illinois, about sixty-five miles south of St. Louis, was founded in 1720. The French from Canada, hunters and traders, were the first settlers in Illinois and Missouri. They came to the river from the Great Lakes, or came overland, on foot or on horseback. They established camps, killed game, and traded with the Indians. Frequently their camps grew into towns—later into cities. The first permanent settlement west of the river was at the town of Ste. Genevieve,

Missouri, in 1735. And the new town, which is the out-growth of the old one, is still thriving. It is some seventy-five miles south of St. Louis.

Some years later Pierre Laclède Liguest and others obtained from the governor of Louisiana a charter for exclusive trade with the Indians of the Missouri and upper Mississippi Rivers. They went up from New Orleans in February, 1760, and established St. Louis as a trading post. For many years this settlement was the principal fur-producing post in the Mississippi Valley. Another post, Carondelet, was founded in 1769, and Florissant in 1776; both these posts lie within twenty-five miles of St. Louis. Portage des Sioux, near St. Charles, was founded in 1780, and Cape Girardeau in 1794.

As the Mississippi assumed more and more importance, there were plots and counterplots among nations in order to secure control of the river and the territory it commanded. Great Britain, France, Spain, and the United States all played their parts. During this time various forts and military outposts were built along the waterway. Some grew into towns and cities; others have disappeared.

The French established Fort Duquesne in 1750; Louisville was planned by Bullitt in 1774, or approximately that time. In 1780 Clark established Fort Jefferson in Kentucky, just south of the mouth of the Ohio River, "for protection against Indians and foreigners," according to Justin Windsor, in "The Westward Movement."

It was in 1786 that the Ohio Company was formed, and members of the company purchased large tracts of land on the Ohio River around the present city of Marietta, Ohio. They built Fort Harmar, at the mouth of the Muskingum River, and brought out a large number of settlers from New England. And it is here that we have our first "blue laws" in the West. These New Englanders did not fall under the spell of the new country and adopt its free and easy ways; on the contrary, they brought with them no end of prohibitions. Here we find, for the first time, ordinances to prohibit the carrying of knives and pistols. And there were other ordinances which seem equally strange when one considers the country into which the settlers had moved. It is interesting to note that many of these settlers did not like the federation of States on the Atlantic seaboard, and in moving to the Ohio River thought that they were escaping from it. (Windsor, p. 296.) Many of these settlers came in wagons; but the majority of them took to the river at Pittsburgh, and came down by boat.

St. Clair, the governor of Fort Harmar, succeeded in obtaining grants to Indian titles west of the Mississippi and north of 41°. Accordingly, another society was formed, secured a grant of land west of Fort Harmar, and established a colony there—Losantiville, afterward Cincinnati. Gallipolis, on the north·bank of the Ohio, a little west of Fort Harmar, was settled in 1790. These settlers were immigrants from France, brought over by Putnam and others.

Vincennes, Indiana, was settled in 1702 by Canadians, or French settlers from Canada, and is referred to as the second oldest settlement in the Mississippi Valley. Soon after that date, Ouintanon, near Tippecanoe, was established. All this section was settled by the French, and very early in the history of the valley we find French names in this vicinity— both in names of settlers and in names of rivers and towns. This is particularly true in the region along the Wabash River.

In 1763 Louisiana was transferred from France to Spain, and in order to escape Spanish rule, many residents of the lower valley went toward the east. In 1763, also, Great Britain acquired Canada by the Treaty of Paris, and as a result of this many French settlers moved from Illinois to regions west of the Mississippi. By the Treaty of Aix-la-Chapelle, in 1748, Great Britain acquired the northern fisheries, Newfoundland, Hudson Bay, Nova Scotia. Shortly after this we find Great Britain claiming the territory south of Canada and west from her Atlantic colonies to the Mississippi. In order to resist this claim, France built Fort Duquesne—which has been mentioned before—to prevent the British encroaching on territory that was considered French. The plan of the French was to build a chain of forts from Canada to Louisiana and thus hem in the British colonies all of the way. (It is interesting here to note that this is La Salle's plan taking shape after nearly a hundred years.) The plan never was carried out, for in 1758 the British captured Fort Duquesne and changed its name to Pittsburgh, in honor of William Pitt. In 1759 the victory of Wolfe over Montcalm on the Plains of Abraham gave Canada to Great Britain. The Treaty of Paris in 1763 ended the matter, and France ceded to Great Britain the valley of the St. Lawrence and all of the territory east of the Mississippi and north of the thirty-first parallel of latitude. And in this treaty Great Britain acknowledged the Mississippi as her western boundary.

It was at this time that France, by secret treaty, ceded the province of Louisiana to Spain, leaving France without any American territory whatever. And so ended La Salle's great dream of empire. New Orleans, Bienville's "Little Paris," was abandoned to its fate, and in 1769 passed under the Spanish yoke.

In 1776 came the Declaration of Independence, and in 1781 Cornwallis surrendered at Yorktown. The next year, by the Treaty of Paris, between the United States and

Great Britain, the United States gained full jurisdiction west to the Mississippi, including the right of its use.

In 1791, Great Britain and Spain were about to go to war over the seizure of a British vessel at Vancouver. Great Britain made a great effort to secure Louisiana and Florida, in order that she might enlarge her territory and thus hem in the United States on land and sea. Spain was afraid that a war would enable the United States to seize the Mississippi River; and accordingly Spain made peace with Great Britain. Thence Great Britain was no longer a factor in the question of the navigation of the river. The matter resolved itself into a dispute between the United States and Spain—for Spain still controlled the mouth of the Mississippi and had control of the territory on the west of the stream. After long diplomatic negotiations, a treaty was signed in 1795. All posts in the territory belonging to the United States, but still occupied by Spain, were to be evacuated within six months; but it was not until 1798 that the United States secured actual possession. Natchez and Chickasaw Bluffs were two important posts that were secured in the end by the United States. The eastern bank of the Mississippi, from its source south to 31°, now belonged to the United States.

In 1800, Spain ceded the territory of Louisiana to France. In 1803, for the sum of $11,250,000, France, under Napoleon, ceded it to the United States. This gave the United States entire control of the river from its source to its mouth, with the exception of a little space just above Baton Rouge which was included in West Florida. The absorption of West Florida, in 1810, and the subsequent cession by Spain, in 1819, completed matters. The United States had now full control of the Mississippi.

For fully five years before the signing of the Declaration of Independence, there had been a great tide of immigration into Kentucky and Tennessee from the colonies along the Atlantic. Men wanted more room. The West was waiting. It seemed to offer possibilities without end. The unknown trail called to the adventurous. Men grew eager to pit their strength against the forest; women were no less eager. As early as 1770 we see the ever-increasing tide of men moving westward.

Waterways offered the easiest mode of travel. And it will be noted that most of the early settlements were beside streams—either the Mississippi or its tributaries. It is difficult to estimate the proportion of settlers that came by water, but many men came down the Ohio from Pittsburgh, and continued down the Mississippi. Others floated down the Ohio and then worked their way up the streams that emptied into that river.

Some came far into the wilderness, settled, and prepared to remain. Neighbors arrived, and settlements grew. But a few years later we find those first pioneers moving on again, seeking new country. It seems, almost, that some great invisible force kept them moving forward, urging them on—a force as great as the Mississippi itself in its endless flow toward the southwest. Why men went so far, it is hard to tell. It would seem that the land itself called them, urging them on from stream to stream and from hill to hill.

Pittsburgh became known, later, as a town where flatboats were built—for it was a favorite place for men to begin their long voyage downstream. Once possessed of a flatboat, it was easy enough to load wife and children, farm animals, and household goods aboard, and strike out for the unknown.

The day of the covered wagon was beginning: from Carolina, from Virginia, and from other eastern States the great caravan was starting its course across America. And for a hundred years after, the march to the West continued, until all of America east and west of the Mississippi was dotted with settlements, with farms, with cities.

By the end of the year 1773, it is estimated, there were about 60,000 people in the country between Pittsburgh and the mouth of the Ohio, including Kentucky. Early settlements were those at Watauga, Carter, and the Nolichucky valley, in east Tennessee, in 1769, 1770, and 1771. In 1772 these were consolidated, under the leadership of James Robertson, into the Watauga Association. And here we have the first organized government "of the people, by the people," under written articles, west of the mountains. From the beginning, these settlements flourished. In 1774 came Daniel Boone to Kentucky, establishing Fort Boonesborough. Soon it was the center of a growing community, and it was here, in that march beyond the mountains, that the first legislative body convened. Robertson, in 1779, established the French Lick settlements, in the vicinity of the present city of Nashville, Tennessee. The Cumberland and Holston settlements began in 1772 in east Tennessee or the western part of North Carolina. Harrodsburg, Limestone, and Lexington, Kentucky, were settled between 1782 and 1784; Knoxville, Tennessee, in 1782, and Nashville in 1784.

By 1785 the number of immigrants had increased. Some historians give the increase as low as 5,000 a year, others as high as 20,000. But on they came, and in ever-growing numbers. There was a tremendous increase in travel on the Ohio and Mississippi. Sometimes as many as 200 boats a day would leave Pittsburgh, one historian states. Travelers began to find these boats stranded and deserted along the river bank. In one year more than a thousand stranded boats were counted along the Ohio River.

At the time of the adoption of the present Constitution of

the United States, in 1789, there were approximately 250,-
000 Americans in the Mississippi Valley. Of these, Kentucky
had most, Tennessee came next, and the country north of the
Ohio third. In 1791, when Kentucky was admitted to the
Union, there were approximately 70,000 white settlers there.
The tide of immigration was now very large. Historians
place it at from 40,000 to 50,000 a year. Most of this tide
was moving north of the Ohio River, but Kentucky, Tennessee, and points south were getting their quota.

By 1812 even a greater increase was noted in the westward movement; many came from Virginia, from North
Carolina, and from Georgia. And always a great tide of men
moving down the Mississippi, settling in the rich and fertile
country along the watercourse. Kentucky, Tennessee, Arkansas, Missouri, Louisiana were growing in population.
The population of the Mississippi Valley has been estimated
as follows: In 1780, 100,000; in 1800, 380,000; in 1810,
1,000,000; in 1820, 2,500,000; in 1832, 4,000,000.

The States south of the Ohio and east of the Mississippi
showed the greatest increase in population. Those bordering on the Mississippi grew more rapidly than those remote
from the waterway. New Orleans became the most important city in the United States, as far as the dwellers of the
Mississippi Valley were concerned; it also became the center
of commerce for all those living west of the Alleghanies.

Down with the current of the great river came the produce
of the fertile valley. An endless stream of gold was pouring
into the city at the mouth of the Mississippi. Ships from all
the seven seas were anchored there, in those days, and the
waterfront was swarming with men. The city became lux-
urious, fine and gay. It was cosmopolitan. At the time of
the Louisiana Purchase, in 1803, many Americans moved
into the city to compete in trade with the French, Spanish,

and Creoles living there. A new "American" city began to grow beyond the confines of the old walled city of Nouvelle Orleans; there were theaters, operas, gambling-halls, horse-races, and sports of all kinds. Money was plentiful, and to those who came down from the upper reaches of the stream the people of the city seemed wealthy. Dark-eyed, languishing women smiled down from lace-like balconies of wrought iron. There were extravagant balls, duels, cock-fights. It is no wonder that the American pioneers who came to New Orleans considered the gay metropolis a veritable "city of sin." For if to laugh and play is a sin, then New Orleans was truly sinful. And it has always been so.

New Orleans drew so much trade from the upper river that Great Britain attempted, time after time, to turn some of it to Canada; and through all the early days the Atlantic colonies tried to divert trade over the mountains to the eastern seaboard by establishing wagon trails through the forest.

The trip down the Mississippi was comparatively easy, but the trip upstream was a tremendous undertaking. It required about forty days to take a small boat from New Orleans to Louisville. To go from New Orleans to the mouth of the Ohio and back, a boat of twenty-five tons, with twenty men, took ninety days. From New Orleans to St. Louis and return took 100 days. For this reason traders would often carry their goods to New Orleans by boat, and either sell them there or take them by boat to Havana, thence to Philadelphia or Baltimore. In one of these eastern ports they would lay in their supply for home use and take it down the Ohio, back to the starting point. This trip would require from four to six months. Many of the farmers would build flatboats, load them with produce, and float them down to New Orleans.

The variety of craft on the river at this period, before the coming of the steamboat, presents an interesting spectacle. It included barges, keelboats, flatboats, ferry flats, scows, skiffs, *pirogues,* canoes, dugouts, and a miscellaneous lot of vessels that we never see today. In going upstream many different methods were used. Smaller boats used paddles and oars, or remained as near the bank as possible and used poles. Boats were invented with a propeller that was worked by horse power; but this was not a success, as the horse's strength was not equal to the current, and the beast soon died of exhaustion.

The French settlers at New Orleans had developed *bateaux-plats* and *radeaux*. The *bateau-plat* was a flat-bottomed rowboat with pointed bow and stern; the *radeau* was more like the flatboat with blunt ends that afterward became so numerous on western waterways. The keelboat was evolved from the *bateau-plat* type; it came into use as an upstream boat. The flat-bottomed boats persisted in hugging the bank and scraping, when propelled by a line drawn from the bank. A keel was found to check this lateral swing toward the shore. A keelboat, by means of rudder or guiding sweep, could be steered parallel with the shore, notwithstanding the slant of the tow-rope with its tendency to turn the boat inshore.

An outstanding type among the Mississippi River pioneers is the riverman: the keelboatman and the flatboatman. He took pride in his strength, in his ability to curse and to fight. He bragged that he was "half alligator and half horse," and that he was impervious to blows that would kill an average man. And it is true that they were a brutal group. In the early history of the river there are endless stories of their escapades. Fables have grown up around them. Fictitious characters abound. A book could be written on "Mike Fink"

alone. Whether or not Fink ever existed is a matter of conjecture, but his exploits of strength remain embedded in
the folklore of America. Many of the stories told of "Mike"
are unprintable—but he was a gargantuan man. He could
eat more than any other man; he could fight more, and
longer; and he excelled in the arts of love. No woman could
withstand him, and he left illegitimate children throughout
the Mississippi Valley. He was said to have had red hair,
and any red-haired child seen playing on the river bank was
dubbed "Mike Fink's brat" by the keelboatmen. He was
killed at last, or so the legend goes, in a fight over a woman.

"Annie Christmas" is another legendary character.
"Annie" was a river tramp, the wife of a keelboatman, and
was said to possess enormous strength. Sometimes "Annie"
is described as keeping a sort of floating saloon aboard a
flatboat. At other times she is pictured as disguising herself
as a man. In such costume she fought, gambled, and made
love to women who did not penetrate her disguise. Numerous feats of strength are described; she could knock down
a strong man; she could throw a man overboard with one
hand; she could lift a barrel of whisky from the floor to
the counter of her saloon—something which few men could
do. There are various stories concerning her sad end. One
is that she committed suicide for love! Another is that she
was shot in a brawl in a New Orleans gambling-house. One
still hears the phrase among roustabouts on steamboats on
the Mississippi, "As strong as 'Annie Christmas.'" In one
version of "Annie's" history, she is pictured as a gigantic
negress, the mother of twelve black sons!

But if "Mike Fink" and "Annie Christmas" did not exist,
their prototypes did. Mark Twain describes these men in
his "Life on the Mississippi," and other writers have given
much space to them. We shall have the report of an eye-

witness in another chapter, but for the present we must confine ourselves to the difficulties of upstream travel in the eighteenth century.

The navigation of the Mississippi, which began as early as 1700, presented many difficulties below the mouth of the Missouri strong currents; eddies of sufficient strength to overturn a rowboat, and in which no swimmer could live; snags or logs embedded in the mud of the river bottom, unseen above the surface of the water, but large enough to break a hole in the bottom of the stanchest boat. And upon the shore of the river there were hostile Indians and renegade whites, waiting their chance to rob and murder the traveler. For mutual protection and assistance, voyages were usually made in convoys of from two to twenty boats. It was usual for these convoys to leave the Illinois country in the early spring, in order to benefit by the strong current during the high-water season on the Mississippi. In returning upstream, the trip was usually undertaken shortly after the first of August, when the river was low and the current not so strong. It took from twelve to twenty-five days to make the voyage downstream, and from three to four months to get home again.

In his book "Mississippi Valley Beginnings," Henry E. Chambers tells something of this upstream travel. "An additional hardship in going upstream," Mr. Chambers writes, "was the many bends that had to be rounded, some of which required a detour of fifty miles to progress five. To avoid the centrifugal sweep of the strong current, the inside of the curve of each bend had to be taken. As these bends were many and sinuous, they compelled many crossings and recrossings from shore to shore to take the inside course. No crossing could be made without dropping back at least half a mile under the force of the midstream current. One voyage from New Orleans to St. Louis recorded three hundred and ninety of these bends on the way."

In the early days, the Mississippi and its tributaries were the highways for the great mass of travel for settlers, just as they played the principal part in mid-American trade. It was only by slow stages that the overland routes increased in importance, and it was not until the coming of the railroads that the Mississippi lost first place as a means of transportation. It would have stimulated early settlement even more rapidly had there been free use of it to the Americans, but during the eighteenth century this was not permitted. As long as Spain held control of the river, Americans were much hampered in their use of it, and seizures of persons and property were frequent.

In the latter part of the eighteenth century we find the Mississippi River playing a greater an greater part in the affairs of the United States. The people in the West wanted the river open for navigation, and urged the people of the East to assist them in demanding that Spain give them this right. The people in the East, however, while pretending to agree in this, gave no real aid; for the colonies on the Atlantic wanted trade to move across the mountains to the seacoast rather than float down the Mississippi to New Orleans. The attitude of the East became so irritating to the West that at one time there was a movement for the West to leave the Union and cast its lot with Spain, in order to clear the river and open up travel and trade. Another group wanted to leave the United States and join Great Britain; still another group wanted to join France. Each of these nations wanted the allegiance of the West, for obvious reasons. At one time, Great Britain thought of sending an army down the river from Canada, and up the river from the Gulf, in order to separate the West from the East. In 1790 there were 200,000 people in the West, and 40,000 of them were able to bear arms. Jefferson ordered the United States Minister to Spain to secure free navigation of the Mississippi at all hazards. In 1795, Spain, fearing that both the United States and Great Britain were about to make war on her, opened up the Mississippi for free trade. This settled the unrest of the western people, and although, even after this time, various schemes were tried by foreign powers to induce the West to join with them, these plots were unsuccessful. And it is interesting, here, to note Washington's Farewell Address. In this speech he admonished the West to forget its unreasonable suspicions of the East, and urged both sections of the country to live together in greater harmony. When one considers the conflicting interests that focused upon the Mississippi River at this time, it is easy to understand what George Washington meant.

Chapter XV

It was in 1781, nearly a century and a half ago, that Molly Glass was executed in New Orleans.

She was hanged in the public square before "a considerable concourse of people," for a murder so atrocious that it puts to shame the crimes in the Newgate Calendar. The Mississippi River plays its part in the story.

Molly Glass was a free quadroon from "the North of the Carolinas" and she had married a renegade white man, a deserter from the English army. She lived in English Pointe Coupée in the district of Baton Rouge. It seems that she had two houses, one on each side of the Mississippi. One of them was in Spanish territory, the other in territory controlled by the British—for it will be remembered that the whole eastern bank of the Mississippi, except New Orleans, fell into the hands of Great Britain as the result of the treaty of 1762. The district above Baton Rouge was known as West Florida, and it was in this section that Molly Glass and her husband, John, lived. But at the time of the American Revolution, Spain declared war against England, in May, 1779; and in September of that year, Governor Galvez of New Orleans captured Baton Rouge and drove the English out of West Florida. He left Carlos de Grandpré in command, and Captain Pedro José Favrot in charge of the fort. Under the terms of capitulation, the English magistrates at Baton Rouge were permitted to con-

tinue for the time being, and it was during this period that
Molly Glass fell under suspicion.

The fact that the court records were written in French,
Spanish, and English, all interlocking, furnishes a mass of
interesting detail.

The quadroon woman had been in trouble before. It was
believed that she helped runaway slaves to escape, if they
were able to pay her for doing so. Her husband was a white
man, a sort of ne'er do well, a lazy, shiftless, weak-willed
creature whom she dominated completely. She was a large,
handsome, strong woman, quick of temper and quick with a
blow. She was known in the neighborhood for her cruelty.

Nevertheless, these were brutal times, and there were
many who dwelt beside the Mississippi who were cruel to
their slaves. But Molly Glass had no negro slaves. Living
in a remote place, she managed to ensnare several free-born
people into slavery. At one time she had taken in a woman,
the widow of a Frenchman, Pierre Dumont. Once in the
hands of Molly Glass, the young widow was forced to do
all the menial work of the farm, laboring in the field, taking
care of cattle and so on. If she failed to do the prescribed
tasks, Molly Glass would beat her and mistreat her otherwise. At last the woman managed to escape, but she made
no complaint to the authorities until later, and it is doubtful
if she would have complained then had she not been brought
to Baton Rouge to testify when Molly Glass was arrested
on the complaint of a pack-peddler called Baronnière. He
had been assaulted by her in an argument over a sale. She
had beaten him, he stated, with a heavy stick, and had injured him so severely that he came down the river to the
fort at Baton Rouge to make complaint against her.

Officers were sent to arrest the woman and her husband;
and these men, arriving at night, found two runaway slaves

hiding in her house. The slaves managed to make their escape, but Molly Glass was arrested, and, with her husband, was brought in a boat down the river to the fort. Now it was known that Molly Glass had a white girl called Emilia Davis living with her; but when search was made for Emilia, she was not to be found. When questioned, Molly Glass said that Emilia had run away with some men who had passed down the river from Natchez in a *pirogue,* and these men had said that it was their intention to pass Baton Rouge secretly and to proceed to Pensacola. But neighbors declared they believed the quadroon had killed Emilia.

Accordingly, many of those who had lived in the vicinity were brought down to the fort at Baton Rouge to testify, and there a most horrifying story came to light.

Emilia was a waif, an orphan, fifteen years old, who had been the indentured servant to one Mr. Walker, who had left the community. Alone, Emilia had gone to live with Molly Glass. As soon as the girl was safely in her hands, the brutality of the woman asserted itself. In view of our present knowledge of abnormal psychology, it would appear that Molly Glass was a sadist, and took delight in torture, for her persecutions of Emilia were such that no sane or normal person could have endured to inflict them.

It was the custom in those days to examine the witnesses out of the presence of the accused, and then to question the latter as the facts in the case developed. In this way the court proceedings stretched out indefinitely, and the prisoner had almost no chance. Having read the thirty-five legal documents which constitute the court records in this case, and finding them so vivid in themselves, I shall take them up in order, quoting the witnesses where it is possible.

First comes the testimony of Odet Baronnière, the pack-merchant. He swears that "the said Molly struck me with

THE SPANISH CABILDO, NEW ORLEANS

It was near this court building, facing Jackson Square, that Molly Glass was executed

her fist in my face until the blood spurted." Friends of Molly's, he said, aided her. Some held him and others handed her sticks with which to beat him. He ends his testimony by begging the court to allow his two negro slaves to testify.

Then comes the testimony of a man who is called simply "Allain." He tells of Molly Glass having attacked his Indian slave; and, had not Allain interfered, the Indian would have retaliated. Allain states that he reported the matter at the time to the fort at Baton Rouge.

Joseph Patin is sworn and says that Molly Glass "insulted me by injuring epithets, even putting her fist under my nose and calling me a rascal, and that this present is the truth. At Pointe Coupée, February 22, 1780."

John Glass, the husband of the accused, is questioned. He states that he is a Catholic, a German, a deserter from the English army, and has legally married Molly Glass, the mulatto woman, in Natchez. He states further that he had not been at home on the day of his wife's quarrel with Baronnière.

Then comes the first examination of Molly Glass herself. She is proud and defiant, and denies everything pertaining to Baronnière. He had insulted her, tried to "make himself master of my house," and so on. She can prove this, she says. When questioned as to her past history, she states that she had come from North Carolina; that she was born of a quadroon and that her father was a negro, both free; that she was of the Anglican religion, and was thirty-seven years old.

Nothing further was done that day, but the next document pertains to the seizure of the household effects of Molly Glass, and an inventory. It was the custom, it appears, to seize the possessions of a prisoner and sell them, in order to defray the costs of the trial. The inventory contains the usual things found in a scantily furnished country house: pots and pans, knives and forks, feather-beds, brass candlesticks, and, oddly enough, a set of fine blue and white chinaware, which seems strangely out of place among the home-made utensils and furniture described in the document. Some of the forks are listed as bent and burned. Note that fact. Also, there were chests full of fine goods, believed to be stolen or smuggled property.

Now we have the testimony of Madame Pierre Dumont, the woman whom Molly Glass held as a slave for a time. The widow Dumont testifies that Molly Glass beat her and punished her otherwise; that the superior strength of the mulatto woman made the white woman powerless against her; and that when visitors came to the place, Molly Glass forced her to go to a distant field to work, and forbade her exchanging a word with any one. Once, she says, Molly Glass struck her upon the bare breast with such force that she was ill for a month, and that she still carries the scar. The scar is exhibited to the court. The witness is excused. She signs her testimony with a cross, as she cannot write.

Then Molly Glass is brought back to the court. She is still defiant. "All lies," she says. The widow Dumont pretended to love her as a sister. But she was shiftless, lazy, "and fond of men." That was the root of the whole trouble. In fact, the only times that she (Molly Glass) had struck her was when she became "exceedingly passionate for anything that was a man."

Molly Glass was then confronted with a small negro boy whom she had in her possession for a time. The court record becomes conversational, easy:

"We asked her why she had held this young Dumont woman against her will, and also a young griff, born free, presented to us by Mr. Alexandre, is scarred from head to foot, front and back, like an Ecce Homo, bearing nine scars on his head and having had his arm broken. She answered that the child had the defect of lying, and was greedy to the extreme and that she did not break his arm.

"We asked her if it was this grievance that caused her to stab him with a knife in the stomach, to inflict nine scars in the center of his head and to have pulled out all his hair.

"The accused answered that she had never subjected him to so cruel a treatment.

"We proved this accusation by exhibiting the naked child to her.

"She answered: 'Is it not so, my child, that I corrected you only when you deserved it?'

"The child, all in a tremble, answered: 'Yes, Mistress.' Thus does she have herself named."

She ends her testimony by declaring in a loud voice that she has nothing to reproach herself with.

Now we have the testimony of her neighbors, both black and white. She boasted that she feared no one, they testified; she flouted the law; she had boasted that she would do as she pleased, and if the Spanish authorities came after her she would cross the river and take refuge on English territory. Samuel, a young overseer, a free man on Mr. Alexandre's plantation, tells of hearing John Glass reproving Molly for her love of liquor and for her bad temper. Molly made scathing response and ended by saying: "I shall talk, I shall drink as much as I choose; it is indifferent to me to be hung; I shall always satisfy myself as much as I can before I die."

And now for the first time the name of Emilia Davis comes into the testimony. Madame Françoise Glause is testifying. She tells a remarkable story. Two little boys came to her house and told her that Molly Glass was beating a young white girl with unusual cruelty. Not content with stripping her in the boys' presence, she had called their attention to punishment that she was inflicting, while the young girl screamed for mercy. The next day, Madame Glause had gone over to see for herself. She found Emilia with her eyes blackened, her face swollen, and in such a condition that she could not speak. Madame Glause asked about Emilia's condition, and Molly Glass said that "a cow had given her the blow." Later, a dispute arising, the mulatto woman threatened Madame Glause, and added that "if she killed a Frenchman, or a woman, there was always the other bank of the Mississippi free for her escape."

Then follows the testimony of Sarah West, Equille West, and Cride West, neighbors:

By order of Don Pedro De Favrot Commander of the Fort at Baton Rouge 8th March 1780.

Appeared before me William Dunbar Esquire, Justice of the Peace for the District of Baton Rouge, Sarah West, who being duly sworn upon the Holy Evangelists of Almighty God, maketh oath and declareth

That about the time of Mr. Willings descent upon the River Mississippi she came from the English side, and took refuge upon the false River and dwelt a considerable time at a distance of about half a mile from the House of a certain free Mulato woman named Marie Glass and that having occasion frequently to be at the House of the said Marie Glass she was a witness of various acts of cruelty and Barbarity exercised upon a certain white girl named Emelia who had formerly lived with and was an Indented servant to William Walker Esq. that particularly one Evening she abused and beat Her accross the neck and Head with a stick larger than an ordinary Cane, to such a degree that the Deponent believed Her unable to speak; after a little time Marie Glass ordered Emelia to get up and carried Her trembling and Bruised all over the

Body to an out Cabin where she stripped Her naked and tied her upon tiptoe by the Hands to a Post and called Her Husband John Glass to View her; this Deponent being much affected, at what she had seen remonstrated with the said Marie Glass and pleaded for the deliverance of the said Emelia, upon which she at that time desisted, after abusing Her with ill language, Curses and threatenings of Vengeance, tho this Deponent knows not any crime she had Committed. This Deponent further declareth she hath upon sundry occasions heard Molly Glass say that she would destroy the said Emelia and throw Her into the River; and that she would Conquer or kill Her and such like expressions.

This Deponent declareth further that after the overflowing of the River the said Molly Glass went to live upon the English side at Browns Cliffs but left the said Emelia in charge of Her House at the false River, where she had in keeping a few Fowls and some Corn and other Bagatelles; that one night a runaway Negro of Doctor Farrar's passing by the place stole some Fowls with a Pot and a little Corn which He stoped to Cook at a small distance and that next morning Emilia missing Her Fowls and etc., went in search of them and found Her Pot with a Basket and a little Corn; that soon after Doctor Farrars overseer and some negroes coming in search of the runaways stoped at the House of this Deponent, who walked over with Him as far as Molly Glass's at which time Molly Glass having come from the other side and finding Her Fowls gone immediately laid hold of Emelia and having tied up Her Rags about Her Girdle, fixed Her upon tiptoe by the Hands to a Post. That Mr. Sterling, Doctor Farrars overseer, observing the situation of the Girl, turned His Head aside, judging it improper for a man to behold so indecent a spectacle; the said Mr. Sterling and this Deponent continued to walk to the River side, and heard distinctly the lamentable cries of the Poor Emelia under the lash of the inhuman Molly Glass for a full quarter of an Hour or more to the best of the Deponents recolection; that upon the return of this Deponent Emelia was untied and Her Petty Coat (unfitt for a negroe slave) being in its natural situation hindered the lower parts of Her

Body from being seen, but Her back was considerably bruised and Her face wounded in several parts so that it was bloody and further that the weals were larger than Her finger the Deponent askt Emelia if she had been flogged on account of the runaway Negroes she answered in the affirmative and at same time most solemnly protested Her own innocence. That during the great rise of the River when this Deponent lived upon the high lands at Browns Cliffs within a few yards of Molly Glass's House, tho she cannot condescend upon Months or Days she was witness to a variety of ill treatment given by the said Mary Glass to the said Emelia that particularly on a certain Day she beat and abused Her exceedingly with a whip armed with a Leather thong and that thinking this discipline not sufficiently severe, she turned the handle or Butt end of the whip which was a stick larger than a mans thumb and with a violent blow on the right side of the Head laid it open to the length of two joints of the Deponents fore finger, that afterwards the said Mary Glass did curse and much abuse the said Emelia ordering Her to begone and never see Her more; the poor wretch answered yes Mamie (as she was wont to call Her) and walked off towards the River side but in a short time after this Deponent Heard the cries of poor Emelia returning up the Hill from the River side Mary Glass following close at her heels armed with Her whip and before her return had received a second Gash or wound on the left side of the Head the full length of the forefinger of this Deponent both wounds being actually measured soon after in the absence of Molly Glass by the Deponent. This Deponent to the best of Her recolection says that the cause of this barbarous usage proceeded from a Pig having taken a Joney Cake from the Fireside out o'Doors which Emelia had been ordered to prepare; that soon after this Deponent observed the eyes of Emelia to be much swelled and inflamed and feeling Her Pulse and judging from the appearance and great heat of Her Body conceived Her to be in a high fever, one Eye was become inservicable and very imperfectly she saw out of the other; all which she the Deponent does solemnly believe proceeded from the barbarous and inhuman usage of Marie Glass, that on a certain Day when Mary Glass was absent at the false River, finding Emelia in this miserable state she advised Her to go to Bed, which she consented to do tho she endeavoured to make Bread and expressed Her apprehension of Molly Glass, upon Molly Glass' return from the false River this Deponent observed to Her that Emelia was very sick and much wounded; to which Mary Glass answered she Emelia fetching a pail of water had fallen down and wounded Her Head upon a stump; notwithstanding this Deponent was an Eye witness to the manner in which she had received Her wounds or bruises from the hand of the said Molly Glass.

This Deponent further Declareth that she left the neighborhood of Molly Glass about the 20th of June last year and returned to Her old house at the false River after which she heard nothing of the said Emelia until on a saturday about a fortnight before Christmass last when the said Marie Glass stoped at the house of this Deponent and took an opportunity to mention that she had lately got clear of the white girl Emelia and added she was glad of it, she further informed this Deponent (after some interrogation upon the part of the Deponent) that on the monday before she had been at the House of a Mr. or Mrs. Ross and on Her return Home, missing Emelia, she went in search of Her and by the assistance of Her Dog found Her lying under a Log that she had been at a Camp of Indians, who after using and abusing of Her, had burned Her in a terrible manner: this relation surprising the Deponent, she asked several more questions and was further told that one Arm of Her Capot was burned off Her fingers so burned that they were all in one gore and the Handkerchief consumed upon Her Head; further that on the wednesday before Mr. Alexander's Nancy had stopped on Her way to point Coupee that then Emilia had got somewhat better and was able to walk a little but had lain down on the appearance of Mr. Alexander's People not wishing to see them. This Deponent question'd Her further and learned with great surprise that the very following Day Thursday Emelia had sett out on a voyage to Pensacola being taken on board a Boat in wh. were two men (according to Her account) one named

Webb and the other Larkins with a woman and child, which People had come past the Natchez and intended to pass the Port of Baton rouge in the night without calling for a passport, that they were bound for Pensacola and by that rout to get to their own Country in Carolina. The Deponent regarding this as an Extraordinary story, could not help at same time observing that Marie Glass in relating it seemed to be much troubled and embarassed and spoke as if she had a Load or oppression upon Her Heart and spirit and further this Deponent says that Molly Glass told her she was very apprehensive of danger from the Indians and that she knew not what had come over her lately for that she could not eat Her victuals nor could not sleep and found Herself inwardly troubled and that Her intention was to sell of Her goods and retire with all expedition to Her own Country. That John Glass Her Husband was also present during this relation; but never opened his Lips upon the subject of Emelia on the contrary He hung down His Head with His Gun between His legs, sitting on a chair and seemed more than ordinary pensive and thoughtful.

The deponent hath further to add that once being informed by her Son, Cride West, that Emelia had been severely flogged by Molly Glass; she was desireous of seeing the state in which she was and happening soon to be at Mary Glass'; She asked Emilia what ailed her, she seemed affraid to declare the true cause, but upon the assurance of the Deponent that she wou'd not acquaint her Mamie (Molly Glass) she lifted up her shift (being unable to bear a petty Coat) and the Deponent saw in her hind parts a wound of about an Inch and a half square and a quarter of an Inch in depth, stuffed full of something which Emilia said was Gum leaves and cream, and that from the small of the back downwards to the hams was in a manner all over gashes or cuts. The Deponent also declareth that of all peoples, Negroes or others, she hath never seen a poor wretch so miserably hacked and cut as this poor white girl was. And further the Deponent sayeth not.

Witness my hand and Seal the date above written.

William Dunbar J. P.   (Seal)

Personally appeared before me William Dunbar Esquire Justice of the Peace for the District of Baton Rouge, Cride West a young Man aged 14 years, apparently of good understanding for his age; Who being duely sworn upon the holy Evangelists of Almighty God, maketh oath and declareth

That he was present when Moly Glass, tied up and flogged with great severity the above mentioned Emilia, resting and whipping her three several times, and at each time rubing her with Soot, salt, pepper, and gunpowder and moreover made a great smoke, the Exhalation of which, in its assent, went all around her, pretending that Emilia had given away the milk to some of Mr. La Blanc's Negroes, tho' the poor girl persisted in declaring her innocence untill her punishment was ended. That after this Correction She remained two weeks hardly able to walk and unable to stand upright but went half bent. And further the Deponent sayeth not.

William Dunbar J. P.   (Seal)

The record goes on and on. Nancy, a free mulatto woman, testifies that she heard Emilia crying out and moaning from a tight-shut cabin, and had tried to aid her, but Molly Glass had driven the other mulatto woman away. Thomas George, a free mulatto boy of twelve years of age, testifies that he came to the house of Molly Glass while the woman was absent, and that Emilia had him help her dress her wounds. All of these testify that it would have been impossible for Emilia to run away, for she was near death and barely able to crawl around.

Now Miss Catherine West is put before the judge, and she tells of seeing Molly Glass tie Emilia up by the hands and whip her unmercifully with a cowhide, afterward suspending her from the branch of a tree, nude, and kindling a fire beneath her—not for the purpose of burning Emilia, but in order to smoke and smother her. "She was suspended in the air by her arms, and her feet did not touch the ground." Catherine West asked what the girl had done, whereupon the mulatto woman answered that during her absence, Emilia had eaten melons from her garden.

Once, Catherine West testified, she had heard cries, and creeping close to Molly Glass's house in the dead of the night, she had seen the mulatto woman seated upon a chair, holding Emilia between her knees. Despite Emilia's screams and struggles, Molly Glass had pulled out Emilia's tongue, between her finger and thumb, and had stuck through it a fork which had been heated in the fire until it was red hot.

"We asked Miss Catherine West if she had anything else to declare against the accused.

"The said Miss Catherine West said that she beseeched Molly Glass to act with more mildness, that Molly Glass answered that she would not forgive her father, nor her mother, and that the girl Emilia was a scapegrace.

"We asked Miss Catherine West what she thought might have become of Emilia.

"She answered that she had seen her too badly treated, that poor Emilia could hardly walk, that she could not be certain that she was dead, but she was inclined to believe that she no longer exists, having had no news of her and not knowing what had become of her, since she saw to what state Emilia was reduced."

Molly Glass was brought in again for further questioning. She denied everything, and repeated her story of Emilia running away down the river. Her story, however, was different in detail from her first account. Now the direct accusation was thrown at Molly Glass: "Did you kill Emilia?" Whereupon Molly Glass denied this indignantly, adding: "If you believe that I killed Emilia, have researches made on my plantation. They will not find her buried." This remark increased the suspicions of the judge, who surmised that the body of Emilia had been thrown into the Mississippi.

"We asked Molly Glass why she had so often maltreated Emilia, with so much cruelty, tying her to a post and whipping her until the blood came, and to have moreover stretched her on a ladder."

Molly glass again denies everything. The statement of Catherine West is read to her.

"The witnesses, like ourselves, see Molly Glass confounded, cursing and damning her accusers, saying that Catherine West tried to excite her to pierce the girl's tongue, but protests that she did not do so; that, to frighten Emilia, she had threatened her with a fork.

"The accused throws herself on her knees swearing and protesting in the name of God that if Emilia is dead, it did not happen at her house, that Emilia had left in a *pirogue* which came from False river, in which there were Englishmen and a woman and her child. That the woman took Emilia to mind the child; that the same woman said that she knew Emilia's mother, who was in America.

"Here is, word for word, Molly Glass' declaration, who swears and says: 'As God is God, I speak the truth!'

"We asked the accused why she had left a young girl go off with folks who were unknown to her. The accused answered that Emilia was such a bad subject that she was glad to get rid of her."

The days passed by. Other witnesses came. All testified to the same facts. The net drew tighter around Molly Glass and her husband. Finally, John Glass, the weaker of the two, confessed. He repeated over and over that "he was not master of his house," and that he was powerless to control the actions of his wife, that he feared her, and that when the sufferings of Emilia became unpleasant to him, he would take his gun and go hunting. At last came the actual confession:

"John Glass swears that towards the middle of last December, on his return to his residence, at the cliff, after having brought meat for the garrison at Baton Rouge, Molly Glass told him that Emilia was very ill, ready to die, and that on the same day of his return, he heard Emilia from the cabin where she was, scream several times and exclaim: 'Ha, Maman, Maman, they have burst my stomach, I am dying!' with these last words, Molly Glass brought her into the house, and she expired. The appearer declareth that Molly Glass cried a great deal on that same day and that he himself fell into such imbecility that he was not able to bury Emilia, and that a runaway negro owned by Mr. Porloe did so; he and Molly Glass burying her near the desert."

He had been afraid to say anything about the matter, and had weakly accepted his wife's lies to the neighbors.

Now we come to the climax of this strange trial. Molly Glass is brought in and asked if she has anything to say. She is still defiant, denying everything, lifting her eyes to heaven, saying that every one is against her. She is then confronted with her husband's confession. She cries out that he is mad, that he has lost his head, that he is an imbecile, a dangerous lunatic. She cries out, "May God damn me, forever," and appeals to all the saints to come to her aid. Finally she falls wailing to the floor. The testimony of her husband is read again to her. She moans and cries; finally she says that it is true in part. But she denies killing Emilia. Emilia died from natural causes, she says. Yes, it is true that two runaway slaves buried her.

Now the two runaway negroes, who have been recaptured,

are brought to court. They testify. Hector, one of the run-aways, testifies that he saw Emilia dying, her lips covered with foam, and, as she lay dying, Molly Glass beat her afresh. He saw Molly Glass tie a rope around Emilia's neck and drag her as though she were a dog. When Emilia died, he helped Molly Glass bury her.

Accordingly, an expedition is sent up the river in a canoe to the scene of the murder. Molly and John Glass are forced to accompany the expedition. He points out the grave, on the edge of the hill, but when it is opened, to the consternation of every one, it is found to contain only the body of a large dog, killed by a blow on the head. No other grave can be seen. John Glass tries to point out another spot; the negro points out still another at the edge of the Mississippi —but Emilia's body is never found.

The party returns to the fort at Baton Rouge. A summary is made of the evidence. Molly Glass and John Glass are convicted. The man's sentence is withheld, but Molly Glass is sentenced "to have her right hand cut off under the gallows, then immediately to be hanged by the neck until she is dead, and when her body is cut down, her head to be severed from the body and stuck up on a pole at her former residence at Browns Cliffs and her right hand to be nailed to the same post." The judge recommended that some mercy be shown to John Glass.

And so, Molly Glass was taken down the Mississippi aboard a flatboat and put in jail in New Orleans. Here she made a last fight for a stay in the execution, regaining something of her old bravado. By claiming that she was soon to become a mother, she had the sentence deferred for several months. Finally, it was declared that she had lied, and the day of execution was named.

On July 26, 1781, in the public square in the city of New

Orleans, Molly Glass was hanged before "a considerable concourse of people." As it was ordered, her hand was chopped off at the foot of the gallows, then "she was hanged by the neck by Miguel the executioner, until she appeared to have died, since she gave not the least sign of life. All of which having been done, the crier, for the crown, made the following proclamation: 'Don Piernas commands that no person, of whatever degree or quality he be, dare to take from the gallows the body of Molly Glass who is hanging upon it, on penalty of life.'"

There is no record of the fate of John Glass. But the judge, in the record of the court, states: "I have the honor to remark that though the said John Glass is very guilty, it is proven that he was no more than the slave of this mulatress who had a despotic power over him, a weak man, who stood in fear of her; I implore you in the name of the assembly to commute this penalty to that of the galleys or to work in the mines for life."

It is probable that John Glass ended his life in the mines. But Molly Glass's head was carried up the river again to the spot where poor Emilia had been tortured and killed. Here the head was stuck up on a pole, and the hand nailed below it, "where," the record concludes, "it remained for some time."

Chapter XVI

A WOMAN PIONEER

WHILE reading some old documents on early days in the Mississippi Valley, I had the good fortune to find, among others belonging to Mr. James T. Flint, of Alexandria, Louisiana, a memoir written by his grandmother, Mrs. Martha Martin. In an old scrapbook she had written a short record of events in her life which she considered worth recording. She wrote simply and well of pioneer days in Louisiana, of her journeys on the Mississippi River, and overland on the old Natchez Trace.

Her maiden name was Martha Phillips. She was called "Patsy," and she was the daughter of Joseph· and Milbry Phillips, of Edgecombe County, North·Carolina. In September, 1809, when she was seventeen years old, she married Thomas Martin, formerly of Bangor, Ireland. The couple went down the Mississippi on a flatboat, to a plantation which Mr. Martin had purchased on Bayou Teche, in southwest Louisiana.

As a child, she had been taken to the funeral of George Washington; later, in her Louisiana travels, she met Lafitte, the pirate, of whom she gives an interesting account. She met General Lafayette when he visited Nashville and sat beside him at a ball. She knew Andrew Jackson well, and he visited her and her husband frequently; she saw him shortly before his death, and describes the meeting in detail. All these things she tells, but her description of pioneer days on the Mississippi and on the Natchez Trace are extraordinarily vivid. Through the courtesy of her grandson, I shall quote from her memoir, eliminating those passages which are of a purely personal nature.

Martha Martin lived to be ninety-three years of age, and died at Nashville, Tennessee, in 1886.

When I married Mr. Martin he was living in Clarksville, Tennessee, and engaged in the mercantile business with Mr. Reynolds. Soon after our marriage, Mr. Reynolds and my husband concluded to give up business there and go South, where farming would be profitable. Louisiana was their preference. They purchased land on Bayou Teche, in the Attakapas country, remaining there for ten months. My husband returned home in October, 1810, having a little boy to welcome his return. The next winter we embarked on a flat boat for our home in Louisiana, leaving Nashville, February 4th, 1811. It was a long, tedious passage of eight weeks, and we stopped at Natchez for a few days. We were frequently annoyed by the Indians when landing at evening, which we were always compelled to do. All the country on the left of the Mississippi was owned by the Chickasaw and Chocktaw Indians. Where the city of Memphis, Tennessee, stands today was a settlement called Chickasaw Bluff, and where Vicksburg, Mississippi, is now located was a small town called Walnut Hills. Well do I remember each place, as they were pointed out to me by the old captain of our boat.

We had considerable trouble after leaving the Mississippi River, passing through bayous and lakes. Many places looked as though a boat had never been on them before. Alligators were so numerous that it was great sport to shoot them in every direction. We landed Sunday at Mr. Reynolds' place, just below our home. He very soon came aboard to welcome us. Mr. Martin in turn presented him our little boy, who was called James Reynolds for our friend. Our meeting was mutually agreeable. I assure you I was glad to get on land and be at our long-looked-for home. All welcomed us with joy.

THE OLD NATCHEZ TRACE

The road is worn deep in the earth by hundreds of years of travel

The country is principally prairie and at that season of the year everything looked well. Cotton and sugar were the principal products of that part of Louisiana. Orange trees were bearing and blooming all the year, and vegetables of all kinds were to be had in abundance.

The mode of making sugar in those days was by grinding the cane with mule power, which was tedious, and from two to three barrels of sugar a day was considered good work, but always demanded a fair price. As long as the war continued between Great Britain and the United States, which was from 1809 to 1815, cotton was cheap, but sugar demanded a good price. As soon as peace was made, cotton went up from seven dollars a bale to twenty-five and thirty dollars.

The first summer and fall I spent there, we had frequent attacks of fever, and in November we lost our darling little boy James, which was sorrow indeed for a young mother away from all her family except my dear husband. Dear child, the Lord has taken him and I can say that it was my first treasure laid up in Heaven, where we will all meet hereafter.

The country was settled by French, Spaniards and Indians principally when we located there, but very soon many from Kentucky, Tennessee and Mississippi came and purchased lands. Having made plenty, quite a favorable change came on our bayou in the addition of three or four Irish families living near us, so Mr. Martin gave it the name of "Irish Bend" and it is called by that name today.

Three brothers by the name of Sumner, from Tennessee, (connections of mine) purchased a large plantation very near ours, the year after our arrival; also Dr. Henning from Nashville, which added greatly to our society and the appearance of things in general. Our communication with New Orleans was by small schooners passing across Berwick's Bay, and up Bayou La Fourche to the Mississippi River, seventy-five miles above the city of New Orleans.

We lived ten miles from the Gulf of Mexico, and two miles from Grand Lake, living just between them we always had a fine breeze. By sending to the bayou we got oysters in abundance; game of all kinds was plentiful and in fishing there was nothing to do but throw your line into the bayou. The red fish we got often from the Indians, and it was superior to any other.

Indians often brought us game of all kinds. Soon after we reached our new home, Alexander Porter, a young lawyer from Nashville, came to see us. He had gone to that country with my husband the year before. He found on his arrival that he would not be able to practice his profession until he could speak French. In six months he was perfect in that language and very soon made a brilliant display of his talents, realizing a handsome fortune in a short time.

He married Miss Baker of that parish, and six years after their marriage Mrs. Porter died while on a visit to his friends in Nashville, leaving him two daughters. Soon after this sad occurrence Judge Porter left for his native country, Ireland, taking his little daughters with him, and leaving them there to be educated.

Soon after the return of Judge Porter to Louisiana he was elected United States Senator, and served many years. Leaving Washington City he returned home to his large estate in Louisiana. There he died and was brought to Nashville and buried by the side of his wife. His daughters returned from Ireland but lived only a short time. Judge Porter left his fortune to his brother, James Porter, except fifty pounds that was to be given to the poor in the county where he was born in Ireland, annually for ten years.

During our stay in Louisiana, we raised cotton, sugar, corn, and rice, which all grew to perfection, finding a market in New Orleans for nearly all we could make.

Two years after our arrival we were blest with the birth of a little girl, which I called Jane. Of course I thought her beautiful and lovely, as all mothers are alike in that respect.

During the war with England, the planters often could not obtain certain articles that were necessary for them to have on the plantation. Mr. Martin, Mr. Patten, Mr. Caffrey and others concluded to take a schooner and go where they had heard they could obtain those things needed.

Having purchased what they wanted and were returning

home, the second night a terrible storm came upon them. They dropped anchor and remained until daylight. The pilot thought they might with safety leave, but very soon they found the vessel sinking. They threw· a portion of the iron out, but still they found there was no hope of saving the boat. They had a yawl and being only about one half mile from the land, all got in the yawl except three or four. Mr. Sumner, Mr. Patten, the pilot, and a servant of ours remained on the vessel, as a part of it was out of the water.

After getting on the beach, Mr. Caffrey and one of the sailors· returned to the vessel where they found Mr. Sumner with his arms around a plank, drowned, while Mr. Patten and the pilot were not to be found. The servant was hanging on the mast perfectly insensible. They brought the servant and the body of Mr. Sumner on shore. Mr. Sumner was buried on the island and the servant recovered. They were all left without any provisions and only a small yawl in which to get home, so those remaining of the party left next morning, making slow progress.

Two days after, they saw some vessels ashore. They immediately made for them, but Mr. Martin concluded that it was most prudent for one of them to go and ascertain who they were. He went himself and found it was Lafitte the pirate. He made his situation known; immediately Lafitte sent for them and treated them with all the kindness possible, taking them aboard his vessel and giving them a bountiful breakfast.

Mr. Martin related their unfortunate disaster to him and how far they were from home. Lafitte ordered a schooner made ready at once, putting in provisions and all that was 'necessary; and in fact, it was just what they had lost by the storm. He inquired of Mr. Martin if he had a family; he replied: "I have a wife and one child," so he sent me a demijohn of Madeira wine, and the first pineapple cheese I ever saw. He told my husband that the schooner and contents was a present to him.

I will say something of the pirate hereafter.

It was several days before they reached home. My husband had lost his hat when leaving the sinking vessel, but Lafitte supplied him with a cap and cape attached, which was very acceptable in December. Mrs. Sumner, my next door neighbor, was with me the evening before they arrived home. We were fearful of some accident, they being gone much longer than we expected, but the sad news came soon enough for her. I have never witnessed greater grief and sorrow, for long did she moan for her dear husband. His brother sent out for Mr. Sumner's remains, which were brought back and buried at his home in 1813.

The brothers after this misfortune were dissatisfied and offered their plantation for sale and soon found a purchaser in Dr. Duncan of New Orleans. They returned to Tennessee the next year.

My health not being good, I often would tell my husband that a visit to my old home was all that I required. My physician thought a trip to the sea shore was all that was necessary. We left in a few days for the coast with several of our neighbors going with us, taking tents and everything in the way of cooking.

General McCall and family went out every season and he went with us that year. I found it very pleasant, plenty of oysters and good company. We remained there for three weeks, and my little Jane was much benefited by the trip, but my heart was set on going to Tennessee—the only place where I thought I would find good health.

On our return I received a letter from my father urging us to come up and spend the summer at my old home. The invitation was readily accepted and in June we left for Nashville. We took two servants with us, also a neighbor, Mr. Theall, who was traveling for his health. He was going to Tennessee and we were pleased to have his company. The first night we spent with a friend, Mr. Crow.

The next day we got to Berwick's Bay, having to cross at night on account of storms and wind, the latter always too high in the day to attempt crossing. While at Berwick's Bay we learned that the pirate Lafitte had been taken prisoner and was sent to New Orleans, but very soon made his escape. A large reward was offered for him.

I think he certainly had many good friends.

We crossed the bay that night on a platform laid on two barges, and at two o'clock in the morning we landed at Breashear City. I had with me a letter to the landlady from her father. I sent it to her by a servant and she immediately came out of her room to see me. She received me with all kindness and attention. The table was all ready for those that had crossed the bay, and all as well as myself enjoyed our supper. We were a mixed company, Americans, French, Spaniards, and Indians. We went upstairs to a large room, with berths all around like those on shipboard. It was late in the morning when we got up, and all the travelers had gone down and eaten their breakfasts. The landlady told me the night before to take my rest in the morning and not to hurry, as I could get my breakfast at any time. My little Jane was not well and I told the servant to remain until I sent for her.

We went down and at the foot of the stairs a servant approached us. I think he was a Spaniard. He inquired if that was Mr. Martin and said that a gentleman wished to see him. Mr. Martin took me in the dining room and then followed the servant. Our breakfast was ready in a few minutes. The lady remarked: "Will you wait for your husband?" and I replied: "He will be in soon." I sat down and commenced eating and after awhile Mr. Martin came in. The lady sent upstairs for my baby. Soon after breakfast we left. I think we were twenty or twenty-five miles on Bayou La Fourche from Donaldsonville. When we arrived there, Mr. Martin told me that he had business with some gentlemen which would delay him a short time.

While we were there we had our dinner, and I inquired often of Mr. Martin who it was that he stopped at Donaldsonville to see, but he evaded answering me. Some time after he told me it was Lafitte the pirate that had been concealed in the inn and that Lafitte had wished him to take some letters to Donaldsonville. On entering the room Lafitte looked at him, saying: "Sir, I think I can trust you." Recognizing Lafitte, Mr. Martin replied: "You can. Your kindness to me cannot be forgotten and whatever I can do for you will be done with pleasure."

Lafitte then said: "You will deliver these letters to such gentlemen as I direct, living in Donaldsonville." He then gave Mr. Martin all the information necessary and handed him the letters, saying: "Sir, I learned you were here this morning, and I immediately concluded to put these letters in your charge, and I feel that they will be safely delivered." Mr. Martin was always quiet on that subject.

The next place we heard of Lafitte, he was fighting the British at New Orleans in favor of the Americans.

Having relatives at Natchez, Dr. McCreary's family, we remained there several days. When leaving there the doctor and my cousin went some miles with us. The doctor reminded my husband of getting a pass from the Governor to carry our servants through the Indian Nation, as this was during the war. Mr. Martin recollected that he had forgotten to get the necessary pass. Mr. Theall proposed taking his horse, and we would drive on slowly until Mr. Martin's return. We were then about twenty-five miles from Natchez, crossing Bear Creek. Our horse got frightened and ran up a very steep bank which did not check him in the least. I thought my only hope of saving myself and child would be to jump out. I threw my little girl out as I made the leap. My left limb was broken, in the ankle joint, both bones crushing through my gaiters, but my little Jane receiving no injury whatever. The horse ran up against a steep bank, breaking himself from the buggy. Mr. Theall had his arm and several ribs broken. So soon as my servant came to me I sent him back for my husband.

Being in a part of the country thickly settled, in a very short time many were there to give me assistance, and they carried me to the nearest house. Very soon Mr. Martin arrived, finding me suffering greatly. He gave full vent to his feelings, which made me feel more sensible of my terrible situation. Two doctors were immediately sent for. They examined my shattered limb and very soon pronounced their opinion that amputation would certainly be necessary to save my life. My husband would not consent to that, but sent for Dr. McCreary, our relative that we had left that morning.

The two doctors remained with me, but during the night I

was threatened with lock-jaw. That alarmed my husband and he told the doctors to act according to their own judgment. Preparations were made just as the sun rose. My heart seemed it would burst, I felt like soul and body were about to separate. My darling child was brought for me, as I thought to take my last leave of her.

My dear husband, his trouble and sorrow none knew but himself. He wished to know if I had any particular request to make, and I told him that my heart clung to my dear little babe, and to take her home to my mother as it was all of myself that I had to give her.

I was taken out on the gallery and laid on a table. The operation soon commenced. Chloroform was not used in those days and my suffering was only known to my God and myself.

Soon after the operation Dr. McCreary arrived. He said that the terrible breaking, the warm climate and the season of the year (it was June) made amputation the safest thing that could be done to save my life.

We remained at that house for twelve days.

Mr. Caradine was a gentleman living near and he proposed having me moved to his house, which was done. Mrs. Caradine, preparing a small bed, I was carried with great ease to myself. In that family I received all the kindness and attention that could have been given to a near relative. They had no children, only a sister living with them, and their love and affection for my little Jane was something to see. I truly prized their tenderness. We remained at Mr. Caradine's for six weeks, during that time Dr. McCreary often visited me. He said so soon as I could leave, he would take me to his house and would remain until I could leave for Tennessee, knowing that my health would not admit of my traveling at that time. Mr. Martin had disposed of our wild horse and purchased one perfectly gentle.

When leaving for the home of Dr. McCreary he insisted I should get in his buggy and ride with him, which I did. About five miles from his place we saw many Indians sitting immediately on the road. When seeing us they rose up, and the horse, frightened, commenced kicking until he broke the entire front of the carriage, I, not thinking of my situation, stood upon one foot and leaped out, falling on the end of my amputated limb, crushing the bone through, which had not yet healed. Blood flowed from the wound, pouring like water from a pitcher. Had the doctor not been with me, I should have survived but a short time.

He was slightly injured by a kick from the horse on his leg. I was put in our own buggy and went on, arriving at the Doctor's house at ten o'clock that night.

For two weeks I was confined to my bed; inflammation was so great that Dr. McCreary feared part of the limb would have to be taken off. My husband mentioned it to me, but I told him never, never, as I preferred death rather than undergo that suffering again. But with great care and skill, in two weeks I was up.

We remained at Natchez until the first of September, when my father, learning of my situation, sent down Mr. Barnes, a man he had great confidence in, and two horses, to assist in getting me to my old home. This was the only mode of traveling at that time. Soon after his arrival, we left for Tennessee. Mr. Martin had sent to New Orleans and had me a Cork leg made, which rendered me great assistance. Still I had to use crutches. We had about four hundred miles to travel through the Indian Nation, Chickasaws and Chocktaws. Many white families were living among them that had been sent there by the United States Government.

The first night after leaving Natchez, we stayed at our dear friends' house—Mr. Caradine and his wife. They received us most affectionately, and the next day we got to Port Gibson, stopping at Mr. Worthner's, a friend of my husband's. We remained there two days.

In a few miles of that place we found ourselves in the Indian Nation. Wherever we stopped they treated us with great kindness, if you showed you had confidence in them.

Traveling on, we heard tremendous howling and yelling, and upon going nearer we found about fifty men sitting on the grass with their blankets over them, moaning for a Chief that had just been buried near the line between two nations.

We stopped to stay all night, finding a great number there. The Agent soon told us that they were to have a war dance there that night, and that the next morning the tribe was leaving for Pensacola. The war dance was truly a sight long to be remembered.

The dance commenced, both male and female taking part, and continued until after midnight. About sunrise they got up, made all join hands, children and all going round and round, crying and yelling. Soon after they made ready for their departure. The men took leave of their wives and children with awful groans and yells. They left and were seen out of sight. The squaws appeared to mourn their departure.

That same day, while crossing a large creek, the horse stopped to drink. I set my daughter Jane in her father's lap. My crutches were fastened to the carriage just in front of me and I took them and threw them into the stream where they soon disappeared. My husband looked at me with astonishment. I told him I could not bear. the sight of them longer. He gently reproved me, saying: "How will you get along without them?" But from that day to this, I have had no use for them.

The next morning we got our breakfast at the house of James Colbert, the Indian Chief. He and his wife had a few days before returned from Washington. He said that his visit there with many others, was to have a talk with their father, the President of the United States, with regard to sending his subjects to fight the British at New Orleans. Mrs. Colbert was delighted with her trip and said the President gave them a dinner, and that all the fashionable gentlemen and ladies were there. At this time she was dressed quite fashionably, except she was bare-footed, and she served us a most excellent breakfast.

Mr. Colbert invited us to stay some days and rest, while Mrs. Colbert gave me lunch for my little Jane that lasted several days. Two days after, we stopped at a house expecting to stay all night. We found the doors and windows all open, and the house had every appearance of having been left in a hurry. We went about two miles and camped in the woods.

The servants made a fire and prepared supper. As we were
ready to partake of it, Mr. Joplin, the mail carrier, rode up, got
down and partook of his coffee, ham and crackers with us.
He told us we were fortunate in not being along two days
before, as a party of Creek Indians had passed along, killing
every one they met.

The next night we got to a place called Big Spring and there
we found many Indians. They had come there to protect the
place from marauding Indians, for three nights before many
of those Creek Indians had passed there. The family heard
that they were coming that route where they had passed before,
and left that night.

Seven boatmen that had gone down the Mississippi River
in their flatboats, sold out their produce and were returning
home from New Orleans, had stopped at that place and five of
the seven men had been killed by the Indians. Their graves
were near the house. They had been buried that day. The
Indians gave us supper, consisting of turkey, corn and potatoes.
Mr. Martin asked the old Indian if he would let me sleep, with
my child, in his house, but the Indian would not consent, as it
their custom not to allow strangers to sleep in the house with
their family. I, not knowing the danger we were exposed to,
slept in the house with not less than fifty Indians, and many
of them drunk. My husband, Mr. Barnes and the servants
sat up all night. The next night we were twelve miles from
Columbia, Tennessee, where we felt safe from all harm.

After more difficulties and hardships, the Martins arrived
at Mrs. Martin's girlhood home "on the Dickerson Pike,
seven miles from Nashville." There she found that two of
her sisters had died. Her mother wept upon seeing her so
painfully crippled, but the tears of Martha Martin were
"all tears of joy."

After recounting various and sundry family matters, she
continues: "My parents would not let Mr. Martin think of
taking me back to Louisiana, and he finally concluded to
remain in Tennessee, which I greatly preferred. In Novem-

ber, Mr. Martin left for our southern home in Louisiana, going with the army under General Jackson that was leaving Nashville for New Orleans, under the immediate command of Generals Coffey and Carroll.

"They all went on flat boats, and arrived in the city of New Orleans, December 22, 1814, and I am told that fighting commenced the next day and continued until the eighth of January, 1815. In that battle, General Jackson gained a victory over the flower of the British army under General Packenham, and this victory crowned General Jackson with laurels that never faded through life."

Mr. Martin did not return until April, but when he did return he reported that he had succeeded in leasing the Louisiana plantation until a time favorable to sell. The Martins then purchased a farm near Nashville, and it was there that Martha Martin was living when she wrote her chronicle.

Their tribulations were not over, however, for an epidemic of "cold plague" visited the community, taking many of their friends and relatives. However, better times were coming, for she writes that in 1817 "we made a fine crop of cotton, corn, tobacco, and hemp, which we sold to good advantage."

She continues her chronicle, recounting births and deaths in her family, telling family history, and giving much interesting information by the way. "The first steamboat, I think, came to Nashville in 1816," she writes, "but goods were brought in wagons some two or three years after steamboats commenced running. The goods were brought to Cincinnati and other points on the Ohio River from New York, and the same wagons hauled them to Nashville."

Six more children were born to the Martins—brothers and sisters for "my little Jane" who played such an important part in the pioneer life in Louisiana. Things prospered; additional land was bought. There was a time of peace and plenty. At the death of her father she shared largely in his estate.

The next item of general interest pertains to the visit of Lafayette. Let me quote again from her own account:

In the spring of 1825, General Lafayette visited Nashville, and well do I remember his noble and pleasant manner of receiving all who were introduced to him. My husband was among those who were appointed to receive him and his party. Taking our little girls into town, we spent some days at our friend Mr. Stewart's home.

There was a handsome arch erected across the street near the public square, and a large platform on which to welcome him. General Jackson, General Lafayette, and George Washington Lafayette were in an open carriage drawn by four handsome gray horses. Governor Carroll welcomed them with much feeling and pleasure. The old Revolutionary soldiers came from every part of the State to shake hands with the old General, who had come across the waters to see them.

I saw one old soldier throw his arms around him with that love of gratitude not often remembered, saying: "You have not forgotten the soldier that brought a bear to your tent, which I had killed when you were out of provisions!" And General Lafayette embraced him saying: "Mr. Hagar, is it possible that you are still with us?"

That night Nashville was illuminated, and the next night there was a splendid ball, which the old and young attended, the ladies displaying the fashions of the day, their beauty and their smiles. A place at one end of the room was raised about three feet for the old ladies and our visitors. On this platform were seated: General Lafayette with Mrs. Jackson, General Jackson and Mrs. Priestly, Mrs. Carroll, George W. Lafayette, Mrs. Stewart, Mrs. McNairy, Dr. Shelby, Mrs. Minick and myself. The young people truly enjoyed themselves dancing. Not less than thirty danced the first set.

The morning before the ball, a large party went up to the Hermitage, General Jackson's home, twelve miles from Nashville, in company with General Lafayette on a steamboat, and they fired a salute in passing the home of Dr. Priestly, in honor of him, who had so recently passed away.

That night his widow replied very beautifully to General Jackson for his kind remembrance of her dear husband.

About two o'clock the next day General Lafayette and his party left for Louisville. Every attention and honor which could be shown our worthy guest was lavished on them. His visit gave Nashville people something to talk about long after his departure.

Writing about Lafayette brings up memories to Martha Martin, and a little later in her memoir she writes of this incident:

"I can remember when I was a little girl about seven years old, my mother taking me to witness the obsequies of General Washington. I had never seen such a large gathering of people before. A coffin and all the form of a funeral and the sad look of all present, made a deep impression upon me. I was impressed by the idea that the great man's body was really in the coffin."

Another of her early memories is given in more detail. It tells of her first meeting with General Andrew Jackson:

"There were many officers that belonged to the army stationed at Nashville. My father invited them all with their wives out to dine, and well do I remember their happy, jovial manner. Among them was General Jackson, a noble, elegant looking gentleman. He wore a long que and powdered hair, which was the fashion in those days. They all appeared to enjoy the dinner and drank freely of the old peach brandy which my father always kept. The company returned to Nashville in the evening, apparently quite well pleased with their visit. My eldest sister, Mary, was then a young lady, much admired and quite pretty."

How tantalizing these entries are! And how brief. It is seldom that Martha Martin wastes even as much as a single word—but how much she could have told us had she seen fit to write a complete account of these incidents! It is proof enough that she considered them important or she would never have mentioned them at all. In her description of her last meeting with General Jackson she gives a complete picture for the first time. The entry is quoted in its entirety:

General Jackson being an old friend of my husband, I feel I must say something in regard to him. As a statesman and a military man, none exceeded him. In 1824 he was nominated for President of the United States but was defeated. In 1828 he was elected and in 1832 he had an overwhelming majority. Mrs. Jackson lived but a short time after he was first elected, which made a great change in him. He never afterward had that happy and cheerful look that he had before her death. The last time my husband ever saw him, he stopped at our home on Gallatin Pike, with some friends, as he was on his way to Washington at the beginning of his second term. He looked sad, and he asked my daughter to play and sing "Old Lang Syne." On his arrival at Washington, he sent my husband his likeness, which I have now.

After his return from Washington, General Jackson remained on his farm, his adopted son and his son's wife living with him. I paid him a visit two weeks before his death.

Although he was not able to come out of his room, he received me most cordially and inquired for all my family. I sat with him until dinner was announced. Before leaving, I walked in the garden and when I went inside again, to take leave of him, he said: "Have you been in the garden?" I replied that I had and I gave him a rose which I had in my hand. He took the rose, then took my hand, saying: "Farewell, my dear, and may God bless you." Two weeks after that visit,

I attended his funeral. Mr. Edgar preached from Revelations
7, verse 14.

His likeness was only finished a few days before his death,
taken by a gentleman that had been sent from France for
that purpose.

After a few more entries of a personal nature, Martha
Martin closes her memoir. It is a simple, dignified document,
meant for her children and her children's children. It is
evident that she had no thought of publication when she
wrote it. But in its very economy of words, it seems to me,
it gives a picture of the times more accurate than many a
longer chronicle of the period. Better still, it gives insight
into a rich and simple nature, and a picture of the true
American pioneer, a woman unafraid.

Chapter XVII

A VOYAGE DOWN THE RIVER IN 1817

It had always seemed to me that the actual chronicle of the times is preferable to an account, reconstructed years later, by a writer unfamiliar with the period. For this reason I have endeavored, in compiling this book on the Mississippi, to give the descriptions of the river in the language of those pioneers who knew the Mississippi for what it was. In order to secure these accounts, it has been necessary to read perhaps a hundred manuscripts and pamphlets. In my search I found among the possessions of the Louisiana Historical Society a journal of a voyage down the Mississippi to New Orleans in 1817. The entries quoted here form but a small part of a lengthy account, written in English, French, and German, covering a period of ten years. The greater part of the journal has evidently been destroyed, and many of the pages still preserved are no longer legible. The author, J. G. Flugel, came from Germany to the United States in 1803, where he remained until 1818. For a number of years he was engaged in trading along the Mississippi River. In 1818 he returned to Germany. Upon the retirement of Friedrich List from the American Consulate at Leipzig, J. G. Flugel was appointed his successor; an office which he held until his death in 1855. This journal belongs to one of his descendants, Felix Flugel, assistant professor of economics at the University of California. Mr. Felix Flugel gave the use of the diary to the Louisiana Historical So-

"BOUND DOWN THE RIVER"
From an old Currier and Ives print

ciety, and it is through the courtesy of Mr. Henry P. Dart, editor of the Louisiana Historical Society Quarterly, that I have received permission to use it here.

This journal interested me more than any other diary examined, for the writer was such a painstaking observer and chronicler. His descriptions of the steamboats and of the life among flatboatmen seem to me extraordinarily vivid.

January 1, 1817. With the beginning of this year I shall keep my journal in the English language. One mile below the fourth bluff is Fort Pickering, which has a tolerable view as it lies very high. It is built of square logs, similar to Fort Massacre. Below this we overtook Picket and about ten o'clock in the morning found Antony who seemed sorry that we did not come with him yesterday. I for my part am not sorry that I had a little business with those good Shawnees. I told Antony that Mr. Strauss has invited me to come on board his boat and that I would accept his good offer as I would be more comfortably situated and besides Strauss could be of service to me since he is going to stay at New Orleans. I went on board Strauss' boat this evening. We had a tolerable day after the fog in the morning. Landed on the right shore near Island number 50.

January 2. Cloudy, foggy and windy, though later in the day the weather cleared up. We passed the grand cut-off, which is certainly the worst place we have passed as yet. Full of sawyers for three miles. I steered the boat, and since I am pretty well acquainted with it I will make this my principal business in the future. We passed this place without difficulty. Landed at Island number 56.

January 3. Hard rain and thick fog. We landed early in the afternoon below the mouth of the St. Francis River, where we found the old man from Tennessee (tobacco cargo). We went up to the habitations but found nothing to trade. The places are poor, and deserted looking. We also walked to the mouth of the St. Francis, but Mr. Parry had nothing to trade or to sell. After we returned we cut loose. Landed in the evening opposite the big Prairie where there is also a settlement. This evening it began to storm.

January 4. After last night's storm, we have this day most beautiful weather. We landed on the Indian side near Island number 62. In the evening three Indians, Delawares, came to Antony to trade. One especially was a cunning chap, but they are dirty looking people.

January 5. Krutz wanted to start last night at 2 o'clock but we did not start until daybreak. The morning was clear. As we came opposite Island number 64, we found a boat which was wrecked on a sawyer and still hanging. The distressed called on us for aid, which we granted. We found it was the man from Tennessee and his company. They started before daybreak, and as the river was smooth before them, ran on the sawyer unawares. The boat is still fast and the current runs through in a violent manner. The upper part of the boat is under water. We went with skiffs to assist them. We first rescued a horse, which had been in the ice-cold water four or five hours. He swam to the Indian shore and by examination was found somewhat injured. We tied him to the cane where he remained the whole day without any other food. We got out five hogsheads of tobacco, which were brought to the shore in skiffs. Ropes were tied to them by which we pulled them to shore with a great deal of labor as the current was remarkably swift. Afternoon I went ashore. Not far from the bank where I was sitting a tree fell on the opposite bank with a tremendous noise—as it fell a large body of sand spread itself around like a cloud. The bank continued to fall nearly the whole afternoon. Late in the afternoon the wrecked boat got loose from the sawyer, and landed three miles below on the right shore (Missouri). Ritter came in the evening. As we were alone I again cautioned him about his uncommon and imprudent liberality. I do not know what to think of this, my friend; I love him but his actions are so very extraordinarily imprudent, and still he looks to me for more help. I am anxious to see the outcome of his Orleans journey. His expenses will amount to three times the profit which in the best market will accrue from his trifling cargo.

January 6. Cut cable. Tied the hogsheads of tobacco to our boat and landed them. The old unfortunate man is much distressed, he told me. His appearance is sickly. Very probably he will fall sick. He will take 1,000 or more staves from the boat, receive the Orleans price for the same, and put in his tobacco and pork. After we started he sent the good Irish sailor (whom I once met near the mouth of the Cumberland River and who had been on board his boat) after his coat, which he had left on board of Anthony's boat. When he came near Krutz's boat, Krutz sent him back, told him that he had not left it there. I called to Antony to send it with his skiff but without avail. The man returned with his canoe and the coat was left on board, for which I feel very sorry, as the poor man had since his wreck exerted himself and appeared to be in a low state of health. Krutz curses him still and calls him every bad name possible, and for what reason? Because he could not take advantage of the poor unfortunate man. And Antony, the tender-hearted, and Bob (negro) also treat him with indifference. The wind began to rise, which scattered us. Picket's boat went ashore, and ours followed after we had laid by awhile. The wind ceased. We went down a little farther and landed in the dark at Island number 68. We had a tolerably good landing, but shallow water. Krutz and Picket had a quarrel about the landing and common words (agreeable to their character) were spoken on both sides.

January 7. This morning it was very cold and foggy. We went several miles and found Antony and Whetstone who had landed. They called us and we put to shore. Staid awhile and started together. The fog again rose and Antony, fearful of it, laid by again. We three kept on through the thick and cold fog. Landed in the evening on the left shore two miles above White River. Two Canadians came on board who live nearly opposite our landing. Apparently good people, with gentle address. I felt tired and soon went to sleep.

January 8. A beautiful morning and calm. Met one keel boat

going up which wanted to hire hands. Passed White River and
the Arkansas or Ozark River, which River has a dark red
color. The weather continued the rest of the day clear, and,
notwithstanding the continual headache with which I have
been plagued, I feel well. Landed opposite the foot of Island
number 76 on the right shore. We had a good landing close
to each other. Ritter and Krutz paid us a visit in the evening,
as usual.

January 9. I saw Antony coming, so we started, but hardly
entered the current when we were obliged to put to shore again
to escape a gust of wind and rain coming from the north east.
It rained very hard, but soon stopped. We started and had
the rest of the day fine weather. In the afternoon, Picket ran
over a sawyer, notwithstanding my caution. The bow was bent
up by the force of the sawyer, but we went over without sus-
taining any injury. At three o'clock three Ozarks with one
squaw came on board to trade. But they were too cunning.
The squaw who was on board our boat was the best looking
one I have yet seen. We landed in the evening below Island
82 on the right shore. It was late when Antony, Krutz and
Ritter came on board our boat. They had been playing cards.
Ritter lost his otter skin. Krutz was the winner. They began to
play cards, which I despise. I gave Ritter caution not to follow
this bad practice.

January 10. A short time after we had cut loose, the wind
rose, so that we had to row continuously to keep off shore.
We at last had to lay by for safety. A whole company of
Indians (Osages) (Ozark) or (Arkansas), which nation, I
understand from a New York State man, who just now came
from the Arkansas River, was at war with the Cherokees on
account of some insults which had been passed by the latter,
who killed seven of the former when at peace. We had to lay
by for the whole day as the wind continued. In the evening
we went to Krutz's boat. They were playing for jewelry, and
at the end for racoon skins. I left the boat soon. Went home
to write some lines in my journal, which I have very much
neglected.

January 11. Cut loose quite early. Passed Spanish Moss

Bend. Fine weather. Here we saw the first trees, full of this hanging moss, which has the appearance of a thick gray domestic thread. This moss, I understand, can be used to stuff mattresses, as it is very much like horse hair. Early in the afternoon we came to Illecheeks settlement, which consists of four families. Tonight we bought some provisions from a Frenchman who formerly lived in New Madrid. The soil here is as rich as I have yet seen in this country, and the tract of land that the improvements are on is handsome.

January 12. We had very fine weather. I started with John Albert, a young man who is on board our boat, in the afternoon with our skiff to trade with some few who are settled along the River below Island number 88, where our boats landed. I did a little trading. I found a very fine old man of seventy years, who had considerable knowledge (Christopher Owen), an Englishman, but he could speak very good German which he had learned while at Lancaster. We found several Indians who had a very large number of furs on the bank near the old man's dwelling.

January 13. We started early. Beautiful weather. Very calm. This morning two Chaktaws came on board. One looked like Lucifer himself, as he wore no clothes. He had only an old dirty blanket round him which, when he paddled the canoe, would fall from his red skin. His long black hair without any ornaments, hung down over his red skin. His dark physiognomy rendered him frightful. He brought very good honey on board, which Mr. Strauss bought. In the afternoon I went out in the skiff to Island number 93. I gathered some Spanish moss and went back on board. Landed this evening at Island number 94. On the left shore Krutz set the cane afire, which cracks as loud as a gun when the joints burst.

January 14. This morning we started in company with the boat from Ste. Genevieve, which had overtaken us. The wind blew a little, though we are blessed with another very fine day. Mr. Strauss and I went out in the skiff to trade. Passed Stack Island, the former seat of counterfeiters, murderers and thieves, but the earthquake sank it and only a bar with a few willows now makes its appearance. At the second house to which we came to trade the dogs nearly bit me. The landlady of this very fine plantation was uncommonly coarse. They lived well and had an elegant stock of cattle which were remarkably fat and that with apparently little feed. The cane and rushes, like other wild herbs, attend very much to the fattening of cattle. We had rather contrary wind. Met a schooner barge going up under sail. Landed above Island number 100 on the left shore.

January 15. Morning, we started early. Ours and the two strange boats were the last. We took another pass, but did not take advantage of the river in time. We came out of the current which kept us far from the other boats for the whole day. We took the last channel between Islands 101 and 102 which was nearer. But as soon as we were out of it we came into an eddy which put us back as much and more than we had gained by that shorter pass of the two islands. A keel boat passed us, going down, and a Chacktaw chief called "Snap Eye" came on aboard to beg. He had a piece of paper, which was written to induce whites to give him assistance. We passed in the afternoon Yazoo River, and as we came within two miles of the Walnut Hills we had a handsome view of them before us, of the different habitations and of Fort McHenry, which was situated on the top of the highest hill I could see. We passed very good settlements all day. Landed opposite Walnut Hills. Mr. Strauss appears displeased that they had to row so long. But I did as much as I could and it pains me that he gives me some reproaches about the steering. I am this evening not well disposed. Vogel and L. argue with Isaac (negro) about religion, Adam's children, Jesus, etc.

January 16. Morning—we started together before daybreak. The two strange boats remained for some time in the right hand eddy, but soon overtook us again. The wind arose. Passed a little village, below the Walnut Hills, Warrington; I counted 25 houses. John made proposals to Mr. Strauss to leave the boat provided he would stop at the various plantations. As this was not in the agreement with him, I am afraid that Strauss and he will have some sharp words before they part. I went to Krutz's boat. Cautioned Ritter how to act in the future toward different persons, then returned to our boat again. I expect we shall soon be separated. The wind rises to such a degree that we are at last obliged to lay by opposite Island number 108. The wind continues until late. I staid on board this evening.

January 17. We started better than an hour before daybreak. Passed an Indian camp. They had a fire and were singing "Oi hi go he jo he," etc. The wind begins to rise again early in the morning and we are obliged again to lay by opposite the foot of Island number 110. We came to a bluff where we landed near a raft of logs which will be taken to Orleans to market. We laid by all day on account of the wind. The wind kept on nearly all night.

January 18. In the morning we started and went about two miles but the contrary and hard wind obliged us to lay by again on the right shore about two miles above the Grand Gulf. It has been since yesterday exceptionally cold, so that we could hardly warm ourselves.

January 19. We saw Picket starting, who yesterday put to shore just opposite us. We put off, but the wind again began to blow against us and so our boats went to shore a little above Black River. Ritter gave me the head of an alligator which he had found a few days ago. It had been washed out of the Mississippi in high water. It is a very large one. I will try to preserve it. We soon started again as the wind ceased. Passed Black River and Grand Gulf by noon. The wind still kept blowing a little all day. Landed above the little Gulf late in the evening on the left shore.

January 20. Passed the little Gulf in the morning, which is a bend like the Grand Gulf and high land—hills on which are scattered a few buildings. The wind again began to rise, and we were obliged to lay by below Island number 111, right shore. I went up to the plantation which was close to us. The lady of the house received us in a friendly manner. We examined the books which belonged to her husband, by which I see that he must be a well-informed man. We went to the plantation below. They both are fine plantations and the owners able men. The lower plantation has an exhaustive cotton gin mill. Soon after our return to the boat Mr. Jacob Bieller, the husband of the lady whom we had seen before, came on board to invite Mrs. Vogel and Strauss up to the house. John went away, too, and I remained on board and finished a letter to N. The wind blew hard all day. I fear for Ritter's boat. As the company came down, I was requested to come up with Mr. and Mrs. Vogel to supper, which I did. The good host pleased me very much. We had a good supper, and spent the evening very agreeably. The wind did not cease until midnight.

January 21. Morning, a little foggy. We started about 8 o'clock. The weather is clear, but later the wind blew again. Passed Cale's Creek. Landed right shore, near plantations which were abandoned, ruined by the earthquake.

January 22. Started about 8 o'clock. Fine weather. Very calm. Arrived at Natchez early in the afternoon. We found Ritter. Antony and Whetstone had already gone. Ritter persuaded me to go up to the lower part of town. We went together—Ritter, Krutz, Strauss, and John. A Frenchman invited us to play cards, but we all refused. Drank a couple of bottles of wine and started. Ritter found an old acquaintance with whom we were obliged to drink, since he invited us.

January 23. In the morning Mr. Strauss and I went up to town. Met Mr. Brune. He invited us to his store.

January 24. I go back on board. A good many boats have come from different parts. The old man whose boat had wrecked at Island number 64 came likewise. Mr. Vogel has taken a place as gardener in Natchez. I remained on board the whole afternoon and cleaned up the boat. Natchez is a very busy place. Ritter started this afternoon for Orleans. I fear the result of his journey to this country, as his expenses will certainly overbalance the profit. He depends too much on me, but I shall in the future think of myself and my family first, second, my creditors, and then my friends. He will never become rich or even in a middle state, as he is too free in spending without the least calculation. His heart is good but he still is not that true being which I once thought to have found in him. I feel sorry for him and his good companion.

January 25. In the morning, a number of boats arrived— from Kentucky and Tennessee. I went on board one of the

Photo by Earl Norman, Natchez

PLANTATION HOUSE NEAR NATCHEZ

boats—from Cape Girardeau, (Captain N. Sears)—to see the old man whom I frequently visited at New Madrid. They had a stuffed panther on board which was killed by them on Flower Island. I would have bought him, had the Captain been on board, to send to my good Hermes in Barby, by Mr. F. Brune, who is going to Hamburg with a shipment of cotton in perhaps a month.

We started about ten o'clock in the morning. Fine weather. Passed St. Catherine's Creek and Ellis' or White Cliffs, which are beautiful. The sides of the cliff still keep falling in and the ground is of various colors—red, blue, yellow, white and handsomely decorated with bright green—date trees and the magnolias, the large leaved tulip tree, a native of this country (Polyandria polyginia). The broken bank has left in some parts a bluff like a wall made by man's hands. All these render a strange sight. We landed about a mile below the cliffs near a plantation belonging to a Mr. Hutchin. Krutz and I went up to see whether they would buy anything of us. We found a most delightful farm. Three very friendly ladies. One, a widow with a beautiful little son. We soon went back to our boats. Krutz had asked for a bottle of milk for which they would take nothing. In the evening two carpenters were on board who work on that plantation. They told me about this country, of the overseer, etc.

January 26. Fine weather again, except for wind. Passed Homochitto River, Buffalo Creek, Loftus Heights. On the left side of the river is situated Fort Adams. I went out with a skiff to visit the fort. The fort is situated at the foot of Loftus Heights. It was built of brick, but all of the buildings, including the fort, have gone to ruins. A small blockhouse stands on the highest hill. It was in 1807 that General Wilkinson was stationed there in a garrison to collect troops to drive away Spaniards beyond the Louisiana line. The ground here is clay, which has a white and iron color intermixed, as if burnt. There are a good many houses in the neighborhood of the fort and the whole forms a tolerably handsome sight. This evening we landed on the left shore one mile below the fort.

January 27. Passed in the morning the line of demarcation,

five miles below the fort, which was drawn before the purchase. It crosses the river 31° north latitude. The great cut off, by land a distance of five miles across, is by water fifty-four miles. We landed this evening about two miles above Red River near a corn plantation. Tolerable weather. Rather windy and cold.

January 28. Passed Red River which was remarkably high at this time. Evening landed in Tunica Bend, right shore. Several negroes came to trade. Night, rain.

January 29. We started in the fog, and went about six miles down stream. Had to lay by on account of contrary winds. It began to rain pretty hard. Landed on the right shore. The rain and wind fill the boat with smoke and almost kill the fire.

January 30. Our boat is full of water, which Mr. Strauss pumps out in anger as John is very lazy. John is a trifling boy. Winds continue all day, but clear weather. Very cold. We cut a great deal of wood.

January 31. This morning at last we start. Landed at Bay Tunica in the morning, ten o'clock. Krutz intends taking in cotton for freight. Beautiful weather. In the afternoon an old French gentleman came on board to purchase a few articles and offered to buy the boat of Mr. Strauss, which Strauss promises him provided he can make arrangements with Krutz. I find him to be a R. A. Mason. This draws him nearer to me. He advises me not to remain in this country. Gives me a great deal of information about the Isle of Cuba to which he advises me to go. He came from there about twenty months ago. He is now residing at Baton Rouge. His name is Jean Fachon.

February 1. In the morning Mr. Fachon came again and Mr. Strauss sold him his boat for Thirty Dollars ($30.00), and Strauss and I bought Krutz's for Forty Dollars ($40.00), in expectation of getting some freight at Point Coupee. We load our things on board the other boat. Fachon on board again. Fine weather.

February 2. Mr. Fachon invited me to breakfast with him. We had a herring salad, and potatoes and a bottle of wine. As I was eating I observed that the cucumbers which were cut in the herring salad were very good. He then observed that he had bought them of a young Swiss a few days ago at Point Coupee. I discovered that it was Antoin of whom he had bought them, and I was eating of the fruit which Helvetie had preserved—1,500 miles from here. John A. and Picket have been up at the tavern and played cards all night. John, I understand, has lost $50.00. The tavern keeper is a mean man, I believe, and has probably taken advantage of John. He is very drunk. It was decided that one of us should go to Point Coupee in order to procure freight. I offered to go. Picket went with me in the skiff. The boat remained in the Bayou this day. We started about noon. As we came below Island number 122 we saw two boats lashed together, toward which we steered. Who can imagine my joy? It was the boat with my friend Silvestre Preve. He was very glad to see me, and I myself not less so. We conversed for a couple of hours, but towards evening the wind blew so hard that they put to shore, and on account of contrary wind and high waves we, with our skiff, could only reach a plantation belonging to Mr. Ludling, about 8 miles above Point Coupee where his brother-in-law, Mr. Martin, Jr., lived. Mr. Martin had gone to the burial of a Captain. I waited until he returned, and then was entreated to stay, to which I agreed, as it was night. His (Martin's) entrance was rather comical, as he came dressed in style française—a sword round his waist. The deceased was in the Battle of New Orleans, therefore, this ornament. Few words passed on either side. He lives with a mulatto woman and six or seven dark-skinned children surround him, who dare not say "father," nor he, "my children." We had a dry supper but a good bed was prepared for me, which was entirely surrounded with white curtains, prepared for that disagreeable little fly, the mosquito. Therefore, these curtains are called mosquito bars or nets. It was the first bed of this kind I have ever slept in. For Picket they had prepared a bed on the floor.

February 3. Morning—extremely cold. As I thought that our host would not make a charge, I did not stay for breakfast. We, therefore, started. It was cold, windy, and the waves were high. We could not reach our destination, so we landed and tied our skiff near a sugar plantation belonging to a certain

Mr. Poydrass, who commands a fortune of nearly two million
dollars. I walked the rest of the way where I saw the first of
the elegant settlements on this river. The plantations are large
and handsomely embellished with orange trees.

We passed a small store which we entered to refresh ourselves, then went to the tavern. On this road I found a poor
negro, wheeling dirt to renew a ditch along the levee. The poor
fellow had an iron with three hooks around his neck, working
in the extreme cold weather. He told me he had not misbe-
haved, but I suppose he had run away. His master's name was
Pierre. Ate breakfast in the tavern. Afterwards went to a
certain Mr. Gross, a Saxon, the sheriff of the Parish of
Point Coupee under Judge I. H. Ludling. He received me
tolerably well. Soon left him. Went to Mr. Ludling's overseer,
a Mr. Steip. I entered the house. Steip, after some time, came.
He is of funny appearance. Invited me to dine with him, which
I did not accept. I left him, as Mr. Ludling, his employer, has
gone to Natchez. Steip toward evening went over to Bayou
Sara. I went with him to see whether freight could be obtained. He, Steip, told me to ask the man about freight—my
letter had so much weight that Mr. Steip could not take the
pains even to ask whether there was anything or not. He is a
man of common stamp. After we returned, I went to the
tavern again. Nothing heard or seen of our boats, for the wind
still blows as in the morning. I do not expect them. As we were
sitting round the fireside, about six in number, a man whom
I had already observed this morning, addressed himself to me.
His appearance was tolerable. His fiery eyes told me of his
deep character and by his language I perceived that he was an
experienced, well-educated man. He was wrapped in a blanket
coat, and his right arm was tied or hung in a handkerchief.
He told me in short that he had been unfortunate lately and
would soon leave for the Isle of Cuba. After supper he called
me out on the piazza, where he told me of the misfortune
which lately happened to him. The last of his riches, 64 slaves,
had been levied upon by his creditors. He at one time had three
ships at sea and was engaged in a large business. As we
were talking I received notice that the door would be locked,

for it was bedtime. I was surprised, and went to bed unwillingly.

February 4. We have this day as disagreeable weather as ever. Rain, frost, and wind, so that I do not expect the boat this day. I remain in the house all day. Picket goes over the river to St. Francisville. Towards evening I visited Mr. Henry Hunt, the unfortunate man of whom I spoke above. After this I went to visit Mr. Gross. We had a pleasant evening. Mr. Gross told me that Henry Hunt was a mean man, and that through his own fault alone his ruin was caused. In the afternoon I gave assistance to an old silversmith in repairing my watch.

February 6. In the morning we winded anchor and tied to a boat which is loaded with artillery pieces from Pittsburgh for New Orleans. Fine weather. We passed Fausse River. Had a beautiful day. Floated all night. About three o'clock passed a steamboat in full flight going down, which was a most delightful sight. The dark night and the bright sparks which were flying out of the cylinder rendered to the eye only an instantaneous, but a magnificent, view. The vessel passed only about 50 feet from us. The water foamed and one could perceive even the wind caused by the swiftness of the boat.

February 7. This day we passed Bayou Manchac. We have to row a great deal. Passed beautiful plantations which continue all the way to Orleans. Landed on the last island in the Mississippi, to get wood. As we weighed anchor a schooner came under full sail bound for Baton Rouge. An elegant sight. It is long since I have seen a large sailing vessel. We intended going all night, but toward midnight it began to rain, and the wind blew us to shore, where we laid by. I got wet since the boat leaks.

February 8. In the morning, when the wind and rain ceased we started. Passed General Hampton's plantation (sugar), where a three-master lies which sight is pleasing to me. Passed Barange's place, which has the best appearance of any I have seen. The houses are built in Roman style. Good weather. Laid by three miles below Contrell's, where we again found a three-master loaded with three hundred hogsheads of sugar, bound

for New York. Some days ago they were driven to shore on
the opposite side of the river because of a broken cable. She
now lies three feet in the mud, and awaits the steamboat to
relieve her.

The people on board our boat become more disagreeable the
nearer we come to Orleans.

February 9. Morning. We intended going last night by the
time the moon rose, but were prevented by contrary winds. The
boat, which contained my friend Sylvestre, landed near us.
We are pleased to meet again. I invited him on board where he
remained awhile, but soon the boat started, and we are again
divided.

We remained at anchor until evening, when a comic scene
occurred. Antony had been playing cards all afternoon with
John (Blanket Coat). Mr. Strauss, Krutz and I had gone to bed
when we heard a noise coming from the other boat where they
were playing. John A. called "Blanket Coat" a cheat, liar, etc.
A few blows followed which the Captain, Mr. Charles Earl,
soon stopped. John A. returned to our boat still cursing. Krutz
laughed heartily to think that John A. had met his match in
gambling. He had lost $14.00. Sharp words passed between
John and Strauss. Mr. Strauss knocked him (John) or rather
clinched him and John fell back on the floor. He kicked vio-
lently. He got up again and cursed. Mr. Earl advised him
that he would gain but little by such behavior. Several negroes
who had asked leave to sleep in our boat because of the storm
(they belonged to a trading boat which had tied close to
ours), as soon as the noise began got up from the floor,
pulled their caps over their ears, and left our boat. I
shall never forget these frightened negroes. The Frenchman
(the proprietor of the boat to which the negroes belonged)
loaded his gun.

February 10. In the morning Mr. Strauss demands an
apology from John, which John refuses. He (John) goes on
shore and later boards Earl's boat with which he intends going
to Orleans.

Very cold. Otherwise beautiful weather. Passed Bona Cara
Church and settlement, which is the prettiest I have seen on

this river. We floated down stream the greater part of the night. I was awake nearly the whole time. Laid by about one o'clock.

February 11. Started after daybreak. Passed most delightful farms and saw about six miles above New Orleans the ship which was sunk last year by the distressing flood. We land around the point about one mile from the city. I went to see Antony, who had landed this morning. Krutz, Ritter, Antony and I went along the levee where we ate some oysters. I am pleased with the order in which the ships are tied and with what I see of the town.

February 12. My intention is going to Havana, as I believe that not much is to be done here, but the hostility which the United States exercises toward Spain renders a passage there not altogether safe. Therefore, I will, with Mr. Strauss, remain on board our boat for a couple of weeks, in which time I can see whether something can be made here or not. Yesterday about twelve ships came in, of which I saw about six or seven come up at once. There are at present about 400 ships here, which, of course, causes a great deal of activity.

February 16. Towards evening I went with Pierre to see the negroes dance. Their dances are certainly curious, particularly to a European. I shall give a more detailed account of them sometime in the future.

February 18. In the morning I clean the boat.

February 20. In the morning the Barge "Eliza" of Cincinnati, belonging to James and Douglass, departed, with which Picket, Bob, and Isaac are going. They only could go to the end of the eddy, a half mile, as the wind was rising powerfully. A barge broke loose and nearly got lost as there was no one on board. Several sailors were drowned in the high waves by crossing the river, and a good deal of damage was otherwise done.

February 22. Washington's birthday. In the morning cannons were fired in honor of the great Washington and in the evening balls were given in the city. I remained tranquil on board.

February 26. Made cider from the spoiled apples. John says

that a man had been overpowered on the street and his money taken from him. Such cases are heard of every day and one must be careful.

March 1. In the afternoon the steamboat "Dispatch" left for the Red River (Natchitoches). This, however, is nothing new. Steamboats, ships and barges go and come almost every hour. A flat boat from Cincinnati has just arrived loaded with sundry produce. A number of gentlemen from that city pass by.

March 2. Last night a couple of men knocked at our door. One of them said that he was a friend and would give us a bargain. I answer that it is not the proper time to do business. They soon departed. A negro woman who had several times bought apples, came to the boat. She told me that she had a good master who would have given her (and the other slaves) freedom, but he died. She was then sold but again has a good master. Later in the afternoon, a couple of gentlemen entered the boat. One of them, a Mr. James Smith, an Irishman, makes inquiry regarding property which he had lost and which Antony had found this side of Point Coupee. He is pleased that some of his papers were saved and a few of his clothes. I direct him to . . . who has the trunk and to whom I gave the papers.

In the evening the men who knocked at our door last night again made their appearance. Since they found that nothing could be done, they disappeared again. We had safeguarded ourselves with three loaded pistols and two guns.

March 7. Morning. Preve tells me that the captain of McCoy's boat with which he came down, started from here with sundry goods, groceries, dry goods, etc., destined for New Madrid. When they were about five miles from New Orleans five men with loaded guns threatened to kill them if they did not give up their boat and cargo. Menard, the owner of the boat, had only two men with him and no arms. He, therefore, was forced to comply with the demands of the robbers, who left with their plunder. I feel sorry for the poor Menard. He lives near New Madrid. Only a short time ago a similar case of robbery occurred, when a number of rogues boarded a boat (brig) and plundered it of valuables.

A COTTON FIELD

Photo by Earl Norman, Natchez

March 10. We had to move our boat in order to make room for several boats which arrived yesterday from Cincinnati. I am tired of this boat life, the constant smoke, etc.

March 11. At last we sold our boat for $20.00 and moved to a house of a merchant in Bourbon Street, for which we pay $11.00 per month for one front room.

March 16. This morning I went to the Bremer ship (brig) to get a book. We found the Captain, Bauermeister, on board, who received us in a friendly manner. Mr. Holt tells me of his earlier misfortunes. The English, he said, did not destroy much of his plantation because he spoke English. However, he added that the Kentuckian, who condemned him for having been guilty of treason, was brought to prison where he remained for a month, being condemned to death. A subscription of $1,500 (obtained from the most respectable men of Orleans) was raised, and General Jackson pardoned him and two others, an Irishman and an American.

March 17. I go to the bath-house for a warm bath. Like everything else, it is very dear (75¢).

March 18. When Brunson returned from dinner he told me that an Englishman had hoisted an English flag above the tri-color of France—to signify, I suppose, that the English were masters over the Napoleonists. He says there will be trouble tonight. Sylvestre, Strauss, Brunson and I take a walk in the afternoon up to St. Louis Street. We looked at the canal which soon will be finished. It will render great service to Orleans, especially on the northeast end. It goes into Lake Pontchartrain and thence into the Gulf of Mexico. A great trade in time will open, of which a beginning has already been made with Mobile and the neighboring country. After we returned we went in the direction of the levee where a large number of people were assembled; some were running with bludgeons. We saw the soldiers, but could see nothing distinctly.

March 19. The whole town is still in an uproar about yesterday's affair, and means are being taken to apprehend the instigator of the mob. The Americans, no doubt, are more enraged than one imagines, as, I understand, the man who was killed is an American. The Orleans Gazette and Commercial Advertiser contained the following statement: "Yesterday afternoon a crowd assembled on the levee in front of the English ship 'Hamilton' in consequence of her having at each mast a vane that bore some resemblance to the tri-colored flag. After threatening a long time, being kept at bay by the crew, who were armed with bludgeons and perhaps one pistol and a sword, the Frenchmen boarded with pistols and swords. A short struggle ensued, the consequence of which was that the crew was overpowered, one of them killed and another severely wounded. The Frenchmen hauled down the obnoxious vanes and otherwise helped the vessel. Further violence was prevented by the arrival of a detachment of U. S. troops with General Ripley at their head. Great credit is due to the General for the promptitude with which he ordered out the troops, and for his decision in suppressing the riot.

Here we blush at being obliged to tell that the mayor was present (C. A. Macarty), if not during the riot, most certainly a moment before, and could not but foresee what was about to happen. Yet did he look on with the most shameful indifference and refused to raise a hand to prevent it, although it was in his power to do so effectually.

I understand that the Captain of the English ship as soon as such measures were taken, gave up his vessel to the Government of the U. S. Attempts are being made to apprehend the man who killed the man on board and others implicated.

March 20. At last the murderer is apprehended. There is proof of his guilt and no doubt he will be obliged to swing.

March 27. A sailor from the Bremer brig "Agnes" came on Sunday evening. He told me he was present when the riot occurred, and that more damage was done than one imagined, that an American sea captain who had cautioned the mob had been shot through the left arm. The pilot of the ship "Hamilton," after some resistance, was shot through the hand, then beaten over the eyes with a pistol and finally thrown into the water. A small boy belonging to the British ship was locked in a cabin after having received a beating. He climbed through a window, however, and by jumping into the water and swimming to a vessel close by saved himself. The damage to the ship was estimated at $5,000. All the riggings were cut, and likewise the masts. What an honorable piece of business!

April 7. After dinner I met Ellis, a German, who frequents Hafner's. I asked him whether he had any business which I might do for him. He suggested that I go on board his barge and receive the cargo. I will go with him to Bayou Sara. It will cost me nothing. This good offer I accept. In the evening I met Hotz. He tells me that those articles of merchandise have to be sold and that Ellis needed a person to whom he might entrust them and that it was probable that he might use me for that purpose.

April 9. After dinner I went on board the barge "Eliza." Agreeable to Ellis' offer I find a very comfortable cabin. Towards evening I go ashore and visit Strauss, who is busy packing his effects. He leaves tomorrow to pursue his Red River expedition, about the novelty of which a great deal might be said. I soon returned to the barge but found it impossible to sleep owing to the fleas. The barge seems to be filled with them.

April 10. This evening a Mr. Rubury, a broker of this place, was stabbed by a countryman of his from St. Domingo. Mr. R. was considered a very fine gentleman and a good citizen in every respect. One knows not why this cruel act was committed.

April 11. This noon Ellis told me that his partner had come from Bayou Sara and wished me to go there and look after his business during his absence. If I felt so inclined he stated he would pay my passage immediately. The salary he would fix upon my arrival. This news is agreeable—but the face of his partner, James Nolasco, is not so agreeable.

After dinner as I was sitting at Hafners, Schones, the instrument maker, entered and told me that the Silversmith, his next door neighbor, had tied the arms of a little boy for stealing a dollar (or rather finding it) and was going to punish him after dinner. I went over to Schones' where I was the spectator of the worst cruelty, the like of which can scarcely be committed among the most barbaric nations. The silversmith

had the boy stripped to his breeches and his hands tied to a
rope which ran on a pulley, fastened to the ceiling of the
piazza. There the poor fellow was suspended while his master
and "disciples" were sitting on the other end eating their dinner, musing, and talking about the poor boy's fate. At last, the
giant-like man arose from the table, took up a cow-skin, which
had been soaked in water and after he had hauled the rope
tight he applied it to the poor fellow's body as hard as he
could; the skin turning black and blue with every cut. This
unmerciful treatment alone would have been sufficient to rouse
my indignation had it been executed in a passion, but his
satanic grin at every cut he dealt, and the sight of the poor
victim began to stir my blood. Schones and I made an effort to
put a stop to it, but without avail. Our interference might have
turned out rather serious. I left this place of horror and
walked alone to the suburb of St. Mary's. Here I hoped to
enjoy an hour of tranquillity, but scarcely had I proceeded a
couple of steps when I met several boxers with bloody faces.
Perceiving them I turned away but had proceeded only a few
steps when I saw two Frenchmen busily engaged in a cock-
fight. The poor animals were nearly exhausted, but they re-
vived them by blowing garlic and whiskey into their bills.
Low, brutish, savage-like has been everything my eyes beheld
today. It is now four o'clock. Later I witnessed a negro dance.
Their postures and movements somewhat resembled those of
monkeys. One might by a little imagination take them for a
group of baboons. Yet as these poor wretches are entirely
ignorant of anything like civilization (for their masters with-
hold everything from them that in the least might add to the
cultivation of their minds) one must not be surprised at their
actions. The recreation is at least natural and they are free in
comparison with those poor wretches, slaves of their passions.
I saw today among the crowd Gildemeister of Bremen, clerk
or partner of Teetzmann. He told me that three of the negroes
in the group closest to us were formerly kings or chiefs in
Congo. I perceive in them a more genteel address. They are
richly ornamented and dance extremely well. As I was looking
on a sailor told me that a few months ago he had come from

Havana where he had sailed with some slaves from the coast of Guinea. Among them was the son of Pepin, a king of Congo, who had been recommended to a merchant-house, Fernandez Fernando of Havana, who were to expedite him to Port au Prince, St. Domingo, where he now lives. By ten o'clock I reach the boat after crossing the levee, which is a rather dangerous time to pass over the levee, since so many persons have been assaulted there and several murdered.

April 15. Today at 9 o'clock we start for Bayou Sara. The steamboat on which I write these lines is elegantly finished. I find among the passengers, about 50 in number, chiefly Kentuckians and the rest creole (French) inhabitants of the coast.

April 16. In the morning it began to rain heavily. After breakfast we met the steamboat "Oliver Evans," now called the Constitution, which had broken one of her wheels and grounded through the Captain's neglect—so we are informed by those of her passengers who sought passage with us. Time passes rather slowly on board. The noise of the passengers is far from agreeable and interferes with my reading and writing. I, nevertheless, read in Pope's *Essay on Man* and *Telemachus*. We stop to discharge several passengers. A number of new passengers board the ship.

April 17. This morning the weather was gloomy. Toward noon it cleared up again. Near Plaquemine we discharged several passengers, among whom was a handsome lady accompanied by a red-faced gentleman with a snuff colored coat. This morning I finished Pope's *Essay on Man*. I again saw several alligators. This evening we reached Baton Rouge, where several passengers left us, among them General Ripley, a handsome, friendly, sensible man. As it is late and dark we cannot come close to the shore owing to the logs. We nevertheless discharge our passengers and that part of our cargo destined for Baton Rouge.

Having had a short interview with the Captain, Mr. A. R. Gale, today, from whom I got some information about the steamboat I am traveling on, I shall take this evening to note with a little more order what he was kind enough to let me

know. He tells me that this steamboat "New Orleans" finished
for navigation cost $65,000. She was built at Pittsburgh in
1815 under the direction of one Hardinger (a German) and
Captain Gale—for a company at New York (Messrs. Rose-
walt, Fulton and Livingston), the same company that built the
old "New Orleans" in 1810. She was built after Fulton's plan
and construction—her machinery alone cost $20,000. She car-
ries, exclusive of her machinery, 200 tons. Her length in keel
is 140 feet and breadth in beam, 28 feet. She carries no sails,
runs from 3 to 4 miles against stream in an hour, and down
stream, 9 to 10 miles. The ladies' cabin is below deck, it being
the most retired place. It is elegantly fitted up. The windows
are ornamented with white curtains and the beds, twenty in
number, with red bombazette curtains and fringes and mosquito bars, besides sofas, chairs, looking-glasses, etc., and an
elegant carpet ornaments the floor. This cabin is 30 feet in
length. Above deck is an elegant round-house of 42 feet in
length and 28 in breadth for the gentlemen. This room for
the convenience of the passengers is provided with 26 berths
in 13 staterooms, 2 berths in each stateroom, with mattresses
of Spanish moss (in which the woods of Louisiana abound).
Other necessary bed-clothes are handsomely flowered. Each
berth had a window. Sofas or settees and chairs, two large
tables, a large gilt framed looking-glass, several elegantly
finished recommendation cards and the regulations of the boat
in gilt frames,—all these adorn the room, and finally an elegant
carpet covers the floor. The Captain's room is on the starboard
side and is tolerably large. Forward of the round-house adjoining the same, on the larboard side is the bar-room fitted
up equal to a coffee house and the present keeper, Louis
Roach, is a very accommodating, pleasant man. Above the
water-wheel on the larboard side is the clerk's office and
lodging. He receives the freight, weighs and measures it,
keeps the accounts, etc. On the starboard side ranging with
the former is a room for the head engineer and the bar-keeper.
Further on the deck forward of the engine is the kitchen and
forward of this is a room for the mate and the pilot. This
appears to be an excellent plan, as these two officers are

placed where they are the most available in case of alarm. Forward of this, immediately under the prow below deck, is the forecastler's lodging with 12 berths, seats and a table for the hands in general. I find that the engine effects eighteen revolutions per minute. This, however, cannot be an exact calculation. The Captain is very particular with her boiler (for I observed him this afternoon stuffing up several holes) it being very old, the same that sank in the old "New Orleans" about two years ago. He is daily expecting a new copper boiler from New York. When he gets the same on board he tells me the engine will perform 22 revolutions per minute. Consequently, it will give the boat a much greater velocity through the water. This boiler, now on board, contains eight tons of water. She consumes 6 cords of wood in 24 hours, which is taken in along the coast where the inhabitants have it in readiness at $2.50 per cord (8 feet long, 4 high, and 4 broad). The vessel can be stopped in an instant if there is any danger and with facility she can be brought to shore, or turned in any direction. Near the forecastler's watch-way is a large bell by which the servants are awakened.

Captain Gale told me that dragging the small boats (which the vessel carries), he had discovered, was injurious to the vessel, as well as impeded her progress. Therefore, he had obtained cranes, by which the small boats were hauled up. This is effected as the boat is proceeding. On the lar- and starboard sides of the bow are two anchors, a provision used only in case of a storm, for commonly they make use of a large cable, which after it has been used is regularly coiled up. As the climate is exceptionally hot and would scarcely be endurable in the summer months on board a steamboat where the heat of the fire and the boilers would be sufficient to prevent persons from traveling, or, at least, would render them uncomfortable when traveling, the boat is completely covered with awning at that time, and above the round-house is an elegantly decorated walk with iron railings and nettings (made by Henry, a German sailor). There the gentlemen passengers sit comfortably and have a commanding view over the boat, river, and land, and enjoy the cool breeze. The awnings, the Captain tells me, have no tendency to impede progress. The sight of these swimming volcanoes on water is very agreeable. They generally have colors at their poop and the American eagle and stars give a very handsome effect. A swivel-gun is carried to signalize their arrival and departure. It is generally fastened at the middle of the bow. The one on board this boat is a little 4-pounder. I might say a great deal more, but have mentioned what I thought to be the most interesting. I add a statement of the persons indispensable on board, also their salaries:

1 Captain, salary per year......................	$2,500
1 Mate, salary month, $50; year...............	600
1 Pilot, salary month, $50; year...............	600
1 Engineer, salary month, $50; year............	600
1 Clerk, salary per year.......................	500
1 Bar-keeper, salary month, $30; year..........	360
1 Steward, salary month, $30; year............	360
1 Steward, Assistant, salary month, $30; year....	360
1 Cook, salary month, $30; year...............	360
1 Cook's Mate, salary month, $20; year.........	240
2 Firemen (each) salary month, $20; year.....	480
	(for both)
8 Sailors (each) salary month, $20; year........	1,920
4 Kitchen servants and waiters who receive from $15 to $20 per month...................	840
	$9,720

These are the expenses for one year for persons absolutely necessary on board. Their maintenance is very costly in this part of the country since everything (especially provisions) are high, for one pays from $20 to $45 per month for board in New Orleans. The expenses in case of damage to machinery, which now and then occur, no one can state, but the final and total expenses are very great. The income obtained is proportionately great, for the Captain told me that on one trip from New Orleans to Natchez, the net proceeds amounted to no less than $4000. There is within the bounds of knowledge no business in any part of the globe which is more lucrative than

Photo by Earl Norman, Natchez

LIVE-OAK TREES, FESTOONED WITH STREAMERS OF SPANISH MOSS

this, but it will not be so in a few years hence, for I know the enterprise of the Americans, and the rivers as far as they may be navigable will be crowded with steamboats, and their enterprise will be slackened in the course of time. I add the prices received for passengers and freight:

Passage upstream from New Orleans:

To Baton Rouge	136	miles	$16.00
" Bayou Sara	173	"	19.00
" Bayou Tunica	195	"	20.00
" Fort Adams	260	"	25.00
" Natchez	314	"	30.00

Passage downstream from Natchez:

To Fort Adams	54	miles	$ 4.00
" Bayou Tunica	119	"	8.00
" Bayou Sara	141	"	9.50
" Baton Rouge	180	"	11.00
" New Orleans	314	"	15.00

Way passengers upstream pay 12½ cents per mile and downstream 6¼ cents. The freight she receives for Bayou Sara is paid at the rate of 30 cents per square foot, and so for a barrel measuring five square feet, $1.50, and for heavy articles such as iron, lead, etc., 75¢ per cwt.

I now shall add the regulations for the conduct of passengers on board:

"1. No gentleman passenger shall descend the stairs leading to, or enter the lady's cabin unless with the permission of all the ladies, to be obtained through the Captain under the penalty of two dollars for each offense.

"2. Smoking is absolutely prohibited in any of the cabins under a penalty of one dollar for each offense, and fifty cents for every five minutes the same is continued after notice.

"3. No gentleman shall lie down in a berth with his shoes or boots on under a penalty of one dollar for each offense.

"4. No passenger shall speak to the man at the helm under a penalty of one dollar.

"5. Cards and games of every description are prohibited in the cabin after ten o'clock at night.

"6. At noon, every day, three persons to be chosen by a majority of the passengers shall form a court to determine on all penalties incurred and the amount collected shall be expended in wine for the whole company after dinner.

"7. For every transgression against good order and cleanliness, not already specified, such fine shall be imposed as the court in their discretion shall think fit.

"8. All damages done to the furniture or boat by any of the passengers, it is expected, will be paid before leaving the boat.

"As the preservation of good order and cleanliness is indispensable to promote the comfort and accommodation of passengers (to which every possible attention will be paid) the foregoing regulations will be rigidly enforced.

"It is particularly requested that gentlemen will not spit on the cabin floors as boxes are provided for that purpose."

So much about the steamboat. For the description of the machinery I am incapable of rendering any satisfactory account, for the engineer is too much occupied to inform me of all particulars and I am not sufficiently acquainted with all the technical terms and various appellations, but the Captain has promised to give me an account at some other time with the greatest of pleasure. This good man (the Captain) deserves notice and credit for his politeness towards everybody and his extraordinary activity and attention which he always displays on board. He is never at rest. The most minute objects do not escape his notice. Moreover, he is just, as he sees that no one is idle. Nor does he allow anyone to suffer—which he extends even to the fowls and pigs on board.

April 18. This evening we reached Bayou Sara. This is the place of my destination, but I feel so indifferent about it that I do not go ashore tonight.

April 19. I have my effects removed to the shore.

April 20. Fine weather. Several boats arrived from Tennessee bound for Orleans. The weather later in the day begins to get gloomy, with a little rain. In the afternoon Mr. Gross came to see the show which is exhibited at St. Francisville. This evening a man who went on board a flat boat to play cards was badly beaten by the boatman, with whom he quarreled.

I heard the fray at the house. I read in *Telemachus* until after midnight.

April 27. In the morning Frauenknecht came over with Ludling. Fine weather. Some more boats from Tennessee arrive. In the afternoon about twenty boatmen took a man, who had stolen $2.00, put him in a cart and pulled him about the streets crying: "Who stole the money?" . . . "Alexander." What else they did with him I know not. They talked of ducking him. I soon closed the door to avoid being a witness of their mean and cowardly acts.

April 30. Fine weather. Several boats arrived from Russelville, Kentucky, and yesterday several from Dayton.

May 2. This morning I went to St. Francisville to pay Mr. Holt a visit. I remained a couple of hours with him (Holt) to see two buffaloes, the first live ones I have seen. A Philadelphia man brought them from the head of the White River and intends taking them to Philadelphia. They looked fatigued.

May 4. At 7 o'clock this morning the steamboat "Washington" passed. Last year the boiler of this boat blew up near Marietta, doing great damage (7 men died at Cincinnati). Just as I turned in the direction of the front door I perceived 1½ miles up stream a large white cloud, which seemed to me something unusual. It rose distinctly, as the blue horizon and the color of the Mississippi contrasted with the white cloud. About 1½ hours later Mr. Stirling, a merchant from St. Francisville, crossed the river with several doctors to give relief to the distressed. I understand that the cylinder of the steamboat "Constitution" burst, scalding a number of passengers. They had to draw her by means of ropes to the shore. There is a continual crossing of the river all day to see the distressed. Eleven persons are dangerously scalded. Two of them were deprived of their senses. It is said that the Captain challenged the "Washington" to a race. A few minutes after he had challenged her the destruction took place. This evening eight of the sufferers were dead. James Nolasco came this morning from Sandy Creek.

May 5. Eleven persons are dead. A good many persons are going to their burial. Among the dead are three Masons. I would like to do them the last honor, but my position here will prevent me from doing so.

May 6. This morning another of the unfortunate from the steamboat was buried. I understand that among them was a gambler, who was buried separately.

* * * * * * *

June 3. Fine weather. Steamboat "Vesuvius" came at 11 o'clock. I went down to see whether she had something for Nolasco. The engineer tells me that nearly all the houses at Natchez were closed on account of the yellow fever, and that the inhabitants had nearly all moved to the country.

June 4. Channon, the young man who discharged the cargo from the keelboat, died this morning, it is generally believed from yellow fever brought from Orleans.

June 7. I go with Mr. Smith (the overseer) to the plantation. The negroes were divided into groups, some cutting and piling wood for the sugar boilers, others hauling the same. We rode over the field, which contains not less than 222 acres of cane, the rest planted with corn and pumpkins. Altogether 300 acres of land under cultivation. Smith told me a negro had recently run away from Mr. More. He showed me some of his footprints. He tells me that the runaway negroes live on pumpkins and corn, and often kill hogs belonging to the negroes. In the night they roast them by a fire in the woods. They then move on to other quarters. I rode an old horse and had much diversion jumping the ditches covered with grass. I ate some sugar cane for the first time.

June 9. Today I started in a gig for the Fausse River. The weather was fine. With the exception of a few mud holes the road was tolerably good. Arrived at the house of Mr. Hanberg at noon. He received me kindly. Mr. H. came from Germany (Danzig) about ten years ago, and is now an overseer on the cotton plantation belonging to the rich Mr. Poidrass. In a short time a good cup of coffee stood on the table for our reception and a plate of fritters. Afterwards I went to Doctor Batcheller, then to a clerk of Mr. Poidrass', a Frenchman, who keeps a small store. When I returned we had dinner. I started back at about 4 o'clock. I took the road along the

Mississippi, which is far more pleasant than the one which I took in the morning. I was pleased with the settlements on the Fausse River. They are very productive. The soil is as rich as any I have seen in America. Poidrass and Fournan are the chief owners of the plantations on the Fausse River. The poorer class of planters go in debt to Poidrass and Fournan, who take mortgages on their plantations; so that many of the plantations fall into their hands. Fausse River has the appearance of a half moon or semi-circle, and when the present passage of the river was formed by the Mississippi the name Point Coupee had its origin. The water of the Fausse River is pleasant to drink. The island is as thickly inhabited as the mainland. I would like to settle there myself. It was dark by the time I returned.

June 10. I again received goods at the warehouse. Francisco engaged Pierre (the fisherman) for $15.00 per month. An Italian, a nephew of the rich Barthold in Orleans, came. He told me of his voyage to England, his adventures, and the profits that could be made, especially from hardware.

June 11. I have the strongest intention of returning to Europe. Unless I can set up an establishment with Ellis I intend going to Orleans in a short time. I will then remain there during the winter and return to Europe with a cargo next spring.

Part Four

LEVEES AND STEAMBOATS

MODERN EXCURSION BOATS ON THE MISSISSIPPI

Chapter XVIII

OLD STEAMBOAT DAYS

OLD steamboat days! How romantic they seem—and how far away. Those in truth were the good old times: it was then that every gentleman conversed with all "the flowers of rhetoric," and singing negro roustabouts rolled cotton bales on the lower deck, chanting their endless songs; it was then that the sleek gamblers paced back and forth, casting languishing glances toward unbelievably beautiful ladies who came tripping up the gangplank, their hoopskirts billowing around them. Ah, yes, if we can only believe the old stories, those ladies were as beautiful as the moon itself, as they came gliding aboard the old packets, shading their faces with tiny black lace parasols tilted against the sun.

As a matter of fact, the men and women of the steamboat days were simple and ordinary persons, who conducted their lives in much the same manner that we conduct our lives today. It is true that conversation was flowery and stilted, and that mock modesty flourished; it was the fashion to be shocked, astonished, indignant before the simple facts of life that constitute the greater part of our conversation today. It is even true, perhaps, that our grandparents were a little ridiculous with all their grand airs; but, after all, are we not also a little ridiculous in our own frank and outspoken era? And is it not possible that our grandchildren will smile in the face of our "realism" and comment that our generation was tremendously *naïve?*

At any rate, there was glamour in the steamboat days, and the men and women recognized it as such; but they preserved their mysteries carefully, realizing, probably, how valuable an asset mystery is to romance.

The first steamboat came puffing down the Mississippi in 1811. In thirty years steamboating had reached its zenith; in thirty more years its glory had departed. Railroads had supplanted the steamboats. But it was a gay and colorful period—a period unique in the world's history, and a development completely and typically American.

It was in 1737, more than thirty years before Watt took out his first patent for the steam-engine, that a certain Jonathan Hulls of London claimed to be the inventor of "a machine for carrying vessels out of, or into, any harbor, port or river against wind and tide, or in a calm," according to Lloyd's Steamboat Directory, published in 1855. A draft of Mr. Hulls's machine is still preserved and it looks astonishingly like an old-fashioned steamboat. It is furnished with chimneys, propelling wheels, and other features typical of the river steamboat. We do not know how Mr. Hulls intended to generate moving forces; but it is evident that fire had something to do with the matter, for in the old drawing there are smokestacks belching forth great clouds of black smoke.

As far as we know, Mr. Hulls did nothing toward building such a boat, but he went on record as an inventor. It was John Fitch, a native of Connecticut, who is usually given credit for the invention of the steamboat as developed in America. Fitch wrote his memoirs—a strange document of melancholy sarcasm. He terms it the greatest misfortune of his life "to have conceived the idea that a vessel might be carried through the water by the force of steam." His disappointment came about through the fact that he had conceived the steam-engine—only to find out that Watt had forestalled him, and had patented just such an invention. But John Fitch was the first man who ever carried the idea of applying steam power to vessels. He took out a patent for the application of steam to navigation in 1788. The earliest experiments of Robert Fulton in steam navigation took place fully ten years later.

Every child's history of the United States tells the story of the first steamboat, so it is useless to go into the matter here; suffice to say that Mississippi steamboating began in 1811 when the *New Orleans* came down the great river on her memorable voyage.

Nicholas J. Roosevelt, uncle of President Theodore Roosevelt, took the *New Orleans* down the river to New Orleans. It was his own boat, built in Pittsburgh in 1809— or, rather, construction was started in 1809, but it was not until two years later that the voyage was made.

Men knew and feared the Mississippi. It was a dangerous stream, full of rapids, eddies, and "boils" in which no swimmer could live. It was full of snags and treacherous sand-bars. The hardiest of the flatboatmen warned Nicholas Roosevelt of the extreme difficulty and danger of his under-taking. When the fact became known that his wife was to accompany him, his friends threw up their hands in horror. It was madness, they assured him. But Mr. Roosevelt was firm in his decision, and his wife was equally assured. Finally, the relatives and friends of the Roosevelts washed their hands of the matter—and the voyage began. Steam-boats were so new and so strange that the people of the United States were dubious. Yes, they admitted, the steam-boat could go downstream, but what about returning? It was ridiculous to assume that such a "floating sawmill" as the *New Orleans* could breast the current of the Mississippi.

But Nicholas Roosevelt was certain that the *New Orleans* could return, if he wished her to. However, it was his intention to take the steamboat to New Orleans, sell her, and return by way of the overland trail, or by boat along the Atlantic seaboard. The *New Orleans* was to be used for freight and passengers between New Orleans and Natchez, Mississippi—then two of the wealthiest cities in the country.

The Roosevelts left Pittsburgh in May, 1811. They arrived at the New Orleans levee on the day before Christmas. They had stopped at many places along the way, remaining for weeks on end for repairs and for work that Mr. Roosevelt had undertaken. The voyage was sensational, to say the least. All along the banks of the Ohio River men and women crowded, cheering as the steamboat made its way downstream. Louisville was reached safely—and here a baby was born to Mrs. Roosevelt. They remained in that Kentucky city for some time, then began their way south again.

Contrary to all predictions, they managed to pass safely the falls of the Ohio, and to reach the Mississippi.

As the *New Orleans* approached New Madrid, Missouri, a great earthquake rocked the country. The river was changed to a raging sea by force of the shocks; the banks caved in, great fissures appeared in the earth; islands dropped from sight beneath the muddy water, and new islands emerged from the slime of the river's bed. The *New Orleans,* tied up at an island, saw the island disappear before the eyes of the terrified crew.

But the Roosevelts continued their course in the face of every obstacle—passing through lands filled with hostile Indians, and braving the river pirates. At Natchez the whole town came crowding to the edge of the bluff to see the marvel of a steam-propelled boat. And it was at Natchez that the genius of Mr. Roosevelt asserted itself. He invited a

"THE NEW ORLEANS"

A replica of the first steamboat to come down the Mississippi to New Orleans

group of leading citizens to dinner aboard the steamboat, and while they were at table the *New Orleans* steamed away from the wharf, carrying the astonished diners *upstream* for an evening's voyage. The men at Natchez were delighted with the experience, for until this time they had been doubtful that the boat could breast the current of the roaring river. After that trip upstream, however, they were enthusiastic, and many of them invested in a company that Roosevelt was forming to build steamboats for Mississippi River transportation.

The city of New Orleans received its namesake with open arms. A holiday was declared, and the entire population crowded the levees. An upstream trip was made, and the crowd cheered wildly. Negroes invented songs on the spur of the moment, extolling the virtues of the steamboat and her captain. It was a great day.

Steamboating on the Mississippi developed slowly at first, although the *New Orleans* began to run regularly between New Orleans and Natchez early in 1812. But from that year forward, the steamboat was one of the principal topics of conversation along the Mississippi. By 1817, as we have seen in a previous chapter, there were many river boats. J. G. Flugel, in his diary, describes one of them in detail, and tells how fine he thought it was.

As we have said, Mississippi steamboating reached its zenith thirty years later. The period just before the Civil War saw the steamboats at the height of their glory. After that came a decline, due to the railroads, which furnished a quicker means of transportation.

The steamboat has not vanished completely, of course, but the great floating palaces have disappeared from the rivers. There are a few great pleasure boats which ply up and down the river for the entertainment of novelty seekers; but the steamboat's day is done. River transportation today is matter-of-fact enough, as we shall see in the chapter on river commerce.

But in the "flush days" the proud owner of a steamboat frequently put as much as $150,000 or $200,000 into the building of one mammoth vessel. Nowadays thirty thousand dollars is considered an ample investment. The steamboats that remain are trim, trig, business-like vessels. The glory has departed.

But what were the steamboats really like? one wonders. Accounts differ. Charles Dickens disliked them heartily— and said so, telling of their discomforts and their gaudiness. But Walt Whitman liked them, and wrote poems about them. And then, of course, there was Mark Twain. In his "Life on the Mississippi" he waxes lyric as to steamboat-racing. Here is what he has to say:

> The public always had an idea that racing was dangerous; whereas the opposite was the case—that is, after the laws were passed which restricted each boat to just so many pounds of steam to the square inch. No engineer was ever sleepy or careless when his heart was in a race. * * * the dangerous place was on slow, plodding boats, where the engineers drowsed around and allowed chips to get into the "doctor" and shut off the water-supply from the boilers.
>
> In the "flush times" of steamboating, a race between two notoriously fleet steamers was an event of vast importance. The date was set for it several weeks in advance, and from that time forward the whole Mississippi Valley was in a state of consuming excitement. * * * As the time approached, the two steamers "stripped" and got ready. Every incumbrance that added weight, or exposed a resisting surface to wind or water, was removed. * * * When the *Eclipse* and the *A. L. Shotwell* ran their great race many years ago, it was said that pains were taken to scrape the gilding off the fanciful device which hung between the *Eclipse's* chimneys, and that for that one trip the

captain left off his kid gloves and had his head shaved. But I always doubted these things. * * *

No way-freights and no way-passengers were allowed, for the racers would stop only at the largest towns, and then it would be only "touch and go." Coal-flats and wood-flats were contracted for beforehand, and these were kept ready to hitch on to the flying steamers at a moment's warning. Double crews were carried, so that all work could be quickly done.

The chosen date being come, and all things in readiness, the two great steamers back into the stream, and lie there jockeying a moment, apparently watching each other's slightest movement, like sentient creatures; flags drooping, the pent steam shrieking through safety-valves, the black smoke rolling and tumbling from the chimneys and darkening all the air. People, people everywhere; the shores, the house-tops, the steamboats, the ships, are packed with them, and you know that the borders of the broad Mississippi are going to be fringed with humanity, thence northward twelve hundred miles, to welcome those racers.

An old New Orleans guidebook published for the Cotton Exposition of 1884-85 gives an excellent idea of steamboat-races on the Mississippi, and the facts in the following paragraphs are taken from that source.

"Back in the thirties" is often referred to by old boatmen as the period when steamboat-races, either with each other or against time, were most exciting. There being no parallel lines of railroad, passengers depended on steamboats for rapid transit, and the boat that could make the quickest time in her particular trade was the most popular with the traveling public. Racing on the rivers was so common an occurrence as to attract the attention of only those who happened to be on board the contesting boats, except when one or both lowered the record of previous performances. The runs against time were usually to test a boat's capacity for speed; and by this means improvements were suggested, from time to time, by which greater speed was obtained, until the building of a railroad rendered great speed unnecessary.

The quickest time ever made from New Orleans to Cincinnati was 5 days and 18 hours, in 1843, by the *Duke of Orleans*. The *Diana* made a quick trip two years later, but no further effort to make fast time was made by any steamboat till the *Charles Morgan,* in June, 1877, left New Orleans twenty-four hours later than the *Robert Mitchell,* passed the latter at Hawesville, and made the time to Cincinnati in 6 days and 11 hours, having made forty-two landings and lost three and one-half hours in getting through the canal at Louisville. In April of the same year the *Thompson Dean* made the run in 6 days and 19 hours, having lost fourteen hours in the canal and seventeen hours at way landings. The *R. R. Springer*, in 1881, came through from New Orleans to Cincinnati in 5 days 12 hours and 45 minutes, which was the quickest made since the trip of the *Duke of Orleans*. Her best time was made while in the Mississippi River. From the time she reached the mouth of the Ohio until she arrived at Cincinnati her speed decreased. She consumed twenty-two hours and five minutes more time from New Orleans to Cairo than did the *R. E. Lee* in 1870. In March, 1881, the *Will S. Hays* made the run in 6 days 17 hours and 10 minutes from port to port, having made fifty-one landings to discharge nearly 3000 packages and meeting with several unusual detentions.

To illustrate further the idea that speed was steadily increasing, it may be mentioned that in 1817 the *Enterprise* made the trip from New Orleans to Louisville in 25 days 2 hours and 4 minutes, and the *Washington* in 25 days. Two years later the *Shelly* made it in 20 days 4 hours and 20 minutes. In 1828 the *Paragon* went up in 18 days and

10 hours. Within the next five or six years the advancement in speed was more rapid, as the *Tecumseh,* in 1834, was only 8 days and 4 hours from port to port. Three years later the *Sultana* made the run in 5 days and 15 hours, and the *Express* in 6 days and 15 hours. In 1842 the *Edward Shippen* was claimed to have covered the distance in 5 days and 14 hours, which time was not beaten till 1849, when the *Sultana* cut it down to 5 days and 12 hours; this was cut down by the *Bostona,* in 1851, to 5 days and 8 hours, and further reduced by the *Belle Key,* the next year, to 4 days and 20 hours; by the *Reindeer,* in 1858, to 4 days 19 hours and 45 minutes; the *Eclipse,* to 4 days 9 hours and 31 minutes, and the *A. L. Shotwell,* to 4 days 9 hours and 19 minutes. In 1838 the steamer *Diana* received from the Post Office Department of the United States a prize of $500 in gold, which had been offered to the first boat that would make the run from New Orleans to Louisville inside of six days. Her time was 5 days 23 hours and 15 minutes.

Steamboat-racing did not end with the decade of the thirties. The prevalent notion has been, and still is, that on these occasions awful explosions of boilers, by which the river was strewn with killed and mangled, were of frequent occurrence. Such calamities may have happened; but if they did, no record of them exists. To generate steam rapidly it was a common practice while racing to feed the furnace under the boilers with pine-knots and tar; but the popular notion that on such occasions the captain would not hesitate to give the command, "Throw in another nigger!" is a fallacy. That explosions did not occur when racing is accounted for by the fact that on such occasions the engineer was more than usually watchful and careful.

It may be noted that in 1844 the quickest trip from New Orleans to Cairo recorded up to that time was made by the *J. M. White,* in 3 days 6 hours and 44 minutes; in 1852 by the *Reindeer,* in 3 days 12 hours and 45 minutes; in 1853 by the *Eclipse,* in 3 days 4 hours and 4 minutes, and by the *A. L. Shotwell,* in 3 days 3 hours and 40 minutes. The time was not shortened until 1870, when the *R. E. Lee* (her second run) "set the pegs" at 3 days 1 hour and 1 minute, which remains the quickest time to this day. The distance is 1013 miles.

From New Orleans to Natchez—distance 272 miles— the quickest time made in 1814 was 5 days and 10 hours, by the *Comet;* in 1815 the *Enterprise* occupied 4 days 11 hours and 20 minutes in making the same trip, and this was cut down two years later to 3 days and 20 hours by the *Shelby.* Two years later the *Paragon* made it in 12 hours less and set the pegs for the next nine years, when, in 1828, the *Tecumseh* consumed only 3 days 1 hour and 20 minutes. This time was first beaten in 1834, when the *Tuscarora* made the trip in 1 day and 21 hours, and it was cut down four years later by the *Natchez* to 1 day and 17 hours. In 1840 the *Edward Shippen* reduced the time to 1 day and 8 hours. In 1844 days were no longer needed in stating the time necessary for the trip, as the *Sultana* made it in 19 hours and 45 minutes, which was not beaten till 1853, when the new *Natchez* again shortened it to 17 hours and 30 minutes. The *Princess* made the same time in 1856. In their great race from New Orleans to St. Louis in 1870 the *Natchez* and *Robert E. Lee* set the pegs at 16 hours 30 minutes and 47 seconds.

No steamboat-race ever excited so much interest throughout the civilized world as that which took place between the *Robert E. Lee* and *Natchez* in June, 1870, from New Orleans to St. Louis. On the twenty-fourth of that month Captain T. P. Leathers telegraphed Captain Perry Tharp, of New Orleans, that the *Natchez* had arrived at St. Louis, having covered the distance from New Orleans, 1278 miles, in 3 days 21 hours and 58 minutes. From the time that she was built at Cincinnati much rivalry in regard to speed had been exhibited between her and the *Robert E. Lee,* which was built at New Albany during the Civil War, and was towed across the river to the Kentucky side to have her name painted on the wheel-house, a measure that was deemed prudent at the time. Captain John W. Cannon commanded the *Lee* and Captain Thomas P. Leathers commanded the *Natchez.* Both were experienced steamboatmen, but, as the sequel proved, Captain Cannon was the better strategist. While each boat had its special corps of friends, the name of the *Robert E. Lee* was more popular along the Mississippi River.

Before the return of the *Natchez* to New Orleans, Captain Cannon had determined that the *Lee* should beat the time of her rival, the fastest that had ever been made over the course. He stripped the *Lee* for the race—removed all parts of her upper works that were calculated to catch the wind; removed all rigging and outfit that could be dispensed with, to lighten her, as the river was low in some places; engaged the steamer *Frank Pargoud* to precede her a hundred miles up the river to supply coal; arranged with coal-yards to have flatboats awaiting her in the middle of the river at given points, to be taken in tow under way until the coal could be transferred to the deck of the *Lee,* and then to be cut loose and float back. He refused all business of every kind and would receive no passengers.

The *Natchez* returned to New Orleans and received a few hundred tons of freight and also a few passengers, and was advertised to leave again for St. Louis, June 30.

At 5 o'clock in the afternoon the *Robert E. Lee* backed

out from the levee, and five minutes later the *Natchez* followed her, but without such elaborate preparation for a race as had been made on the *Lee*. Captain Leathers was confident that he could pass the latter within the first hundred miles.

A steamer had preceded the boats up the river many miles to witness all that could be seen of the great race that was to be. The telegraph informed the people along both banks of the river of the coming great struggle for supremacy in speed; and the world looked on with as much interest as if it had been an event local to every part of it. Wherever there was a village the people collected on the bank of the river to watch the passage of the two steamers. The *Lee* gained slightly every hundred miles as the race progressed, and at Natchez, three hundred miles from the starting point, this gain amounted to ten minutes, attributable more to landings that had been made by the *Natchez* for fuel than to anything else. The people of the whole city of Natchez viewed the race. At the bend at Vicksburg, although the two steamers were ten miles apart by the course of the river, the smoke of each was plainly seen from the other. Thousands of people were congregated on the bluffs. At Helena and other points it seemed that the population for miles back from the river had turned out to witness the race.

At Memphis ten thousand people looked at the passing steamers, neither of which landed, the *Natchez* by this time having adopted the *Lee's* method of receiving fuel. At every point where there was a telegraph instrument the hour and the minute of the passing steamers were ticked to all points of America that could be reached, and the newspapers throughout the country displayed bulletins showing the progress of the boats.

THE FAMOUS RACE BETWEEN THE "NATCHEZ" AND THE "ROBT. E. LEE"

From an old print by Currier and Ives

The time of passing Memphis, Vicksburg, and Cairo was cabled to Europe. When Cairo was reached, the race was virtually ended, but the *Lee* proceeded to St. Louis, arriving there in 3 days 18 hours and 14 minutes from the time she left New Orleans, beating by thirty-three minutes the previous time of the *Natchez*. The latter had grounded and run into a fog between Memphis and Cairo, which detained her more than six hours.

When the *Lee* arrived at St. Louis, thirty thousand people crowded the wharf, the windows and the housetops to receive her. No similar event had ever created so much excitement. Captain Cannon was tendered a banquet by the business men of the city, and was generally lionized while he remained there. It was estimated that more than $1,000,-000 had been wagered on the race by the friends of the two steamers. Many of the bets were drawn, on the ground that the *Lee* had been assisted the first one hundred miles by the power of the *Frank Pargoud* added to her own; and many men have since regarded the *Natchez* as the faster boat, but outgeneraled by the commander of the other.

So much for steamboat-racing. Books have been written about these races, just as other books have been written about the romantic side of steamboating, of the gamblers of the Mississippi, and of steamboat disasters. But for a plain and homely story of actual conditions aboard a river boat in the eighteen-forties, I know of no more straightforward account than that given by Eliza Ripley in her delightful memoir, "Social Life in Old New Orleans." Mrs. Ripley had no illusions concerning life on the Mississippi, but she writes with kindly toleration and with quiet humor. She tells of a trip up the river from New Orleans to Kentucky in her childhood.

Grey Eagle was the finest and best [she writes] and therefore
most popular boat. I recall with amusement an eight or ten
days' trip on that palace. The cabins were divided by curtains,
drawn at night for privacy. The ladies' cabin, at the stern, was
equipped with ten or twelve small staterooms. The gentlemen's
cabin stretched on down to the officers' quarters, bar, barber
shop, pantries, etc., ending in what was called Social Hall, where
the men sat about, smoking and chewing (the latter as common
a habit as cigarette smoking is now) and talking—in other
words, making themselves sociable.

On that same *Grey Eagle* I was for the first time promoted
to the upper berth, in a stateroom shared by an older sister.
The berth was so narrow that in attempting to turn over I fell
out and landed in the wash basin, on the opposite side of the
room! My sister had to sit on the lower berth to braid my
pigtails, then sent me forth so she could have room to braid her
own. Trunks and other baggage more unwieldy than carpetbags
were piled up in the vicinity of Social Hall. A carpetbag, small
enough to be easily handled, was all there was room for in
the stateroom. There were no valises, suitcases or steamer
trunks in those days of little travel, and unless you are three-
quarters of a century old you can't imagine a more unwieldy
article than a carpetbag of seventy years ago. Only toilet articles and things that could not muss and tumble could be safely
stored in one.

In the stateroom, where we had to sleep and dress, and, if
we could snatch a chance, take an afternoon nap, there was
a corner shelf for a basin and pitcher and one chair; two doors,
one leading out and the other leading in, transoms over each
for light and ventilation—and there you are for over a week.
The cabin was lighted with swinging whale-oil lamps, and
one could light his stateroom if one had thought to provide
a candle.

Every family traveled with a man servant, whose business it
was to be constantly at beck and call. Of course, there was
always a colored chambermaid, and, equally of course, she
frisked around and seemed to have very little responsibility—
no bells, no means of summoning her from her little nodding

naps if she happened to be beyond the sound of one's voice. The man servant's duties, therefore, were almost incessant. If an article was needed from the trunks he was sent to the baggage pile for it, and often he brought trunk trays to the staterooms. When the boat stopped "to wood" every man servant rushed to the woodman's cabin to get eggs, chickens, milk, what not.

And those men had the privilege of the kitchen to prepare private dishes for their white folks. I wonder how long a boat or hotel would stand that kind of management today. * * * There was no ice chest, no cold storage; in a word, no way of preserving fresh foods for any length of time, so passengers resorted to such means as presented themselves for their own bodily comfort. Those who had not the necessary appendage —a man servant—foraged for themselves.

Mrs. Ripley has much to say of the passing flatboats and keelboats, of the steamers which came gliding out of the darkness nosing their way upstream. She tells of long days spent on the decks and in the salon. She has this interesting anecdote to relate about the meals served aboard:

The table for meals extended the length of the gentlemen's cabin, stretched out and out to its utmost length, if need be, so that every passenger had a seat. There was no second table, no second-class passengers—anybody was the equal of anybody else. If you could not possibly be that, you could find accommodation on the lower deck and eat from a tin plate.

It was quite customary, as I have mentioned, for passengers to have private dishes, prepared by their own servants. I recall with a smile, on one occasion, a very respectable-looking stranger boarded our boat at Helena or some such place. At dinner he reached for a bottle of wine. Cuthbert Bullitt touched the bottle with a fork, saying "Private Wine." The man, with a bow, withdrew his hand. Presently he reached for a dish of eggs. My father said, "Excuse me, private." There was something else he reached for, I forget what, and another fellow passenger touched the dish and said "Private." Presently dessert was served, and a fine, large pie happened to be placed in front of the Helena man. He promptly stuck his fork into it. "By gracious! this is a private pie." There was a roar of laughter.

After dinner the others, finding him delightfully congenial and entertaining, fraternized with him to the extent of a few games at cards. He was wonderfully lucky. He left the boat at an obscure river town during the night, and the next day our captain said he was a notorious gambler. From his capers at table the captain saw he was planning a way of winning attention to himself, therefore under cover of darkness he had been put ashore. My father, who did not play, was vastly amused when he found the smart gambler had carried off all the spare cash of those who had enjoyed the innocent sport.

There is an old book called "Gambling Unmasked," by one J. H. Green, who styles himself "a reformed gambler," which recounts many wild stories of gamblers and gambling on Mississippi River steamboats, but unfortunately for the reader, Mr. Green's reformation made him such an extremely moral man that his discourses on the evils of gambling occupy more space than an actual description of his methods of approach to the card-table. He does, however, tell something of "Rock-in-Cave," the rendezvous of many notorious criminals of the eighteen-thirties. Here, in a cave beside the river, a hundred miles below Louisville, gamblers and all manner of fugitive criminals assembled and played at various games of chance. Here, also, they brought the spoils of piracy on the river, of robbery, and the loot taken from the bodies of the men whom they had murdered. It must have been a strange place, lighted only by candles and dim lamps, and filled with as desperate a crew as one can imagine. Here, in this dank place, the men made exchanges—money, jewels, clothes. Here they perfected their disguises, growing whiskers, or dyeing their

THE STEAMBOAT "HENRY FRANK" LOADED WITH A RECORD SHIPMENT OF 9226 BALES OF COTTON

hair and beards. The men boasted to each other of their exploits, each trying to outdo the other in brutality. A gang of counterfeiters made "Rock-in-Cave" their headquarters, and from their presses a stream of counterfeit money went forth—some to be used by gamblers aboard steamboats, some to be distributed by men who made a specialty of visiting communities with the purpose of changing as much counterfeit money as possible for *bona fide* legal tender.

Some of the men operated alone; some worked in couples, and would board a steamboat as seeming strangers. Meeting at the card-table, these "strangers" would play into each other's hands at the expense of the other players. They used marked cards, loaded dice, and trick roulette wheels, which they had "doctored" until they could make them operate at will—and could win or lose as they saw fit. A common practice on steamboats was for a gambler to bribe the barkeeper and gain possession of all the packs of cards, which he would take to his stateroom and mark in such a way that he could identify them at a touch; then the marked cards were neatly sealed into their original packages and taken back to the bar. Later, when a new pack was purchased—which happened many times during the evening—the gambler was equally familiar with all. And the ignorant passengers were fleeced of all they had.

Numerous suicides and duels grew out of these card games. There are stories without end of wealthy planters who lost everything to these steamboat gamblers—money, land, slaves. But it is unlikely that such occurrences were common. The average gambler was glad to "make" two or three hundred dollars a week at the card-table, by the "honest practice" of using marked cards! "For," Mr. Green remarks, "such is a gambler's standard of honesty!"

Natchez-Under-the-Hill was a favorite hang-out for these gentlemen of the gambling fraternity. There were a "dozen or more gilded dens" in which an honest man could lose a fortune at the turn of a card, Mr. Green assures us; and as for New Orleans! . . .

Royal Street, the main thoroughfare of the old city, was filled with gambling-houses. Here the visitor found keno, roulette, faro, craps, the "six-and-eight" dice game, and every card game known to man—with the possible exception of "Old Maid." In these gambling-houses, in an atmosphere of luxury, the games went on in carpeted rooms, by the light of many glittering crystal chandeliers. Gilt-framed mirrors many feet wide reflected the tables and the players, and soft-footed negroes went to and fro, bearing trays loaded with whisky, wines, and liqueurs.

Gambling remained popular in New Orleans until recent years. Although prohibited by law, these houses flourished and operated openly. Even today there are many gambling-houses in New Orleans and in the immediate vicinity, just beyond the city's limits. But, like the steamboats, their glory has departed. No longer do the rich planters from "up-river" come to town to throw away the profits from a year's cotton crop; no longer do beautiful adventuresses trail their silks and velvets through the carpeted rooms, marking out their victims. For there are no more rich planters, no more gorgeous steamboats—and alas! no more gilded adventuresses. The women who work with the gamblers nowadays are rather a sorry lot. Can it be possible that our generation is tiring of these "gilded dens of vice"? Mr. Green assures us that they prospered in the eighteen-thirties and eighteen-forties.

Natchez-Under-the-Hill is no more. The Mississippi River has taken it. Lying below the bluff, near the river side, it was the favorite meeting-place for the men passengers from steamboats in the old days. But steadily, with the changing years, the river has eaten into the land. One by one the old brick houses crumbled and slid into the river. Today there are only three or four of these old houses left, and they hang precariously above the river, ready to crumble and disintegrate. They are deserted, abandoned. Spiders weave their webs across the doors. And below them the river rushes by, washing always at the foundations. In another year or two Natchez-Under-the-Hill will be only a memory.

I spoke just now of duels resulting from the card-table, and, from all accounts, they were frequent enough; but perhaps the strangest cause for a duel was an insult to—the Mississippi River!

Some seventy years ago there appeared in New Orleans a learned academician known as the Chevalier Tomasi. He published a volume on the hydraulics of the Mississippi. He had many ideas—all of them forgotten today. Nobody seems quite sure just what his method of flood control was, but he was certain that it was the only one. Frequently he said so. The creoles became tired of hearing about Chevalier Tomasi's plans for damming or draining the river. Some of them even dared say so. They insinuated that his ideas were impractical, and while they might work very well on some of the smaller European rivers, the Mississippi presented a different problem.

So Tomasi, describing his plans to a creole gentleman, remarked that the control of the Mississippi was mere child's play for such a mind as his. The creole suggested that the Mississippi was a very headstrong stream, and it was possible that Tomasi's scheme would fail. Whereupon Tomasi remarked:

"How little you Americans know of the world! Know

that there are rivers in Europe so large that the Mississippi is a mere rill, figuratively speaking!"

To this the enraged creole replied:

"Sir, I will never allow the Mississippi to be insulted or disparaged in my presence by an arrogant pretender to knowledge!" This he accompanied by a flirt of a glove in the face of Tomasi. A challenge resulted, and the Chevalier Tomasi was wounded (it is hoped) mortally.

In "Lloyd's Steamboat Directory and Disasters on Western Waters," no less than two hundred steamboat disasters are described with sickening reality. Almost no steamboats escaped an unhappy end. Many were burned, wrecked on snags, or—as the phrase went—"destroyed through the explosion of the boiler." And in "Mississippi Steamboatin'," that very delightful volume by Herbert and Edward Quick, many pages are given to wrecks, fires, and explosions aboard packets. But perhaps the best story by an "eye-witness" is found in a very old and rare volume with this truly magnificent title: "Shipwrecks and Disasters at Sea; or, Historical Narratives of the Most Noted Calamities and Providential Deliverances from Fire and Famine on Ocean and River."

Among the "noted calamities" is a description of the "Fatal Explosion of the Boiler on board the Steamboat 'Helen MacGregor,' at Memphis, Tennessee, on the Mississippi." And as it seems to be as typical a disaster as can be found in any of the books pertaining to steamboats, I give it here, just as it is given in that now-forgotten book. But first, I must try to describe the thrilling picture which accompanies the description. Eleven men are seen hurtling through the air. Some of them carry their hats in their hands. Two women in hoopskirts are floating in space, making gestures of appeal, while the boat bursts to pieces amidships. Nor is this all; for in the foreground six luckless chaps have fallen into the water and are being devoured by alligators.

On the morning of the 24th of February, 1830, the Helen McGregor stopped at Memphis, on the Mississippi River, to deliver freight and land a number of passengers, who resided in that section of Tennessee. The time occupied in so doing could not have exceeded three-quarters of an hour. When the boat landed, I went ashore to see a gentleman with whom I had some business. I found him on the beach, and after a short conversation, I returned to the boat. I recollect looking at my watch as I passed the gang-way. It was half-past eight o'clock. A great number of persons were standing on what is called the boiler deck, being that part of the upper deck situated immediately over the boilers. It was crowded to excess, and presented one dense mass of human bodies. In a few minutes we sat down to breakfast in the cabin. The table, although extending the whole length of the cabin, was completely filled, there being upwards of sixty cabin passengers, among whom were several ladies and children. The number of passengers on board, deck and cabin united, was between four and five hundred. I had almost finished my breakfast, when the pilot rung his bell for the engineer to put the machinery in motion. The boat having just shoved off, I was in the act of raising my cup to my lips, the tingling of the pilot bell yet on my ear, when I heard an explosion, resembling the discharge of a small piece of artillery. The report was perhaps louder than usual in such cases; for an exclamation was half uttered by me, that the gun was well loaded, when the rushing sound of steam, and the rattling of glass in some of the cabin windows, checked my speech, and told me too well what had occurred. I almost involuntarily bent my head and body down to the floor—a vague idea seemed to shoot across my mind that more than one boiler might burst, and that by assuming this posture, the destroying matter would pass over without touching me.

The general cry of, "a boiler has burst," resounded from one end of the table to the other; and, as if by a simultaneous movement, all started on their feet. Then commenced a general

race to the ladies' cabin, which lay more towards the stern
of the boat. All regard to order or deference to sex seemed to
be lost in the struggle for which should be first and farthest
removed from the dreaded boilers. The danger had already
passed away. I remained standing by the chair on which I
previously had been sitting. Only one or two persons stayed in
the cabin with me. As yet no more than half a minute had
elapsed since the explosion; but, in that brief space, how had
the scene changed! In that "drop of time" what confusion,
distress, and dismay! An instant before, and all were in the
quiet repose of security—another, and they were overwhelmed
with alarm or consternation. It is but justice to say, that in this
scene of terror, the ladies exhibited a degree of firmness worthy
of all praise. No screaming, no fainting—their fears, when
uttered, were not for themselves, but for their husbands and
children.

I advanced from my position to one of the cabin doors for
the purpose of inquiring who were injured, when, just as I
reached it, a man entered at the opposite one, both his hands
covering his face, and exclaiming, "Oh God! Oh God! I am
ruined!" He immediately began to tear off his clothes. When
stripped, he presented a most shocking spectacle: his face was
entirely black—his body without a particle of skin. He had been
flayed alive. He gave me his name, and place of abode—then
sunk in a state of exhaustion and agony on the floor. I assisted
in placing him on a mattress taken from one of the berths,
and covered him with blankets. He complained of heat and cold
as at once oppressing him. He bore his torments with manly
fortitude, yet a convulsive shriek would occasionally burst from
him. His wife, his children, were his constant theme—it was
hard to die without seeing them—"it was hard to go without
bidding them one farewell." Oil and cotton were applied to
his wounds; but he soon became insensible to earthly misery.
Before I had done attending to him, the whole floor of the
cabin was covered with unfortunate sufferers. Some bore up
under the horrors of their situation with a degree of resolution
amounting to heroism. Others were wholly overcome by the
sense of pain, the suddenness of the disaster, and the near

approach of death, which even to them was evident—whose pangs they already felt. Some implored us, as an act of humanity, to complete the work of destruction, and free them from present suffering. One entreated the presence of a clergyman, to pray by him, declaring he was not fit to die. I inquired —none could be had. On every side were heard groans, and mingled exclamations of grief and despair.

To add to the confusion, persons were every moment running about to learn the fate of their friends and relatives—fathers, sons, brothers—for in this scene of unmixed calamity, it was impossible to say who were saved, or who had perished. The countenances of many were so much disfigured as to be past recognition. My attention, after some time, was particularly drawn towards a poor fellow, who lay unnoticed on the floor, without uttering a single word of complaint. He was at a little distance removed from the rest. He was not much scalded; but one of his thighs was broken, and a principal artery had been severed, from which the blood was gushing rapidly. He betrayed no displeasure at the apparent neglect with which he was treated—he was perfectly calm. I spoke to him: he said "he was very weak, but felt himself going—it would soon be over." A gentleman ran for one of the physicians. He came, and declared that if expedition were used, he might be preserved by amputating the limb; but that, to effect this, it would be necessary to remove him from the boat. Unfortunately the boat was not sufficiently near to run a plank ashore. We were obliged to wait until it could be close hauled. I stood by him, calling for help. We placed him on a mattress, and bore him to the guards. There we were detained some time from the cause we have mentioned. Never did anything appear to me so slow as the movements of those engaged in hauling the boat.

I knew, and he knew, that delay was death—that life was fast ebbing. I could not take my gaze from his face—there all coolness and resignation. No word or gesture indicative of impatience escaped him. He perceived by my loud, and perhaps angry tone of voice, how much I was excited by what I thought the barbarous slowness of those around: he begged me not to take so much trouble—that they were doing their best. At length we got him on shore. It was too late—he was too much exhausted, and died immediately after the amputation.

So soon as I was relieved from attending on those in the cabin, I went to examine that part of the boat where the boiler had burst. It was a complete wreck—a picture of destruction. It bore ample testimony to the tremendous force of that power which the ingenuity of man had brought to his aid. The steam had given everything a whitish hue; the boilers were displaced; the deck had fallen down; the machinery was broken and disordered. Bricks, dirt, and rubbish were scattered about. Close by the bowsprit was a large rent, through which I was told the boiler, after exploding, had passed out, carrying one or two men in its mouth. Several dead bodies were lying around. Their fate had been an enviable one compared with that of others: they could scarcely have been conscious of a pang ere they had ceased to be. On the starboard wheel-house lay a human body, in which life was not yet extinct, though apparently there was no sensibility remaining. The body must have been thrown from the boiler-deck, a distance of thirty feet. The whole of the forehead had been blown away: the brains were still beating. Tufts of hair, shreds of clothing, and splotches of blood might be seen in every direction. A piece of skin was picked up by a gentleman on board, which appeared to have been peeled off by the force of the steam. It extended from the middle of the arm down to the tips of the fingers, the nails adhering to it. So dreadful had been the force, that not a particle of the flesh adhered to it. The most skilful operator could scarcely have effected such a result. Several died from inhaling the steam or gas, whose skin was almost uninjured.

The number of lives lost will, in all probability, never be distinctly known. Many were seen flung into the river, most of whom sunk to rise no more. Could the survivors have been kept together until the list of passengers was called, the precise loss would have been ascertained. That, however, though it had been attempted, would, under the circumstances, have been next to impossible.

Judging from the crowd which I saw on the boiler-deck immediately before the explosion, and the statement which I received as to the number of those who succeeded in swimming out after they were cast into the river, I am inclined to believe that between fifty and sixty must have perished.

The cabin passengers escaped, owing to the peculiar construction of the boat. Just behind the boilers were several large iron posts, supporting, I think, the boiler-deck: across each post was a large circular plate of iron of between one and two inches in thickness. One of these posts was placed exactly opposite the head of the boiler which burst, being the second one on the starboard side. Against this plate the head struck, and penetrated to the depth of an inch; then broke, and flew off at an angle, entering a cotton bale to the depth of a foot. The boiler head was in point blank range with the breakfast table in the cabin; and had it not been obstructed by the iron post, must have made a clear sweep of those who were seated at the table.

To render any satisfactory account of the cause which produced the explosion, can hardly be expected from one who possesses no scientific or practical knowledge on the subject, and who previously thereto was paying no attention to the management of the boat. The captain appeared to be very active and diligent in attending to his duty. He was on the boiler deck when the explosion occurred, was materially injured by that event, and must have been ignorant of the mismanagement, if any there were.

From the engineer alone could the true explanation be afforded; and, if indeed it was really attributable to negligence, it can scarcely be supposed he will lay the blame on himself. If I might venture a suggestion in relation thereto, I would assign the following causes :—That the water in the starboard boilers had become low, in consequence of that side of the boat resting upon the ground during our stay at Memphis; that, though the fires were kept up some time before we shoved off, that the head which burst had been cracked for a considerable time; that the boiler was extremely heated, and the water, thrown in when the boat was again in motion, was at once converted into steam; and the flues not being sufficiently large to carry it off as soon as it was generated, nor the boiler head of a strength capable of resisting its action, the explosion was a natural result.

Chapter XIX

COMMERCE ON THE MISSISSIPPI

THE history of commerce on the Mississippi River and the history of commerce in New Orleans are so entangled that in writing of one you must, necessarily, write of the other. For today, as in the beginning, New Orleans is the key to the Mississippi Valley.

In an earlier chapter I have spoken of *pirogues* and canoes, of flatboats and keelboats which floated down the Mississippi and tied up at the New Orleans waterfront. Conspicuous factors in the early colonial trade were corn, both shelled and in the ear; rice, hulled and in the straw; tobacco, indigo, and sassafras, occasionally. Pecans are mentioned in the old invoices as early as 1725. Deerskins and beaver hides, bear's grease and tallow counted very significantly, to judge from the large bills and shipments incidental merely to court business (as testified by the papers on file of early lawsuits). Tar and pitch were produced early in the history of New Orleans. A pottery concern was noted as early as the lumber trade; oak and ash were named in shipments. In 1738 there is record of a shipment of "Mississippi wood" which speaks of its preservative resin—this must have been pine. In the old accounts of a plantation-owner in 1740 we find produce listed, and among the items are: milk, cucumbers, greens, peas, plums, peaches, figs, pomegranates, and oranges.

We find eggs quoted at ten sous an egg in a document

235

of 1724; flour sold at 20 sous a pound in 1721 and 1722
(the latter year was known as the year of the famine);
whereas in the last quarter of 1742 the plentiful stage is
reflected in the invoices of laces and silks, gold watches and
"jackets of luxury"—embroidered, it is noted, in "white
and yellow, blue and cherry."

Most of the early shipments down the river consisted of
furs from the Northwest and Canada. In 1720 the exports
from New Orleans were valued at only $62,000 a year, of
which 65 per cent. was skins from the upper country, according to Norman Walker, in his chapter on "Commercial
and Mercantile Interests," in Henry Rightor's "Standard
History of New Orleans." Quoting from the same source:

As early as 1705 the Mississippi had suggested itself as a
means of communication between the far North and the Gulf
of Mexico. In that year, only six years after Bienville had first
visited New Orleans and had seen in it the best site for the
capital of the new colony and for the port of the great valley,
the first cargo came down the Mississippi. * * *

A number of French voyageurs settled in the Indian country
around the Wabash, collected from the several hunting posts in
the neighborhood 10,000 deer and 5,000 bear skins and shipped
them down the Mississippi as the only way by which they
could reach Europe, as it was impossible to pack them
across the country and over the mountains to Canada or
Philadelphia. * * *

The Canadian voyageurs who brought down their first cargo
on the Mississippi traveled 1,400 miles without seeing a settlement or a white man, and through a country filled with hostile
Indians. It took them nearly six months to make the trip, but
they got through all the difficulties and reached the Gulf in the
early part of 1706. As New Orleans did not exist then or
until twelve years later, these primitive merchants floated down
the Mississippi only as far as Bayou Manchac, then a navigable
stream (it was closed by Gen. Jackson in 1815 as a protection

against the British fleet), and sailed through Bayou Manchac and Iberville (now Amite) river into Lake Pontchartrain. Thence they went through Mississippi Sound to Mobile (then known as St. Louis des Mobiles), where their cargo was marketed. The furs were sold in France and the voyageur merchants made a handsome profit, but they did not care to repeat the experiment. They did not return home, but settled in Louisiana. * * *

During the first years of the new city its trade consisted almost exclusively in the products of the chase, and these figured very prominently in its business for nearly half a century afterward. During all this early time New Orleans was one of the chief entrepots of the Northwestern and Canadian fur trade. * * *

In 1763 Louisiana was ceded to Spain. The commerce of New Orleans at that time amounted to only $304,000 a year, less than the value of a single cargo shipped from the city today. Of these exports only half came from the country around New Orleans. The items are as follows: Indigo (the main product of the colony at that time), $100,000; deer skins and furs from the Upper Mississippi, Missouri and Ohio, $80,000; lumber, $50,000; naval stores, $12,000; rice, peas and beans, $4,000; tallow $4,000. The smuggled trade was put down as $54,000, but may have been more. * * * As for the food products brought down from the Illinois country they were all consumed in and around New Orleans and did not find their way abroad.

Spain took Louisiana in 1763, and Mr. Walker relates how, following that country's colonial policy, all legitimate trade was confined to Spain alone. This put the settlers at the mercy of Spanish merchants, deprived Louisiana settlers of articles that were needed in the colony, and encouraged a smuggling trade that was almost as large as the legitimate commerce and far more profitable.

From one-fifth to one-half of the imports received in New Orleans were smuggled in; and this business was easily enough conducted because by treaty Great Britain had reserved to itself the right for British ships to enter the Mississippi and supply the British settlements on the east bank of the river, above Bayou Manchac, with such articles as they needed. These vessels were supposed to be handling the trade of the English settlements in West Florida and in what is now the State of Mississippi; but their voyages up the Mississippi gave them a splendid opportunity of dealing with the colonists below Fort Bute (at the junction of the Mississippi River and the Manchac).

British trading vessels on the way to Fort Bute or Baton Rouge landed part of their cargoes in Louisiana. The center of this smuggling trade was at a point about six miles above the city of New Orleans, where entire cargoes were disembarked and where the city merchants had their agents and representatives to purchase the British contraband goods. The slave trade formed a very considerable proportion of this smuggling, and the Louisiana planters were supplied with "Guinea negroes" mainly by the British vessels. In all the earlier commercial reports this smuggling was spoken of openly. There was, indeed, very little secrecy about it, and during the French régime it was winked at by the authorities, many of whom found it personally profitable. * * *

When the Spaniards took possession of New Orleans they set to work to break up the smuggling, which not only cut down the colonial revenue, but injured the mother country. Governor O'Reilly found the commerce of the city very much demoralized by this contraband trade. He reported to the Spanish government that he found the foreign commerce of New Orleans almost wholly in the hands of the British. "They have their traders and their ships here," he reported, "and they pocket nine-tenths of all the money spent in New Orleans and Louisiana."

During and following O'Reilly's *régime,* foreign import privileges alternately grew rigid and relaxed, and during Galvez's administration the colonists were allowed to trade with any port in France, and later, "in consideration of the bravery of Louisiana troops" at the capture of Pensacola

(Spain then being at war with Great Britain), the commercial facilities of New Orleans were still further extended, and it was allowed to trade with Mexico, which country had previously been closed against it. In 1770 the exports of New Orleans had risen to $631,000 a year, having more than doubled during the seven years of Spanish rule.

In the meanwhile, events occurred which completely changed the commerce of New Orleans—the Americans came. The first of these was Oliver Pollock of Baltimore, who entered the port during O'Reilly's governorship. It happened to be at a time when provisions were scarce in consequence of the non-arrival of Spanish supply ships. Pollock had a cargo of flour, which he sold to the governor for $15 a barrel, two-thirds of the then current price, in return for which O'Reilly granted Pollock the right of free trade with New Orleans during his lifetime.

Pollock was the first American merchant to establish himself in New Orleans, and had his agents and representatives in the city, who did a very large business. This commercial venture proved of the utmost importance to the American cause in the end, as much of the ammunition and arms furnished the Continental army was obtained through Governor Galvez, being carried by boat up the Mississippi and Ohio to Pittsburg, and thence distributed to the American forces. At the close of the Revolutionary war New Orleans was receiving produce to the value of $225,000 a year from the settlements in Tennessee and Kentucky, mainly flour, tobacco and similar produce, and was supplying in return manufactured goods, principally cottons and other dry goods, imported from France.

Governor Galvez was anxious to make New Orleans a free port, but Spanish policy would not allow this. However, exceptional concessions were allowed. By a royal decree made public in New Orleans in 1782, "the reshipment to any South American colony of goods received from Spain" was permitted; but this was not permissible with goods from other countries. Negroes were allowed to be imported free of duty from the colonies of neutral or allied powers, save from Martinique, "whose negroes had the reputation of being too partial to voudouism."

The commercial importance of New Orleans and the Mississippi River was now fully recognized by all powers, and American politics for the next twenty years was to center around New Orleans and the Mississippi. The Treaty of Ghent, which ended the war between the United States, Great Britain, France, and Spain, provided that the Mississippi from its source to the Gulf should remain free to the United States and Great Britain forever.

This stipulation was never carried out in good faith by Spain; but it became the origin of a series of Spanish and American intrigues, the aim of the Spaniards being to keep the Yankees away from New Orleans, and of the Americans to secure the free use of the river, if not to annex New Orleans and the adjacent territory, as necessary for the prosperity of the country above, whose outlet was through "the Crescent City." In 1786 a large number of American flatboats loaded with provisions and breadstuffs, which had been floated down from the Ohio and the Cumberland, were seized at New Orleans and confiscated by the Spanish government on the ground that they had violated some of the revenue laws of the colony.

In 1787 General James Wilkinson succeeded in obtaining valuable commercial concessions from Governor Miro, and the flatboatmen were no longer interfered with. * * * The uncertainty of the trade, and the obstacles placed in the way of the American flatboatmen, led the Ohio settlers to demand of Congress that it show itself more interested in their affairs and better protect their interests; indeed the demand was coupled

ON THE MISSISSIPPI, TODAY

A river steamboat pushing three barges upstream

with threats, and the Kentucky pioneers talked secession very loudly. * * * The result of their agitation was the treaty of St. Ildefonso in 1795, the first treaty made by the United States with Spain.

The treaty dealt with boundaries, but the most important provision was that the Mississippi was to be free to Americans, and they were allowed to deposit at New Orleans for three years, without payment of any sort except for storage. At the end of three years a new arrangement was to be made of similar nature, Spain reserving the right to name another point than New Orleans where American goods could be stored.

At that time, only thirty-two years from the date of the Spanish acquisition of the colony, the trade of New Orleans had increased more than four-fold, and had very radically changed. Indigo no longer constituted the largest item in the exports, for indigo was fast disappearing as a paying crop in Louisiana and sugar was taking its place. The largest single item was Western produce, which constituted more than one-third of the total.

The several items were as follows: Cotton (200,000 pounds), $50,000; furs, $100,000; boxes (shipped to Cuba for the sugar crop), $225,000; sugar (40,000,000 pounds), $320,000; indigo (100,000 pounds), $100,000; tobacco (200,000 pounds), $10,-000; timber, $50,000; rice (2,000 barrels), $50,000; Western produce, $500,000. Total, $1,421,000. The furs came from the North and Northwest; the sugar, indigo, rice and timber from the Spanish possessions in Louisiana; and the rest from Kentucky, Tennessee and Ohio.

The treaty of San Ildefonso and the opening of the Mississippi gave a stimulus to the American trade through New Orleans. In 1798 the Western produce received there was valued at $975,000, and was increasing at the rate of $300,000 a year with the heavy emigration pouring into the Ohio Valley.

When the three years named by Spain elapsed during which American goods could be stored in New Orleans, Morales, the Spanish intendant, gave Americans to understand that he interpreted the treaty to mean that Americans were to lose all rights of deposit. This, with other growing friction, precipitated the Louisiana Purchase. The Revolutionary War, and later wars between England and France and Spain, closed one European port after another to New Orleans exports and tended to concentrate trade along the Mississippi.

The annexation of Louisiana to the United States was followed by a large increase in the trade of New Orleans. In 1795 its exports were $1,421,000, of which $500,000 was estimated as coming from Kentucky, Tennessee and Ohio. In 1801 the shipments from Kentucky and Mississippi alone were $1,626,-672, and from all the American possessions in the Mississippi Valley, $2,111,672. In 1802, the last year of the Spanish rule, the trade ran up to $2,637,564. * * * Two-thirds [of the total receipts] were from American territory and included 34,500 bales of cotton, of an average weight of 300 pounds each; 4,300 hogsheads of sugar, of an average weight of 1,000 pounds; 800 casks of molasses, of 125 gallons each, equal to 2,000 of the barrels in which molasses is exported to-day, 4,000 casks of tafia or rum made from Louisiana molasses, each of 50 gallons; 3,000 pounds of indigo; lumber and (sugar) boxes to the value of $300,000; peltries and skins to the value of $120,000; rice and various other products amounting to some $80,000. These were the products of Louisiana.

Among the chief articles of Western produce coming from American territory were 50,000 barrels of flour, 2,000 barrels of pork, 1,200 barrels of beef, 2,400 hogsheads of tobacco, 25,000 barrels of corn, besides butter, hams, beans, lard, staves and cordage. Not only did the Americans control the interior trade, but they were rapidly getting control of the exterior trade of New Orleans, for of the ocean vessels leaving that port in 1802, a total of 265 of a tonnage of 31,241, there were 158

Americans and 104 Spanish and French. The British were shut out altogether by the war.

After the transfer of Louisiana, there was an influx of American merchants, mostly from the Atlantic coast cities; but the first few years of American rule did not see the increase in commerce that was expected. It was not until 1807 that the receipts of western produce passed the $5,000,-000 mark. In that year, produce reached New Orleans in 314 keelboats and barges and 110 flatboats. The flatboat and keelboat period lasted about ten years and were years of commercial prosperity in spite of the disadvantages under which the flatboatmen labored. The flatboatmen, after making the voyage to New Orleans and selling their cargo, usually broke up their boats, sold the lumber and walked home to the Cumberland or Ohio overland. The upriver freight was almost prohibitive, five or six cents to the pound, with not much profit at that.

The flatboats usually landed above the corporate limits of New Orleans, and their produce was loaded on ocean-going vessels at the Place d'Armes, now Jackson Square. There were usually twenty or more vessels tied up there. These sailed on no definite schedule but only when they had received their full cargo. It was not until after the invention of the steamboat that Mississippi River traffic was to take on the proportions it assumed during the most prosperous period.

In 1810 the arrivals by river were 679 flatboats and 392 keelboats, a total of 1071. These brought to New Orleans a most miscellaneous character of products, which included sugar, molasses, rice, cotton, flour, pork, bacon, whisky, apples, cider, corn, oats, cheese, beans, lumber, butter, lard, onions, potatoes, hemp, yarn and cordage, linen, tobacco,

beer, horses, hogs, poultry, and other things. Three-fifths
of these originated above "the Falls of the Ohio" (Louisville) and two-fifths below this point.

In 1811, the arrival of the New Orleans, the first steamboat
to navigate the Mississippi, created a revolution in the river
business of New Orleans. The change was somewhat slow at
first, because the steamers were possessed of so little power
that they could with difficulty resist the mighty current of
the river, and found it a most tedious matter to go upstream.
There were only five steamboats built in as many years.

Navigation was also handicapped by legislation. A company had been formed with Fulton and Livingston at the
head.   This company secured from the Louisiana legislature
the exclusive right to navigate the Mississippi within the
state bounds for fourteen years, with the privilege of re-
newing their charter at the expiration of that time. However, the *Washington,* first high-pressure steamer on the
Mississippi, openly violated the charter, carried the matter
into court, and won, it being decided "that the Mississippi
River was the heritage of the people, and that neither Congress nor any state legislature had the right to give control
of its navigation to any person or company."

The decision hastened the development of steamboating,
and from 1814 on there was a diminution of the number
of flatboats and keelboats visiting the city. In 1814 the
arrivals at New Orleans were 508 flatboats, 324 barges and
twenty-one steamboats. The products received from the
interior showed an increase in agricultural items and in
rum and whisky. Most of the importers in New Orleans
were French or creoles, who shipped up the Mississippi fine
French goods. It is interesting to note that the Kentuckians
and Tennesseans of a hundred years ago were supplied with

COMMERCE ON THE MISSISSIPPI TODAY

A modern steamboat towing eight barges, the cargo totalling a value of one million dollars

French prints and broadcloths, while their neighbors on the Atlantic seaboard were supplied almost wholly with products of the English looms.

The introduction of the steamboat as a means of transportation on the river brought about a radical change in trade lines and gave an immense impetus to the business of New Orleans. The quarter of a century between 1815 and 1840 was the golden age commercially of that city, when it saw its greatest prosperity. Its trade is larger in the aggregate to-day, but not relatively and proportionately, and there is not as much profit in it. During the early steamboat period New Orleans, in spite of epidemics, rose to be the wealthiest city in the Union, the third in point of population, and disputed with New York the rank of the first port in America. * * * Indeed, no other American city ever occupied the metropolitan position that New Orleans filled for half the century during its "flush days."

The opening of the Mississippi to steamboats without let or hindrance in 1816 saw a total of $8,052,540 of produce shipped down, about double the receipts of the first year of the American dominion. Cotton still constituted only a small part of this commerce, amounting to 37,371 bales, or twelve per cent in value, and the bulk of the receipts were from the Ohio Valley and included breadstuffs, provisions, tobacco, and other Western produce, or eighty per cent in value of the receipts. * * * The river traffic at that time required six steamboats, 594 barges and 1,287 flatboats, of a total tonnage of 87,670.

The trip down the Mississippi was full of danger, because of the many snags and other river accidents, and a rough estimate placed the losses at 20 per cent; that is, only 80 per cent of the goods which started down from the Ohio to New Orleans ever reached that port, the remaining fifth being sunk or burnt in the Mississippi on its way down.

Transportation on the Mississippi increased tremendously with the advent of assured, regular transportation. In the period of four years, between 1816 and 1820, the river commerce doubled; nor did the improvement stop here. The

Middle West was being more thickly settled, and as the number of steamboats steadily increased, the flatboats were relegated to second place.

The first steamboat reached New Orleans the day before Christmas, 1811. In 1815, when the Fulton-Livingston monopoly was declared unconstitutional, there were forty steamers to make the voyage downstream. There were 198 arrivals in 1820; in 1830 there were 989, and in 1841, 1958 steamboats arrived at New Orleans.

There were other forces at work at this time that changed the character of the produce coming down the Mississippi. The opening of the Erie Canal did much to divert western produce which had formerly gone down the river. In place of the produce, steamboats began to make larger shipments of cotton, which hitherto had had a smaller place in the percentage of shipments. The ocean commerce of New Orleans had increased proportionately with river transportation, and European demand for cotton was another encouraging factor in the swing toward that staple.

By 1832 the waters of the upper Ohio were connected with Lake Erie by canal and the latter with the Hudson River by the Erie Canal. Over this route the State of Ohio shipped to New York 86,000 barrels of flour, 98,000 bushels of wheat, and 2,500,000 staves in 1835. This was the first blow in trade the Mississippi River had received, but at the time there was so much produce coming down the stream that no attention was paid that slight diversion of traffic. A greater enemy to river traffic was to come—the railroad.

A few miles of railroad had been constructed in 1830. More were built each year, but for a long time the river traffic had nothing to fear. The railroads were mostly local, with great gaps between lines, and for a long time were considered as expedients for getting goods to the river, where they could be shipped to their destinations. In 1849 the receipts from commerce, in spite of canals and railroads, reached the magnificent total of $81,989,692. This was the time when New Orleans was entering its career as the cotton city of the world.

In 1845 it was estimated that half the product of the Mississippi Valley shipped to seaboard found its way to market via the canals, railroads and other routes, and half by way of the Mississippi to New Orleans, thus showing how much business had been diverted. * * * In 1846 the receipts of flour and wheat at Buffalo exceeded those of New Orleans for the first time. This created a sensation. The New Orleans press expressed the sentiment that this diversion was merely temporary, that an artificial waterway could never compete successfully with a natural one; and that the flour and wheat trade would return; but it never did.

Thereafter, such grain and flour as passed down the Mississippi was reshipped to Cuba and other countries of Latin America. In 1852 the lead trade of Illinois and Missouri, which formerly passed down the river, was diverted by railroads, connections having been made with Galena, the center of the lead industry. Lower Mississippi merchants did not bother; there was more money to be made, and the South staked its fortune on "King Cotton."

Another trouble manifested itself again and again. This was the difficulty of getting produce from the river to the ocean on account of the bar at the mouth of the Mississippi. The use of steam had greatly increased the size of ocean-going vessels, and these encountered difficulties, first at Northeast Pass and then at Southwest Pass. In 1837, Northeast Pass shoaled up, and Southwest Pass came into vogue until 1850 when its sixteen-foot depth became too shallow.

The draft of many of the vessels was sixteen feet or more and those of one thousand tons or over encountered great difficulty in getting over the bars in this Pass. In 1852, within a few weeks there were forty vessels aground on the bar, suffering a detention there of from two days to eight weeks. Many of them could not get over the bar with their cargoes and had to discharge the latter into lighters.

In 1853 the same difficulties occurred, and in a memorial presented to Congress by the merchants of New Orleans, it was represented that vessels with cargoes valued at $7,367,339 were delayed at the mouth of the Mississippi, being unable either to get into it or to get out. This naturally increased the freight rate from New Orleans and tended to injure the commerce of the city. The trouble was constantly recurring for the next twenty years or more, and was only cured in 1874 by the construction of the Eads jetties.

In the seventies the question came to a focus. Three plans had been proposed, a canal, dredging, and jetties. By the latter plan, the river would be contracted so that its increased current would wash away the obstructive bars. The dredging was tried and proved a failure; and Congress then, with rare good luck for New Orleans, allowed Captain Eads to try his jetty plan. It was a success.

Completed in 1879, it afforded a depth of thirty feet in the center of the channel and opened New Orleans to the largest vessels then afloat.

The lower Mississippi then was assured an adequate outlet for its shipping.

To return to the period before the Civil War. The lower Mississippi Valley began concentrating on shipments of cotton as its supply of foodstuffs from the north and west was diverted to New York and the Atlantic by rail and canal. Several economists of the time pointed out to merchants that single crop and single kind of shipments were likely to be the undoing of river transportation. But the

THE LEVEE AT NEW ORLEANS—TWENTY YEARS AGO

merchants were making too much money to listen to "calamity howlers."

The season before the Civil War, 1859-60, saw the largest receipts of produce at New Orleans, and the heaviest and most profitable trade the city had ever done; and it stands on record to-day [1900] as the summit of its commercial prosperity. The number of steamboats arriving at New Orleans was, it is true, not as great as in 1846-7, but the boats had in the meanwhile more than doubled in size, and the tonnage reaching New Orleans by the Mississippi has never been equaled since. The total receipts amounted to 2,187,560 tons, and the total river trade to reach the city was valued at $289,565,000 for the year.

There were no less than twelve steamboat arrivals from Cairo, Illinois, in direct communication with New Orleans. From Cincinnati 206 steamboats arrived during the year; from the Cumberland river, 66; from Evansville, Indiana, 8; from Louisville, 172; from Memphis, 110; from Pittsburg, 526; Paducah, Kentucky, and St. Louis, 472; Tennessee river, 16; Wheeling, 9; and White river, Arkansas, 4.

The Civil War, the backwardness of the lower Mississippi Valley people in seeing the advantages of railroads, numerous causes have been set down for the decline of river traffic. Possibly all these factors influenced. Certainly no one in the fifties would have suspected that the golden days of river transportation were nearing their end.

The commercial business of the city, instead of being hidden away as it is to-day, at the railroad depots, was concentrated on the levees; and "the levee" was one of the show places of New Orleans, to which strangers were taken to give them some idea of the city's immense commerce. * * * The description of the levee in those ante-bellum days reads like fairy tales from The Arabian Nights. The levee was the storehouse for all the great Mississippi Valley. Along the wharves lay steamboats or steamships two or three deep, for the wharfage was not sufficient to accommodate all the vessels loading at the port.

All was action; the very water was covered with life. It was beyond all question the most active commercial center of the world, with which not even the docks of Liverpool and London could merit comparison; and whenever any one expressed fear that the railroads would sap the commerce of New Orleans, he was taken to the levee and asked if that looked like commercial decay.

The Civil War was a serious blow to river transportation. The year before the war, commerce was at its peak and the next year dropped because of the blockade. Thereafter, until the close of the struggle, river traffic was almost entirely a matter of military transportation.

The value of produce received in New Orleans during the war is misleading as to volume, Mr. Walker points out. During the year 1864-65, it is given as $113,649,280. This was for 275,015 bales of cotton, at a price greatly inflated by the blockade. River commerce was practically dead, and this depression existed for several years after.

In 1865 the shipments of western produce through New Orleans had declined 75 to 90 per cent. Not only did the war have the effect of crippling river transportation but it encouraged the building of railroads, which have carried on the bulk of inland transportation ever since. In 1859-60, 46 per cent. of the cotton crop had gone down the river. This figure dropped to 33 per cent. in 1870-71 and to 27 per cent. in 1876-77.

From then until recent years river transportation has been of secondary importance. The urgent demand for speed in getting cotton to markets gave more and more business to railroads. But a balance was reached at last when higher freight rates did not justify the speed of transportation.

For such non-perishable articles as steel and coal, when delivery was not urgent, the Mississippi again suggested itself as a proper carrier. River steamboats, offshoots of the palatial fleets of yesterday, now paddle the river alongside small tugs guiding a train of modern steel barges.

These tows sometimes represent a million-dollar investment with their cargoes. The Jones & Laughlin Steel Corporation of Pittsburgh regularly makes shipments down the Ohio and Mississippi of steel weighing 10,000 tons. A photograph printed in a brochure put out by the corporation, "Our Runaway Rivers," shows twelve barges unloading at the rail terminal in Memphis. These twelve barges, if loaded to capacity, would require 600 freight cars, averaging forty tons to the car, to carry away their cargoes.

Many other shipping concerns have turned again to the Mississippi as a faithful and less expensive carrier. During the war the United States Government established the Mississippi Warrior service, designed to relieve the overburdened rail lines. The service was established as a common carrier upon the Mississippi River between New Orleans and St. Louis and upon the Warrior River in Alabama, and was operated under the Railroad Administration in coordination with the rail carriers.

Quoting from the Jones & Laughlin brochure:

"It has since been incorporated as the Inland Waterways Corporation, and provided by Congress with a capital stock of $5,000,000. It has assets of approximately $15,000,000 and its organization functions along lines of great private transportation practice, the Secretary of War representing the stockholders, controlling its functioning through an executive corresponding to the president of a railroad. This executive is chairman of an advisory board, composed of six representative business men from various sections of the country."

The extent to which the Inland Waterways Corporation serves the nation was recently stated by Major-General T. Q. Ashburn, executive and chairman:

"The corporation, operating its fleets as a common carrier, transports into and from 42 states of the Union through joint rail-water rates, approximately 80 per cent. of the all-rail rate for the same service, where the service performed is partly by water and partly by rail.

"It operates on 2,500 miles of river, touching 11 states, has interchange relations with 165 railroads, and is planning to extend its service to the remaining six states, so that every state in the Union may be benefited by its operations."

By complete reorganization of the service effective in August, 1924, it was put on a profit-making basis, and from a loss of $973,305 per annum hitherto, it has produced a profit in two and a half years of $219,511.96.

The success of the Mississippi as a carrier has suggested the development of waterways and canals in other parts of the country, which cannot be discussed here. That Mississippi traffic is beginning to benefit by another season of growth may be judged by the statements of political leaders when the matter of inland waterways came before Congress for legislation. To quote Herbert Hoover:

"If we are to make a survey of all the opportunities of physical progress in our nation that lie before us, the development of our internal waterways would stand in the forefront. Above all, expenditure on works of this type increases the wealth of our country. It is a reproductive expenditure that increases the area of tax distribution and becomes in the end an actual economy to the government."

THE WATERFRONT AT NEW ORLEANS AS IT APPEARS TODAY

Chapter XX

WHEN de Soto and his men came first to the shores of the Mississippi, they found the river in flood; La Salle and other explorers who came later speak of vast portions of the country suffering from inundation; the first settlements of white men on the banks of the river in the lower valley were almost destroyed by freshets which came sweeping down upon them in early spring.

The delta of the Mississippi River subject to overflow extends from Cape Girardeau, forty-five miles above Cairo, to the Gulf of Mexico, nearly 600 miles in an air line, and varies in width from twenty to eighty miles. Its area amounts to 29,790 square miles.

It was formed in the geological ages of the past, we are told, by sediment carried to the sea by the streams draining the basins tributary to the Mississippi. This alluvial formation, or delta, which is now the richest and most fertile soil in the United States, was gradually elevated, so that it stands now above the ordinary floods that occur in the Mississippi; but in times of extraordinary rainfall, and, therefore, of excessive floods, it is subject to overflow by the abnormal flood heights of the river. The river flowing through this delta carries the drainage of 1,240,050 square miles, which is 41 per cent. of the total area of the United States. The area drained extends from the Rockies to the Alleghanies and from Canada to the Gulf of Mexico. It covers 1800 miles in longitude and 1500 miles in latitude. It drains ten entire States, parts of twenty-two other States, besides a part of two provinces in Canada. The area drained by the Mississippi is as great as the combined area of Austria, Germany, France, Holland, Italy, Spain, Portugal, Norway, and Great Britain.

Here we have, then, thousands of miles of streams and rivers which carry this drainage to the main body of the Mississippi, and of these, 15,000 miles are navigable streams. There are six main drainage basins: the Ohio River basin, comprising 201,700 square miles; the upper Mississippi River basin, 165,900 square miles; the Missouri River basin, 527,150 square miles; the Arkansas River basin, 186,300 square miles; the Red River basin, 90,000 square miles; and the central basin of the Mississippi River, 69,000 square miles. This brings us a grand total of 1,240,050 square miles drained by the Mississippi and its tributaries.

These facts and figures are taken from a report made by Arsène Perrilliat, member of the board of state engineers of Louisiana, and by former Governor John M. Parker, of Louisiana, in 1927 appointed by Secretary Herbert Hoover as flood dictator for the State of Louisiana.

The Mississippi, flowing in a sinuous course from Cape Girardeau to the Gulf of Mexico, a distance of 600 miles in an air line, as I have said, has a length, owing to its constant bending and curving, of 1115 miles. As long ago as 1904 it was computed that the average rainfall carried annually to the sea amounted to 785 billions of cubic feet, or 159 cubic miles of water; and this was estimated as being only 25 per cent. of the total rainfall over the basin, the remaining 75 per cent. being lost in evaporation, and in percolation and absorption in the ground. These figures are twenty-three years old, and it is needless to point out that the volume has increased greatly since that time; for every year, as the country becomes more open, better tilled, and therefore better drained, the volume of water finding its way to the Mississippi increases and also reaches the river more rapidly, thereby swelling and increasing the intensity of floods.

Moreover, the period of heavy rainfall is limited to two or three months in the spring; and this enormous volume of water drained, instead of being spread throughout the year, is carried to the sea in its enormous bulk during a short period of the year, thereby causing intense and excessive flood waves.

In order to protect this fertile land in the valley from yearly overflow, it has been necessary to build levees from Cairo to the Gulf of Mexico. These levees have grown gradually, and each year more and more land has been reclaimed behind them. The additional drainage, the reclaiming of 'swamp land—which formerly served as a reservoir for part of the flood waters—the cutting away of forests, and the growth of cities along the Mississippi are given as reasons for the ever-increasing flood levels of the river.

Now a great deal of nonsense has been written about the Mississippi in the past, and even greater nonsense has been written about the river during the floods of 1927. The principal piece of misinformation that has been printed and reprinted during the 1927 flood is this: that the bed of the river has filled up, and in some places the river bed is above the level of the land beside the river. It would be difficult to pin the original assertion to any one man, but many parrots have repeated it, and today many uninformed people believe it to be true.

Albert Bushnell Hart, professor emeritus of government

of Harvard College, writing in "Current History" for
June, 1927, corrects this statement. He writes: "The theory
that the Mississippi builds up its bed until the bottom of
the stream is higher than the country behind the levees is
entirely and literally without foundation. The bottom of the
Mississippi is always lower than the country outside its
banks, but the level of the surface of the flowing stream is
frequently much higher than the back country." And if you
doubt Professor Hart's assertion, you have only to read
the findings of the government engineers, who, year after
year, have taken soundings of the Mississippi. This miscon-
ception is found almost entirely among those who live away
from the Mississippi River, for those who live beside its
banks can see for themselves. The dwellers beside the Mississippi know that in times of low water the river falls to
as low a stage as it ever did. There are gauges beside the
river in nearly every town and village on the Mississippi,
and upon these gauges the observer can learn the stages
of the river for himself. And it stands to reason that, if
the bottom of the river were filling up, the water in the
river would not fall to its former low-water level—for we
know that more and more water comes pouring down the
Mississippi every year. But in addition to what the dweller
beside the Mississippi can see with his own eyes, there are
the soundings by government engineers as to the river's
depth, from year to year.

Now, as for the levees themselves, a book could be written about them, but I must be as brief as possible. Accordingly, I quote again from the best authority I can find:
Humphreys and Abbot's "Physics and Hydraulics of the
Mississippi River," also from government reports and the
reports of state engineers:

Photo by Marshall Gray, U. S. Engineers' Corps, 1927

"TOPPING" TO PREVENT WATER WASHING OVER THE LEVEE-TOP

The first permanent settlements by Europeans in the valley of the lower Mississippi were made at Natchez and at the present site of New Orleans. At Natchez the bluffs were occupied, but at New Orleans precautions had to be at once taken to protect the colony from inundation.

According to Dumont, De la Tour, the engineer who laid out the city of New Orleans in 1717, directed "a dyke or levee to be raised in front, the more effectually to preserve the city from overflow." Although this work was so early contemplated, it was not completed until November, 1727, when Governor Perrier announced that the New Orleans levee was finished, it being 5400 feet in length, and 18 feet wide on the top. He added that within a year a levee would be constructed for 18 miles above and below the city, which, though not so strong as that at the city, "would answer the purpose of preventing overflows."

In the meantime, colonists continued to arrive slowly and occupy the land along the river banks, so that in 1723, according to François Xavier Martin, "the only settlements then began below the Natchez were those of St. Reine and Madame de Mezieres, a little below Pointe Coupée—that of Diron d'Artaguette, at Baton Rouge—that of Paris, near bayou Manchac—that of the Marquis d'Anconio, below Lafourche—that of the Marquis d'Artagnac, at *Cannes Brulées*—that of de Meuse, a little below, and a plantation of three brothers of the name of Chauvin, lately from Canada, at the Tchapitoulas."

In 1728 Dumont says there were five colonies "extending for 30 miles above New Orleans, who were obliged to construct levees of earth for their protection." The expense of constructing these embankments was borne by the planters, each building a levee the length of his river front.

In 1731 the Mississippi company gave up the colony to the French crown. In 1735 Du Pratz states that "the levees extended from English bend, 12 miles below, to 30 miles above and on both sides of the river." The same year, the insufficiency of the works was demonstrated, as "the water was very high, and the levees broke in many places." It is certain that this difficulty continued to be felt, for in 1743, according to Gayarré, "an ordinance was promulgated requiring the inhabitants to complete their levees by the 1st of January, 1744, under a penalty of forfeiture of their lands to the crown."

According to Monette, in 1752 the plantations extended "20 miles below, and 30 miles above New Orleans," and in that distance "nearly the whole coast was in a high state of cultivation, and securely protected from floods."

Captain Philip Pittman, who published a work in 1770, defines the settlements at that date as extending only "30 miles above, and 20 miles below New Orleans." In other words, the inhabitants for twenty years had been devoting themselves to the cultivation and improvement of those districts already partially reclaimed, instead of trying to extend the levees farther along the bank. The wars between England and France, the cession by the latter power of all her territory on the Mississippi to Spain in 1763, and the impolitic course pursued by the Spanish governors, doubtless contributed to retard the growth of the colony at that epoch. It also appears to have been supposed that the settlements could not be extended farther down the river, "on account of the immense expense attending the levees necessary to protect the fields from the inundations of sea and land floods," which would render it advisable to defer the settlement of that section of the country "until the land shall be raised by the accession of soil." (François Xavier Martin.)

In the year 1800 the territory was ceded back to France, Napoleon being then First Consul. In 1803 it was ceded to the United States. Its condition may be inferred from the following extracts from the Abstract of Documents of the State Department and of the Treasury, 1802-5:—

"The principal settlements in Louisiana are on the Mississippi river, which begins to be cultivated about twenty (20) leagues from the sea. Ascending, you see them improve on each side till you reach the city [New Orleans]. Except on the point just below Iberville, the country from New Orleans is settled the whole way."

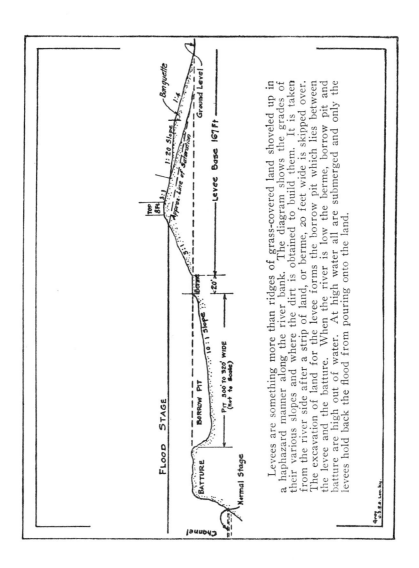

Levees are something more than ridges of grass-covered land shoveled up in a haphazard manner along the river bank. The diagram shows the grades of their various slopes and where the dirt is obtained to build them. It is taken from the river side after a strip of land, or berme, 20 feet wide is skipped over. The excavation of land for the levee forms the borrow pit which lies between the levee and the batture. When the river is low the berme, borrow pit and batture are high out of water. At high water all are submerged and only the levees hold back the flood from pouring onto the land.

"Above Baton Rouge, at the distance of 50 leagues from New Orleans and on the west side of the Mississippi, is Pointe Coupée, a populous and rich settlement, extending 8 leagues along the river. Behind it, on an old bed of the river now a lake whose outlets are closed up, is the settlement of Fausse Rivière."

"There is no other settlement on the Mississippi except the small one called Concord, opposite Natchez, till you come to the Arkansas river, 250 leagues above New Orleans. Here is a small settlement. There is no other settlement from this place to New Madrid."

"On both banks of this creek [bayou La Fourche] there are settlements one plantation deep for near 15 leagues."

"Bayou Plaquemine, 32 leagues above New Orleans, is the principal and swiftest communication to the rich and populous settlement of Atacapas and Opelousas."

Louisiana was admitted to the Federal Union in 1812. Stoddard, in his history of Louisiana, published in that year, states: "These banks [levees] extend on both sides of the river, from the lowest settlements to Point Coupée on one side, and to the neighborhood of Baton Rouge on the other, except where the country remains unoccupied."

"Few settlements are formed on the west bank of the Mississippi between the Red and Arkansas rivers. They are thinly scattered along from Red river to the mouth of the Yazoo."

Brackenridge states: "From Pointe Coupée to La Fourche, two-thirds of the banks are perfectly cleared, and from thence to New Orleans the settlements continue without interruption on both sides, and present the appearance of a continued village."

In 1828 the levees were continuous from New Orleans nearly to Red-river landing, excepting above Baton Rouge on the left bank, where the bluffs rendered them unnecessary. Above Red river they were in a very disconnected and unfinished state on the right bank as far as Napoleon. Elsewhere in the alluvial region their extent was so limited as to make it unnecessary to mention them.

In 1844 the levees had been made nearly continuous from New Orleans to Napoleon on the right bank, and many isolated

Photo by Marshall Gray, U. S. Engineers' Corps, 1927

A SAND-BOIL UNLESS ATTENDED TO IMMEDIATELY WILL CAUSE A CREVASSE

Here sand bags have been piled around the boil until the water is level with that of the surface of the river beyond the **levee.**

levees existed along the lower part of the Yazoo front. Above Napoleon, few or none had yet been attempted.

In September, 1850, a great impulse was given to the work of reclaiming the alluvial region below the mouth of the Ohio by the Federal Government, which, by an act approved September 28, 1850, granted to the several States all swamp and overflowed lands within their limits remaining unsold, in order to provide a fund to reclaim the districts liable to inundation. The States of Louisiana, Mississippi, Arkansas, and Missouri soon organized offices for the sale of the swamp lands, and appointed commissioners for the location and construction of the levees. The systems adopted were generally faulty, and have undergone many modifications.

Careful examinations and inquiries made by parties of the Delta Survey, in the autumn of 1857 and the winter of 1858, resulted in the following exhibit of the actual condition of the levees at that date. Each bank of the river will be noticed in turn.

Beginning at the head of the alluvial region, on the right bank the inlet between Cape Girardeau and Commerce bluffs was closed by a macadamized road, some 4 feet high, which crossed the low ground about 2.5 miles from the river bank. From Commerce bluffs to a sandy ridge above overflow near Dog-tooth bend, the levees were nearly completed. Thence, they were finished to a point 6 miles below Cairo. Here was a gap of 3 miles, but upon land so elevated as to be overflowed only in the highest floods. Next was a strip of high land above overflow, 3 miles in extent. Next came 8.5 miles of completed levee; next 0.5 of a mile of high land above overflow. This point is about 5 miles above Hickman. Thence to bayou St. John, there was a continuous levee. Thence to Point Pleasant, the land is entirely above overflow. Thence to the northern boundary of Arkansas, the levees were nearly completed. Between the northern boundary of Arkansas and Osceola, there were about 2.5 miles of unfinished levees. In the bend below Osceola was a gap, 1.5 miles long. Opposite Island 34 was another, 1.5 miles long. Between Islands 36 and 37 was another 2.5 miles long. At foot of Island 37 was another, 4 miles long.

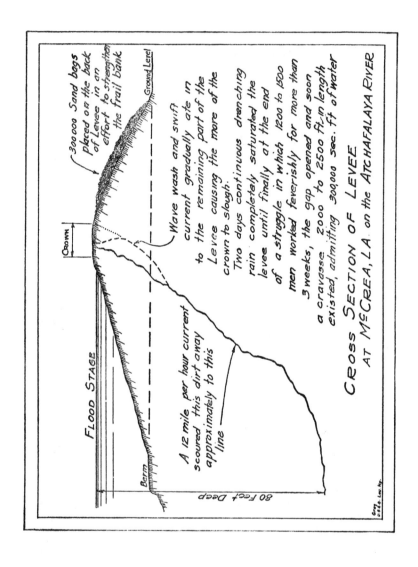

300000 Sand bags placed on the back of Levee in an effort to strengthen the frail bank

Ground Level

Crown

Wave wash and swift current gradually ate in to the remaining part of the Levee causing the more of the crown to slough.

Two days continuous drenching rain completely saturated the levee until finally at the end of a struggle in which 1200 to 1500 men worked feverishly for more than 3 weeks, the gap opened and soon a cravasse 2000 to 2500 ft. in length existed, admitting 300000 sec. ft of water

Flood Stage

Berm

A 12 mile per hour current scoured this dirt away approximately to this line

80 Feet Deep

CROSS SECTION OF LEVEE
AT McCREA, LA. on the ATCHAFALAYA RIVER

LEVEES   263

At foot of Island 39 was another, 1.5 miles long. At foot of
Island 41 was another, 0.3 of a mile long. Six miles below Memphis was another, 1.5 miles long. In Council bend, near Island
53, was another, 3 miles long. In Walnut bend, near Island 56,
was another, 1 mile long. The above list includes the whole
St. Francis bottom. By summing up the different gaps, it will
be found that they were about 25 miles in length. It would be a
great error to imagine that the bottom was securely leveed with
the exception of these breaks. The levees had all been made
since the flood of 1851, and consequently had never been
tested. They were much too low, hardly averaging 3 feet in
height, although some of them, across old bayous, were of
enormous size, as, for instance, a short one near the northern
boundary of Crittenden county, which was reported to be 40
feet high, 40 feet wide at top and 320 feet wide at bottom.
Generally their cross-section was much too small, and, upon
the whole, they were quite inadequate to effect the object for
which they were intended.

From the mouth of St. Francis river to Old Town, the
levees were complete. Between this place and Scrub-grass
bayou, there were several gaps, amounting to about 14 miles.
Thence to Napoleon there were no levees. Between Napoleon
and the high land, south of Cypress creek, there were only
about 3 miles of levee. Thence nearly to Point La Hache,
below New Orleans, the embankments were completed.

On the left bank, excepting a few unimportant private
levees, there were no artificial embankments between the mouth
of the Ohio and the southern boundary of Tennessee. The near
approach of the hills to the river, throughout the greater part
of this region, has the effect of flooding by hill drainage the
narrow belts of swamp land, and there is no immediate prospect
of any attempt to reclaim them. Whether leveed or not, they are
too trifling in extent to have any sensible influence upon the
high-water level of the Mississippi river.

The Yazoo bottom below the Mississippi State boundary
was considered to be well protected by levees. They, however,
averaged only about 4 feet in height, and, having been mainly
constructed since 1853, had never been tested by a great flood.

They were much too low and too narrow, as the flood of 1858 proved. The levee which closed the Yazoo pass was an enormous embankment across an old lake. It was 1152 feet long, and 28 feet high, with a base spread out to the width of 300 feet. About 10 miles of gaps in Coahoma and Tunica counties (between Islands 51 and 67) had been closed in the winter of 1858, and consequently the levees had not had time to settle properly before the occurrence of the high water. There was only one open gap. It was nearly opposite Helena, and had been caused by a caving bank.

Between Vicksburg and Baton Rouge, on the left bank, the levees were complete where there was any occasion for them. The hills approach so near to the river in this part of its course, that the bottom lands are limited in extent, and hence somewhat liable to injury from sudden upland drainage.

From Baton Rouge nearly to Point La Hache, the whole river-coast was leveed.

This memorandum brings the history of the levees down to the Civil War, during which no progress in construction was made, but, on the contrary, great destruction prevailed from neglect, the great flood of 1862, and cutting from malice or for military purposes on both sides of the river during extreme high water.

Immediately after the war desultory efforts were made at restoration, but progress was slow owing to bad administration and general poverty. Between 1880 and 1890, the present State levee organizations were perfected, except in the St. Francis basin, where it was considerably later.

In 1882, one of the most disastrous floods ever known devastated the entire delta, and the loss of lives, live stock and property was appalling. During that memorable year there were 282 crevasses, and the outlook was most disheartening.

President Arthur, in a special message to Congress, strongly urged the importance and duty of the National Government to protect its people and safeguard the great Mississippi river, and annually since that time the Mississippi River Commission has been untiring in its efforts to lend all assistance possible,

A REMARKABLE "CLOSE-UP" OF A CREVASSE BREAKING THROUGH THE LEVEE, MELVILLE, LOUISIANA

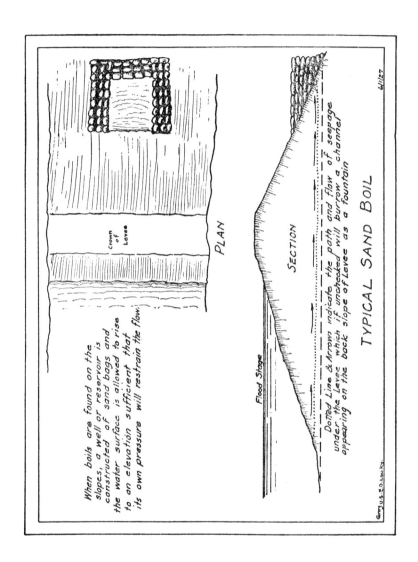

When boils are found on the slopes, a well or reservoir is constructed of sand bags and the water surface is allowed to rise to an elevation sufficient that its own pressure will restrain the flow.

PLAN

Crown of Levee

Flood Stage

SECTION

Dotted Line & Arrows indicate the path and flow of seepage under the Levee which if unchecked will burrow a channel appearing on the back slope of Levee as a fountain

TYPICAL SAND BOIL

6/1/27

Greg U.S. E.D. Louisky.

with the result that in 1903, with the highest and most prolonged high water ever known, there were seven crevasses and
but a small percentage of tilled land was overflowed.

Levees constructed entirely under the supervision of United
States engineers have shown the greatest strength.

Since the inception of levee building, most of the work done
has been by individual effort or State effort, and no united
effort under uniform rules has ever been made by the various
States at interest.

The present system of raising funds for the erection and
maintaining levees is by taxation of the land and products. In
Louisiana, the tax is on sugar, per barrel, $.10; rice, per sack,
$.05; cotton, per bale, $1.00; land per acre, $.05; in addition
to the usual *ad valorem* tax, which varies in the different
districts.

"Properly protected and cultivated, the overflow delta
area of the Mississippi alone can for years to come supply
the cotton for the world, and at the same time raise ample
corn, hay, and other farm products," said John M. Parker
in 1927.

"If this Government announces to the world that it intends to protect the delta inhabitants from the waters of the
States which pass our doors, within a few years what is
now a vast swamp will develop into most prosperous farms,
and the great wilderness now known as the Mississippi
delta will prove one of the best populated and most prosperous farming sections of this great country, and add hundreds of millions annually to its exports."

In 1879 the Mississippi River Commission was formed
and was given control of the flood situation on the Mississippi. From the very beginning, there have been two groups
in Congress: one favored outlets, spillways, reservoirs,
source-stream control in addition to levees; but another
and stronger group has stood for "levees only" and con-

finement between dikes. All this agitation during the flood of 1927 for spillways and reservoirs is nothing new. If one has the patience to look through the Congressional Record, one will find that the fight has been renewed at intervals since the very beginning. In 1914, Colonel C. McD. Townsend, of the United States engineer corps, and president of the Mississippi River Commission, made a speech in New Orleans (afterward included in the Congressional Record), in which he stated the attitude of the Mississippi River Commission and its policy as regards flood control. Inasmuch as the commission has followed its program from that time to this, it is interesting to see just exactly what that policy is. Here is Colonel Townsend's speech, and in 1927 it makes very interesting reading in view of the floods of this year—the greatest in the history of the Mississippi Valley:

It is not my purpose to appear before you as the advocate or opponent of any bill which is being considered by Congress, but I believe that the people have always a right to demand from an executive officer an account of his stewardship, and that you are entitled to a frank statement from its president of what the Mississippi River Commission has done and what it proposes to do, no matter what its bearing on proposed legislation.

During the thirty years work on the Mississippi River has been under the direction of the Mississippi River Commission there has been a marked improvement in its navigable channel. While in former years pilots complained of depths of 4½ feet on its bars, and I can personally recall a case where the river was so obstructed at President Island, below Memphis, that vessels drawing 3½ feet went aground, during the past low-water season, for a distance of over 275 miles from its mouth, there was a channel of over thirty feet depth, which was buoyed and lighted so that steamships loaded above Baton Rouge to the draft they could carry over the bar at the mouth.

For a further distance of 800 miles there was a depth of not less than nine feet, which vessels could navigate night and day, unless stopped by fog; and for the 190 miles between Cairo and St. Louis there was a channel depth of not less than seven feet, not only shown by lights and day beacons, but, wherever the channel was narrow, further marked by buoys. Moreover, the depth of seven feet existed only for a few days on two bars, which were deepened to the project depth of eight feet as soon as dredges could be towed to the locality.

It may surprise you to learn that such depths exceed those found at low water on any river in the civilized world, except the St. Lawrence system, where, due to the Great Lakes and the canalization of the channels connecting them, fourteen feet has been obtained to Lake Erie, and over twenty-one feet thence to Lake Superior and Lake Michigan.

For the far-famed Rhine, carrying a commerce of over 50,-000,000 tons, a channel depth has been adopted of three meters (less than ten feet) at mean low water on its lower reaches and of two meters between Bingen and Goar.

Moreover, the channel in the Mississippi River is being maintained at a cost not exceeding one-third of that expended per mile for maintenance by the average railroad in the United States, and affords a very cheap means of transportation.

Coal is towed from Cairo to New Orleans at the rate of 0.3 mill per ton-mile, which is the price charged for coal transported on the Great Lakes as a return cargo; cheaper rates are only offered for ocean transportation over long distances in vessels of deep draft.

But while in many parts of the United States commercial advancement is so rapid that the General Government has difficulty in developing navigation facilities as fast as they are required, along the Mississippi the utilization of the river channel has not kept pace with the increased depths obtained. The reasons are obvious. The surrounding country is sparsely settled, there being but one city of over 25,000 population between St. Louis and New Orleans, a distance of over 1100 miles, and but eight towns exceeding 5000. These communities are not

Original Line of Crown of Levee →

MEN ARE SHOWN HERE THROWING BAGS OF DIRT INTO THE RIVER IN A VAIN EFFORT TO SAVE A CAVING LEVEE

Two days later this levee "went out" endangering the lives of hundreds of workers, and flooding thousands of Louisiana's richest farming country. McCrea, Louisiana

natural manufacturing centers. There is no coal, iron ore, or other mineral wealth along its banks, and even the logs and lumber, which were formerly large items of commerce, are rapidly disappearing. The commerce derived from its banks is, therefore, largely confined to the products of agriculture, and such supplies as are necessary to sustain an agricultural community, and can never become very extensive, as the railroads will carry all farm products that are not produced in close proximity to the river. It is popular to-day to assail railroads as the foes of river transportation, but, in my judgment, the wagon road is the greater offender. With such roads as exist in the delta, a long haul of agricultural products by wagon rapidly absorbs the profits of farming, and if the railroads did not exist, there would be only a comparatively narrow strip of land along the rivers that could be profitably cultivated, and the interior of the basins would remain undeveloped.

If the Mississippi River is ever to become a great transportation route, other sources than those at present existing along its banks must create its commerce.

Over 100,000,000 tons of freight annually passes through Pittsburgh, much of which is of a character which seeks cheap water transportation. The Ohio Valley is teeming with factories whose products naturally would move down a river. The flour of Minneapolis and the grain of the Northwest are demanding cheaper transportation; and it is from these sources that we must seek the commerce that will justify a further development of the main stream.

It is folly to expend hundreds of millions of dollars in creating a deep channel in the lower Mississippi River so long as boats navigating the tributaries cannot utilize existing depths. During the past low-water season there were few tributaries of the river which had a navigable depth of four feet, and its commerce was practically suspended, not for lack of depth in its channel, but because there was no source from which freight could be derived.

If a 24-foot waterway existed from St. Louis to the Gulf,

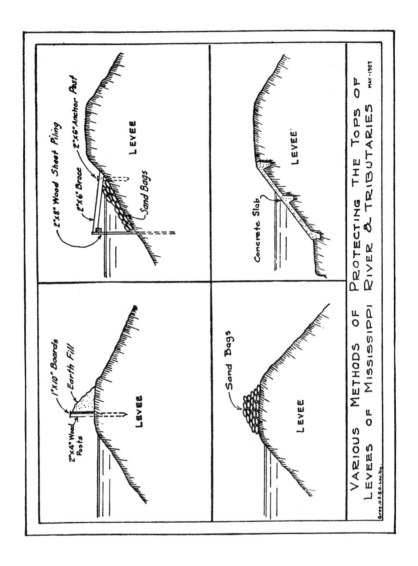

VARIOUS METHODS OF PROTECTING THE TOPS OF
LEVEES OF MISSISSIPPI RIVER & TRIBUTARIES   MAY 1927

the entire commerce of the city of St. Louis that is at present seeking water transportation could be carried in a single large lake freighter.

We are maintaining a sufficient depth of channel for the existing navigation, and the problem of the Mississippi River which demands immediate attention is one of flood protection.

When the Mississippi River Commission assumed charge of the river, a flood having a discharge of 1,100,000 second-feet created disaster throughout the entire delta, but there has been constructed a levee line which can now successfully restrain a flood of 1,750,000 second-feet at the head of the levee system, and one of over 1,400,000 second-feet at New Orleans.

The maximum discharge of the floods of 1912 and 1913 was about 2,000,000 second-feet. A simple, direct solution of the problem is to increase the size of the levees until they can safely pass 250,000 second-feet more than they do at present. The estimated cost of such an enlargement of the levee system is about $60,000,000, less than $4 for every acre of land protected. When levees of these dimensions are constructed, we cannot afford to permit them to be destroyed, and it will therefore be necessary to protect the river banks wherever caving threatens their destruction. For this purpose an appropriation of from $2,000,000 to $4,000,000 annually will be necessary. The revetment of banks will, however, react on the river channel, tending to prevent the immense deposits which are now formed from the material which is precipitated into it as its banks cave, and will thus gradually prepare the river for increased depths, should they be required as the population increases or commerce develops. This solution involves no new theories of river hydraulics, and has the advantage that it has been thoroughly tested on foreign streams and has been successful.

But Job's comforter appears and bemoans the fact that a levee that was built to resist a discharge of 1,500,000 second-feet is overtopped when a flood of 2,000,000 occurs. This is to him ample proof that a levee system is a failure, and that further investigation is necessary so that the subject can be treated in a scientific manner.

I have at other times pointed out the difficulties which surround the controlling of the floods of the Mississippi River by methods other than by building levees, and have summarized them as follows:

1. *Reforestation.* While forests may have some influence on a river during mid-stages, they produce little effect either during extreme floods or extreme low water. It takes too long a time for trees to grow and the humus to form under them for reforestation to be a practical solution of flood prevention in the Mississippi basin. It would also require the abandonment of too much land needed for agricultural purposes.

2. *Reservoirs.* In a mountainous country, where short high dams can create reservoirs of great depth and volume, or in a comparatively level country, where low dams can form lakes of large area, it may be practicable to control floods by means of reservoirs. There is but a comparatively small section of the Mississippi basin that fulfils either of these conditions, and in such areas the rainfall is generally light. The rolling country which forms the greater part of the Mississippi Valley, and from which the water that produces its floods is derived, can be protected from floods by reservoirs only by an enormous expenditure.

3. *Cutoffs.* By cutting off the bends in a river, its length is diminished and slope increased. This would increase its discharge at a given height. This method of relief cannot be applied to the Mississippi River, as it would seriously injure its navigability during low water and increase the caving of its banks, which is now excessive. While it would afford relief in the upper portions of the section of the river thus straightened, it would increase flood heights at the lower end, benefiting one locality at the expense of another.

4. *Outlets.* Outlets, while locally reducing flood heights, have only limited application as a means of relief from Mississippi floods. They cannot be constructed above the mouth of Red River; their influence on flood heights extends only a comparatively short distance above the locality where they are constructed; there is a tendency for the river to diminish its area of cross section below them; they have to be protected

Photo by H. J. Harvey, New Orleans

THE MISSISSIPPI'S CRESCENT AT NEW ORLEANS

by levees of the same dimensions as the river itself, and there is danger, if the outlet is made sufficiently large to be of practical value, that the river may abandon its present channel and adopt that of the outlet.

5. *Diversion of flood waters into channels parallel to the main river.* The maximum flood discharge of the Mississippi River exceeds 2,000,000 second-feet, while it discharges about 1,000,-000 second-feet at a bank-full stage. A side channel which would discharge the excess flood waters would therefore require an area of cross section equal to that of the river itself at bankfull stage, and with the same characteristics as to depth and velocity.

6. *Levees.* Levees afford the only practicable means of preventing the damages which might be caused by floods in the lower Mississippi Valley. They have been successfully employed on European rivers, and are the only means of flood protection of large rivers that have been tested, or, if tested, have not failed. To restrain floods like those of 1912 and 1913 will require in the existing levee line about twice the yardage now in place.

A scientific investigation of all the problems of river hydraulics and their proper coördination may be exceedingly desirable, but to make such an investigation necessitates an accurate survey, and such surveys cost money and require considerable time for their execution. The survey of Austria cost $400 per square mile, that of Great Britain $186, and of Germany $79. The survey of the Mississippi River by the Mississippi River Commission exceeded $50 per square mile, and has been in progress over thirty years. It is none too accurate for the solution of all the problems in hydraulics which can arise on a river, and if such a survey were extended over the entire United States it would cost over $180,000,000. It is also very questionable if there are enough surveyors in the country to complete such a work in ten years.

This meeting appears to be a fitting occasion to emphasize the fact that if Congress will appropriate the requisite funds, the Mississippi River Commission can construct a levee line which will give adequate protection to the Mississippi Valley before any body of experts can collect the data necessary to even prepare an intelligent report on a scientific coördination of the hydraulic problems which arise in the rivers of the United States.

Writing in "Collier's Weekly" for July 9, 1927, Owen P. White remarks, somewhat bitterly:

"In its annual report for 1926 the Mississippi River Commission held out its hand for its yearly appropriation of $10,000,000. Coincidentally, it boldly stuck out its bemedaled chest and asserted that the Mississippi flood-control work 'is now in a condition to prevent the disastrous effect of floods.' This was just a few short months prior to the unexpected descent upon us of the greatest disaster of peace time in all our disaster-freckled history!

"Think of a commission which has had absolute control of the improvement of the Mississippi for forty-eight years and has spent more than $228,000,000 on it, knowing so little about the tragic possibilities of the situation, that it could go on record with so colossal and mistaken a boast! Yet, there it is, in black and white, embodied in the report submitted by the chief of engineers of the United States army."

Every American who has read newspapers during 1927 is familiar with the policy of the Mississippi River Commission: to build the levees higher and stronger, to cut off all natural outlets from the Mississippi, with the theory that the additional water in the main stream would dig a deeper channel and carry the flood waters more quickly to the Gulf of Mexico.

It is an interesting theory, but it does not appear to work.

"Although the cost of adopting some different plan for controlling the Mississippi may be enormous, and the blow to the pride of the commission terrible, some other plan must be adopted," Mr. White continues. "And some new set of engineers should be put in charge of it, and an end put to the army connection—maintained, it seems, for purposes of revenue only."

In conclusion, Mr. White quotes a warning made by Lyman E. Cooley before a Senate committee in 1916:

"You are going to build levees, you have been building them, and this is the proposition that you are up against: You wipe out all natural overflow regulation and constrain the entire volume to the river channel and take it as it comes. The maximum volume is greatly increased, the flood heights raised, the velocity accelerated. You have greatly increased the dynamic energy of the stream. You have not only magnified the surplus horsepower but you have also increased the speed of the application, thus multiplying the destructive powers; in other words, you have stimulated the energy, filed the teeth, and ground the claws of your tiger."

Mr. Cooley speaking in 1916 was not alone in his criticism of the Mississippi River Commission, but the commission went blandly upon its way. No doubt, those in charge of its destiny thought they were right—but the floods of 1927 have proved conclusively that "levees only" are not enough, and can never be enough.

The headquarters of the Mississippi River Commission are maintained in St. Louis. The members of the commission for the fiscal year covered by the 1926 report of the chief of engineers, United States Army, were: Colonel Charles L. Potter, corps of engineers, president; Charles H. West, civil engineer; Robert L. Faris, assistant director, United States Coast and Geodetic Survey; Colonel G. M. Hoffman, corps of engineers; Jerome O. Christie; Edward Flad, civil engineer; Colonel C. W. Kutz, corps of engineers. It will be interesting to hear what they have to say when Congress convenes. Of course, it is needless to say that the blame—if the commission is to blame—does not rest upon the present members of the Mississippi River Commission in any greater degree than it does upon all former members of the commission, for the policy has been unchanged and unchanging through the years.

WATER FROM A CREVASSE SWEEPING DOWN UPON A TOWN

Part Five

1 9 2 7

Chapter XXI

THE RISING RIVER

In the spring of 1927 the Mississippi River rose higher than ever before in its history. Before its floods were over, the river had turned the Mississippi Valley into a series of lakes, several of which could have cupped a European nation apiece without showing a rim of foreign ground. It has taught us that though we have been building levees for two hundred years, they never have been and never will be strong enough; but the knowledge cost us something like a quarter of a billion dollars and misery indescribable. Now the valley is considering what to do about it.

The public memory is short-lived; recollections of 1918 are not deterring the world from arming diligently for the next war, and the valley cannot help wondering if this flood to end floods will result in nothing but patched levees. The valley is demanding that it lead to something more than that. It is tired of living on the good-natured supposition that next time the crevasses will flood somebody else's property. The valley hasn't forgotten those terrible days in April and May when the dikes were crumbling from Illinois to Louisiana, while the river swallowed towns and farms with insatiable appetite and reached out hungrily to where New Orleans crouched in terror behind her levees. The valley wants assurance that it will not happen again.

The flood of 1927 began six months or more before it happened. Rains in August and September, 1926, filled the watersheds that ran down to the Mississippi and its tributaries. In September, little floods occurred in several small rivers that are normally at low-water mark at that time, and by mid-October a number of Middle Western streams were high, with floods along the Illinois River and in the Indiana streams tributary to the Wabash. In December the Tennessee and Cumberland rivers, both tributaries of the Ohio, went over their banks; in January the lower Ohio flooded, and the Mississippi rose to flood heights on its way through Missouri. With the rivers already high, the unprecedented rains throughout the valley in the early spring sent them higher, straining the weaker levees till the farmers in the rich alluvial lands along the river should have heard them creak. But the people of the valley had faith in their levees—pathetic faith. The levees were higher and stronger than they had ever been before. They might give way in a few isolated places where nobody lived—that was no rare occurrence—but not the mighty ramparts guarding the towns and the rich river plantations. Since the high water of 1922 there had been unceasing work on those levees, till by now they were vast walls of defense, constantly watched lest treacherous spots appear. The water was always high in the spring; with the river laden with melted snows from the north, how could it be otherwise? If it reached too near the top of the levee, sandbags were ready for capping. To be sure, the river was high, but it could not break our levee. Somebody else's levee, perhaps . . . but then it was somebody else's business to make his levee stronger. But certainly not our levee.

There had been 308 crevasses in the Mississippi dikes since 1882. That sounds ominous to those who do not know the river. But the residents of the valley would have explained to you, with the pleasant patience of old residents

FRANTIC WORK TO STOP A SAND-BOIL WHICH THREATENS TO WIPE OUT THE
RAILROAD EMBANKMENT

showing the sights to tourists, that 268 of these had come before 1900, and that since the flood of 1912 there had been but a bare dozen. Most of these had been breaks in unimportant sections and were quickly closed and forgotten. The Poydras crevasse of 1922 was the only one anybody remembered, except the weather bureau employees and the members of the levee boards, and that only because it came at a time when New Orleans was believed to be in danger and' the crevasse loosed the river on the plantations below.

The whole story of the levees seems strange to one not familiar with them. The gauge, which reads a certain number of feet "Cairo datum," is simply an arbitrary standard that means nothing unless one has lived under the levee and has seen the river heights; for instance, when the gauge reads forty-seven at Vicksburg, there is no danger, while New Orleans would be frightened if the gauge there read twenty-two. Levees in New Orleans—or, rather, around New Orleans, for they circle the city on three sides, the streets extending to where the levees begin—are from twenty-three to twenty-five feet high. The normal depth of the river is said to be about 125 feet at Carrollton Avenue, the upper border of the city, and 200 feet at Canal Street, near the lower end.

There was talk of high water in New Orleans in March, but nobody was expecting the flood that devastated the valley and threatened to make New Orleans another Atlantis. Planters in south Louisiana remarked that the river was high, glanced complacently toward their levees, and went on hoeing their bean-patches. Louisiana and Mississippi did have excellent levees, gigantic earthen ramparts enclosing their tawny, lazy-looking river on either side; they were stronger than ever, and they could have withstood the floods of the past—any flood except the one that crashed upon them. The valley residents do not trifle with the river. When they say a levee is strong, it is strong. They know that their river, indolent as it looks gliding along between opulent plantations and jungle-tangled bayous, can behave like a mad giant when it goes on a rampage, and they take care that it shall be kept where it belongs.

The river is always very evident to the valley dwellers. The farmer has only to lift his head to see the levee, and in New Orleans a short ride to any of the three leveed sides of the city ends only when the street jams into the embankment. A ride to the fourth side ends at Lake Pontchartrain. In the city a favorite form of entertainment is a moonlight party on the levee. These are usually held on the Carrollton levee, just behind one of the most beautiful of the uptown residential avenues, and they are romantic parties. The boys and girls sit in pairs or in little groups on the thick grass of the levee crest, while the yellow tropic moon climbs out of the palms and throws flakes of light over the water. The valley residents are fond of their river, but they also feel for it a deep respect.

It was a wet spring. From Cairo, Illinois, where the Mississippi levees start, to New Orleans, the valley was full of snow in the north and rain in the south. In New Orleans, 11.16 inches of rain fell during February, exceeding the average February rainfall over a period of thirty-four years by nearly seven inches, the average being 4.4. The river gauge at Carrollton registered eighteen feet, Cairo datum, for several weeks, dropping to 17.9 feet March 9.

New Orleans lies in a semicircular bend of the river, which curls down to the Gulf in a series of similar bends, the crookedest long river in the world. It flows due south past Carrollton Avenue, where the official river gauge is situated, then turns east, then gives another twist, so that at the lower end of the city, as it passes the Canal Street dock, it flows due north. When it has journeyed north for a few miles it bends again, going southeast this time, and makes its way through the parishes of St. Bernard and Plaquemines. This writhing of the river has much to do with the difficulty of making it behave, as men count good behavior, for it has frequently been known to cut across a curve or make a new one in an unexpected place, especially in the days when its levees were easily conquered.

Toward the middle of March several cloudbursts in quick succession in the lower valley added to the burden of waters and met the deluge from the north with streams already swollen. A sudden downpour in north and central Louisiana March 12 crippled train service and highway traffic around the town of Alexandria and drove dozens of small streams over their banks. All the highways in Lincoln parish were reported under water for several hours. News of rains causing tied-up traffic was sent down from Winfield, Monroe, and several smaller north Louisiana towns that day. Similar cloudbursts prefaced short-lived floods in Alabama, Tennessee, Mississippi, and Arkansas.

A newspaper dispatch from Jackson, Mississippi, March 17, reported that the levee protecting the town of Darling, in Quitman county, was to be patroled by National Guard troops, as the river was higher than it had been for ten years past, and rumors were stirring that a scheme had been laid for dynamiting the levee. On March 20 two high school boys of Kansas City were drowned in the flooded Davis Creek near Sweet Springs, Missouri. The creek, ordinarily hardly more than a brook, had become a raging river following the downpours of several days before. Still, there was almost no flood apprehension among the general public in New Orleans and other cities near the Gulf. There were

a few professional pessimists who made dire prophecies,
but they got metaphorical cabbages pitched at them and the
show went on. Flood? Flood in south Louisiana? Idiotic.
Look at our levees!

But by the end of March the pessimists had several excuses for saying "I told you so"—not that anybody was
listening, but they could say it to one another. An appeal
for tents for twenty-six families of Tarbet, Mississippi,
made homeless by the river overflow, was made March 24
by Congressman Percy E. Quin. On the same day the
Louisiana state board of engineers announced that in view
of predicted flood levels, no permits for blasting would be
issued to seismograph oil operators in any of the organized
levee districts.

A special meeting of the board of Mississippi levee commissioners was held in Greenville, Mississippi, March 23,
to discuss preparations for meeting the flood in case the
Mississippi should become dangerous. (The river later
spilled over into Greenville with such force that the town
was nearly swept away; but for the present, Greenville
was high and dry and sorry for its drenched neighbors.)
The same day a call for five hundred tents to shelter refugees
from the flooded river bottoms around Helena, Arkansas,
was received by the Arkansas National Guard stationed at
Little Rock. A mild flood warning was issued in New
Orleans the next day—on page 34 of the paper!—"Dr.
I. M. Cline, meteorologist of the weather bureau, Wednesday issued a flood warning covering the Atchafalaya and
the Mississippi rivers from Natchez southward, predicting
almost record stages by the latter part of April." ("The
New Orleans Times-Picayune," March 24.)

By this time floods formed a good dinner-table topic in
New Orleans. Stories of the floods of 1912 and 1922, both

Photo by Marshall Gray, U. S. Engineers' Corps, 1927

NEGRO LABORERS FILLING SAND-BAGS ON THE LEVEE TOP

of which had caused considerable damage upstate, were recounted for the benefit of new residents. It would be pretty serious for the planters if the levees in upper Louisiana should break, it was agreed, though, of course, that was hardly to be expected; they were a good deal stronger than they had been in 1922.

"But how about New Orleans?" a resident of one year would suggest timidly.

New Orleans? Who had ever heard of the levees breaking at New Orleans since the beginning of modern levee-building? The levees were twenty-five feet high and more than a hundred feet thick at the bottom. Nobody was really troubled about Louisiana—just look at our levees! (A month later the river would be smirking, "Yes—just look at them!")

Then, March 29, the levee broke at Laconia Circle, Arkansas, and the water surged over the alluvial farm lands, sending two thousand persons fleeing before it. "Twelve thousand three hundred and fifty acres of fertile Arkansas land, some of it in cultivation, was today being gradually covered by waters from the Mississippi River, the result of a break in the levee at Laconia Circle," said a newspaper dispatch sent by the Associated Press from Memphis March 30. "The crevasse was gradually widening today, while a fifty-one foot stage on the Mississippi River poured water on the alluvial soil. About two thousand persons, in the main negro tenant farmers and their hands, were forced to flee their homes when the break became inevitable. The area enclosed in the Laconia Circle covers fourteen square miles." Farmers who lived in Arkansas and along the northern edges of Mississippi and Louisiana began to move their live-stock to higher ground.

Though the dikes along the main line of the Mississippi

were still intact, those guarding the tributary streams were crumbling here and there, and warnings were issued urging care in navigation. The first of April Major J. H. C. Lee, of the United States engineers, issued letters of warning to all navigation companies, masters, and pilots along the river, advising them to navigate their vessels with extreme caution while the river was at flood stage.

Torrential rains fell in Kansas, Missouri, and Oklahoma the first week in April, causing floods in Oklahoma and Kansas April 8, which took the lives of eleven persons and inundated several hundreds of homes. Several streams in southeast Kansas rose to the highest stages on record following the rains.

Still, however, the main line levee between Cairo and New Orleans showed no sign of weakening. The press dispatches from cities along the Mississippi itself were encouraging. "Despite local rains, levee conditions along the twisting length of the Mississippi River from Cairo, Illinois, to the mouth of the Arkansas and White rivers below Helena appeared good late today," said an Associated Press dispatch of April 8, "and government engineers believed the great dikes were prepared to stand the strain of the tremendous weight of waters moving southward." Other optimistic reports came that day from Natchez, Vicksburg, and other cities along the levee line. Apparently, there was very little suspicion that in a few days more the Mississippi would go mad and fling famine and destruction across the valley.

"Vigilance and confidence prevailed tonight along the wide and turbulent course of the Mississippi River from Cairo, Illinois, to New Orleans, and river engineers predicted that the government levees would continue to hold in check all the water in sight," said an Associated Press dispatch from Memphis April 9. "Acute distress at Columbus,

Kentucky, where a private dike defends the town against the floods, was somewhat relieved during the day as the water there, far above the level of the town and almost at the top of the embankment, began to fall slowly."

During the next few days a realization of the power of the Mississippi began to seep into the lower valley, like water through a crawfish hole in the levee. There was very little real apprehension, but there was a ruffle of uneasiness here and there, and questions that refused to be choked. But everywhere the burden of river-conversations was the classic recurrence, "Floods here? Hardly. Look at the levees!"

Engineers looked at the levees and were confident. "The New Orleans Times-Picayune" of April 14 reassured its readers:

"All levees above New Orleans were found to be in good condition, and except for repairs occasioned by washing from the wake of vessels and wind waves, little need be done fully to protect against flood danger from the Mississippi River high water, according to Major W. H. Holcombe, army engineer in charge of the Fourth Mississippi River District, upon his return from an inspection of the levees above New Orleans. Although the Carrollton gauge registered a stage of 19.6 feet Wednesday and the river continued its slow rise, Major Holcombe remained confident that the crest of the spring rise would be passed without difficulty." In the same issue the "Times-Picayune" carried dispatches from Natchez and Memphis, forecasting high water for both cities. On April 13 Governor Dennis Murphree of Mississippi had called on the people of the State to contribute to the relief of the four thousand persons affected by the floods in the lowlands of the upper valley. He expressed some apprehension for the safety of the delta when backwaters from the river should flow in. Governor Murphree had been less than a month in office, having taken the official oath March 21, upon the death of Governor Henry L. Whitfield. The governor of Louisiana, O. H. Simpson, had also risen recently to his office from that of lieutenant-governor, the death of Governor Fuqua having occurred the previous October.

Still, the south valley waited, secure behind its dikes. The flood was annoying, of course; when one saw workmen patrolling the levees one was reminded that the river was high and the flood crest was tearing downstream at a great rate; but again one reminded one's self that no flood the Mississippi had ever brought down would be strong enough to crash through such mighty walls as these. The levees guarding the tributary streams in the north were weaker, of course—they might be expected to break occasionally at flood seasons. So the south valley went about its business.

But on the sixteenth of April there flashed along the wires a paragraph that made even the optimists of the south pucker their foreheads as they read the morning papers, and scold the cook because there was an unpleasant taste to the scrambled eggs. The main line levee of the Mississippi had broken.

"The first break in the main line levee of the Mississippi River occurred near Doreno, Mississippi county, Missouri, early today, flooding a stretch of land for forty miles, according to reports here today," said an Associated Press dispatch from Memphis. "Thousands of acres of lowlands in the vicinity were under water. Water lapping over the top of the levee as a result of a heavy wind washed out a gap ninety feet wide, and as the waters rushed through it widened greatly, reports said. Doreno, across the river from Hickman, Kentucky, where floods made more than eight hundred persons homeless yesterday, was apprehensive; and

Photo by courtesy of American Red Cross

REFUGEES, WITH ALL THEIR WORLDLY GOODS PILED AROUND THEM, WAITING TO BE TAKEN ABOARD A RESCUE BOAT

New Madrid, near where St. John's Bayou flows into the Mississippi, was anticipating the worst flood in its history."

It was a rather bad break, though no worse than breaks that had come in the tributary river levees, but it was made doubly terrifying by its being on the main river. Those main river levees were levees to command the respect of anybody.

But now the river is rushing southward, tearing down between quivering dikes. Is the water stronger than those walls that were reared with such confidence? Nobody can answer now, on the sixteenth of April. But the main line levee has begun to topple. The river has asserted itself. The preliminary overflows are over, ladies and gentlemen, and now begins the Biggest Flood on Earth. Move out, lest you get splashed.

Chapter XXII

THE FLOOD SWEEPS ON

WHILE the river was bursting its levees as a fat man bursts his last year's coat, the calendar came to April 15, Good Friday, one of the biggest holidays of the year in New Orleans. Every business in town that can do so closes up on Good Friday, and houses that do not close grant their employees time to go to church.

But the day dawned black, and by mid-morning the heaviest rain in the history of the weather bureau was pouring into the city. It rained and rained—more than fourteen inches that day. Lightning struck the sewerage pumping-plant—without which a downpour would fill up New Orleans as the faucet fills up the kitchen sink—and one of the pumps was put out of commission. The pumping system was further demoralized by the absence of half the workmen, who had been granted the holiday in which to burn candles. By noon streets in the lower sections of town were brimful of water and were spilling it over the sidewalks; by three o'clock residents found water climbing over their front lawns; by five it was crawling up the front steps; and by nightfall miles of city streets were under from eight inches to three feet of water, automobiles were stalled in rivers up to the tops of the wheels, and street-car traffic was paralyzed, with scores of cars halted half way downtown, unable to go forward or back.

"Many thousands of persons homeward-bound found

themselves marooned on street corners of the business section when many car-lines went out of commission because of the inability of cars to traverse water-covered streets," reported the "Times-Picayune" the next morning. "The accumulated rainwater in many areas was from one to two feet deep. In the South Claiborne Avenue section from Napoleon Avenue to Broadway the water was reported to be even deeper. * * * Virtually all of the streets between St. Charles Avenue and the river were inundated, including the riverside roadway of St. Charles Avenue. Uptown, down and back of town were hundreds of stalled automobiles, in many of which were persons who in preference to sitting in the cars all night waded knee deep to their homes. At midnight both roadways of St. Charles Avenue became flooded. A count later revealed one hundred and twenty-six automobiles stalled in the avenue. * * * The special delivery service of the post office was partly put out of commission early in the night when messengers found it impossible for their motorcycles to travel the inundated area."

Came the dawn. The sun shone gleefully over yesterday's waters and grinned at the stalled automobiles. The streets in the low section between St. Charles and Claiborne avenues had become canals, where a brisk rowboat traffic was being carried on. Patients were brought to the Baptist hospital on Napoleon Avenue in rowboats and unloaded upon stretchers at the door. Two or three husky negroes quit their jobs and made a month's wages that day lifting men to their shoulders and carrying them across the inundated streets. Hundreds of workers got an extension of the Good Friday holiday, when they telephoned their offices that water was two feet deep around their homes and that they had rather get fired than wade through it and get pneumonia. Streets where the water had subsided were crowded with men and women walking to work, unable to ride because their automobiles were stuck in mud up to the axles and the cartracks were still submerged. Telephone service was interfered with, not because of serious damage to the lines, but because scores of operators were marooned in their homes and unable to reach the exchanges.

"In the uptown-rear section conditions were said by the sewerage and water board to be most serious," said "The New Orleans States" Saturday afternoon. "Residents of these sections said that in many instances the water had crept inside their houses, forcing them to remain on the second floor or risk collision with floating furniture." A negro mammy living on Clara Street, near Claiborne Avenue, one of the lowest sections of town, woke in the gray dawn of Saturday to find water up to the mattress of her bed, while her baby, who had been put to bed on a low crib, was sleeping blissfully on its own mattress, which the water had lifted from the crib and had carried to the other end of the room.

"Indignant property-owners became clamant," according to Charles P. Jones, a New Orleans newspaper man, in an article in "The New York World" May 8. "Hostility was directed at the sewerage and water board, a branch of the city government, and at the city government itself. There were excuses, denials, recriminations. The buck was passed so fast that friction scorched it. Indignant housewives looked at their pianos standing in six inches of water and shrieked to high heaven for scalps. There weren't any scalps available, so the victims settled down to air their grievances. They told everybody."

It was that Good Friday rain that started the flood-scare in New Orleans. Orleanians looked out of their windows Friday night and saw the rain still plunging down through

REFUGEES CROWDED LIKE CATTLE ON STEAMBOAT

TWENTY MILES TO THE NEAREST DRY LAND

the darkness as if there were fourteen inches more hurrying to fall into the bubbling canals that were streets yesterday. They remembered their mud-dressed autos and their runnel-slashed gardens, and they swore at everything, from the pumping system to the family cat. Then, suddenly, the city recalled that just as much rain had fallen into the river as had fallen around it, and the afternoon papers were reporting similar cloudbursts that day throughout the south end of the valley. People began to say to each other: "These rains put more pressure on the levee. And if one day's rain can do this to the city, what on earth would a crack in the levee do?"

While New Orleans was drenched with the rain of Good Friday, and while Orleanians were knitting their brows over the troublesome prospects the rain had suggested, the misfortunes up the river were deepening into tragedy. Red Cross camps crowded with farmers' families who had fled before the first breaks woke to a hopeless Easter. The Scott levee in Pulaski County, Arkansas, twenty miles southeast of Little Rock, broke April 18, flooding fifteen thousand acres of plantation country. Water from the Arkansas River swept across North Little Rock, and into low-lying sections of Little Rock itself. A hundred thousand acres were under water within a 250-mile radius of Pine Bluff, Arkansas, and Red Cross workers at St. Louis estimated that there were 35,000 persons homeless between Cairo and New Orleans.

Fear mounting to panic ran along the towns and farms under the levees. The river was wildly earnest now, tearing relentlessly from the north, and men and women looked in terror to the dikes that a week ago had seemed so strong. Levees along the lower river were patrolled with frenzied vigilance. Labor was asked for, then demanded, then conscripted. Andrew H. Gay, president of the Atchafalaya basin levee board, outlined the plan of patrolling the levees in his district in "The Baton Rouge States-Times" April 18:

The one hundred and twenty-two miles of levees in this district from Red River Landing to Donaldsonville on the west side have been divided into sections of thirty miles, each in charge of an inspector. Each thirty miles is divided into three ten-mile sections, with a foreman and necessary labor to drain and do any other work necessary under the direction of the inspector. Each foreman is required to go over the levee in his section constantly and report to the general inspector over him as frequently as necessary. The general inspector covers his thirty miles constantly by automobile. The section foreman is not permitted to travel by automobile, but must be on foot or horse. All inspectors are under the chief inspector, and must report to the office of the board at Port Allen once a day, or by phone if anything demands attention.

As the water rose along the southern levees emergency calls for workmen met a varied response. Any healthy man who appeared within shouting distance of the levees got a job at two dollars a day, whether he wanted it or not, unless he could show evidence that he was already employed. Policemen scattered through the towns to round up more workmen, and many a cheerful negro who had been getting a tolerable livelihood from his Mandy's talent for taking in washing found himself confronted by an officer of the law who presented him with a man-size job demanding immediate attention.

Hoboes ready to start north for the summer took the chance to pick up a few extra dollars for the trip, and so augmented the scarecrow clan. But all the workmen were soon at it in dead earnest. It was alarmingly obvious that they had to be. It was not only that inspectors were on hand to see to it that they earned their two dollars a day. They saw that unless they worked, there was no telling what might happen to the levee. Their own lives were not charmed, they knew, and neither were the lives of the wives and children behind the levee, whose husbands and fathers were working with the laborers to keep their ramparts tight.

By April 22, twenty thousand men were working on the levees between New Orleans and Baton Rouge. There were tons of sandbags ready, and the levee between the two cities must be capped from one to three feet higher along its entire length before the crest of the flood arrived. The river was swelling steadily between New Orleans and Vicksburg, and the uneasiness in New Orleans was growing into consternation. The overflows and breaks above, contrary to belief outside the flood-threatened area, were not aiding New Orleans, for it was making the time of the arrival of the flood crest harder to prophesy, and the consensus among engineers was that the water loosed to run wild over the country would flow back into the main stream when it had done all the damage it could. If this backwater should arrive when the river was nearing its height at New Orleans, as there was a lively chance that it would, the strain on the levees would be terrific.

"Flood waters that swept onward with irresistible force drew nearer today as New Orleans lost some of its assurance," said an Associated Press dispatch April 22. "From up the river came reports that the Father of Waters had been victorious in spots where his strength had been given preliminary tests. In New Orleans itself a thousand men were at work placing a frail-looking line of sandbags to hold back the deluge pouring down from the north."

Levees in north Louisiana and Mississippi were crumbling fast by this time. The efforts of hundreds of workmen and voluntary assistance by students of Louisiana State University at Baton Rouge were unavailing in a desperate attempt to save the dike near Greenville, Mississippi, which broke April 21 at Stops Landing, about fourteen miles north of town. Telephone officials in the neighborhood of the break supplied their employees with stoves, groceries, and boats, urging them to stay on the job and keep the lines open. The water poured through the break upon the Mississippi delta, threatening a quarter of a million acres of the richest farm land in the world and sending thousands of persons scattering in terror over the State to the homes of friends or to the hastily set up refugee camps on the edges of the flooded districts. Adjutant-General Curtis T. Green "immediately ordered a refugee camp to be established within the city of Greenville, which, although in the path of the waters, is protected by a protection-levee itself, and forces began work at once to build up this levee around the city. Adjutant-General Green estimated that eight thousand refugees could be cared for in the city and provided with food and shelter." (Associated Press dispatch from Jackson, Mississippi, April 21.) The same dispatch continues: "The Stops Landing crevasse is the second major break in the main line of the Mississippi levee system, the first occurring Saturday at Doreno, Missouri. From Doreno the waters are flowing southward, swelling the inundation of New Madrid, Missouri, and moving down to cover millions of acres in the St. Francis River basin of Arkansas. * * * At Clarendon, Arkansas, the White River still rode through the streets in tragic triumph today, while inhabitants crouched in upper floors or on tops of buildings. * * *

"Death, famine, pestilence, and war between men and the elements rode the ever-increasing tide of the Father of Waters gulfward today in the greatest flood in the history of the Mississippi Valley. Thousands of square miles of fertile soil lay inundated. Damage to property had already

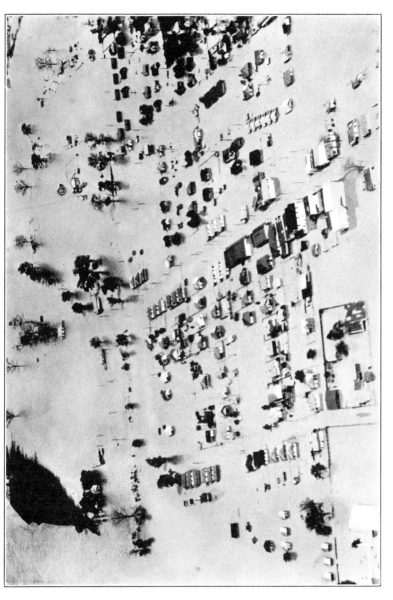

A PART OF LITTLE ROCK DURING THE FLOOD OF 1927

reached an unestimated figure in the millions of dollars. Thousands of persons, driven from their homes by the angry waters, were suffering for food, clothing, and shelter, while others who had braved the flood to stay in their homes had perished.

"The four horsemen rode on, doomed to be subdued, but wreaking a mighty wrath on a suffering people. The end was not yet in sight.

"Seven States, Arkansas, Missouri, Illinois, Kentucky, Mississippi, and Louisiana, were battling valiantly against the encroachments of the river, which gives them a boundary each. Texas was receiving a quantity of water from western tributaries. Diseases due to conditions in camps have broken out among refugees at Wynne and Parkin, Arkansas. Nearly six hundred cases of measles, mumps, and whooping-cough have been reported there. Medical officers of the Arkansas National Guard were rushed to the stricken encampments yesterday."

Along with the human victims of the flood, there were other less important but no less frantic refugees. "Bears and snakes have come out of the cache river bottoms to refuge here with hundreds of humans whose homes are under water," said an Associated Press wire from Cotton Plant, Arkansas, April 21. "The bears are so hungry and exhausted from swimming through the turbulent floods that they have lost most of their fear of people, who are feeding them from their scant store of food. The snakes are resting in trees. There are many reports of snakes dropping in an apparent attempt to land on vehicles or persons."

Gigantic rescue organizations shrunk to Liliputian size before the enormity of the disaster. Before the millions of ruined acres and the thousands of sick and starving human beings, rescue-workers felt as if they had come out with hardly enough equipment to fight a tempest in a goldfish bowl. But they kept at it, and the heroism of the workers in the Red Cross, the Salvation Army, the government rescue corps, and the volunteer brigades is and will remain the most inspiring chapter in the chronicle of the Mississippi rampage.

The Indians of the delta fought for the white men as bitterly as their fathers had fought against them two hundred years ago. It was the Indians who, when the waters were pouring over the lowlands, remembered the burial mounds of their ancestors, and the hills of the aborigines became places of refuge for the civilized white men when everything else was submerged. Snakes crawled up from the flood edges to take a chance of safety on the burial mounds, and the refugees had no heart to kill them—especially as the snakes apparently intended no damage to their human co-sufferers. Half-starved animals crawled up from the woods and farms, and men and women fed them from the scraps of food they had been hoarding. Many a sleek pig who is nibbling acorns in the Mississippi farmyards today owes his being alive to the generosity of some human being who saw him only as another flood sufferer squealing for food. Two hundred deer were corraled on the levee just south of Helena, Arkansas, by game authorities, who feared the total extinction of the wild life of the valley. The Conservation Commission, to prevent the shooting of muskrats and other fur-bearing animals, ordered confiscation of all fur pelts with shot-holes that should be offered for sale.

The levees fell to pieces faster than the wires could twang the news to the papers. Men saw marvels of modern engineering topple like toothpick fortresses, and they realized again, what they had been about to forget, that the river was no less than it had been in pre-levee days, but remained in spite of human efforts the same muddy miracle it was when de Soto found it. They did not wonder that the Indians prayed to the Mississippi. They knew why the Nile and the Tiber had been gods. There is something terrible and yet maliciously gleeful about the river when it breaks its man-made manacles, something human with a kind of Frankenstein-humanness.

Something of this was expressed by "The New York World," in an editorial published April 20, while the flood was rising to its climax:

In spite of all efforts, men have never succeeded in reducing the Mississippi River. That stream, by reason of its great size, has set at naught all efforts to conquer it. By reason of its great size? By reason of something else, too. There is something sinister about the Mississippi; it almost seems alive, on account of the devilish schemes it thinks up to circumvent man. Did somebody have the idea that the thing to do was to straighten the channel, then it rushed along at such speed as to tear out all redoubts that have been erected. Did somebody else have the idea that erosion must be stopped at a certain bend, then it deposited fifteen feet of silt on his jetty and ate for itself a channel somewhere else. As a result, there developed the policy of "persuading" rather than forcing it to stay within bounds. From that phrase can be deduced the extent to which it has harassed the engineers. And after it has been persuaded by all sorts of gigantic embankments, then, by the sheer power that it possesses, it gives a shake and bursts its bounds again.

Now, in all the lower river States, we see the same old drama again. There are, according to the dispatches, a dozen people dead and twenty-five thousand homeless as a result of the present flood. Will we ever get the best of this river? That remains to be seen. But we have fought it for two centuries now, and the score is all its way so far.

Thus an Eastern newspaper views the river, and it has as yet only begun its ghastly carnival. Meanwhile, in the

Mississippi Valley, there are thousands of refugees huddled on the levees, little boys clinging to their dogs and little girls to their dolls, and mothers wrapping their babies in mud-caked aprons to keep off the night wind from the river. There are thousands of others gathered in the tents of the improvised Red Cross camps, thanking heaven for dry blankets and food. And the river goes on its way toward the Gulf, cracking its walls that it may throw itself still farther over the lowlands; while all day men work piling up sandbags on the levees not yet reached by the flood crest; and all night guards prowl along the river-walls lest a tricky spade or stick of dynamite make a hole for a terrified farmer who had prayed that the water be dumped somewhere else than on his plantation, and who is now helping Providence answer his prayer. The beleaguered city of New Orleans is reinforcing its vast levees and is beginning to send its wives and children for a spring vacation on the other side of Lake Pontchartrain. New Orleans is sober. The Mardi Gras city, "the city that care forgot," as it loves to call itself, is for once passionately earnest.

TWO VIEWS OF GREENVILLE, MISSISSIPPI, MAY 27, 1927

THE ENTIRE CITY WAS INUNDATED WITH FLOOD WATERS

Chapter XXIII

WE are gathered together on the levee-top—white and black men, rich and poor—or, rather, yesterday we were rich and poor; tonight we are equal in misery, for the Mississippi has taken everything from us.

The old Devil river! Rightly enough do the negroes call it so. "The old Devil river, pushin' and shovin' at the levees," they say. These walls of earth, man made, erected at tremendous cost and endless labor, are built higher and higher every year in order that our homes, lying behind the levees, may be safe from the ever-rising stream. And now—all useless, all washed away.

The broken levee-top is like a long narrow island. Twenty feet wide, perhaps, and water washing on both sides—black water that extends out in all directions, mile after mile, dotted now with wreckage of our homes and covering the land endlessly.

We are tired out, hungry, wet, miserable. There are perhaps fifty of us, near the end of the levee. Ahead of us lies the crevasse . . . the water rushing through, inundating the fields and cotton land deeper under the yellow flood. Yes, yellow by day, but at this hour only a vast black torrent, with never a light anywhere. There is no moon. There are no stars tonight. A soft rain has fallen, making us, shelterless, even more miserable.

We sit upon the ground, in groups, afraid to sleep, too

301

miserable to cry, waiting, with forlorn hope, for a rescue boat.

We have been here for more than twenty-four hours, ever since the alarm came which sent us running out into the night. . . . Can it be only twenty-four hours ago? It seems eternity.

We have no water except the yellow, foul stuff that is all about us. We drink sparingly of it, grimacing, wiping our lips. There is no food.

There is no wood. We have no fire. This afternoon some one broke up a packing-case, kindled a fire, and made coffee. There was only enough for a few. The aroma made the rest of us sick with its fragrance.

Only two white men. We sit with bowed heads, leaning forward, looking out into the darkness. Near-by a group of negro men lies sleeping. A young negro woman, separated from her family, lies moaning. She is going to give birth to a baby before morning, or so the old negro women say who have gathered around her. She is having a hard time. They have tried every charm and spell they know, but nothing works.

What can you expect with the old Devil river pounding all around you, and with no help in sight?

The black woman cries. Sometimes she screams aloud. An old negro man lies near her, his head pillowed in the lap of a woman, almost equally old. The old man doesn't say anything. This afternoon we tried to talk to him, but nothing was gained by it. His mind ran back to the old days, to other floods and disasters. This one, he says, is no worse than others. The old woman, his wife, grunts and groans and holds his head:

"De ole man's mighty bad," she says. " 'E won't las' long."

The girl's moans, muffled by the rushing of the water around us, worry the old man. He mutters to himself.

I sit disconsolately, thinking of the cotton fields and the fields of young sugar-cane, lying deep under all these miles of black water. Gone, all gone. All that we of the South have labored for, hoped for, lived for.

Not myself alone. My own loss is so slight that it does not seem to matter in the general *débâcle*. But the old Devil river has done for us all, at last.

For years we have curbed it, fenced it into its channel. But now it has taken its land again, as it did in the old days, when it spread out as the Nile does, enriching the country for the coming year. We thought we were cleverer than the men who lived thousands of years ago. We would tame the old river and make our lands safe.

Ah, yes, I have heard my grandfather, an old planter, say over and over again: "We have worked always to tame the river—but the river waits and waits. Sooner or later it will take what it wants. May I not be here to see it!"

Thank God that he is not here to see it! For he would suffer to see the land laid waste by the torrents of never-ending water that pour over the fields, taking everything before the flood. It is like an old horror tale of Bible times, a plague, a judgment. But what have we of the Mississippi Valley done, save try to wrest a living from the land? For two hundred years our forefathers have lived here, planting the land, fighting the river. Here they built their homes, rough ones at first—later the large, white pillared brick houses that we call our homes today. Furniture came from France, or from "up North," to furnish them. Our fathers knew great prosperity. Then, Civil War, loss of labor—the "hard times" came. Then a sort of renaissance in the eighteen-eighties, when the Cotton Exhibition was held in New Orleans, and "King Cotton" became a slogan.

Then the boll-weevil, and high water, and labor hard to get; the negro migration north; and hard times again. I was born at the end of the Golden Age—as a child, I saw the last of the prosperity and knew the pinch of hard times. The times have been hard for plantation people ever since, for we are rooted in the old ways. We are planters rather than farmers. Other people may plant truck gardens. We plant cane or cotton—or nothing. Well, let it be nothing from now on. The old Devil river has finished us.

But who cares for my thoughts? There are other sufferers far more deserving of sympathy than men of my type. We have a sort of resignation that we call philosophy; but our simpler brothers have nothing. For them everything is lost. All they labored for is destroyed tonight.

And the negroes. Their homes are gone, they are destitute, adrift. And yet, what lessons they can teach us in taking trouble with ease. . . . "They're used to adversity," says the man at my elbow. "They don't mind."

Something else is there, though—these black men who have sung their way up from slavery, now they weather this storm which has laid the white folks low. They seem tireless. All afternoon they have been wading about in the water, salvaging things from the wreckage about us. It was the negroes who found the wood for our puny fire, now burned down to a few ashes.

It was a negro who gave me a piece of stale bread this afternoon. Never have I tasted cake half so sweet as that crumbling loaf handed me by black fingers. He sits near me now, his head hanging down on his breast. I turn to him:

"Is that a light, out yonder?"

A FRANTIC EFFORT TO SAVE A CAVING LEVEE—WITH WATER LAPPING AT THE VERY TOP

The surface of the water, here, is twenty-five feet higher than the land behind the levee

His head snaps up, he looks. "No, suh, I can't see nuttin'. . . . Yo' done fool me, boss!" he laughs.

He laughs!

How can he laugh in the face of this terrible night and the black water?

"Where are you going when we get away from here—if we get away?" I ask.

"Maybe to New Awlins! Maybe somewhere else. . . . I got to find Mattie—she's done got los' somewhere."

"Mattie?"

"Yassuh. She done gone up to de schoolhouse wid her maw and sister when me and the rest of the niggers come out to work wid Mr. Jim. Dat was fo' days ago." He paused. "Mattie's my wife," he added as an afterthought.

So he had a wife out there somewhere in the black expanse of water. Safe? Drowned? Who could tell? We had no news. We knew nothing and could only conjecture.

All around us lay the flood. No light anywhere. And always the rushing sound of water going by in its mad race toward the lower river and the Gulf. Two hundred miles or more to the south lay New Orleans under her levees. Day before yesterday—years ago—I had seen a paper . . . the water was almost at the top of the levees . . . the people of the city were "carrying on business as usual." Good, brave people, those folks in New Orleans, carrying on their business and their lives, although every man knew that the menace of the river was worse this year than ever before. And what now? To what would the city resort—with crevasses on all sides—and yet the crest of the flood somewhere "up river," where I am sitting on a levee-top with homeless negroes?

My mind runs back to the activities of yesterday. A backbreaking, heart-breaking day. In a small motorboat we plowed through the inundated section, trying to rescue some of these poor devils who clung to their homes until too late to get away.

We moved slowly among the branches of the trees, in danger of upsetting as we crossed submerged fences. In the afternoon we approached a cabin, standing to its eaves in the yellow water. On the roof a strange group was gathered. An old negro mammy, very placid, was in command of the situation. She was cooking on a wood-burning cook-stove which had been balanced in some miraculous way on the ridge-pole. The fire was fed with shingles ripped from the roof—nearly half of them gone already. A half-grown boy sat on the edge of the roof, patiently fishing. Evidently he had had luck earlier in the day, for a fish was sizzling now in the pan. A young negro woman with a baby in her arms squatted against the chimney, feeding fish to the infant. They greeted us, when we came chugging up in the motor-boat, with cries of welcome—offered us a portion of the fish, and seemed greatly relieved when we refused. No, they wouldn't come to the levee-top; they preferred to remain where they were. "De watah ain't goin' no higher, an' we's safer heah dan on de levee."

All their meager household goods were piled on the roof-top and they refused to leave them. They promised to signal us with a torch if the water rose higher, or if the house crumbled beneath them.

It was well for them that they refused to enter our boat, for not half an hour after we struck a snag and ripped a hole in its bottom. For two hours we hung, wet and shivering, in a tree, until an old negro man in a flat-bottomed row-boat picked us up and brought us to the other refugees on the levee-top. And here we have remained since.

The white man beside me is a civil engineer. He has remained near the river, studying the levees—working to build them higher, year after year. Two days ago we both joined in rescue work, as everybody else did. Tonight we were waiting to be rescued. He has said little, except to talk to the negroes, reassuring them, although he has small hope himself. Surely there will be a rescue boat along in the morning. He has said that over and over.

I fall to thinking of the greatest flood that the Mississippi has ever known: Minnesota, Iowa, Wisconsin, Illinois, Missouri, Kentucky, Tennessee, Arkansas, Mississippi, and now Louisiana—every State bordering on the great river suffering. The Mississippi Valley, a third of the United States, draining into the river which now washes around us. And all the dwellers in the lower valley, fighting year after year, against this ever-increasing terror that has now engulfed us all.

The sword of Damocles has fallen!

For we never have the river "off our mind"—those of us who live behind the levees. Every year we work and fear— and the floods come just as our crops are rising from the good black earth. We should know whereof we speak, for we have thought of little else for many years. And year by year we have seen the river rising higher, always higher than the levees that rise to combat its flood stage. New Orleans built its levees in the year that the city was founded by Bienville in 1718. But the new levee is inadequate today as the old was inadequate then. Now, at this moment, New Orleans is facing the greatest danger in its history, with water lapping at the very top of these man-made embankments—and the crest of the flood still up the river. There were floods in 1785, 1828, 1858, 1862, 1867—every one worse than the one before. The high water of 1882 set high-water marks, and other disastrous floods occurred in 1883,

1897, 1912, 1913, 1922—and now this flood of 1927, the worst in the history of the river.

And it seems that it will be worse always until some other plan than "levees only" is worked out. I speak to the civil engineer about it. He answers angrily:

"Of course! Since 1879 that fight has been waged. 'Levees only. Confinement of the river into its channel.' It can't be done, old man. Look about you now. This is the result.

"It's hard for me to talk about it calmly, when I think of the millions of dollars and hundreds of lives sacrificed to the levees—and this flood proves conclusively that levees are not enough and can never be enough.

"Look! From Cairo, Illinois, to the Gulf there are no outlets. Just confinement between dikes. Once there were thirty thousand square miles of natural reservoirs in the Mississippi. Twenty-seven thousand of these square miles have been partially reclaimed by the levee system. All this storage space for water is gone. The water must go somewhere, and it is forced into the main channel. Ever since 1879 there have been two groups considering floods on the Mississippi. One group advocated spillways; the other group advocated higher levees, cutting off all natural outlets, and forcing the water into the main channel, the theory being that additional water would dig the channel deeper.

"What folly! Look about you!

"The warning has been plain enough, but people will not understand. 'Levees only' and 'confinement' plans have proved futile now. This—our worst flood—and two natural outlets closed: Cypress Creek, an outlet into the Tensas basin below Arkansas City, and the Atchafalaya, which gave directly into the Gulf. That is, money given to erect levees has been used to partially close the natural outlet into the Atchafalaya. Formerly there were eight miles of opening

BEHIND THE LEVEE AT CAERNARVON, NEAR NEW ORLEANS, JUST
BEFORE THE LEVEE WAS BLOWN UP WITH DYNAMITE

THE SAME SPOT, TWENTY-FOUR HOURS LATER

there; now there are only three miles. And Cypress Creek is completely closed. The great volume of water is forced back into the main channel. And always more and more water—from lands swept bare of their forests, and from natural reservoirs, now reclaimed behind the levees.

"This year the levees all along the Mississippi were higher than ever before in their history. Yet they fall like paper before the flood. We can never build them high enough or strong enough, unless there are spillways and reservoirs in addition to the levees.

"Surely levees alone can never protect the lower valley from the floods of the Mississippi. It may be that this disaster will bring home the fact. God knows, I hope so!

"Think of it, old man, there are only fifty of us here on this bit of broken levee-top, and up and down the valley there are perhaps ten thousand like us, marooned. It makes me shiver to think of it.

"And every year conditions grow worse. And they will continue to grow worse until there are spillways to carry off the flood waters.

"Oh, yes, I know what you are going to say. It will be a gigantic task—as gigantic, perhaps, as the Panama Canal. But it seems to me that this is the only solution. Levees plus spillways—controlled spillways for the lower part of the lower Mississippi Valley, and levees plus source-stream control above the Yazoo River. I don't see any other way out. And it can be done. It may be that this flood will make the people of the United States see—and make Congress act."

Behind us the negro girl is screaming again. The old negro women are trying to fortify her with one of their remedies—an open pocket-knife placed under her body, "to cut de pain"; but this seems to give no relief, although it is one of the negroes' favorite superstitions. Over and over the woman cries out: "Oh, Jesus! Please, Jesus!"

And the old negro women nod, mumbling: "Gawd, help! Hab mussy!"

The big negro man at my elbow leans forward, trying to see into the darkness. "Seems to me, I heahs screams in de wind," he says.

We shiver, relapse into silence.

After a time a woman's quavering voice is heard:

> In de time o' dyin'
> Ah wan't yuh all tuh draw nigh;
> Dey's one mo' favor dat I wan' to ask,
> Come close muh dyin' eye.

And then every negro joining in the chorus, their voices rising sweet and clear above the rushing waters:

> Well! Well! He's a dyin'-bed maker!
> Well! A dyin'-bed maker!
> Well! Well! He's a dyin'-bed maker!
> Ah know He's goin' to make-up muh dyin'-bed!

The negroes are excited; they move about in the darkness. They cry and moan aloud. The big negro man leans toward me and says: "De ole man's done die."

The young black girl's screams of pain now blend with the moans for the dead man and the rushing sound of the water:

"Oh, Jesus!"

"Hab mussy!"

"Please, Jesus!"

"Gawd, help!"

There are two groups discernible in the darkness now. One group of the negroes is around the old man, who still lies with his head in the lap of the old woman, and the other group is about the young woman.

The two white men, powerless to help, lean forward, burying heads on folded arms. The sky in the east is beginning to show gray.

The black man beside me speaks again: "Ah'm worried 'bout Mattie—Ah shore wish daylight wuz heah!"

"The sun will be up before long," says the civil engineer.

Another hour drags by. As the light increases we can see an old woman crouching at the levee's edge, holding something in her arms. She dabs a rag in the muddy water. And then, in the silence, comes a thin cry, like a cat mewing.

One man is dead, but there is another life on the levee-top. We all crowd around to see the baby, lying naked in the old woman's lap. The mother, covered with sacking, lies with closed eyes.

"Hit's a fine big boy!" the old woman announces.

Immediately there is a chorus of comment:

"Great day!"

"Gawd knows!"

"What yo' goin' tuh name 'im, sister?"

The black mother opens her eyes in the dawn and smiles a twisted smile. "Ah specks Ah'm goin' tuh name 'im Refugee," she says.

There is instant agreement.

"Dat's right!"

"Sho' nuff!"

The old woman, leaning with bowed head over the body of the old man, continues to moan to herself. Above the horizon comes the broad face of the sun, round and red.

We all look about. On all sides desolation. Only a strip of levee-top, an island, on which we are gathered, and

beyond, to the left, the mighty river, roaring toward the
Gulf, its surface dotted with drifting logs and uprooted
trees. To our right are the inundated fields, with the tops
of trees visible, and in the distance the tall tower of a sugar-
house, standing clear of the flood. Wreckage is floating
about—a chicken-coop, a barrel, a broken chair from some
water-swept cabin.

But there—up the river—plainly seen in the first rays of
sunlight, is a steamboat. It is far off, but approaching. Above
it, a plume of smoke from the smokestacks rises black in the
clear air. A shout rises from the levee-top.

"Thank Gawd! De boat done come!"

Slowly it draws nearer down the river. A small steamboat, the *Daisy B*—usually in some placid bayou—now playing its part as a rescue boat. Already the decks are crowded
with other refugees, but there will be room for us. It is not
dangerous for the boat to come near us now, for the water
has stopped roaring through the crevasse ahead of us; the
water in the fields is at the same level as the water in the
river outside the levee.

A white man is in the bow. He greets us, hails the negroes
with a cry: "Well, we'll take you folks to land somewhere."

Negro men carry the body of the old man aboard. Those
already on deck roll their eyes in superstitious awe. Bad luck
for a boat to take a corpse aboard. But the bowed figure of
the old woman quiets their comment. The young negro
mother with her new baby is greeted with a shout: "Lawzee!
De flood done brought dat gal a baby! Um-Umph!"

The negro man who sat at my elbow all night goes from
group to group, asking for news of his wife: "Is yo' seen
anything of a light brown gal dey calls Mattie?" he asks.

The white man in charge of the refugees asks where she

MUSKRATS LOST THEIR FEAR OF MAN WHEN DRIVEN OUT OF THE
SWAMPS BY FLOOD WATERS

Photo by Stanley Clisby Arthur

A TRAPPER OF ST. BERNARD PARISH, LOUISIANA

Preparing a raft to house muskrats in order that the animals be not exterminated
altogether

was, and, on hearing his reply, becomes grave. He shakes his head : "No, I haven't seen her."

Then, turning to the civil engineer, he says : "How can I tell that black boy that fifteen nigger women were drowned up there at the schoolhouse? Yes, sir. The building collapsed some time yesterday. We were there this morning. There's not one of them alive."

From group to group the big negro goes, asking his question : "Yo' ain't seen Mattie nowhere, have you? A light brown gal. . . . She wuz headed fo' de schoolhouse when I las' seed her. I just got tuh find Mattie. She's done got los' somewhere."

Chapter XXIV

WHAT HAPPENED AT NEW ORLEANS

HERE is New Orleans, then, a city loved of its people as few cities are loved, fighting the rabid river. The whole town has become a camp of Cassandras, and from the Cotton Exchange to the bargain-counters run predictions of disaster. On April 21 there are ten thousand men on the Louisiana levees, working to strengthen them against the flood sweeping down from the north. The levee board assures New Orleans that six hundred and forty thousand sandbags have been procured for topping the levees in the crescent that holds the city, and Commissioner John Klorer, head of high-water precautions, announces that by the time the flood reaches the crescent the Carrollton levees will be two feet higher than ever before. Owners of river boats have been warned that, as it is imperative to avoid any extra wash against the levees, unless pilots move their vessels at a very slow rate of speed they will be prosecuted.

But if New Orleans had no literal river flood as yet, she assuredly had a metaphorical one, for she was wading waist-deep in a deluge of everything but water: fear, rumors, stories of how this and that had happened up the river, and how only the grace of God could keep it from happening in New Orleans. The river was straining at its manacles too obviously to be ignored. The thousands of persons who visited the docks every day went out to the edge where the docks are built far over the water, and between the boards they could see the river lapping but a few inches below. When they went away they were frightened in spite of their determination to be sensible. Then there were the papers, those from out of town even more frightening than those published in New Orleans.

In spite of reiterated announcements from the levee board that there was no immediate danger for New Orleans, the city was a long way from believing them. Head-lines were growing ominous. On April 22, one week after the Good Friday rain, "The New Orleans Times-Picayune" bore its first flood streamer, leaping across eight columns:

"Death Toll Mounts as Two Levees Collapse Up River.

"Rushing forward with unexpected fury, the great wall of water tearing through the break at Stops Landing lashed against the Greenville protection levee just before midnight and within a few minutes had climbed to the top, a distance of ten feet. Fire engines screamed the alarm through the city."

A few paragraphs below one read of a break near Vicksburg which had flooded two Arkansas counties and two Louisiana parishes. A dispatch from Memphis announced that Governor Murphree of Mississippi had appealed to President Coolidge for troops, to be stationed at Yazoo City, Vicksburg, and Greenwood. Another dispatch reported that water lapping over the levee at Albemarle Bend, near Jackson, Mississippi, had submerged it to a depth of ten inches, and that the levee was momentarily expected to crash. The known death toll amounted to thirty, with scores reported missing. Fifty thousand persons by this time were taking pitiful refuge in tents hurriedly pitched by the Red Cross on the rim of the flood and on the levees. Epidemics of typhoid and dysentery, the result of drinking the river water unfiltered, had appeared in the improvised camps.

Aeroplanes sent out from Red Cross centers dropped packages of smallpox vaccine and typhoid serum into the camps marooned on the levees. Disaster, pestilence, and death were stalking the delta.

"There is no reason for alarm in New Orleans," the "Times-Picayune" assured its readers April 22. Perhaps there was not. "Hundreds of false reports that levee breaks, storms, and other imaginary disasters were threatening the city were circulated in New Orleans Thursday," continued the newspaper. "Needless to say none of these was true. The 'Times-Picayune' is keeping in closest touch with river and weather conditions and is giving its readers as complete and as accurate information as possible. The 'Times-Picayune' will be glad to give information by telephone at any hour."

But it needs more than a can of oil to quiet a maelstrom. The people of the city continued to rush for each succeeding edition of the papers, and read with avid apprehension. How could they help it? Here, for instance, was the news that six hundred and forty thousand sandbags, which were to have given the city perfect protection, had been increased to six million. At the bottom of the page on which appeared the notice that there was no reason for alarm blazed the far more convincing head-lines, "Scores of Hysterical Refugees Scream in Attics of Clarendon; Four Cling to Roof as Boat Sinks." Clarendon is in Arkansas, just across the river from Louisiana. Were things like that going to happen in New Orleans?

The river had fallen four-tenths of a foot at Cairo, but it was rising along the southern banks. At Memphis it was 45.6 on April 22; at Vicksburg 55.4, at Baton Rouge 44.2, and at New Orleans 20.5, all of them dangerous readings. At a downtown ferry-landing in New Orleans the river

Photo through courtesy of Red Cross

AN OLD ACADIAN WOMAN TELLS STORIES TO A GROUP OF CHILDREN IN A MISSISSIPPI REFUGEE CAMP

was a foot above the street level, but was held back by sandbag topping.

During this week the city had but one topic of conversation. "Have you been down to the levees lately? What do
they look like along Carrollton Avenue? I drove down to
the Congress Street wharf yesterday, and the water is nearly
up to the top of the normal levee, but there is a three-feet
layer of sandbags on top and workmen are still adding to
it. Looks pretty bad to me."

Shopping was suddenly limited to necessities, and the
march of trade assumed the pace of a funeral *cortège*.
Hotels and hospitals began to close their upper floors, because there were no guests and no patients. Eighteen stores
in the city were closed by a single chain-store company. Why
buy clothes or furniture when the town might be under water
within a couple of weeks? Why begin to build houses when
the planks were likely to float away before they were nailed
into place? Why buy land for the devouring of that glutton-
ous river? Why do anything, in fact, except leave town if
you could? And if you couldn't, make daily pilgrimages to
the river's edge and watch the water seething up against the
levees. New Orleans was just plain scared, and well it might
be.

"Going down to the levees" became the great civic enterprise. All day long, especially during the lunch hour and
in the evenings, it looked as if half the cars in town were
parked along the city's river front, and the levees were so
thronged that it finally became necessary to station armed
guards in the most accessible spots to keep away visitors and
give the workmen a chance to work.

The waters were dashing madly across Arkansas and
deluging the delta. "Tales of appalling anguish are told
by people coming in from the various areas where the waters

have wandered so wantonly," reported the Associated Press correspondent at Greenville, Mississippi, April 22. "Pictures of young mothers, mired in mud, crying out to be saved from cold and starvation, with their newborn infants whimpering at this new world, clinging to their breasts, were painted by incoming refugees. Stories of men, women, and children who had climbed into tree-tops to save their lives were told in heartrending terms, punctuated by descriptions of shrieks and cries of agony from those who could climb but little higher to save themselves from destruction. A great engulfing pestilence was scourging the land."

It was at this time that President Coolidge issued an appeal for aid from the entire nation to help the seventy-five thousand persons who were already driven from their homes. The Red Cross announced a campaign to raise five million dollars for the relief of the valley.

New Orleans, with its long, winding streets, its waving palms, the dilapidated beauty of its Vieux Carré, began to assume an uncanny color. The stores and offices and banks were still running; outwardly things were too normal. To sit before an impersonal typewriter writing "Yours of the fifteenth instant—," when all the time one knew that a madcap river was whirling upon the city, became harder and harder to accomplish. One's nerves were strained, and all one wanted to do was to study the newspapers and go down to the levee. Yet "business as usual" had to go on. Nobody could say definitely whether the city was in peril, and there were of course the incurable optimists who refused to go near the levee and who laughed boisterously at the apprehensions of other people. Orleanians began to compare their plight to that of the ancients who lived in dire terror of the Chimera, knowing that it might come and then again that it might not; and they yearned for a hero who could bestride a submarine Pegasus and teach the Mississippi that its place was at home in bed and not in the homes of other people.

Hysterical parents in other States again wired their sons and daughters at Tulane and Loyola to come home. Others, whose homes were in the sections already threatened, wired: "Stay where you are. It's safer there than here." The river was tearing like mad across Mississippi; troops were guarding the refugee camps, and new detachments of Red Cross workers were hurrying to the stricken towns. Then, April 23, a black streamer flashed across the front page of the conservative "New Orleans Times-Picayune":

"FOR GOD'S SAKE, SEND US BOATS!" PLEADS MURPHREE

CRAFT NEEDED IN EVACUATION OF GREENVILLE
2000 Cling to Crumbling Levee Screaming for Aid

"For God's sake, send us all the skiffs and motorboats you can to Vicksburg," was the heartrending plea for assistance received by long distance at the "Times-Picayune" late Friday night from Governor Dennis Murphree of Mississippi. "Our immediate need is to get all the motor- and row-boats possible," said Governor Murphree, whose emotion in this hour of distress for his State was discernible in his voice.

"The Illinois Central Railroad will handle these boats and rush them to Vicksburg," he said. "We make the plea that all craft of this kind be rushed to us without delay by any persons or concerns having them.

"Tonight we are trying to get everybody out of Greenville. There is a great flooded area in eight counties from which thousands of persons must be rescued—and this rescue can be made only by boats. For God's sake send us boats!"

Below was a series of dispatches:

Greenville, Mississippi.—Rescued from death in the flood water which stretches away for scores of miles, hundreds of exhausted men, women, and children formed a human topping for the Mississippi River levee here tonight, as, wrapped in blankets, they slept on the dikes. Below them was this city, flooded by water flowing from the levee break eighteen miles to the north. Its water supply was cut off, and by nightfall boats had become the only means of transportation, as the city streets were covered with from two to five feet of water.

Helena, Arkansas.—Two thousand refugees are on a crumbling levee two and a half feet wide at Knowlton's Landing on the Mississippi River screaming for help.

Vicksburg, Mississippi.—Firebells rang a loud alarm in Vicksburg just before midnight tonight as two breaks in the sea wall admitted the Mississippi River floods.

Other dispatches reported that twenty-three babies were born in the refugee camps near Helena, April 22. One mother in a box-car on a siding gave birth to twins, while ten other women in box-cars had one baby each. Another baby was born on a barge carrying refugees out of the flooded district around Helena. The others were born in comparative luxury, in the tents of the refugee camps.

By April 23 Little Rock, Arkansas, looked like a neglected little stepbrother of Venice, with seventy-five blocks under water, its streets turned into canals, and boats being used for such transportation as was found necessary by the citizens who had not been able to leave the city, or who were staying in a desperate determination to stick to their property. Conditions in other parts of the State were described in a newspaper account the same day, appearing in "The New Orleans Item," April 23:

Pine Bluff, Ark.—Tales of men and women suffering and dying on housetops, in trees, and on levees surrounded by flood waters were brought to Pine Bluff tonight by Lieutenant Griff McSwine of the Little Rock airport and Captain Harry Wilson

Photo by Ewing, Baton Rouge, La.

PART OF THE RESCUE FLEET ANCHORED IN THE MISSISSIPPI

The scores of small boats trailing out behind are being towed upstream for use in rescue work behind the levees in flooded areas

of the National Guard, who spent the day surveying the situation for the Government from an airplane. On one housetop were fifteen people, some lying still as if dead. Others were making feeble attempts to rise, and the remainder shouted and waved for help. At another place about fifty negroes were marooned on a drainage ditch levee, while the fliers could see the levee crumbling at both ends and could hear the distress cries of the refugees.

Meanwhile, through the southern end of the valley work was going faster. Another half million sandbags was being rushed from Atlanta to be added to the six million already being piled on the lower levees. Stories that somebody was going to cut the levee to save his own land had terrified the rural districts. "Friday, thousands of men were called out for work on the levees in the lower valley, reinforcing the army of men already at work," reported the "Times-Picayune" April 23. "In addition a line of sentries has been stationed from the latest break at Stops Landing to far below New Orleans, and every foot of the levees is being patrolled night and day and all strangers are being halted."

On April 24, A. B. Broussard, a general contractor living in Baton Rouge, turned up a blue-print of proposed locks, made in 1868, on which it appeared that the government engineers in those days figured that there was no chance of the river's ever rising to more than thirty-eight feet at Baton Rouge. The blue-print was drawn up by Brigadier-General M. D. McAlister, of the United States army engineers, when a plan was on foot to connect Bayou Manchac and the Mississippi, thus making an inland waterway from Lake Pontchartrain through to Berwick Bay. When the blue-print was found by Mr. Broussard, the river was already pushing the gauge up to a reading of 45 feet, and official forecasts placed the crest to come at 48.5 feet—ten feet and six inches more than the forecasters of 1868 believed could possibly come.

The situation in New Orleans was bad. One could see the city, green and gold in the spring sunshine, with new flowers appearing in the parks and pale new fronds jutting out of the palm-trees, and yet one knew that the river was rushing down in unprecedented fury, with levees popping down the line as if they had been made of pasteboard. At first it had been hard to realize the city's danger, New Orleans was so steeped in security. Outwardly, people were buying and selling, marrying and giving in marriage; it had seemed impossible that a few miles above, an ever-rising river was tearing upon the city. But now New Orleans had no doubt about its danger.

"New Orleans today began to realize how serious the flood menace was," said an Associated Press dispatch Tuesday, April 26. "The assurance that the flood could not reach the city has disappeared and anxiety has taken its place. Every unusual steamboat whistle in the harbor sounded like the dreaded four long blasts which means that a levee has given way, and the newspapers were flooded with inquiries about their safety."

A call for the registration of every Red Cross nurse in the city had been issued Monday night, and four squads of policemen were ordered on duty to patrol the levees around the city. The student council of Tulane University announced that the students had been organized, and could be put on duty at any relief work at a moment's notice. Hospitals were notified to store food supplies for several weeks' use, in the event of flood, and to buy oil cook-stoves and set them on the upper floors; for if the levees broke, the gas-plants would be inundated. Things were tense in New Orleans; even the incurable optimists were not so sure that the levee was as strong as the river and maybe stronger.

"Rumor painted full of tongues" was wagging every one of them, and the staidest resident was half willing to believe what he heard, because the absurdities of the stories were no worse than accounts of events that had actually happened up the river.

In the event of a break, wagged rumor, boats were ready in some secret place (kept hidden for fear of alarming the citizenry) to convey the populace to buildings chosen as the strongest in the city, which were to be commandeered as rescue camps. The newest hospital, several of the school buildings, the main buildings of the banks, the public library—hardly a building in town known to have steel girders but whose owner heard it would be full of flood refugees before long. Stories of armored cars bearing supplies of crackers and cheese and sardines to unknown but unutterably strong vaults ran through the downtown section. Somebody communicated the tidings that the Red Cross had on hand thousands of blankets and twice as many thousands of safety pins, and that each refugee (whose clothes, it was assumed, would be drenched and torn beyond repair) was to be given one blanket and two safety pins, the blanket to be slept on at night and pinned into a garment à la Swiss Family Robinson during the day.

The unorganized tales of disaster to come met in one unmistakable peak—the demand that the city be saved. Something must be done! There has been enough talk. There are no more synonyms for watchful waiting. New Orleans must be saved at any price. New Orleans is the key to the valley, and with New Orleans lost the commerce of the valley would receive a death-blow.

Eager citizens gathered in little knots on the corners.

Again they said that something must be done. And again and again, in these little unofficial conclaves, there occurred the query, "Why not cut the levee below the city?"

Whispered fearfully at first, it rose in a panicky crescendo. Rumors of weak spots ran wild through town. Have the Carrollton levees been examined today? What's this about a sandboil at the Oak Street levee? Water is seeping through at the Dumaine Street docks. What is going to happen? Something, obviously, and it's up to us to see that it doesn't happen to New Orleans.

Even before the downpour of Good Friday the people of New Orleans were remembering the Poydras crevasse. In 1922, when the river had reached a hitherto unprecedented high-water mark, and when questions as to the strength of the levees were raining anxiously upon the Association of Commerce and the city engineers, the levee suddenly cracked at Poydras, eleven miles below the city. The waters poured across the plantations—and there was no disaster in New Orleans.

The Poydras crevasse was providential—too providential, according to the Poydras residents. When one has had one's farm and home and cattle, representing the savings of a lifetime, swept away, one is likely to be enraged with everything. Ugly accusations were made in undertones against the powers of New Orleans. But, as there were no definite accusations and no possibility of making any, the Poydras crevasse by 1927 had been accepted as an accident that was happy for the city and unfortunate for the planters concerned, while new farms were being cultivated and new homes had been built in the face of the mended levee.

But with the rise of the 1927 flood, thoughts of the Poydras crevasse came back. Providence had pointed the way of salvation for New Orleans by breaking the levee five

Photo by American Red Cross photographers

REFUGEES

Horses, mules and all living things take refuge upon the slope of the levee in order to escape death by drowning.

years ago; why not let man do it again? The furtive murmur swelled into a howl, and the levee board warned all residents of the district not to approach the levees below the city after dark, lest they be shot as emissaries from New Orleans charged with the mission of making a secret cut.

The hesitating question, "Do you think cutting the levee below the city might be possible?" became a frantic demand. Business men meeting downtown for lunch called it the only way to avert the danger. Laborers on the city dikes wondered why they were working under such pressure when a cut below New Orleans would force the river to spare the city. Housewives who met at the back-door garbage-can with the breakfast scraps assured one another that the levee must be cut to save their homes from the fate of homes upstate. Children at school played at building levees during recess, and chose the roughest part of their sand breastworks as the Poydras dike, and broke it there. From the uptown avenues to the downtown alleys came the appeal, sometimes frantic, sometimes hysterical, sometimes with the stern insistence of conviction—"Cut the levee!"

A few frightened farmers began to move out of Poydras, certain now that somebody was going to slip up some dark night and break the dike. The first refugees to reach New Orleans arrived April 26, when N. Nicosla, a truck farmer, came to Red Cross headquarters with his wife and ten children. "Hardened flood veterans," the Associated Press writer called them, "they told of having to flee their homes in 1922; then there were eight children. The children, eight of the ten, were piled in the back of a truck upon mattresses, all they could bring from their home. The other two children stayed behind to take care of their mule, which they felt they could not afford to lose or leave to its fate."

But most of the farmers below the city stayed stolidly at

home, while the city poured its petitions on the governor, the mayor, the Association of Commerce and the levee board. They prayed for a cut, and they prayed that it might be soon. Sunday, April 24, business leaders of New Orleans went to Baton Rouge to call on Governor Simpson and impress on him the crisis confronting the city. Meetings of lawyers, financiers, engineers, and government officials were in progress all day Monday. The city was fairly quivering with excitement. Suppose the levee should break before they decided anything? Why didn't they hurry?

The governor demanded that business men assure him that the ruined parishes would be indemnified for their losses. They promised. The people of the parishes below the city, St. Bernard and Plaquemines, would be brought to New Orleans, supported during the refugee period and compensated by the city for the loss of their property—that and more. Whatever they asked. But they begged the governor to hurry. Breaking the levee near Poydras would divert the water of the river into Lake Borgne, and thence through the Mississippi Sound into the Gulf. It would ruin the farms, but New Orleans would pay. But hurry!

The trappers of St. Bernard and Plaquemines were angrily resentful at the news that their homes were going to be flooded to save the city. For weeks the trappers had been patrolling the levees with guns in their hands and every intention of using them if anybody appeared in the neighborhood who could not give satisfactory reasons for his being there. Inundating St. Bernard would destroy the fur-bearing animals and cripple the trappers' trade for several years to come. It sounded very well, the trappers were saying sullenly, to talk about saving the key to the valley; but judging by reports from up the river, there wasn't very much left to unlock, was there? And every trapper knew that his own home was worth just as much to him as the houses of St. Charles Avenue and Audubon Place were to their owners, and his job was as much his job as if it had been the presidency of a bank on Carondelet Street. But though the trappers blustered, they were acquiescent enough when they were warned Monday night that the governor had wired to Washington for permission to cut the levee. They knew the river and the things it could do. Most of them understood that New Orleans must be saved. "It's hard," said the sheriff of St. Bernard; "but I guess it's fair enough."

The farmers said little. They are Cajans, children of the race of Evangeline, stolid, quiet, but somehow intense; their name, Cajan, is a corruption of their old name, Acadian. They speak English to outsiders, but among themselves they speak a soft *patois,* neither French nor English nor Spanish, but something of all three, a *patois* peculiarly Cajan. They didn't know much about all this fuss in New Orleans.

But New Orleans was turning eager, desperate attention to the section just below the city. How strong is the levee there? How soon can it be cut? Will the trappers have a riot? Suppose they do—what difference will it make? For heaven's sake, hurry and bring them into the city! Promise them compensation for all they lose—double compensation. Give them brocaded curtains to sleep under when they get here, if they want them. Take everybody's car and fill it up with farmers and trappers and their families—only hurry! Hurry and make the cut at Poydras or Caernarvon or anywhere else you like, only make a cut and make it soon, and let us burn candles to every saint in the calendar that the city levee will hold until you do.

By Sunday the city engineers had joined with the public

in demanding a cut. On Monday, April 25, after many conferences, Secretary of War Davis received a telegram from Governor Simpson of Louisiana, asking for permission to cut the levee below New Orleans to save the city from destruction. Secretary Davis wired the governor that the War Department would interpose no objection to the cutting of the levee if national flood authorities agreed that it was necessary to save the city. Major-General Jadwin, chief of United States army engineers, sent a similar telegram. Business men in the city had already passed a resolution to place $150,000 at the disposal of the governor, to be used in caring for the fugitives who would be forced to flee from Plaquemines and St. Bernard. At 9:45 Tuesday night, immediately upon receiving the telegrams, Governor Simpson signed the proclamation that lay on his desk. Head-lines were clapped upon the front page of the extra that had lain all day in the composing-room of the "Times-Picayune." Then newsboys ran through the streets waving over their heads papers announcing in damp head-lines that the levee would be cut Friday.

The extras sold like food in a famine. Men and women tossed nickels from street-car windows, while the newsboys outside chased the cars and stood on tiptoe to give them the papers that bore the news. Motorists who heard the shouts of the boys halted their cars in the middle of the block and yelled for papers, and nobody seemed to mind. Windows were flung open in houses whose occupants had gone to bed, and ex-sleepers in pajamas leaned out to grab papers. The levee would be cut in two days more—New Orleans would be saved—thank the saints and the governor! There is probably not a saint in the category who lacked a prayer from New Orleans that night.

The governor's proclamation read in part as follows:

Photo by Simes, New Orleans

REFUGEES

Dressed in their Sunday best, fleeing from a small town in southwest Louisiana.
Ten hours later the town was under water.

An unprecedented flood now holds in its grip the lower Mississippi Valley. Large areas of the State of Louisiana, and the entire city of New Orleans, are seriously threatened. The levees of this State are now holding, but the strain to which they will be subjected in the next fifteen days seriously aggravates the present danger, and imperatively demands that drastic steps shall be taken to avert the menace. * * * In the face of this danger, and with the opportunity of averting it effectively, the governor of the State of Louisiana, charged with the supreme executive authority of the State, is confronted with the necessity of employing the police powers that inhere in the State. * * * I am impressed with the danger, and I am determined to avert it. The people in the affected area will be removed to safety and properly cared for. No lives will be sacrificed. Relief measures have been provided, and will be put into immediate effect. The damage to property resulting from this act will be paid. * * * Therefore, by virtue of the powers invested in me by the constitution and the laws of the State of Louisiana, I, O. H. Simpson, governor of the State of Louisiana, do hereby declare that a public emergency exists, and, in order to deal adequately with this situation, an artificial break in the levee of the Mississippi River is hereby ordered to be created at or near Poydras plantation in the parish of St. Bernard, Louisiana, at 12 o'clock noon on Friday, April 29, 1927.

New Orleans relaxed and went to sleep. Let the levees hold but two days longer, and then would come salvation. Two days more—could the levees hold that long? Of course, there were stories instantly on the wing that they could not. But as the crest of the flood was still upstream, most Orleanians believed that they could. At any rate, the extra Tuesday night loosed the tight nerves of the city and started a new "Hold-the-fort-for-I-am-coming" spirit. For the first time in the troubled days that had followed Good Friday the people of New Orleans realized that Lent was over and they could celebrate.

Chapter XXV

It was decided to blast the levee at Caernarvon, two miles
below Poydras. Excitement ran high in New Orleans, but
the frenzy of fear that had gripped the city had given place
to the thrill that precedes a big show. Herbert Hoover,
secretary of commerce, and Major-General Edgar Jadwin,
chief of army engineers, arrived in New Orleans April 27.
Up the river, along the three-hundred-mile levee from New
Orleans to Vicksburg, the fight against high water went on,
the climax of the struggle being on the levee along Bayou
des Glaises, which guarded the "sugar bowl" section of
Louisiana and its six-million-dollar sugar-cane crop.

The evacuation of St. Bernard and Plaquemines began.

The levee was going to be cut, messengers from the city
had told the residents of the two doomed parishes. New
Orleans had promised them compensation for their losses.
New Orleans would take care of them while the flood lasted.
They listened, somewhat bewildered. Most of them lived
on farms, in cottages by the side of the road that wound
for miles just under the sloping green wall of the levee.
And now New Orleans had called upon them to give up
their homes, to pile up their household goods with the
utmost possible speed, and come into the city, there to be
herded in a rescue camp—a camp where they would be fed
and clothed and sheltered, it is true, a camp out of reach of
the river, but where they must remain for lonely weeks

330

upon weeks, remembering their carrots and their bean-patches, their whitewashed cottages under the levee, remembering home. Compensation or not, they knew it was time to go.

And so they began to leave. While their parents loaded the mattresses and tables on wagons, the children gathered their dolls and their pet kittens into their arms and looked back at their homes. There was not much time for sentimentalizing or leave-taking. They had to go, and most of them said little about it. The trappers talked, but these Cajan farmers are a tight-lipped clan. As when they made their other great migration from Acadia in the days of Evangeline, they obeyed orders with a kind of hard-shelled acquiescence. They did as they were told, perhaps realizing subconsciously that by a strange destiny they, who learn to love their homes so deeply, are doomed to be a foot-loose race. At any rate, there was no outspoken bitterness among them when men from the city told these children of the Acadians that it was time to move again.

Wednesday and Thursday were the days of the exodus. It was noon Wednesday when the bugles echoed from building to building at Jackson Barracks, notifying the troops stationed there that the road leading along the foot of the levee to the lower parishes must be guarded from incoming vehicles, to keep it clear for the trucks of the evacuating planters.

Army trucks, Red Cross trucks, trucks belonging to the State Highway Commission, every available vehicle was hurried into Plaquemines and St. Bernard for the use of the people, for many of these farmers have no vehicles of their own save a rickety wagon or two hardly strong enough to bear the weight of a load of cabbages brought to town for sale.

Some of them were reluctant to leave their gardens and their homes till the last minute. Wouldn't tomorrow do? they asked the officers. Or maybe Friday morning? Occasionally a group of sunburnt trappers threatened defense of their levee.

But they came. New Orleans was ready to receive them, the scouts from the city said, describing the vacation they would have. All that was humanly possible to give them, she had made ready. The refugee camp had been arranged at the army supply base in the vast building alongside that of the International Trade Exhibition, covering a space as large as a city block. Here were storage rooms for furniture, sleeping quarters, a well-manned kitchen, Red Cross nurses ready to treat anything from grandpa's rheumatism to Jimmy's toe where the thorn stuck in while he was getting ready to leave home. In a few days a school would be arranged for the children, with their own teachers, imported from the district schools in their parishes. Free newspapers would be sent them every day. There would be vaudeville twice a week. There were abundant supplies of clothes. Their rich neighbor was eager to pay them for their sacrifice, and was holding out every inducement she could offer. It's not every day—

The farmers listened when all this was described to them. But as there had been little bitterness at the news that they were to be flooded, there was little enthusiasm over seeing the sights of the city. They shrugged, and looked at their bean-patches, and then looked up at their high grassy levee.

"Guess we better move," they said.

Wednesday morning the dusty caravan began to wind its way from Plaquemines and St. Bernard. Trucks, wagons, automobiles impudently chalked up with flivver jokes in less strenuous days, even push-carts, carried the Lares and

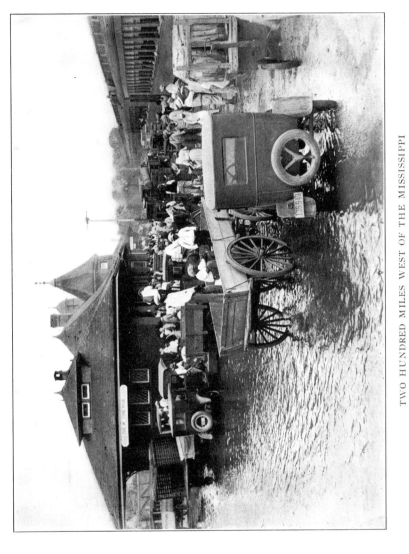

TWO HUNDRED MILES WEST OF THE MISSISSIPPI

Refugees fleeing from the rising waters at New Iberia, Louisiana

Penates of the Cajans along the road to New Orleans. Some of the travelers were sad, others merely bewildered. Some of them looked resentfully at the well-kept homes along the roads, other men's homes that were spared at the price of their own. Some of them were frightened, as if they were momentarily expecting the sound of a blast or of rushing waters behind them. Negroes were trundling wheelbarrows laden with the last crops of beets or carrots from their gardens just under the levee. As the day wore on, they trudged more wearily under the sunshine, which burns with summer heat in a Louisiana April.

But they went on, a steady, stoic procession of men and women bred to the endurance of exile. Here and there a thrifty farmer drove a wagon piled high with green vegetables he expected to cry for sale in the streets of New Orleans. Boys in high glee at the adventure ran up and down, keeping chickens and cattle in line. A curious babble of tongues, English, French, Spanish, and the soft Cajan *patois,* rose with the hoof-beats of the long caravan.

At last they were all corraled into New Orleans, and New Orleans was set for one of the most spectacular episodes of all its spectacular history—the blasting of the Caernarvon levee. A conclave of notables had come to town for the occasion, such as not even the most brilliant Mardi Gras had ever been able to draw. Cabinet members, United States army officials, world-famous writers, engineers who had built skyscrapers and bridges as well as levees, and who were learning for the first time that blasting a levee is as complicated a feat as building one, all joined the corps of the reporters and photographers and moving-picture men and trekked down to Caernarvon. Half forgotten in the *mêlée* of famous folk were the cases of dynamite and the laborers who were to plant it.

At eight o'clock Friday morning the story of the flood and the contemplated crevasse had been telephoned to "The London Evening News" by the "Times-Picayune." It was an awesome occasion in journalistic circles, described by the London paper April 29 as follows:

At seven o'clock tonight, British summer time, which is noon in New Orleans, a mighty gap is being blown in the Mississippi embankment south of the great city, in the attempt to save it from engulfment by the raging Father of Waters. How this will be done is described below in a wonderful telephone conversation that took place between New Orleans and the "Evening News" office over 4500 miles of land and sea this afternoon. * * * The voice of Mr. L. R. Brooks, city editor of the "Times-Picayune," noticeable for its soft southern drawl, was heard clearly and strongly throughout the conversation.

The account is perfectly accurate, except for the reference to Mr. Brooks's soft southern drawl, which wasn't there. Mr. Brooks was born and brought up in Minnesota, and had been in New Orleans less than two years when the British reporter mistook his healthy twang of the plains for a southern accent. But that didn't lessen the thrill that both cities got out of the conversation, and it made good atmosphere. Bernard Krebs, who had been "covering" the flood, gave a detailed report to "The London Evening News."

Friday morning the roads leading down to the sentenced parishes were closed and patrolled by armed guards. Only the privileged with their official permits could pass. But they came, a new caravan going down toward Poydras by the same road the Cajans had traveled in the opposite direction yesterday. They came in automobiles, boats and aeroplanes, eager for the big show.

In New Orleans everybody set his clock and watched

the hands climb toward noon, waiting for the noise of a blast that would shake his window-panes with a fourteen-mile echo from Caernarvon.

The clock struck twelve, and the sound of the strokes was the only noise. New Orleans waited tensely. Nothing happened. Pretty soon the clock struck twelve-thirty, and still there were only the noises of street-cars and traffic whistles from the street below. New Orleans was troubled. What had happened to the levee?

As a matter of fact, something very definite had happened to the levee, and the water was bubbling over the plains of St. Bernard, but it wasn't as definite as everybody had been expecting. It wasn't a big show. The plain truth was that the Caernarvon levee was about as tough a levee as there was to be found along the Mississippi, and it was very much harder to break than anybody had anticipated. But it was broken, all the same, and the farms of St. Bernard and Plaquemines were at the bottom of a tawny lake, and New Orleans was saved.

But the show was a fizzle. Meigs O. Frost, one of the newspaper reporters who went along, wrote an account of it the next day for "The New Orleans States":

They dynamited the levee, all right. Nearly a ton of dynamite, sixty Senegambian pick and shovel specialists, a governor, a major-general, a brace of brigadier-generals, colonels and majors galore, engineers, more captains and first and second lieutenants than Mr. Burroughs has invented machines competent to count—all were there, Friday afternoon. Saturday morning the Mississippi River was flowing gayly through the gaps in the East Bank dike at Caernarvon Beacon. * * *

As an engineering feat, the operation is pronounced a success by those who issued the official communiqués.

As a military manœuver, announces Brigadier-General Allison Owen, of the militia, the affair was also a success.

As a spectacular show, your correspondent, back from the battle-front, announces that it was a flop.

Some fifty reporters, cameramen and movie-camera crank-grinders agree with him. They had come from all over America to see something approximating the end of the world. There was to be flame and smoke and a thundering detonation heard for miles, the report ran. There was to be a mighty wall of water suddenly unleashed, Niagara-like, ripping, tearing all before it; swirling down toward the Gulf of Mexico like the onrush of Attila's horde of Huns.

Was there? There was not.

But it was a great day for the officials. And a great day for the militia.

Your correspondent, accompanied by other distinguished correspondents properly equipped with passes to enter the danger zone, headed down toward Caernarvon Friday morning. The road was closed to the general public. It was darn near closed to the reporters. Seven times between the Orleans parish lower boundary line and Caernarvon the party was stopped and ordered to show its papers. At last they got through.

There on the levee was the towering shaft of the Caernarvon Beacon. About it the sixty laborers delved, hidden by a crowd of official spectators. Your correspondent and the other correspondents naturally started for the scene, up the levee. They were halted successively by a private, a corporal, a sergeant, a lieutenant, a captain, a major, and a colonel. They descended the levee to the road and again started for the scene. They were halted by the same line-up and a few more. They retired to the spot on the levee where such things as newspaper correspondents were herded for the day. On the way back they were halted a few times. Your correspondent desires earnestly to look up the remaining eight members of the Louisiana militia and get halted by them so he can have a hundred per cent. record. * * *

Your correspondent at last saw Fire Chief John Evans of New Orleans far within the lines—also a brace of New Orleans detectives. He managed to slip through to their side in an

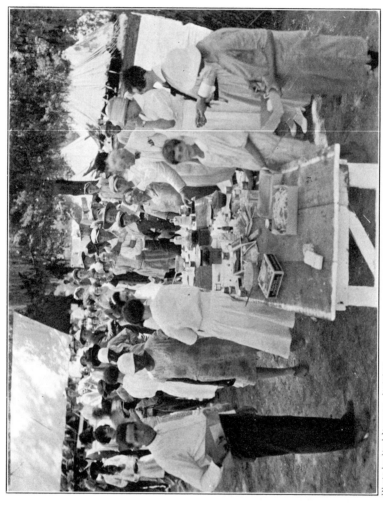

REFUGEES BEING VACCINATED AT CAMP WHITFIELD, NATCHEZ, MISSISSIPPI

effort to learn something of how you dynamite a levee. But the eagle eye of Colonel James E. Edmonds found him there.

"What are you doing here?" demanded the colonel.

Your correspondent modestly explained that he was endeavoring to report the events of the day.

"I know what you are doing," said the colonel. "I'm an ex-newspaper man. You're trying to put something over. Get out of here."

Your correspondent got out of there.

By now it was getting toward zero hour, which had been set by Governor Simpson's proclamation at high noon, just like a society wedding. Ripples of excitement went through the crowd, two hundred feet back of the dynamite squad up the levee. Sheriff L. A. Meraux, in knee-high laced boots, olive-drab riding-breeches, khaki shirt, Colt six-shooter in his waistband, frontier handkerchief about his neck and a soft gray felt hat pulled over his eyes, stood in the center of a group of newspaper men and waxed wroth.

"We're letting 'em do it because we can't stop 'em," he said. "You can't fight the Government. * * * I have a hell of a time trying to get my people to see that. A lot of them don't see it yet. But a lot of them have been moving out. They wanted to go to the levee first with their women and children and their weapons, and tell the State of Louisiana to come ahead and cut the levee—but it would be cut over their dead bodies first. We managed to talk them out of that for their own good. But this ruins us.

"Here's the parish of St. Bernard. Supplies more furs to the world than Canada and Russia put together. The trapping will be ruined for from three to five years. We've got the best oysters in the world. The oyster trade will be ruined, and the shrimpers and the fishermen. The truck farms are gone. The cattle and the canning industries will be wrecked. And we haven't got a line in writing for any kind of a guarantee that we're going to get anything back out of all we lose. Right here in the path of this crevasse that's coming in a few minutes I own land that I was offered two hundred and fifty dollars an acre for only three weeks ago. I refused it. If any of you men want any of it you can have it for ten dollars an acre right now. Just say the word. Speak up."

Nobody spoke up.

Overhead, seaplanes No. 20 and No. 22 of the United States navy began to circle a groaning path. Far out for two miles in every direction from the place where the dynamite was planted, they scouted looking for human beings. Evidently they found none. Back they circled, closer and closer. Presently from one fell fluttering three sheets of white paper. Blasts sounded from whistles on the river. Evidently all was clear.

Cameras were focused. Somebody in a loud voice tolled off minutes, minute by minute, until the moment of the blast.

"Three minutes left—two minutes—one minute!"

Movie-cameras began to grind. Reporters cocked one eye on synchronized watches and the other eye on the levee. Beatrice Washburn put her hands over her ears.

Then—Pop!

Out there in the open air it sounded like the discharge of a French seventy-five. Up from the levee, maybe a hundred feet in air, shot a fan-shaped screen of dark earth from the levee. Above it shot a cloud of dove-gray smoke that thinned and filmed. Then under the feet of the newspaper men and photographers, now herded five hundred feet back of the break, the solid levee rose like a wave, as the force of the dynamite spent itself along the heavy earthen rampart.

Eager eyes swept the landscape for a last look at a scene of sun-bathed beauty that so soon was to be swept by a raging torrent. * * * It stayed there, undampened. Three painful minutes passed before a shout announced that a trickle of water had appeared on the land side of the levee. Then, at 2:22 P.M., the second blast shot earth in air, while the acrid fumes of the dynamite filled the throats of those who watched, and again the levee shook beneath the feet of the spectators. And at 2:24 P.M. the same unspectacular setting marked the third blast. Many a New Orleans gutter runs more water after half an hour's mild rain than was going through the first gap by now. * * *

Sheriff Meraux started forward. He walked straight to the edge of the first gap. Above him stood the Caernarvon Beacon, that had not even been shaken by the three explosions at its base. Cameramen and reporters, after another skirmish with the militia, followed him.

"Gentlemen, you have seen today the public execution of this parish," said Sheriff Meraux. * * *

The hour of 3:30 P.M. had now arrived. Water was running at the rate of five miles an hour in a stream ten feet wide and some two or three feet deep through the levee. Investigation showed that some of the original charges of dynamite had not exploded. This information beat the militia seven ways from the jack when it came to getting the crowd back.

At 3:45 P.M. Governor O. H. Simpson in person, not a moving picture, appeared on the levee. * * * To your correspondent's question he said: "I have nothing to say. I am here on a trip of inspection."

Two minutes later, at 3:47 P.M., the fourth blast went off. Adjutant-General Toombs solemnly walked over and shook hands with Governor Simpson.

"Permit me to congratulate you, Governor," he said. "You have been under fire."

Governor Simpson looked impressed.

At 3:50 P.M. the fifth dynamite charge was exploded. Nobody congratulated the governor for being under fire this time, though the clods rained all about the group.

The river fell one-tenth of a foot during the first seven hours after the crevasse. But even the river, so demoniac in its fury where it wasn't wanted, seemed mild to the engineers at Caernarvon. They wanted a big crevasse and they wanted it in a hurry, and the river wasn't wearing down the gap fast enough by itself. The engineers wired to New Orleans for two more tons of dynamite, which they put to work Saturday. This time they retired with the satisfaction of having done a good day's work. The crevasse was two thousand feet wide, and New Orleans realized for the first time how much water she had been spared when she saw the flood that finally poured in upon the empty parishes.

Poydras, by the way, the town that got so much publicity over being sacrificed, never was at all until it leaped into prominence on maps of the crevasse. Poydras had very little more existence than Asgard and El Dorado. "The charming little southern town, wiped away that the queen city of the South might be saved," etc., etc., consisted of a crossroads filling station, a tumbledown mansion uninhabited for years, and six or seven scattered houses of two or three rooms apiece.

Loosed at last to do as it pleased, the Mississippi poured through the Caernarvon gap and over the lowlands. The people of New Orleans drew a long breath, remarked to one another "Good! Now that's over," and went back to work.

Miraculously the tension loosened. People looked at each other as if they were together for the first time after a long separation. It was queer to have everything so normal. They saw with surprise that the town looked just as it always had.

REFUGEES, WITH ALL THEIR WORLDLY GOODS, ARE CARRIED TO SAFETY

Chapter XXVI

REFUGEES

NEW ORLEANS was safe, but there was yet to come perhaps the most disastrous battle won by the river—the conquest of the Bayou des Glaises levee and the emptying of the Louisiana "sugar bowl."

Hardly had the last blast of dynamite blown into the air its Caernarvon dirt when news came that the dikes guarding the "sugar bowl," the opulent valley in central Louisiana that produces nearly all the sugar-cane and molasses produced in America, were tottering under the weight of the flood, to which had been added the backflow of six crevasses upstream. Bayou des Glaises acts as a kind of funnel, through which the water from upstate is poured into the Atchafalaya River and the Mississippi. It is less than a hundred miles in length, extending from the southwest corner of Rapides parish to Simmsport, where it flows into Old River, a branch of the Mississippi.

The crevasse waters were piling up against the levee, straining it to its utmost, with the flood crest still fifty miles upstream. The planters of the "sugar bowl" had rushed to their dikes, and there followed days and nights of almost superhuman struggle to protect the teeming Tensas and Atchafalaya basins. The State sent workmen from all quarters. By May 10 the eyes of all Louisiana were on Bayou des Glaises. It was probably the finest fight of the flood period that the sugar- and rice-planters made to save their homes.

"Seepage is reported in that vicinity to be so bad that it is with considerable difficulty that mules are able to drag levee-scrapers up the embankments," reported "The New Orleans States" May 10. "Small tributaries of the Atchafalaya basin are sending their backwaters into the Big Bend district, hampering the movement of levee-fighting supplies. * * * John W. Monget, veteran levee man, after an inspection trip through the Bayou des Glaises districts, said, 'The levees in that locality are too low to hold back the volume of water thrown against them by the breaks above and they are too narrow to stand necessary topping.' * * * Accompanying the rise of the flood crest through the extremities of the Mississippi Valley is a prediction of stormy weather, high winds, and possible rains, making suspense more tense as flood waters mass about the mouth of Old River before descending into the lower valley, either through the expected breach in Bayou des Glaises or down the main stream.

"Roofs of houses, fences, and trees floating down the swollen channel of the Mississippi indicate the return of waters from breaks in north Louisiana to the main stream. National guardsmen and civilians patrolled the main stream levees in the teeth of the gale, battling to strengthen the ramparts in the face of the charging water, which ate gradually into the banks and battered at sandbags thrown into the breaches thus created. Fifteen hundred workers labored along the Red River, Bayou Rapides and Bayou des Glaises in Alexandria and that vicinity as the fight in central Louisiana approached its critical point."

But pessimistic predictions did not stop the fight of the planters. The waters streamed down upon the embankments from the crevasses above Natchez and Vicksburg, from the flooded lowlands of Arkansas and from the backwater of the Red River. On May 12 the prophesied rain saturated the levee crust and diminished its strength, but still the men on the levee, drenched by the downpour, silently refused to leave their job long enough to find dry clothes. "With hungry waters of Bayou des Glaises biting into the hastily constructed sandbag topping within six inches of its summit, and in many cases running through this barrier, a thousand wan and weary men continued their fight Thursday against the break threatened between Bordelonville and Sarto in the Big Bend district," said "The New Orleans Item" May 12. "With the exception of the thousand levee workers, who have toiled day and night for the past two weeks, the countryside has been practically deserted."

But they lost. On May 13 the waters suddenly burst through two crevasses in the Big Bend section of Bayou des Glaises, seventy miles north of Baton Rouge. The planters staggered into the refugee concentration camps, weak from cold and exposure. There was little they would say to newspaper correspondents. They had lost their fight, and the "sugar bowl" was gone.

By the next afternoon the Bayou des Glaises levee was honeycombed with breaks. Five parishes had gone under the flood—Avoyelles, St. Landry, St. Martin, St. Mary and Iberia. A hundred and fifty thousand new refugees were straggling into the Red Cross camps.

The Tensas parish jail, in the town of St. Joseph, had opened its doors to the most distinguished guests who had ever slept there. Leading citizens of St. Joseph and the Tensas rural districts fled from their drenched homes and took refuge behind the bars of the jail, crowding out the prisoners, who were summarily packed off to Natchez. The jail and the parish court-house were both turned into sleeping quarters for men who stuck by the town in spite of the flood, which had intruded itself into the second story rooms of their houses.

The loss of the "sugar-bowl" country is declared by economic experts to be the only flood disaster for which efficient reconstruction work can offer no compensation. The comments on this episode of the flood are summed up by "The Literary Digest" in the issue of June 18:

> The only possibility of a lasting effect of the Mississippi flood is seen by observers of southern conditions in the Louisiana sugar-cane industry, we read in "The New York Times." Louisiana's sugar bowl may be empty this year, reports an Associated Press correspondent in New Orleans, because of the prolonged inundation of the Tensas and Atchafalaya basins. Practically all our American-grown sugar-cane and molasses come from Louisiana, the papers remind us on every hand. A sugar-grower, quoted in Facts About Sugar (New York) as an authority, declares that such cane as escaped destruction will be needed as seed cane for next year's planting: "It is quite likely therefore that there will be no grinding this year in Louisiana except at a very few isolated factories."

With the sugar parishes turned into lake bottoms, the river continued its journey southward. The Atchafalaya broke its east levee May 24, flooding five more parishes of the sugar section—Pointe Coupée, West Baton Rouge, Assumption, Iberville, and Terrebone—as well as part of Ascension parish. On May 27 backwaters from Spanish Lake and Bayou Teche, both of which had flooded some time before, converged and inundated the towns of New Iberia and Morgan City. The last-ditch fights between man and the 1927 flood were being fought in the basin of the Atchafalaya River the last of May, now the river and now the levees gaining the upper hand. By the first of June the flood was draining lazily into the Gulf of Mexico.

BAYOU DES GLAIZES, LOUISIANA

Men and women marooned on the second floor of a house, chickens on the roof, and hogs fighting for life upon the top of the submerged levee

Louisiana had become a rim of land cupping a vast lake two hundred miles long and varying from fifty to a hundred miles in width. Ten thousand square miles in twenty parishes had been submerged, and the river had collected a bill totaling tens of millions of dollars. Reluctantly but steadily it was emptying itself into the Gulf, and the energies of the Mississippi Valley were turned to caring for the refugees huddled in Red Cross camps, and reconstructing the stricken country, while the country's foremost engineers considered plans for making this catastrophe the last of its kind in America.

Four hundred lives, seven hundred thousand persons made homeless, thirteen million acres engulfed, and three hundred million dollars' worth of destruction—this is a postage-stamp story of the Mississippi flood. When the people of America, who had been focusing attention on New Orleans for several weeks past, turned to survey the general wreckage, they saw disaster through the valley from Cairo to the Gulf. "There are thousands of persons still clinging to their homes where the upper floors remain dry," said Secretary Hoover in a radio address broadcast from Memphis April 30, "more thousands needing to be removed in boats and established in great camps on higher ground, and yet other thousands camped upon broken levees." A statement from the Red Cross May 10 showed that at that time there were 323,827 persons under the care of the organization. Ninety-five thousand persons had been given typhoid fever serum, eighty-five thousand vaccinated against smallpox, and one hundred and twenty-nine thousand had been given quinine in a preventive campaign against malaria. It was estimated that more than half a million persons received Red Cross aid during the flood period.

Relief work from the beginning of the flood had been conducted by the Red Cross from centers established in each of the stricken States. The Louisiana relief station, though probably the most highly organized rescue office in the valley, is typical of these. Former Governor John M. Parker, flood relief director for the State, was a veteran at dealing with the river's rampages, having helped to fight every flood in Louisiana since 1882. He knew the geography of the levee lines, and which branches of the river had been the most turbulent in times past; he was personally acquainted with levee board members in nearly every town along the river; and his familiarity with the regions under water led him to judge where isolated groups were likely to be found clinging to levees or Indian mounds. Having been governor of the State during the 1922 flood, he had had experience in directing relief work.

Mr. Parker's headquarters were established in the State capitol at Baton Rouge, four rooms housing the officers who directed the relief service: L. A. Toombs, adjutant-general of the Louisiana National Guard; T. G. McCarty, national Red Cross representative in the State; Major J. H. Elliott, commander of planes and ships assembled for rescue work; and Mr. Parker, general director. There were days when they were all on duty sixteen hours or more, working and waiting for news. The offices swarmed all day with national guardsmen, army officers, members of the state flood relief committee, Red Cross nurses, directors of volunteer corps, newspaper correspondents, all eager for news, news, news, all grabbing for telephones when they rang, or running half way downstairs to meet the boys who brought telegrams. The State was being watched over by the three relief divisions: the National Guard, whose business it was to warn the inhabitants of threatened regions and to supervise the task of getting them out of the danger zone; the ship and aeroplane corps, which carried the refugees to the Red Cross camps or other places of safety; and the Red Cross proper, to care for the fugitives. Reports by wireless, telephone and telegraph were sent constantly to the main office at Baton Rouge from these agencies, in addition to periodic reports made by seaplane pilots sent out to watch the developments of the flood as it swept over the State. The levees were patrolled by members of the National Guard.

An Associated Press dispatch sent from New Orleans May 3 described the work of collecting the refugees:

Craft of almost every type, from the lumbering river steamer to the flatboat propelled by an outboard motor, were converging upon wide stretches of northeastern Louisiana, moving the homeless to the safety of concentration camps in many sections of the State and near-by Mississippi towns. Directing the rescue work from the air were many swift seaplanes of the navy, which roared over the more isolated inland places to locate refugees clinging to rooftops, trees, and the tops of promontories projecting above the swirling flood waters. Playing a prominent *rôle* were bronzed life-savers of the lighthouse department, men who had fought the mountainous waves of the Atlantic, the Gulf and the Great Lakes for years, to find a new and strange enemy in the roaring waters of a mighty river writhing in the throes of its greatest flood force of history.

Before the flood had given more than an indication of the havoc it intended to wreak, the Red Cross had taken charge of rescue work and had called upon the people of the nation for aid. Their response had been immediate. The Red Cross asked first for five million dollars, and within three hours the first half million had been subscribed. The appeal was later made for ten million, and then for more; and the fund raised by midsummer amounted to about fifteen million dollars.

Relief centers were opened in the cities of the valley that were not built on the river banks, but which were near the flooded sections, where supplies were collected and refugees from the inundated territory were taken care of. Volunteer workers were mustered into service and appeals for clothing and other supplies were broadcast. Contributions poured in from the safe cities of the valley and from other cities all over the country, while refugees fairly swarmed in, many of them sick from exposure and the contagious diseases that had begun their epidemics in the improvised camps on the levees. Relief boats flying Red Cross flags went to and fro between these hamlets and the cities where food and clean beds and medical attention awaited the fugitives. Students of Louisiana State University set up a tent city to care for eighteen hundred negroes at the old experimental station on the Bayou Sara road, and with this and camps in the city, Baton Rouge alone is said to have been a place of refuge for ten thousand sufferers. Other camps were established at Natchez, Vicksburg, Delhi, Bastrop, Oak Grove, Monroe, Alexandria, Marksville, Rhinehart, Harrisonburg, Columbia, Winnsboro, and other towns beyond the flood limits, where refugees were continually streaming in.

Big Jim Hursey, a gigantic black Hercules, constituted himself the guardian of the public peace in the refugee camp at Vicksburg, where five thousand negroes were concentrated under military control. Jim was officially in charge of the hospital isolation ward, and unofficially custodian of good behavior. When one of the negroes disturbed the tranquillity of the camp, Big Jim approached the commanding officer and there was held between the two a long undertone *tête-à-tête*. A moment later Big Jim would stride over to the sinner, pick him up (Jim could pick up anybody on the

Photo by Marshall Gray, U. S. Engineers' Corps, 1927

ON THE LEVEES ALONG BAYOU DES GLAIZES

For weeks refugees lived on the levees until rescued by the members of the U. S. Coast Guard operating under the direction of the Red Cross

premises), and carry him off down the hill. When they re-appeared the offender always seemed eager to promise that he would be good in future.

Religious meetings were frequent, especially in the camps where the negroes were gathered, and many a negro who had lost his mule and cabin in the flood forgot all his troubles to the tune of "Swing Low, Sweet Chariot" or "Go Down, Moses." While their elders were praying, at the Memphis refugee camp negro boys played baseball with as much gusto as though they were kicking up the dust of their own back yards. Relief workers distributed full sup-plies for baseball, much to the delight of the little negroes, most of whom had never played with anything more ortho-dox than the sticks and rag balls supplied by their mammies.

The town of Greenville, Mississippi, if it didn't exactly enjoy the flood, at least had a picturesque time of it. With the bravado characteristic of the territories that long ago learned to say "It's the way of the river," "The Greenville Democrat-Times" continued to appear daily, though its plant was surrounded by water, providing news of the world to the inhabitants of the town who had not fled before the river and to the refugees from elsewhere who had crowded into the tent city on the levee. With no electric power to run the printing machines, the staff of the "Democrat-Times" assembled the news in bulletin form and set type and turned presses by hand.

The daily edition consisted of a single sheet, printed on both sides with six columns of news. The doings of the world at large were chronicled under the head-line "Received by Pat Scully over Radio from Memphis." There was local news, gleaned by reporters who made daily rounds of the refugee camps and the offices of the Red Cross, the army, and the government workers. News was published about flood conditions in Greenville and near-by towns along the river; bulletins of the depth of the river at the levee and the depth of water in different parts of town; local items concerning the departure of residents and the arrival of refugees; and notices sent out by relief stations and by private citizens more fortunate than the rest, who were offering aid of various kinds. A typical such notice was this:

John Hardin, colored, told the "Democrat-Times" today that he will give away to both white and colored vegetable dinners from his café on South Walnut Street. There are entrances to the café both front and rear. The front entrance is for white people and the rear of the café will be used for serving colored. Hardin says that he has plenty of vegetables and will be glad to give as many as possible to those marooned.

Or this:

Any man, either able-bodied or intelligent, will please report to E. D. Davis in the brown tent on levee for assignment of work. The work will not be romantic, but necessary. The need for white volunteers is urgent. When you volunteer, stay near Mr. Davis until you are assigned, on the job till it is completed. Any man, either able-bodied or intelligent, who will not work, I request to leave town on the next boat. I request all ladies to keep off the boardwalks and levee unless on business.

There was also a lost-and-found column, the advertisements being for missing men and women rather than spectacles and pocketbooks. A typical paragraph announced:

A rumor went wild over the city this morning that C. L. Schlom was drowned, but Mr. Schlom has turned up O. K.

These extracts are from the issue of April 26. Copies of the paper were cherished by the marooned citizens as their grandparents had cherished the issues of the Vicksburg newspaper of Civil War days which was printed on wallpaper during Grant's long siege of the city.

The government officials had parked an automobile on the levee, near the refugee camp, and had designated it as the post office, under the name of Greenville Substation No. 1. Here mail deliveries were made by postmen who had sworn to carry on through the flood, delivering letters by boat to refugee camps in a grim determination to beat the river at something, anyway. A new post office, christened "Refugee Dock," was established at Natchez to receive mail for the fugitives there. River steamers and Coast Guard cutters laden with cargoes of mail plowed regularly through the water-covered country. The steamer *Augustin* went every other day from Natchez, Mississippi, to St. Joseph, Louisiana, stopping here and there at little camps cut off from the world on the bank of the river. The *Tuscumbia* went on alternate days from Natchez to the mouth of the Red River, while every third day the *Coal Bluff* made a precarious trip up the Red and Black rivers, bringing the scatterlings news; while outlying tent towns got more or less regular visits from Coast Guard cutters.

Life in the Red Cross camps continued for weeks after the peak of the flood was past, until the waters had receded sufficiently for the farmers to go back home and start again. One of the most thoroughly organized of these camps was the refugee headquarters in New Orleans equipped by the Red Cross when word went out that the people of Plaquemines and St. Bernard would be brought into the city to leave the river a clear field around Caernarvon. This camp, instead of being a tent city like most of the camps which sprang up overnight to receive the frantic hordes from the river bottoms, was located in three connected buildings, and was organized and equipped beforehand for the expected visitors. The buildings were those housing the International Trade Exhibition and the army supply base, and the people of New Orleans, realizing that they were paying a debt rather than extending charity, entertained their refugees in addition to feeding them.

The negro refugees were housed on the sixth floor and the white refugees on the fifth. As soon as they arrived, they were given typhoid serum, and general physical examinations were made by Red Cross physicians. The Red Cross nurses, who were in constant attendance, took the temperature of every one in the camp twice a day, and if any fever was present that appeared not to be a direct result of the serum, the patient was isolated in bed until the next visit of the doctor, who made daily rounds. If the patient's ailment was found to be contagious, he was at once taken to the charity department of some local hospital.

Hospital treatment was given to scores of farmers and members of their families who were found to be suffering from chronic ailments that could be cured or improved. The enforced stay in New Orleans was far from being an unmixed evil for most of these refugees; their general health was vastly improved, both by medical aid, balanced diet, and rest, and the vacation at the concentration camp provided the first that many of the poorer men and women had had in years. An open-air playground was provided for the children in the park opposite the trade exhibition buildings, and a school was arranged for them at the army barracks, with the teachers from the district schools they had attended in their home parishes. A bus called for them every morning and brought them back every afternoon, and on the return of the bus they were given a mid-afternoon lunch of cookies and milk.

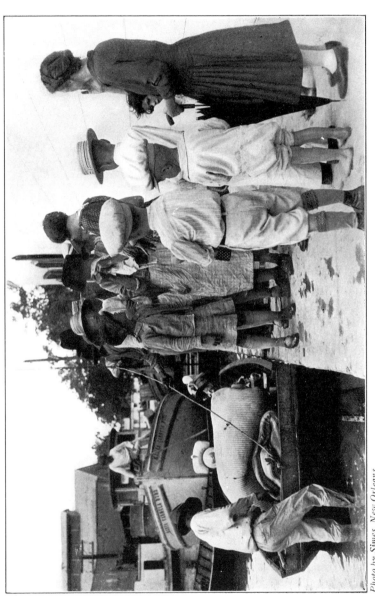

Photo by Simes, New Orleans

FEW TEARS WERE SHED, ALTHOUGH MANY LOST EVERYTHING IN THE FRENZIED EFFORT TO ESCAPE
BEFORE THE FLOOD

Life at the camp was described in the "Times-Picayune"
May 9:

One look into the great dormitory of the fifth floor, where
the white persons sleep, gives a good cross-section of the
everyday life at refugee headquarters.

The army cots have been folded up and put away, and the
two vast rooms, one of which is used as sleeping quarters for
men and one for women, are used as sitting-rooms. Suspended
from the ceiling, directly opposite the elevator, is a great Red
Cross banner, and beyond this is a table covered with pens
and hospital charts, thermometers in glasses of antiseptic solution, record cards, and other hospital equipment. A Red Cross
nurse is at this table all day, taking temperatures and bandaging
bruises acquired by the boys and girls in too zealous play.

Every refugee in the building has been vaccinated and given
antitoxin against typhoid and scarlet fever. * * *

In one corner of the room are two women pressing clothes
with electric irons before up-to-date ironing boards, while one
of their friends rocks back and forth in a wicker rocking-chair
near-by, reading a new magazine donated by some friend of
the Red Cross. On the other side of the room is a group of
men sitting around a phonograph, which is grinding out the
latest jazz tunes. Near them is a mother showing a little girl of
three or four how to dress her doll. A short distance from the
nurse's table is a table covered with a blue checked cloth, on
which is an electric stove, where milk for one of the babies is
being prepared. All the milk given the refugee babies is
pasteurized and prepared by the nurses according to hospital
formulas. * * *

Breakfast is served to most of the refugees at eight o'clock,
but those who have to be at work early are served in time to
leave. The dining hall is on one of the long covered porches
that are on all sides of the building, and the cooking is done
on a great range placed on this porch. Here is a row of long
tables, each with benches on the side, and a glass of flowers in
the center of each table. Breakfast consists of fruit, bacon, and

toast, and coffee or milk. The menu is frequently changed. At eight-thirty the bus arrives and the children pile in with their books to go to school in the improvised schoolhouse at Jackson Barracks.

Meanwhile those who have jobs have gone to work. Many of the men still have their jobs in factories where they worked before the crevasse; others have secured employment in New Orleans.

The social service department, which is headed by Miss Susan Gillean, keeps a list of men and women wanting employment, and supplies household servants or other employees to families in town.

Nobody at the refugee camp was required to get a job. However, many of those who had worked in factories at some distance from their homes, which were not destroyed by the flood, held on to their jobs for fear of losing them for good. Others, after several days of idleness, went out into New Orleans and got jobs for themselves, evidently thinking it a good time to lay up some money for the winter, or desiring to be able to afford the price of city amusements; for though a vaudeville show was given at the camp twice a week, the city theaters and shops were enticing.

The New Orleans camp, however, provided a far easier life than that made possible by most of the camps that dotted the valley. Life in a typical hurry-up tent city was described by R. B. Pixley in "The New Orleans Tribune" for May 29:

Life in flood refugee camps has taught a hundred and fifty thousand men, women and children in Louisiana one lesson—the value of discipline, patience, and a little hardship now and then. * * * It is not exactly a picnic for the refugee.

In some of the Louisiana camps—they are scattered through all the western side of the State—the people came with a rush and before any preparations were made to care for them. Towns of a bare thousand population suddenly had to feed and house five thousand visitors, every family with small children needing pure milk, and nearly every family demanding some medical attention if sickness was to be kept away.

A night spent in one of these camps, at Delhi, in Morehouse parish, where thirty-seven refugees were sleeping in army tents, showed how this community met these problems. * * * For instance, in Delhi the thousands of women and children are fed first, and the men come later. First the white women and children, then the negro women and children, then the men in order. They stand in line with tin plates and cups, and as they pass huge tanks of prepared food, an attendant heaps the plate full. You may have coffee black or with hot milk, as you prefer. The meals during weekdays are plain—meat, potatoes or rice, and bread. Not always butter, although the day we were there they gave us butter and it was being served to all the refugees. On Sunday there was pudding and stewed corn. * * * In this camp there is milk enough for children under three years of age. It is rationed to the families who present cards.

Delhi has the best appearing streets in its camp of any found in the State. A grading contractor took his teams and tractors off all his jobs and graded up the streets between the rows of tents, and then used scrapers to make them almost like pavement. Gutters run around each tent, and there is a perfect system of drainage.

Over in Monroe, a city of twenty thousand, with an organization ready to meet any emergency, they had a camp in order two days before the Red Cross arrived, and had a thousand refugees registered and at home. Monroe has natural gas, and the result is one of the finest groups of kitchens that could be imagined. Being a refugee in Monroe is like going to Sunday dinner every day in the week. They took a lot of sheet iron and welded it together some way so as to make a long pancake griddle that bakes four hundred and forty cakes at one time. Pipes with natural gas run under it and they turn on the gas and feed their three thousand refugees hot cakes and maple syrup for breakfast. * * * They have fed the three thousand on an average of twenty-nine cents a day. * * *

In all the camps, except at Lafayette, where they had to care for twelve thousand five hundred refugees who arrived in three days—and Lafayette has a population of about two thousand—the homes are regulation army tents. Each family is given a tent, and there are many with ten children. Whenever it has been possible the families have been allowed to bring their bedroom furniture, or at least one set, and there is a dresser nearly always. Here the mother washes and combs and dresses her flock, and they all look miraculously clean.

.

VACCINATING NEGROES AGAINST TYPHOID AT A CAMP IN
VICKSBURG, MISSISSIPPI

Chapter XXVII

EPISODE: ACADIANS IN THE FLOOD

IF you will look at a map of Louisiana you will see that nearly the entire State is a network of waterways. Trace with your finger the progress of the Mississippi River from Natchez toward Baton Rouge, and between these two points you will see Red River where this stream empties itself into the Mississippi. Here the main river divides itself, part of the current going down the channel past Baton Rouge and New Orleans, and another part going by way of the Atchafalaya River directly to the Gulf of Mexico. The meeting-place of these three rivers is known as the "Old River District," and it is just here that the worst flood in the history of the whole valley is taking place in May and June, 1927.

For, with the breaking of many levees, a torrent has descended upon Louisiana, covering the central and south-western portion with a roaring sea, and flooding sections that have never known flood before. If you will trace with your finger a line from the mouth of Red River, west of the Mississippi, but covering the land on both sides of the Atchafalaya toward the Gulf, you will gain some idea of the magnitude of the flooded area. Let your finger-tip pass through the towns of the Evangeline country, Morgan City, New Iberia, Saint Martinsville. . . . No, even with a map it is hard to make you see. . . . Think, rather, of an inland ocean of muddy water more than twenty miles wide, extending for two hundred miles through the center of the

357

State, covering farm- and pasture-lands, covering towns and villages, turning houses over, battering churches down, blotting out everything as it goes. Think, then, of the water spreading out, moving slower, covering the more distant towns with only two or three feet of water, but with enough to ruin the crops, destroy all growing things, and kill all small animals. Think of a flooded area so large that the island of Manhattan could be dropped into it with hardly a splash.

Look at your map once more, and if it is a large map you will see, just at the mouth of Red River, a winding stream—Bayou des Glaises. From this bayou, south, is the country of the Acadians. Driven from Nova Scotia in the latter half of the eighteenth century, they came to Louisiana; being simple farmer folk, they sought homes along the streams of the State, spreading out farther and farther as the families increased. They are quiet, happy people, tilling the soil and raising families; they are hospitable, laughing people—pretty, demure little women; men with black eyes and flashing white teeth; children that prefer laughter to tears.

We who remember Bayou des Glaises from other summers, recall a verdant, peaceful country of small farms and large plantations. Cotton and sugar-cane fields simmering in the sun; good black earth with green things growing in it; fruit trees bending under the weight of peaches, plums, pears, and purple figs; a land like a flower garden, covered with lush, semi-tropical growth; pink crêpe-myrtle-trees, red and white oleanders, pale yellow banks of acacia blossoms, and fern-like mimosa-trees bearing flowers the summer through. And everywhere, half buried in vines, stand small white cottages with faded blue-green window blinds, quiet and cool in all the simmering heat. Here women are busy at their household tasks while men labor in the fields. And from the houses come the laughter of children and the babble of soft French, slurringly spoken.

Today the whole section is inundated with muddy waters which spread out on every side, with never a dry spot anywhere—an endless expanse of desolation. For the water has risen above the houses, above the trees, above the levees. Here and there a small island, a part of a broken levee, shows above the rushing water. On these islands are huddled cows, horses, dogs, mules—lost and abandoned. On every side the water rushes by. The animals are hopeless, dying.

The surface of the water is filled with floating objects—furniture, chairs and tables, chicken-coops, bee-hives, barrels, floating downstream toward the Atchafalaya and on toward the Gulf of Mexico. On some of the larger pieces of wreckage chickens are perched—chickens which have taken refuge on levee-tops, levees which are now inundated, levees upon which men, and even women, toiled fearfully two weeks ago. And while they were toiling, the crest of the flood came, wiping out the levees like paper, rushing over the levee-tops. The "big bend" of Bayou des Glaises was chaos within the space of a few hours. So swiftly did the whole terrain fill with water that men had no time to salvage anything from their homes except those articles which they could carry in their hands. The first rush was for the levee-tops or to the tops of houses, and there the people remained while the water climbed higher and higher. They were marooned until the rescue boats came.

Anchored in Old River, between the Mississippi and Red River, the rescue boats were waiting, in charge of Red Cross officials. It was with four men from the coast guard —a rescue squad—that I got into the heart of the flooded area. Our squad was one of a hundred operating there.

Bronzed and blistered men are these, working at this grim business of life-saving for many weeks, moving farther and farther down the Mississippi, following the crest of the flood. Here are large river steamboats, picturesque vessels of another and happier age than ours; here are submarine chasers, manned by sailors; here are the stanch river tugs and smaller river boats; here are hundreds of motor-driven surf-boats, small enough to ride through the holes in the broken levees and cruise about the inundated country where hundreds of men, women, and children are marooned, helpless and hungry, on levee-tops, in trees, and in water-swept houses.

For days I went with the coast guard men in these surf-boats into the back country of the Bayou des Glaises section. The hours dragged on under the burning sun, brighter still reflected from the water. The flood is vast and terrible. Picture to yourself this great inland sea, mile upon mile of muddy water, with never a bit of dry land anywhere; houses askew, roofs fallen in, and the water filled with dead animals. On ridge-poles of houses are roosting chickens, marooned and left to starve. Abandoned dogs bark pitifully from housetops—hunting dogs mostly, pointers and setters, left behind in the mad rush to escape.

And everywhere, rising above the water, are half-submerged trees, pink crêpe-myrtles, blossoming magnolias, the creamy blossoms beginning to turn brown already from the surrounding water. Floating here and there, the household treasures are seen, prized possessions which were carried to the levee-tops, only to be abandoned there in the mad rush for safety as the water rose higher and higher. Beds and bedding, chairs and sofas, objects having a mute and tragic quality of their own.

What is the story of this red and blue patchwork quilt,

Photo by Ewing, Baton Rouge

DEVASTATED COUNTRY LEFT BY THE RECEDING WATERS AT BAYOU DES GLAIZES

lying in the mud of the levee-top? Where is the miserable and terror-stricken woman who has dropped it here in her flight? To what child did this doll belong, a doll dressed as a baby, wearing a knitted jacket of light blue—some child's prized possession, now lying half in, half out of the water? Where is the girl who dropped the mirror which lies face upturned in the sunlight, sending out blinding radiance into our eyes as we come chugging beside the levee in our motor-boat?

As we go farther along Bayou des Glaises—farther from the Mississippi—we find more and more refugees, negroes mostly, living in rough board shacks which they have constructed on the levee-top. Here, surrounded by their chickens, their hogs, and their meager household treasures, they wait for the rescue boats to come for them, preferring to remain near their possessions rather than go to safety:

"No, suh . . . Ah's rather wait till de big boat come fo' us. . . . Den Ah can tek muh mule wid me . . . muh mule and muh dawg. . . . Dat's all Ah got lef'." Then, after a pause: "But, boss, Ah shore is hongry. . . . Ain't yo' got nuthin' tuh eat in dat boat?"

Who can blame the negro, or the white man, for refusing to leave the little that he has? Born and bred in this quiet, peaceful country, he fears the unknown—and what assurance can we give that his possessions will be restored to him?

We press on, farther and farther into the flooded country. Now we have left even Bayou des Glaises far behind and are in the inner country. Chickens, pigs, dogs upon housetops, starving. Chickens in trees—sometimes in close proximity to snakes which coil among the branches, seeking safety from the water. There are squirrels, opossums, 'coons, other small animals, high in the branches above us. And over all this desolation comes the clear, high call of the mocking-bird, winging its way from tree to tree. Cardinals fly low over the water, their crimson feathers glinting in the sunlight. Herons, white and blue, swoop down, undismayed by the flood. And high in the air, black buzzards, circling lower.

Upon a housetop we find an aged negro, crying out to be rescued, but when we come close and urge him to enter our boat, he refuses to leave his beehives—six of them— over which the bees, disturbed, are buzzing angrily. The bronzed and blistered sailor beside me, throws up his hands in exasperation: "And how the hell," he asks, "can we take your beehives into our lifeboat?" The old negro is stubborn. "Ah'll wait fo' de big boat," he says.

We have crossed the "big bend" now and are back in Bayou des Glaises once more. A clear hail comes across the water toward us. A man in a rowboat is calling. We come close. Near-by is his house, the roof projecting above the rushing water which washes about the eaves. Upon this roof is a strange gathering: two half-grown boys, four dogs, a cat and kittens, and perhaps thirty chickens. Red roosters stand like living weather-cocks upon the chimneys.

The man's name is Ambrose Lemoine: "An' I tell you, my frien', this is one hell of a mess to happen to a man. *Mon Dieu!* I assu' you, I was workin' on the levee when she break under me! *Sacre!* How my wife scream! I look behind' me and I see my l'il children flopping like fish in the water! Ah, I tell you, my frien', I work like the devil to get my l'il children on the roof! But what I wan' know is: where my wife an' chile got to?" All this delivered so rapidly that we can hardly understand.

His wife, we learn, along with the smaller children, has been picked up by a rescue boat and taken out to safety aboard one of the large river steamboats anchored in the Mississippi. We tell him that he will find his wife safe in the refugee camp in Baton Rouge, but he is dubious.

"Ha! You don't know my wife! You never can tell what that woman going to do! She got sister in New Iberia. She got brother in Houma. She got cousin in Natchez. God knows where she gone!"

When we try to get him to come with us into the life-boat, he refuses: "What! Me leave my cow and my mule and my dog and cat? I tell you no!" We point out that it is extremely difficult to get food to him in this remote spot, and that he may go hungry many days, but he is determined to stick it out. He has been able to find food for his cows and horses by breaking off leaves from half-submerged trees; a little canned food was left for himself, his sons, the cat, and dogs.

Fastened to the eaves of the house is a hastily constructed raft of logs, and upon this are the cow and calf, the mule, and two horses. The raft rises and falls in the rushing water.

The household treasures which he has taken to the roof make an incongruous picture in the blinding sunlight: a photograph album bound in red plush, a patent rocking-chair, quilts and blankets, a water-cooler, trunks, a bicycle, and—oddly enough—half a dozen potted plants, red geraniums, a gay splash of color. A hen and a brood of young chickens are pecking about on the shingles. In the shadow of the chimney a cat lies, regarding us with mild yellow eyes, her paws folded under her.

As we chug on our way he calls after us: "Hey! If you see my wife, tell her we're all right, and we'll stay here till she come home again!"

With my inner eye I see that sad homecoming—ruined crops, ruined houses—the savings of a lifetime destroyed. But Ambrose Lemoine is making the best of it.

His psychology is not peculiar among those who dwell behind the levees in Louisiana. And his stubborn refusal to leave his home is characteristic of the Acadian. Everywhere they have been reluctant to leave; and who can blame them? For they leave behind everything that they have loved and labored to attain. Yet, this refusal to leave the threatened areas has proved one of the greatest problems of the 1927 flood. The people will not take the warnings seriously, and remain at home until the crevasse comes; then they grow hysterical with fright.

In the face of all difficulties, the Red Cross is doing a magnificent work, rescuing these people and feeding them. Eventually they will be sent home again when the waters have receded.

In Baton Rouge and in Natchez there are camps where the refugees are housed, where they are fed, and where they are given medical attention when ill. Every precaution is taken to prevent an epidemic. Ten thousand refugees are housed in the city of Baton Rouge. Even more in Natchez. And these are but two of the camps.

Late in the afternoon, when our surf-boat has taken as many refugees as it will hold, we go back through the flood to the *Kankakee,* a large steamboat which is anchored at the mouth of Red River. Here our refugees are put aboard, here they are fed, here they remain until the river steamer *King* comes by to pick them up and bring them down the river to Baton Rouge.

It is twilight, and the big boat is crowded. Men and women stand mute, looking out over the rushing river. Children, blistered from the sun, cry in their mothers' arms.

AIRPLANES USED IN RESCUE WORK FORMED A PART OF THE EMERGENCY FLEET AT
THE STANDARD OIL COMPANY'S REFINERY AT BATON ROUGE

It is like some horror of war—only this time the enemy is the Mississippi.

And yet there is always a glamour about the river, even in this tragic time. Twilight deepens, blotting out the distant line of trees which marks the place where land had been a few weeks ago. All about us is movement—motorboats go chugging by; submarine chasers lie alongside, their decks filled with sailors; other river steamboats are seen, the red and green lights upon the twin smokestacks bright in the gathering dusk. The air becomes cooler since the sun has set, and the breeze is filled with the scent of crushed, wet willow-trees.

Out of the darkness comes a large steamboat—the U. S. S. *William R. King* of St. Louis. All the refugees —286 of us—are put aboard. We swarm over the decks. The *King* pushes three large barges before her, abreast. The center barge is filled with negroes, under a tent, all their worldly goods piled around them. To the left is a barge packed tight with cows which low incessantly. The barge on the right is similarly loaded with a mixed cargo of horses and mules, cows and calves. The animals are crowded with no regard to their torture—this through direct necessity. So tight-packed are they, that they rise one above the other. The horses whinny; the cows low. Their torture is like some dream of hell.

The women and children are crowded together inside the cabin and upon the rear decks of the steamboat; the white men are on the forward deck above the negroes, the mules, and the cattle. Other barges are towed alongside the *King,* and the whole presents the picture of a floating island—an island loaded with as miserable a freight as can be imagined.

The searchlight, playing from the upper deck, lights up the barges before us, showing the milling animals, the crouching negroes, the whole miserable scene. Acadians, thin and bronzed, go about the edges of the cattle barges, trying to do what they can for the animals there. One tall, thin boy wearing a tattered red sweater stands watching a calf being trampled beneath the hoofs of frightened cows.

The animals kick and bite each other, showing the whites of their eyes. And always the pitiful cries of distress, of thirst, of hunger, of fright. I go forward upon the barge and speak to the boy in the red sweater—one refugee to another. I speak of the plight of the animals, and he says: "Po' things . . . they've been there since yesterday." Then he forgets me, watching again the black and white calf which is now flecked with blood from the crushing hoofs of the larger animals.

I go back to the steamer again. Here the decks are filled with sprawling figures, men and boys, making a pretense of sleeping. The breeze is cool, but the deck is hot, for beneath us are the boilers.

A whisper is in circulation. Something is wrong. Fear of the unknown stalks among us. There is a rumor, the captain says, of a crevasse in the river below us. If this is true, he must tie the *King* up for the night—for, should this heavily laden boat come within the area of a crevasse, we might be carried through to death.

The searchlight plays along the distant banks, picking out the levee-tops, standing a scant two feet above the rushing water. Between us and the levees are fringes of willows— growing on the batture, or that part of the bank which extends beyond the levee in low-water time, but which is now completely flooded. The pilot has found trees large enough to offer secure anchorage, and the *King*, with its barges before it, is headed for the bank. The boat and barges nose into the willows, crashing down the smaller trees before us. How green the leaves appear in the glare of the searchlight! How unreal it all seems—the barges of animals, the crouching negroes, the white men, leaning forward, watching anxiously.

The smaller trees crack off like match-stems. Large trees fall before the weight of the cattle barges; then, after a long moment, there is a jolt, a cry. Men run along the edge of the barges, throwing out ropes. We are made fast, and swing about with the current. We find ourselves against a gigantic tree, which stands half out of the water. The green leaves are all about us, reaching to the upper decks. The boat seems to be in a wood—were it not for the rushing water below decks.

The crowded cattle grasp hungrily at the leaves which are just out of their reach. A brown and white spotted cow falls and is trampled upon. The little black and white calf is dead now, flecked with blood. Frenzied mules kick each other with fiendish force.

Above, on the deck, we talk: "Yes, sir! Four thousand acres I had under cultivation. There's not one acre above water. It was the richest land in the State. My hay alone would have brought $10,000 this year." The man sits huddled up, figuring on a scrap of paper by the reflection from the searchlight. He talks to any one who will listen.

Near-by a man of middle age, an Acadian, mumbles excitedly to himself: "A day laborer . . . that's what I'll be. . . . Not a thing left. All I had was two hundred hogs. I didn't get one of them out. Yessir! All of 'em drowned. I'm too old to begin again. . . . I can't." And he wanders off into the darkness.

Another man: "I'll never go back. No, not me! I never want to see that country again. All my life I live there—and now!"

Still another: *"Sacre,* man! Sure you'll go back! We'll all go back! What I say is this: 'If you haven't got, you can't lose!' Ain't that the truth?" He laughs.

A little boy, round-eyed, holding his father's hand, says: "When will it be mawnin', Papa? Is it nearly mawnin', Papa?" And the man says: "Sh-sh! Let the poor people sleep!"

". . . And out at Bayou Choupique where I come from, we go on the roof. . . . But what you know? The house capsize . . . like that! I tell you, man, I see trouble this year!"

A woman is walking up and down the deck, moaning. Nobody knows what the trouble is, and she will not answer when spoken to. She has been walking so for an hour. Another woman comes and leads her away.

A boy of perhaps fourteen years comes close to me in the darkness: "Mister, for God's sake, tell me what to do when we get to Baton Rouge . . . me and my cow. . . . There she is, brindled like . . . see? She's going to have a calf. She'll get trampled to death sure . . . sure!"

Down on the barge before us, where the negroes are camped, an aged negro man has lumped down among drums of gasoline and bundles tied up with clothes-lines. A young negro girl kneels beside him, putting a cup to his lips. The searchlight moves on, blotting out the picture.

We settle down to sleep as best we can, waiting for safety, and sunrise, and dry land.

JAMES FEISER, ACTING NATIONAL CHAIRMAN, AMERICAN RED
CROSS; HERBERT HOOVER, SECRETARY OF COMMERCE, AND
DWIGHT DAVIS, SECRETARY OF WAR

Photographed at Vicksburg while on tour of inspection of refugee camps

Chapter XXVIII

THE WAY OF THE RIVER

THERE was no more danger from the river this year, the engineers promised, but there was work to be done, and done in a hurry, if the valley was not to be impoverished for the next generation. This was the work of rebuilding a new civilization on the mud and slime left in the wake of the river.

The homes and farms of the valley had been turned into a gigantic pile of *débris*. The condition of the wreckage was described in an editorial in "The New Republic" for May 18:

A third of a million persons live in the areas affected. Of these, many have lost everything they had in the world. The work of rehabilitation will be as difficult and expensive, in proportion, as was the restitution of the devastated areas in France and Belgium after the war. * * * The damage to property is estimated at various amounts, from two hundred million up. Since a great part of this comes from the pockets of poor people who have lost all they have in the world, the work of rehabilitation will require huge sums, which are not now in sight. Fields must be replanted, cattle and work animals replaced, houses repaired or substitutes built, roads reconstructed.

But the flooded States dug down into their pockets and with the aid of the Federal Government brought funds into sight. Credit corporations were organized for the benefit of

369

the impoverished planters, and seeds and work animals were bought for distribution. The work of closing the gaps in the levees, though it got very little publicity, was a work as expensive as it was important; the New Orleans levee board, in an estimate presented June 29, reported that the repair of the Caernarvon crevasse alone would cost $150,-000. There was, however, a large group who advocated leaving this crevasse open permanently as part of a spillway system. There was widespread discussion during the early summer as to whether the rebuilding of the levees should be done by the States or the Federal Government, the consensus in most cases being that the Federal Government should pay the cost, both because work of rehabilitation was already straining the finances of the lower valley, and because it was generally felt that since the lower valley had been the dumping-ground for the drainage of thirty-odd States, flood control was a national problem.

"Secretary Davis of the war department and General Edgar Jadwin, the chief of engineers, spent a considerable portion of the day discussing the matter of local contributions for the reconstruction of levees for the replacement of Federal funds used during the high-water fight," reported Paul Wooten, the Washington correspondent of the "Times-Picayune," in the issue of June 30. "While there are some legal obstructions still to overcome, there is every reason to believe that there will be no insistence upon local payments conditioned upon the action which Congress itself will take. The conferences today were with Senator Broussard and other Louisiana representatives. * * * Senator Broussard was told that orders had been issued to proceed as rapidly as possible with the work of closing the gaps in the levee line."

The condition of the flooded districts when the river had

become safe enough to permit tours of inspection was sufficient to justify Governor Simpson's exclamation, "Louisiana has been stricken to her knees!" ("New Orleans States," May 15.) The flooded parishes as they appeared to the inspection party were described by Meigs O. Frost of the "States" in the issue of May 15:

Governor O. H. Simpson and Adjutant-General L. A. Toombs of Louisiana this morning at Monroe finished the first lap of the governor's tour of the battle-fronts of flooded Louisiana. Four hundred miles through six parishes they had gone in the conservation cruiser *Louisiana* since Thursday. They found an area of more than four thousand square miles stricken down, fathoms deep, beneath the swirling waters of such a flood as Louisiana has never known.

From daylight to dark they sailed through the parishes of Avoyelles, Concordia, Catahoula, and Caldwell, for two days without seeing the faintest sign of land except for the tops of two Indian mounds at Jonesville, the heights of the Catahoula hills at Harrisonburg, the other heights of Sicily Island, and the hills back of Columbia in Caldwell parish. It was a land utterly desolate, inhabited only by refugees crowded in emergency camps and by those who stayed by their homes fighting to save their water-soaked possessions. More than twenty thousand are refugees in the area through which the governor passed. * * * "Louisiana has been stricken to her knees!" said the governor, as he stepped ashore at Monroe this morning.

While government engineers considered plans for making similar disasters impossible in the future, the people of the Mississippi Valley regarded the other problem before them —that of rehabilitation of their country. It means very little to a farmer to tell him that the Government will see to it that his farm will not be turned into a lake again, when all that is left of what used to be his farm is a swampy waste, bare of crops and live-stock, his home and outbuildings lashed to pieces and perhaps even the pieces floating down to the Gulf, while he in his tent on the levee has not so much as a mule for plowing nor a handful of cotton seed to start a new crop. The farmers of the valley had the task of pioneering in a desolate country, and the States saw that it was up to them to give their citizens a new beginning. So in the cities of the valley—New Orleans, Natchez, Vicksburg, Memphis, Little Rock, Baton Rouge, and others—men and women settled down to tackle the problem of rehabilitation.

"Rehabilitation" is an unwieldy word. Secretary Hoover preferred to call it "reconstruction." But "reconstruction" still has an unpleasant effluvium in the South. They always spell it with a capital R, and it always carries an indefinite connotation of carpet-baggers and scalawags, and its proper place is in the classic line, "It wasn't the war, it was Reconstruction." Cæsar Augustus knew he could govern Rome as long as he didn't call himself a king; and the southern farmer is glad to remedy his farm with northern capital as long as nobody calls it Reconstruction.

In discussing what he termed "the greatest peace-time calamity in the history of our country," in a radio address from New Orleans May 29, Secretary Hoover described the work of rehabilitation as it was being conducted:

But, unfortunately, our problem does not end when the waters have receded. We are faced with the difficult task of reconstruction. These people must be returned to their farms and villages. They must be put upon the road to self-support. Thousands have had their homes washed away or damaged, businesses have been prostrated, the crops already planted for this year have been drowned out, hundreds of thousands of animals have perished, their resources of food and forage are

Photo by Marshall Gray, U. S. Engineers' Corps, 1927

WATER POURING THROUGH THE BREAK IN THE LEVEE AT MELVILLE, LOUISIANA, INUNDATING MILLIONS OF ACRES OF THE "SUGAR BOWL"

gone. Much of their implements are lost and household furnishings gone or damaged. Often enough there is but the bare land to welcome them back.

It is our duty as citizens of a great and prosperous country to assist those people back on the road of self-support. The majority are farmers, and therefore the beginning of the road to self-support to the majority means that we must enable them to replant their fields. It must be done at once before it is too late to make this year's crop. If our help is sufficient and our organization effective, the crop can be got in over most of the territory in Mississippi and north Louisiana, Arkansas, and the States above. Southern Louisiana will be a more difficult problem, for their crops are planted earlier than in the north and the flood will be on for a month yet.

We have not been idle in preparation. All this reconstruction involves many and difficult problems in which the people of the South themselves alone have the experience for determination and leadership. In this direction the governors of the three most affected States have each of them appointed state reconstruction commissions of able men, and we propose that our national agencies shall coöperate with and support them. Jointly, as between the state commissions and the Red Cross, we are erecting in every county a county reconstruction committee comprised of their leading citizens.

The committees are engaged in examining the condition of each of the flooded citizens who needs assistance. They are authorized to take emergency steps while fuller measures of help are devised. It has quickly developed that the problem is one of credit to carry on the usual wheels of production as well as relief assistance to get them started. The agriculture in the flooded country even normally depends largely upon credit to carry on from month to month in producing the crop. In addition to physical destruction and the necessity to plant all over again, the volume of credit has necessarily been impaired, due to the large losses in the South, so that to remedy any deficiency we have jointly with the State commissions coöperated with the leading bankers of each State to organize special farm loan companies through which liberal loans can be made to all those who have or whom we can by relie. measures build back to the substance of credit. These special loan companies to assist in reconstruction have now been created in three States with a capital of half a million dollars each, subscribed by their own citizens.

We have arranged to rediscount their loans in the intermediate credit from Washington at the ratio of four to one, thus multiplying their credit resources. The United States Chamber of Commerce has announced an appeal to the industrial and financial institutions of our Northern States that they should subscribe additional sums to the capital of these loan companies for the flood territory. It is a service of the utmost importance. The local banks and merchants will find a large part of the credit necessary to carry on, but to have the whole situation buttressed against the deficiencies in this direction is vital if we are to succeed in our job of raising these people up out of the flood to within reach of the credit rope; and they do not want relief a moment beyond that time. They want to fight their own way back.

Our immediate problem is imperative: that we get the crops in, or the dimensions of the catastrophe will be enormously increased. Therefore, those who are destitute, and whose homes and household furniture are gone, have been given the use of their camp tents and bedding. We have authorized for them the purchase by the county committees of the very minimum of work animals and seed and the implements that will get in the crop. Upon their return home, we are giving to them food and feed for their animals for from two to four weeks.

All this is a race with the season to get the planting in time. If we can get the crop safely above the ground, the position of many of them will be much the same in their ability to command credit to carry them on until harvest as it was before the flood. That part of the flooded people who are wage-earners and tradesmen are also receiving consideration. Some of them we can rehabilitate with credit, others we must continue to sustain until we can find employment for them. We are receiving the coöperation of the railways and the government agencies in securing this employment on emergency repair works.

All this is the emergency state of reconstruction. It is already working in the northern part of the valley, and we are following down the receding waters with this organization just as our rescue and exile organizations have followed in turn. Beyond this first emergency action we must help to rebuild homes to replace the tents, we must supply further animals and implements. We must assure safety against disease by widespread measures of sanitation, lasting for months. In many ways, reconstruction is more difficult than the other stages. The excitement and appeal of the human life in jeopardy, of women and children in distress, stir the sympathies and energies of all decent men and women. This is now passing, and the public loses its interest. Yet, let us not forget, we must return this one-half million of our fellow-citizens to the road of self-support.

"The New Orleans States" for May 29 reported: "Already in Arkansas and Mississippi the planters are working to salvage the largest possible crop, though the flood waters are receding from their lands more slowly than ever before in history, the United States agricultural experts have just reported to Secretary Hoover."

It took longer to get started in Louisiana, because the State had received the last of the flood, and drainage was slow. L. O. Crosby of Picayune was made rehabilitation chairman for Mississippi, and Colonel W. H. Sullivan, mayor of Bogalusa, chairman for Louisiana. Mr. Crosby, a veteran at flood relief, gave the Louisiana commission a pat on the back and told them things would be easier when the waters went down, according to "The New Orleans Tribune," May 29:

That things will turn out better than we think, was the statement of Mr. Crosby, who described rehabilitation work in

Mississippi, where it is considerably further advanced than here. * * * "As soon as the people gain confidence in what you are doing," he said, "you will be amazed at the way they will take hold. The secret is not to wait for the waters to go away, but to plan to work in skiffs. We in Mississippi have never been more than two days behind the waters in getting the people back in their homes and preparing for another crop."

Definite steps toward rehabilitation were reported in the "Times-Picayune" the same day:

With flood waters beginning to recede from the overflowed areas of northeast Louisiana, the machinery for assisting in the restoration of the devastated regions is rapidly being assembled, it developed at a meeting of the Louisiana Rehabilitation Commission at the Canal Bank building Saturday morning.

Organization of a finance corporation, which will probably be known as the Louisiana Farm Credit Company, has reached the point where a capitalization of $750,000 can be assured, it was announced by James P. Butler, president of the Canal Bank. This means that ultimately credit facilities to the extent of six million dollars will be available to help the farmers make their crops this year.

Administration of this credit fund will primarily be directed by local committees in the affected parishes. The Red Cross organization will be used for this purpose to a large extent, with the members of the Rehabilitation Commission strengthening the committees in the parishes in their districts by the addition of financial and other representatives. * * * The plan is for Louisiana financial interests to supply a capitalization of $750,000, which will be doubled by a subscription of the same amount from the fund being raised nationally by the United States Chamber of Commerce. This would give a working capital of $1,500,000, which can be discounted with the Federal land banks at a ratio of four to one, thus furnishing a total credit of six million dollars for rehabilitation of Louisiana's farmers. * * *

J. L. Feiser, acting chairman of the National Red Cross,

Courtesy of Red Cross

REFUGEES LIVING ON THE SLOPE OF THE LEVEE

said that in the overflowed districts of Arkansas and other States to the north, assurance and even enthusiasm are becoming apparent as the problems are met and solved. The sixteen million dollars or more that is going into the various States for relief work, he asserted, is being so administered that it serves a constructive purpose and forms a basis for the extension of considerable banking credit. When the refugees return to their homes, he pointed out, they must obtain shelter, sustenance, seed, a minimum of agricultural implements, feed for their live stock and other essentials.

The rehabilitation work in the valley in general was outlined by an Associated Press correspondent in a dispatch sent out May 30:

Out of the greatest flood disaster in its history, Secretary of Commerce Hoover is hoping to bring through his reconstruction plans new and improved conditions of life and health to the seven hundred thousand homeless persons in the Mississippi Valley. The machine created by the cabinet member who has directed the immense task of rescue, relief, and now rehabilitation of the victims for the past five weeks, augurs two improvements—better health conditions and probably greater diversification of the agricultural crops of the inundated regions, so that in the future its farmers will not be dependent solely upon one staple crop's market value. * * *

The improvement of health conditions in the flood region, it is expected, will result from two phases of Mr. Hoover's relief and reconstruction plan. The six hundred thousand refugees who were under the care of the Red Cross received typhoid and smallpox inoculations, the greatest single precautionary movement against these most dreaded diseases of the valley ever accomplished in the region. After the waters recede, Mr. Hoover has ordered the health authorities of the three flooded States of Arkansas, Louisiana, and Mississippi to make a thorough inspection and sanitary clean-up of the inundated lands, burying dead animals and eliminating all disease menaces.

In giving the farmers a new start in life when they return to their homes, Mr. Hoover's reconstruction scheme will encourage the diversification of crops by grants of vegetable seed for the raising of "sustenance crops." Mr. Hoover believes the rehabilitated farmers should raise their own food supplies to tide them over until their basic crops of cotton, rice, and sugarcane are matured. The Federal agricultural experts are inclined to think this method of rehabilitation will mean in the future more sustenance, and vegetable crops may be grown in the valley, and the farmers will not tend to put all their eggs in one basket with the one basic crop.

Sometimes the residents of Maine or Wisconsin are puzzled to know why so many millions must be poured into the Mississippi Valley to restore it to prosperity, and why so many more millions must be spent to make it safe from future floods. Is it essential that people live so close to the river?

To which the inhabitants of the valley answer yes, and shrug their shoulders. If the dwellers in other parts of the country had ever seen the green and gold lowlands of the subtropic lower valley, they say, there would be no question of why people must live there. However, in years of dealing with the river, they have got used to the lackadaisical attitude of the rest of the country with regard to floods. They complain sometimes, it is true. As Charles P. Jones remarked in "The New York World," May 8:

What's wrong with the river floods, contend the chief sufferers, is the fact that the rest of the country apparently forgets them as soon as they are off the first pages. A few hundred persons are drowned, a few million acres are inundated, half a dozen States suffer staggering losses; then the floods subside, the levees are rebuilt, and life proceeds on the theory that maybe, in the next flood, the crevasses will be somewhere else.

However, the 1927 flood has roused both the philosophical valley population and the skeptical inhabitants of
the rest of the country. Most persons agreed that the
deluged States must be restored to normality, and that
floods must be curbed. For those who doubt the wisdom
of filling the valley with cash as it has been filled with water,
residents of the river edges give two reasons.

The first, and the most important to the rest of the country, is that the river bottoms are the most fertile land in
the world, with the possible exception of the valley of the
Nile. The alluvial lands that lay in the path of the 1927
flood are marvelous in their richness, justifying the remark
of Longfellow's Acadian, who boasted to his friends that
more grass grew in Louisiana in a night than in a whole
Acadian summer. Farmers of the section declare that the
entire nation could be fed and clothed from the lands along
the lower Mississippi. Floods that recurred at intervals during the ages before men came and demanded the valley for
their own use have left the country so wonderful a heritage
in the soil that it would be economic madness to give the
land back to the river for a playground.

But there is another reason why the Mississippi country
must be first rebuilt and then made safe for all time. The
people of the lower valley love their homes with an intensity that apartment-dwellers of more business-like sections cannot understand. These little farms are theirs. Nothing under heaven can make them want to give up their
homes. Even among the farmers who had seen their cattle
and their beds and tables swept downstream, there was
little talk of going somewhere else to live. Crowded together in tent-towns, they smoked slow pipes and asked the
rescue workers how soon they could go home. Among
themselves they said that if they could get back in June

they could raise new crops and get through the year; with their opulent soil and abundant sunshine they knew they could. They will not give up.

They cannot be blamed, after all, when one remembers the loveliness of the country in which they live, with its palm-bordered roads, its bayous trailing their way under live-oak-trees that dip into the water their festoons of gray moss, trees filled with southern birds in the nine-months summer and northern birds in the short cool winter. When rescue boats were making their way up the bayous to the flooded sections above, they found it necessary to blast the water-hyacinths out of the way with dynamite, so thick they grew. It is a gorgeous country, and its people love it with an almost unbelievable fervor.

About the middle of May, coast guard cutters were sent out through the thirteen deluged parishes north of the Red River in Louisiana, to count the persons who insisted on remaining near where their homes had been. They reported to state relief headquarters that they had found eight thousand men and women camping on the levees and on the tops of their houses, or living on log rafts in the water wilderness. These people refused to move. Tales of dry beds and abundant food moved them not at all. Over there, where you saw a chimney sticking through the muddy lake, was home. Eventually the waters would go down. They'd stay, thank you.

An Associated Press dispatch from Vicksburg, May 5, described the tenacity with which they clung to home:

Difficulty is being experienced in evacuation work, because many persons express a decision to stick with their belongings or run to the levees with the hope that the flood will not be so bad as the warnings pictured it. Many go to the levees, see that the water is rising very slowly, and return to their homes be-

Photo by Marshall Gray, U. S. Engineers' Corps, 1927

THE MAIN STREET OF A LOUISIANA TOWN WHICH REMAINED UNDER WATER FOR NEARLY TWO MONTHS

fore the rescue boats arrive. * * * In addition, a number of ridges scattered through the flooded area provide places for refugees to gather, often in sight of their homes. Many prefer to sit there and wait for rations to be hauled up to them rather than go to the refugee camps.

About three fourths of the population of Concordia parish, Louisiana, remained on their housetops or on their levees while the waters covered their plantations. The parish normally has about 12,500 inhabitants. They built rafts when the floods threatened, or scaffoldings on their houses, and when the water came they took refuge there. Some of them who lived in large houses stayed on the upper floors, or on the upper floors of their barns. Rescue workers reported that these people, white and black alike, insisted that nothing but physical force would make them desert their land.

Whether, then, the valley is ever made absolutely safe or not, it will not be empty of its people. They will go back and build new houses if theirs have floated down to the Gulf. If their homes are left standing, they will scrape the mud off the floors and put new panes in the windows. Meanwhile, they will have planted their farms. The valley soil is so rich, the valley climate so glorious, that war with the river is worth an occasional defeat. They are philosophical about it. They know this is the way of the river.

Chapter XXIX

AND THE WATERS RECEDED

THIS is the first day of July. Officially, at least, the 1927 flood in the Mississippi Valley is over. Newspapers assure us of this fact. Everybody says so; it must be true.

Nevertheless, figures made available by the Red Cross on June 21 show that 590,530 persons have been cared for during the emergency; on that date there were still 63,378 persons in refugee camps, while 242,484 persons were being fed. In addition, relief forces were feeding 157,628 animals. In Louisiana 203,966 persons have been cared for, while 150,200 were still being cared for on that date. In Mississippi the total number cared for was 168,936, while 101,400 persons were still receiving help. Also, on that date, there were still two million acres of farm and pasture land under water.

Heavy rains in Arkansas, Oklahoma, Tennessee, Mississippi, and Louisiana have prolonged flood conditions in Louisiana and Mississippi by diminishing the rate of the river's fall. Cotton acreage in northern Louisiana, Mississippi, Arkansas, Missouri, and Tennessee has been reduced 529,000 acres by the flood waters, as compared with the acreage in this section in 1926, according to the bureau of agricultural economics. Nevertheless, the flood is over, and the people of the lower valley are beginning again.

Secretary Mellon has announced that, at the close of the fiscal year, there will be a surplus in the Treasury, from this year's taxation, of $600,000,000. This is an amazing amount of money, even for the richest country in the world—an overflowing treasury; but as yet there has been nothing said about using any of this surplus for rehabilitation of the flooded areas of the Mississippi Valley. And by the general term rehabilitation, the people of the lower valley mean protection from future floods.

America gave $20,000,000 to Russian and $100,000,000 to European sufferers, in wartime, but not one cent from the National Treasury has been suggested, at this writing, to safeguard the future of the vast and fertile valley which lies in the heart of the United States.

The people of this country, however, have not been so slow to show their sympathy. They have contributed $16,-100,000 already to the Red Cross. Herbert Hoover, secretary of commerce, gave this as the official figure while in New Orleans on June 28. With this sum a wonderful work has been done. This money has saved lives, fed refugees, and maintained camps for many thousands of homeless persons; it has given medical attention to the sick, and is now helping the farmers toward a new start. But the $16,100,000 will go no farther than that. What assurance have the people of the Mississippi Valley that there will not be bigger and worse floods next year? What will Congress do about it?

Maps by United States engineers show the actual drainage area of the Mississippi River. Waters from the Red, the Arkansas, the Missouri, the upper Mississippi and the Ohio rivers must flow, finally, into the main channel of the lower Mississippi, thence to the Gulf of Mexico. This drainage area is like a gigantic funnel, narrowing as it approaches the Gulf. Roughly, the outline of this funnel is like this: a line runs northwest through Louisiana, across the northern part of Texas, passes through a third of New

Mexico, bisects Colorado, on into Wyoming, which it crosses
from corner to corner; the line encircles the State of Mon-
tana and runs up into Canada, and, descending, passes
through North Dakota and curves upward again through
Minnesota, skirting just below Lake Superior; it descends
through Wisconsin and Illinois, below Lake Michigan, then
through northern Indiana and Ohio, northward again
through Pennsylvania and into lower New York; here it
drops down through Pennsylvania again, passes through
West Virginia and Virginia, then into North Carolina, and
takes off a corner of South Carolina; it includes a part of
Georgia and upper part of Alabama; the lower end of the
funnel narrows suddenly as it approaches the Gulf, and the
end of the funnel is a wide strip which includes nearly all of
Louisiana and more than half of Mississippi. Such States as
Arkansas, Kansas, Oklahoma, Nebraska, South Dakota,
Iowa, Missouri, Tennessee, and Kentucky lie wholly within
the area.

More than half of the States receive all of the benefits
of Mississippi River drainage and but few of the hardships which this drainage brings about in flood-times. The
high waters in the Mississippi, to which all the States mentioned contribute, must be taken care of by the States lying
along the rivers—the Mississippi and its largest tributaries.
In the past, each State looked to its own levees as best it
could, using its taxes and such sums as it could beg from
Congress. From Cairo to the Gulf, where levees are used
to protect the rich bottom lands, the same policy has been
followed: "If our state levees hold—well, those folks downstream must watch out for themselves."

More and more water drains into the Mississippi every
year, owing to the growth of cities along the river, the cutting away of forests, the closing of natural outlets, the

ST. MARTINSVILLE, LOUISIANA

A beautiful little town in the heart of the bayou country, covered with floodwaters. The famous "Evangeline Oak" is shown at center

reclamation of natural reservoirs into farmland protected behind levees, and also to increased drainage facilities.

Added to all these reasons for high water in 1927 came simultaneous rainfalls over nearly all of the drainage area. The tributaries rose at the same time, and these swollen streams and rivers poured their torrents into the main stream. If all the levees along the Mississippi, from Cairo to the Gulf, had remained intact—which they did not—the water would have poured over the tops of most of them.

The States that suffer mostly from overflows are those which are unfortunate enough to lie at the lower end of the narrowing funnel: Arkansas, Mississippi, and Louisiana. The case of Louisiana is typical. The State has spent every cent that it could raise by taxation and bond issue upon levees that proved inadequate. It has not only spent all the money it has for levees, but it has gone into debt to boot, and today is confronted by a vast area still under water, ruined crops, and, in some sections, a population that is penniless. Despite the work of the Red Cross—and it is notable work—the restitution is not a hundredth part of the loss.

The 1927 flood—"the greatest peace-time disaster that the United States has ever known," to quote Herbert Hoover—was a good news-story: interesting, dramatic, terrible. For a time, every newspaper in the United States was full of it. Hundreds of journalists wrote about it. Some of the articles were excellent, some were not so convincing; but it will be observed that the men who knew least about the history of the Mississippi were those who, with a gesture, solved the problem of the river's future. The men who have lived their lives beside the Mississippi are not so sure: sure that a solution *can* be worked out, but not so sure that it *will* be worked out.

It appears, at this time, that the solution will include higher and stronger levees, built to government specification; outlets or spillways—call them what you like—in several places below the mouth of the Yazoo River, and some method of source-stream control or reservoirs above that point. Part of these things—probably all of them—must be done before there will be any safety from overflows. And yet, there are arguments against each of these solutions. Since 1879 there have been men who advocated controlled outlets or spillways, and there was another and stronger group in Congress which opposed such spillways and has stood for "levees only," or confinement of the river between dikes. Some members of the latter group have changed their minds this year.

But opponents of spillways tell us that these outlets are useful only to the lower valley and would be ineffective at points higher up in the stream; they say that such outlets mean the building of sand-bars by the river's current as it sweeps through the new opening; they point out that each spillway calls for hundreds of miles of additional levee building, as these artificial streams or outlets must be protected on both sides, all the way from the river to the body of water into which they empty. Despite the arguments against such spillways, a levee at Poydras, some twenty miles below New Orleans, was dynamited to make a similar outlet when the flood waters were threatening New Orleans. Such desperate measures had never been taken before—officially, at least.

But already the propagandists are announcing, in fairly good-sized type, that "New Orleans has always been safe from the Mississippi; New Orleans will always be safe." If this be true, then some one blundered rather badly in dynamiting a levee which sent thousands of acres of rich farmland under water, made nearly four thousand people homeless, and destroyed hundreds of thousands of dollars' worth of property and an enormous number of the fur-bearing animals which have made this section the richest fur-producing region in the United States.

Such obvious propaganda defeats itself. The question is not, "Was New Orleans safe this year?" but rather, "Will New Orleans be safe in the future?" The answer to the first question is immaterial now, but the answer to the second is of paramount importance. I do not doubt that New Orleans will be safe in the future, for it has learned its lesson, has paid dearly for it, is still paying and will continue to pay for some time to come. At this moment New Orleans is caring for three thousand or more refugees from the flooded district where the artificial crevasse was made, and the city has promised restitution to those whose properties were destroyed.

Engineers seem to agree that there must be levees always, no matter what other steps are taken to prevent future floods—and they back up their statement with facts and figures taken from the conquest of the valley of the Nile, and from the past history of the Mississippi. If levees are abandoned, they point out, millions of acres of the most fertile soil in the world will be taken by the river's overflow. These fertile acres, now protected, are needed by the people of the United States.

The question of reservoirs is one even more difficult to solve, for where in the Mississippi Valley can such storage spaces for water be built? Storage spaces which must be as large as the State of New Jersey, and may not be large enough even then! This seems to be a question of bottling the flood, rather than draining it. Yet, the run-off must be slowed up in some way, for, from the Rockies to the Appalachians, erosion is taking place, and every year much of the richest top-soil is carried off down the Mississippi. It was this rich top-soil that built up the Mississippi delta; a considerable amount of it now goes out to sea in the river's muddy stream. This loss continues day after day, year after year. Unnoticed, unchecked, a great part of the country's richest farming land is being destroyed; in time, it will be unfit for cultivation. If one considers this, one can readily see that flood control is not the problem of the dwellers in the lower valley only, but a matter of real concern for the entire nation.

It is hardly possible that erosion can be checked, and improbable that floods can be done away with for all time. But the Mississippi can be slowed down and curbed. This must be done if the permanency of our agriculture is to be assured.

Theodore H. Price, writing in "Commerce and Finance" for June 15, points out that prosperity will follow the flood, as it has, he says, nearly all of the wars and other disasters of modern times. The Civil War made business hum in the United States, he writes; increased business followed the San Francisco earthquake and fire; the World War made America the richest of nations. All this may be true, may be sound reasoning, but what Mr. Price fails to point out is that one man's disaster is another man's gold. The 1927 floods may produce good business in the country at large, but those who suffered most will gain nothing from it. Many farmers who have been ruined will never recover.

The Mississippi River belongs to the United States. It is too large and too powerful for the individual States to control. Many of the States lying beside it have spent all the money available, and given all their strength to a losing fight. They are incapable of fighting it further. The river

MAIN STREET, VIDALIA, LOUISIANA, MAY, 1927

drains a vast area unaffected by flood but which should be held equally responsible for its ravages.

The United States undertook the building of the Panama Canal, the protection of Cuba and the Philippines. Surely it can take over the problem of the Mississippi; we have the brains and money. Curbing the river is a man's-size job, but it can be done. The solution, perhaps, will be slow, but relief can be given, and it must be given quickly, for not so very long after Congress meets, spring will be here, and torrents will be sweeping down the Mississippi toward the Gulf.

We are a strange people—we Americans: we so soon forget. Before the water had begun to recede, and while some of the worst floods of the year were taking place, newspaper readers had become tired of the disasters along the Mississippi. It was already an old story. Newspaper men in the flooded area were fed up on horror, fed up on bravery, bored with the terrible sameness of destruction. Even the rescuers were sated. They had seen too much suffering, had endured too much. The heat, the blistering sun and blinding water, the mosquitoes, the frightened, miserable refugees, the drowned animals. . . . There was no end to the suffering. The men who had seen the most could not talk about it.

Lindbergh flew to Paris while the waters were at their highest, and the glad news of his great triumph ended the Mississippi flood so far as American newspapers were concerned. And yet the flood waters from the McCrea break and from the Melville crevasse on the Atchafalaya River— one of the outlets from the Mississippi to the Gulf of Mexico —were sweeping down through the "sugar bowl" of Louisiana, and a body of water as wide as the Mississippi itself was flowing across country into the land of the Acadians, two hundred miles west of the Mississippi, a land that had never known flood before within the memory of living man. Had either of these disastrous breaks occurred a month earlier, every paper in the country would have been full of the horrors. But the flood was officially "over."

The day that Lindbergh landed in Paris, this was happening on Bayou Teche in southwest Louisiana:

Afternoon. A sleepy little town, swooning in the simmering heat. A negro funeral procession moving slowly down the street; a hearse bearing a coffin; many negro men and women walking slowly after it. The women wear white, the men black, for this is a member of a "burying-society" who lies dead to-day. Black shadows on the yellow dust of the road. A mangy cur follows the hearse, its tongue lolling out, keeping close in the shadow.

Hot. Hot. Palmetto fans sway back and forth as the feet of the marchers stir the dust of the long, dry street; a fine gray film settles upon black, sweat-streaked faces. Slowly the procession passes out of the town to the negro cemetery at the edge of Bayou Teche. Here moss-draped oaks stand beside the water, long streamers of gray moss dipping into the stream. The stream is level full—higher than any one remembers it in other years. The cemetery is cool and seems dim after the simmering heat of the road.

The hearse stops beside the open grave. The fresh earth is piled beside it. Men and women stand in a semicircle, holding red lilies in black hands. The coffin is placed upon the ground, and a song rises, hangs, poised in the air, for a moment, then dissipates thinly into the sunlight beyond the trees: "Death ain't nuthin' but a robber . . . in dis lan'! No, Death ain't nuthin' but a robber, in dis lan'! 'E come in yo' house, but 'e don' stay long. . . . When yo' look aroun' somebody is gone. . . . Death ain't nuthin' but a robber, in dis lan'!"

They begin a second verse, voices stronger, surer, now: "Death ain't nuthin' but a robber. . . ."

An old woman lifts her eyes as she sings, and sees across the stream, already full, a white wall of water moving silently toward them, covering everything as it comes.

The singers continue: " 'E come in yo' house, but 'e don't stay long. When yo' look aroun' . . ."

But the old woman's voice rises suddenly to a shriek: "Oh, muh Gawd! Look at dat water!"

The hymn breaks off short. The mourners stand motionless for a long second, looking at that wall of advancing water. How white it appears against the dark green of lush foliage! Then panic. The preacher cries: "Quick! Throw de coffin in de grave!"

Many hands grasp the wooden box. It drops into the hole. Men grab spades and begin to shovel in the earth. Women fall upon their knees and scoop in the earth with their hands. When the grave is half filled, the water has crossed the bayou and is upon them, the stream rushing now, widening every moment, and the cemetery ankle deep before the mourners leave, running in terror.

Water is all around them. The negroes scream. Many rushing to the hearse. Women and children are packed inside where the coffin rested only a few moments ago. Horses are lashed. The widow, already hysterical from sorrow, is lifted to the driver's seat. As the hearse reaches the cemetery gate, she looks back to see the open grave full of water, and the red lilies and white roses floating in the rushing stream. She screams but nobody listens.

They run, splashing through the deepening flood. The

homing instinct is strong, but their cabins are already knee-deep in muddy water. Frightened dogs whine from the galleries, men on horseback gallop, splashing through the streets.

"Run! Run!"

"Gawd help!"

"Hab mussy, Jesus!"

"Jesus save!"

No time to stop now. To the railroad embankment they run, crying out, falling in the water. A train is waiting, already packed full of townspeople, white and black. The mourners clamber aboard, empty-handed, as the train pulls out. Those left behind stand on the railroad track, for this is the last train out, and they must wait on housetops or in trees until the rescue boats can come—when the water is deep enough.

A hundred such scenes were enacted in Louisiana, after the flood was officially over.

This is the first of July. I write in central Louisiana, where the refugees have returned to their homes and are making a new start. Let me try to tell you what I see from the window of this house in which I write. A bare expanse of muddy field; fences down and drainage ditches obliterated. The one house that lies within my range of vision has drifted from its foundations and is askew upon the ground. Its chimney has fallen. All of its outbuildings have been washed away, and there, in the center of the field, the green-painted cistern which formerly held rainwater for drinking purposes lies half buried in mud.

Nevertheless, there are people living in that house. In the field four men working—four men who are "walking in" their seeds with bare feet, because the ground is still too

Photo by Earl Norman, Natchez

FOUR LITTLE REFUGEES, A LONG WAY FROM HOME

muddy to bear the weight of the plow and mule. There is one mule left for that family. Three were drowned or lost in the overflow. Once there were some forty hogs here. There is none here now. Once there was a flock of chickens. They are all drowned. Once there were beehives, and a cow. Not now.

In that house yonder a woman is preparing dinner for the men who work in the field; she cooks on a rusty, wood-burning stove which has been set on the sloping veranda, its pipe extending only a few feet into the air. In that house is a supply of food given by the Red Cross when the family left the refugee camp; enough food to last ten days. Leaving Baton Rouge yesterday, where they had been sheltered and cared for for a month, they were given the following things to take with them: two bushels of soy beans, three bushels of corn, ten bushels of cotton seed and one dollar's worth of garden seed. Each man was given a shovel and a hoe, and his work stock was returned to him by boat from pastures on the highlands near Baton Rouge. In addition to this, the members of the family had rations to last ten days. They were cautioned to boil all drinking water.

The Red Cross has done its part, and a glorious part it is too. The people are truly grateful, and with reason; had it not been for the organized life-saving crews working for the Red Cross, the loss of life would have been enormous.

Here in central Louisiana, among these people who have lost everything, it is difficult to look at the matter of future flood control calmly and dispassionately. For these people are beginning over again with almost nothing to start with—not even an assurance that their lands will not be inundated next year. No matter how their crops may prosper—and it is late in the summer to plant a crop under all this blistering heat—there are hard times ahead. Many of them will be hungry this fall. School-houses have been washed away, and the funds of the State are insufficient to replace them in time for the autumn session. Many churches are damaged beyond repair, and the land itself is covered with silt and sand from the receding waters.

But no matter for all that. We of the lower valley have known overflows before and each time we have begun again; but each time it is harder to begin. What we want is security from overflows. We can "get by" this time, perhaps, if there is any promise of safety for the future.

What we want is assurance that the Government of these United States will take over the task of curbing the Mississippi. We ask that, and we feel we have the right to ask it.

Appendix

EVER since the first levees built by the French colonists crumbled before the onslaught of waters, the valley has been demanding higher and stronger levees. The floods came again, always followed by .the call for higher levees. In the flood of 1882, the greatest before 1927, the levees broke in two hundred and eighty-two places. Then came 1927, and now, loud as the demand for higher levees used to be, comes the demand for something else. The valley has found that higher and stronger levees do not suffice.

Gifford Pinchot is quoted by "The Outlook" for May 18, 1927, saying: "To depend on levees alone is like depending on curing disease instead of trying to prevent it. What is needed is to avoid calamitous Mississippi floods, and that cannot be done by local measures alone. We must deal with the river system as a whole." Mr. Pinchot advocates storage reservoirs for source streams, which would be, he says, at least partly self-supporting by furnishing electric power.

Secretary Hoover and Chief of Engineers Jadwin, after visiting the flooded sections, favored levees. Their statement on the subject is condensed in "The Outlook" for May 11:

Secretary Hoover and General Jadwin, army engineer, have united in a statement the conclusion of which asserts that "levees are the practicable, feasible, and economical means for affording flood protection for the valley as a whole." * * * It contradicts what is called the most widespread fallacy about levees—namely, "the assertion that they raise the bed of the river, so that in the long run they will merely result in the formation of an elevated trough," adding that "the surveys and measurements carried on for more than a half century do not show that the levees have very appreciably raised the bed of this river."

However, "The Outlook" goes on to call attention to an editorial elsewhere in the same issue, in which the Mississippi is likened to the Hwang-ho, or Yellow River, "China's Sorrow." The Chinese, says the editorial, have been pursuing the "levees-only" plan for a long time, with disastrous results :

To stop the river from meandering, to overcome the consequences of the reckless destruction of their forests, the Chinese have from time immemorial been building dikes. As the river bed has risen they have built their dikes higher. They did not foresee, or if they foresaw they did not care, what would happen. As human life is measured, the process of confining the river has been a slow one. John R. Freeman, the famous American hydraulic engineer, has estimated the rate of elevation of the bed of the Yellow River as "hardly more than one foot in a hundred years." But as hundreds of years have run into thousands, the bed of the Yellow River is now in some places as much as twenty feet above the level of the surrounding country. The river, instead of running in a channel, thus runs on a bridge.

What happens when the Yellow River bursts through its dikes appalls the imagination. No man can conceive the terror, the suffering, the desolation. * * *

We have begun by imitating the Chinese. Of course, we have not gone so far as they. We have checked, but not stopped, the practice of destroying forests. But we are building levees along the Mississippi with the same disregard of the future that the Chinese have shown in building their dikes along the Hwang-ho.

We have let the floods come, and then we have futilely tried to control them.

Is there no better way?

Lincoln Colcord, writing in "The Minneapolis Tribune," urges that in controlling the Mississippi we employ the engineering principle of Li-Ping, a Chinese engineer of 175 B.C., who advised, "Dig the bed deep, keep the banks low"— the principle that has controlled the water of the Min River in the province of Szechwan since the day of Li-Ping.

"Dig the bed deep, keep the banks low." It should be obvious to any layman's mind that the thing to do with the Mississippi River is to dredge the bottom and deposit the annual sediment on the surrounding country as fertilizing material. This would help to pay the cost of the enterprise; such sediment would have commercial value. Mechanical progress has given us all sorts of efficient mud-sucking dredging machinery. The gift of science to us is the ability to do what China has been unable to do with the Yellow River. But the correct principles must never be departed from. Mud-sucking dredgers should be put to work up and down the Mississippi River. The river should be brought back, if possible, to the level of its old natural bed. The levees should be abandoned wherever possible as the level is lowered. In connection with this, there should be a system of dams and reservoirs on the tributary streams for impounding the flood waters. The improvement in navigating conditions alone on the Mississippi River would return the cost of the enterprise to the wealth of the nation.

But the main item of this centralized plan must be the constant dredging of the river. "Dig the bed deep, keep the banks low." The question is not whether we can do it; there is nothing else to do. All other plans only lead to ultimate disaster.

T. G. Winter, of Minneapolis, in a letter published in "The Outlook" for May 18, observes:

The great floods now ravaging the Mississippi Valley are considered by many to be an "act of God." They are, on the contrary, most distinctly the work of man. For generations we have been doing our best to produce them. Had our sole object been to flood out our neighbors on the lower Mississippi, we could have done nothing that we have not done for years to bring about this catastrophe.

At the headwaters of the great river and its affluents we have drained every possible marsh. We have put in endless dams to keep the river from overflowing into lowlands that would hold back the flood waters. We have deepened the channel so as more quickly to deliver the flood southward. We have turned the waters of Lake Michigan into the river instead of its natural outlet, the St. Lawrence. And worst of all, we have swept off our forests and burned off the great sponge of forest floor that once covered a vast territory at the headwaters and held the snow water for gentle delivery all through the summer.

John R. Freeman, in "The Outlook" for June 8, contends that levees alone cannot hold back maximum floods, even with the aid of revetments. After saying that the levee line between Cairo and New Orleans has never been fully built to the size and strength advocated by the Mississippi River Commission, he adds:

With the levees completed to the full height, great flood dangers will still remain. The problem of holding this meandering river to its course, so as to prevent its attack from undermining levees, is a far more difficult, far more slow, and far more expensive matter than all of the levee construction involved from beginning to end.

The accepted methods of restraining the river from undermining levees and threatening farms or populous cities with inundation, by holding it back by revetment of these banks with mattresses composed of interwoven willow-trees, wires, and slabs of concrete, cost at a rate of nearly one third of a million dollars per mile of shore line. At the rate of construction of the past twenty years, two hundred years would be required to protect all of the shore line, and beyond this cost

Photo by Ewing, Baton Rouge

RECEDING WATERS LEAVE RAILROAD TRACKS A MASS OF TANGLED WRECKAGE

of original construction would be added many millions of dollars per year for its maintenance. Work of this kind could not be largely hurried without extravagant cost, because of lack of willow mattress material and other reasons. * * *

Levees costing fifty million dollars and revetments costing four hundred million dollars more would not be a perfect or a permanent remedy, and yearly maintenance costs will be enormous. The facts should be collected and looked squarely in the face.

The dangers of the "levees-only" plan, as outlined by Mr. Freeman, fall into four classes: first, the danger of sandboils, or water whirling against a layer of sand under the levee and penetrating the embankment from underneath, which sometimes happens as the result of the meeting of opposing currents in the river; second, the caving-in of the foreshore, caused by heavy *débris* floating downstream; third, seepage through old or hastily-built levees, which causes tiny streams that ultimately undermine the bank; and fourth, the work of crawfish, which burrow under the levee and release the water in tiny but disastrous streams.

There are nearly two thousand miles of levee on the Mississippi River alone, protecting thirty thousand square miles of property. Advocates of the "levees-only" plan have said something about "unbreakable levees"—but is there any such thing? The residents of the Mississippi Valley never saw one, and they know that floods even more severe than the flood of 1927 are possible. Great stretches of land are being artificially drained into the river channel, and the river is being called upon to bear an ever-increasing burden of waters. If all the seven rivers of the North that drain into the Mississippi should be in flood at once, the Mississippi would have to carry enough water to break through any levee ever built by man.

If levees alone won't protect the valley—and authoritative opinions seem agreed that they won't—what will?

Leading engineers, as we have said, are advocating reforestation, reservoirs, or spillways, or a combination of the three methods. All three of these have been suggested before, and still we have sworn by our levees as in a more faithful age we would have sworn by the knuckle-bones of our saints; because building a levee injures nobody's property, but rather gives it a visible protection, while planting forests, constructing reservoirs, or cutting spillways spoils somebody's good land.

Engineers who have studied the problem of flood control seem to be equally divided as to the value of storage reservoirs and spillways. The former method is advocated in "The Independent" for May 7:

After the disastrous flood of 1921, Dayton and the other industrial cities in that broad, fertile valley set the genius of Arthur Morgan to work upon the problem of permanent flood control. The result is a series of reservoirs for the storage of flood waters, which have since withstood every challenge of the elements. The Mississippi already possesses a number of reservoirs primarily intended to assist navigation by furnishing additional water when the normal flow is low. Every calculation upon the possibility of Mississippi flood control is based upon equalizing flow in order that low water may be avoided as much as flood water. With enough storage reservoirs on the tributaries of the Mississippi, presumably the great river can be kept in check precisely as the Miami is kept in check.

Such a system would absorb vast amounts of capital and require continuous effort through many years, perhaps half a century; but in its major outlines it presents few if any problems beyond the competence of modern engineers. * * *

During this long prospective development, the levee system would have to be maintained, but gradually its function would change from first-line to second-line defense. More and more the impounding reservoirs would take up the load, leaving the levees as part of the margin of safety between the securities of life and raging waters.

"The Review of Reviews" for June has this to say of reservoirs:

The removal of forests and the drainage of farmlands, of towns and cities, and of improved highways, swell creeks and small streams and bring water to the main channels much more rapidly than in former times. All this serves to put a strain upon the protective dikes of the lower Mississippi, and now necessitates engineering works of a new and elaborate character for which the Federal Government ought to assume responsibility. That existing dikes or levees ought henceforth to be maintained and strengthened is evidently true. But it is also true that there might be a large number of reservoirs created in the headwater districts of numerous tributary rivers. The impounding of flood waters by this system would, to a certain extent, help to protect the lower alluvial lands against inundation. Also, it would help to maintain flow for navigation purposes in the low-water months of the year. Furthermore, the release of water from these impounding reservoirs would provide a large aggregate amount of hydroelectric power, and this would help to pay for the necessary engineering works.

Mr. Freeman, in the article already quoted, objects to reservoirs on the headwaters, because, he says, the great floods do not originate on the headwaters, and because possible reservoir sites are insufficient. Though the Hoover-Jadwin report advocating a continuation of the "levees-only" system condemned the reservoir plan, saying, "The construction of reservoirs around headwaters are not solutions, as they would cover lands virtually equal to the lands subject to overflow," Jadwin gave authority to the reservoir board in Washington to draw up a report on the reservoir system, to be ready by September 1.

"A thoroughgoing engineering report covering the use of reservoirs as a means of flood control on the Mississippi River and its tributaries is to be pushed to its conclusion as rapidly as possible and will be available by September 1 at the latest, Colonel Kelley announced today at the close of a two-day session of the reservoir board, of which he is chairman," said Paul Wooton, Washington correspondent of the "Times-Picayune," in a dispatch from Washington June 16.

"A detailed plan which will be followed in the development of this report has been agreed upon. Despite the magnitude of the task, Colonel Kelley is certain that the control facts will be available on September 1, thereby reducing the reservoir question to one of exact information rather than one of personal opinion. To accomplish this it will be necessary to divide the work among a large number of engineers. Authority to do this has been given by General Jadwin, chief of engineers."

Spillways, reduced to their simplest terms, would provide safety-valves for the flood waters. The whole plain close to the river served as a safety-valve for floods before human beings took the river and tried to bottle it up. Since the river has been loudly refusing to be bottled up, the advocates of spillways call them the nearest thing possible to a back-to-nature movement. They had been discussed as possible solutions of the flood problem before 1927 by the Mississippi River Commission, and a conference on the value of the spillway system was held in New Orleans shortly before the 1927 flood. A series of spillways would provide that the water at times of high level would be turned off into certain designated marshy areas, making temporary artificial lakes and relieving the pressure on the levees.

F. H. Newell, in the "Review of Reviews" article already referred to, advocates spillways.

Every engineer when he builds an earth dam makes elaborate provision for a spillway so placed that the floods cannot rise to the top of the dam and flow over it. A dike or levee is merely a long, low earth dam. If overtopped, the waters quickly cut it out. Recognizing this condition, many engineers now contend that instead of trying to build these hundreds of miles of levee high enough to be safe from overtopping, there should be constructed at suitable intervals long spillways at flood heights so that when the flood begins to threaten the levee the excess water creeping up over these spillways may flow back into the basins provided by nature. This means that occupation of these basins for farms and towns should be discouraged or reduced to a minimum and the land devoted largely to the production of trees. It does not mean necessarily a wholesale destruction of improvements already made, but rather a gradual readjustment by which the less valuable lands may be so handled as to be least injured by these occasional extreme flood flows.

Note in this connection that the river has done this very thing during each successive flood. It has found the weakest point in the levees, has cut crevasses, and has spread out, thus lowering the flood crest and reducing the danger to the other levees. The difference is that these points where the river overflows should be selected by experts, far in advance, and with a view to minimum damage, and with provision made for the safety of whole communities. Here, however, is the rub. Each local politician naturally urges that the water be dumped not upon the lands of his constituents, but somewhere else.

Mr. Freeman, on the other hand, outlines the objections to this means of control ("Outlook," June 8) :

The chief objections to permanent controlled spillway sluices at this point [below New Orleans] are possible injury to navigation channels that may be caused by diminished power for the scour and transportation of sediment in the main channel, and the uncertainty of maintaining with safety the outflow channel from the spillway. There are better possibilities for a spillway here at Caernarvon or at Poydras than farther upstream, due to the small value of land flooded by the breach, but it is an open question if it is not better to rely on the possibility of an artificial temporary breach, like the present, in rare emergencies—perhaps once in twenty-five years—rather than incur the vast expense of permanent sills, sluices, and safe discharge channels.

Later, however, he adds:

There are possibilities for an emergency spillway opening into the Atchafalaya that are well worthy of thorough investigation, because of the much shorter, straighter channel thence to the Gulf, and its position upstream from New Orleans and Baton Rouge.

In the same article Mr. Freeman advises the building of safety mounds all through the bottom-lands, rising four feet above flood level, which can be used as places of refuge as the Indian burial mounds were used in the 1927 flood.

Reforestation is usually brought forward as an accessory system of control. Says George D. Pratt, president of the American Forestry Association, according to an Associated Press dispatch from Washington May 10:

No well-informed person will pretend that the Mississippi River can be controlled by reforestation alone, but it is one of many measures of possible relief which must be developed to its maximum of possibilities. The extent of these possibilities is not now known and cannot be known until a systematic survey is made of the lands in the several States involved which are suitable for and in need of reforestation.

It has been objected that the land concerned is more valuable in farms than in forests; and Mr. Newell, in the article quoted, adds: "A checking-up of the time and place of the occurrence of the floods indicates that, so far as the lower river is concerned, the flood height would probably not have been lowered more than a fraction of an inch if all the headwaters had been kept in primeval forests." Others who think reforestation would be of little value remind us that the floods of 1844 and 1858—probably the most disastrous floods that occurred before that of 1882—came before the forests had been cut away.

But "The New Republic" for May 18 urges reforestation:

Along the western slopes of the Appalachians, where the Ohio and its tributaries rise, there were extensive forests. In several ways these served to retard the creation of torrents of water. The air above a forest is cooler, producing frequent slight precipitation instead of an occasional deluge. The fall of the water is slackened by its striking the leaves and by the necessity for its forking through the spongy mass of dead vegetable matter which covers and interpenetrates the top layer of the soil. The roots hold the earth together and prevent its washing down into gullies which form a convenient channel for the flood current.

In the same issue this magazine quotes H. H. Bennett of the United States bureau of soils as saying: "Terraces and grass woodlots, forests, and other soil-binding crops will vastly improve the flood situation; not only will they slow up the run-off of water, but they will save the most valuable part of the soil, and will reduce the clogging of streams which cuts down their carrying capacity and adds to the flood danger."

The flood control conference called by the mayors of Chicago, St. Louis, and New Orleans, which met in Chicago the first three days of June, comprised representatives of the twenty-seven States of the Mississippi Valley. While the conference did nothing definite except call for aid for flood sufferers and demand a solution of the flood problem from the National Government, it brought together the leaders of the valley States, gave them an expert analysis of the problem, and placed before the President resolutions from the Mississippi Valley as a unit.

Past dealings of men with the Mississippi were cordially condemned. "The trouble is that we are not directing our engineering and mechanical ability to human welfare," declared Senator Shipstead, of Minnesota, in an address delivered June 3. "Until now we have not really tried to control the Mississippi, and the present flood is a symbol of economic error. Looking at such a flood in any other country, we would say that the country is ill-governed, but here we ourselves are the government."

"The present disaster might not have happened if the Mississippi River Commission had not insisted upon levees only," said Gifford Pinchot the same day. Mr. Pinchot characterized the "levees-only" policy as the "most colossal blunder in civilized history."

"The need for a revision of the Government's project," said General Jadwin, "rests primarily on the following propositions: That this flood has shown that protection must be furnished for greater floods than existing works were expected to meet, even had they been completed; that levees necessary for the protection of the endangered area, not now under Government supervision, must be reduced; that the laws should be so modified that the Government shall have authority to locate the works where sound engineering dictates they be built, whether this involves the construction of larger levees, or spillways and reservoirs, or a combination of all these."

The conference unanimously adopted resolutions characterizing the flood control problem as one that should claim the attention of the National Government, and demanding that Congress take immediate steps toward a satisfactory solution of the problem.

The text of the resolution follows:

Whereas, The time is here for the Federal Government to attack the flood problem in a broad and comprehensive way because of the present Mississippi Valley disaster, the greatest of its kind in the nation's peace-time history, resulting in an incalculable amount of damage to life and property; and

Whereas, The need for a comprehensive plan for national flood control is made apparent by this disaster, and there are in general three proposals for flood relief set up by competent authorities, viz.: Levees, spillways, or by-pass outlets and storage reservoirs, all of which should be considered; and

Whereas, It is contended that this problem cannot be adequately met by the application of any single remedy, and that levees, spillways, and reservoirs should be used in combination where practical, together with such additional remedies as may from time to time be developed; and

Whereas, Floods in the Mississippi basin have not only brought disaster to those immediately concerned, but have resulted in economic loss to the whole nation, and the people of this country now demand that effective and permanent remedies be applied, and they will willingly approve the expenditure of the public moneys necessary to this end; therefore, be it

Resolved, That the flood control conference, assembled at Chicago, does hereby declare that the control of the flood waters of the Mississippi River and its tributaries is a national problem, and that the sole responsibility therefore should be assumed by the National Government; and

Resolved further, That we urge immediate and effective relief to be extended to all present sufferers, that the measures which may be commended by existing Federal agencies for relief to the lower valley, so as to protect it against a recurrence of the present disaster, be carried out promptly, and that the necessary appropriations therefor be made; and

Resolved further, That without delaying the carrying into execution of such necessary measures as may be recommended by existing government agencies, the President be urged to call a conference to draw up a comprehensive plan for navigation and permanent flood control, said conference to be composed of army engineers, civil engineers, conservationists, geologists, financiers, agriculturists, and other experts representing the various interests of our country; and

Resolved further, That the conference petition the President and the Congress energetically to undertake and carry to a speedy conclusion comprehensive and effective measures for permanent flood control of the Mississippi River and all its tributaries.

The problem of flood control is so tremendous that one is almost tempted to shrug one's shoulders, like the Cajans under the levee, and voice the philosophic "It's the way of the river." For two hundred years we have been trying to govern this lazy, giant Mississippi, and for two hundred years we have had but mediocre success. It is a gorgeous river—a mile wide, swirling slowly down to New Orleans, with palms sticking spiky fingers into the current and hyacinths damming the bayous. Its current is only about five miles an hour. To one who watches the river in its indolent seasons it seems impossible that this is the lustful enemy that men have fought, whipped to frenzy by a sense of their own impotence.

But this is the Mississippi, giver of the valley's wealth and the valley's desolation, strong, slow, deceptive. Whether or not we shall learn to govern the river remains to be found out. But though it can be cajoled, it cannot be forced, and whatever is done must be done according to its own way, giving it the only thing it really wants—a royal road to the Gulf.

II—THE WORK OF THE AMERICAN RED CROSS IN THE 1927 FLOOD

WHEN it became apparent that the Mississippi flood would assume such tremendous proportions, the American Red Cross and government departments began preparations commensurate with the emergency. On April 22, President Coolidge, who is also president of the Red Cross, appointed a special Red Cross committee composed of five cabinet members: Secretary of Commerce Herbert Hoover, Secretary of the Treasury Andrew W. Mellon, Secretary of War Dwight F. Davis, Secretary of the Navy Curtis D. Wilbur, and Secretary of Agriculture William M. Jardine.

Secretary of Commerce Hoover, as chairman of this special committee and also as a member of the central committee of the American Red Cross, assumed the direction of relief work. This special Red Cross committee made available to the organization the entire resources of the government departments and played a tremendously important part in coping with the disaster.

The 3,200 chapters of the American Red Cross were instructed to begin the collection of a $5,000,000 relief fund, and later, when it became certain that this would be an inadequate sum, another $5,000,000 was requested. The fund on August 13, 1927, totaled $16,852,724.36.

Secretary Hoover and James L. Fieser, vice-chairman of the American Red Cross, proceeded at once to the flood area and throughout the critical stage of the disaster personally supervised the relief work. They continued this personal supervision even after the emergency period was over and the reconstruction work had begun, making periodic visits to the area and keeping in close touch with the situation.

The latter part of April and throughout the month of May, the Red Cross was facing three major problems. Of first importance was the rescue of those who had sought refuge from the flood waters on levees, housetops, and other high places, and removing them to concentration centers or other places of safety. Thousands of persons were transported by the rescue fleet, which consisted of more than 900 power-boats and literally thousands of small auxiliary craft. The second problem was that of sheltering, feeding, clothing, and protecting the health of the refugees in the 138 camps established by the Red Cross in unflooded territory in and adjacent to the flood area. At the same time adequate preparations had to be made for impending levee breaks farther south as the crest moved toward the Gulf.

From the relief headquarters at Memphis, and later at New Orleans when the crest had moved into Louisiana, these three stages of relief were directed. Besides the 330,000 persons who were cared for in camps, the Red Cross aided 277,000 others during this emergency work, whose homes were flooded but who were quartered in places other than refugee camps, such as the second stories of their homes, churches, halls, and other buildings. In all, 607,000 persons were under the care of the Red Cross during the first stages of the relief work.

During this emergency period the relief organization, in coöperation with the state departments of health of the seven affected States and the United States Public Health Service, instituted a health program for the prevention of disease on a scale which possibly surpasses anything that has been attempted in this country during peace times. Approximately 300,000 persons were inoculated against typhoid fever and 120,000 were vaccinated for smallpox. More than 8,335,989 grains of quinine were used as a preventive against malaria. Public health experts were stationed at strategic points over the entire area to see that every possible precaution was taken to safeguard the health of the sufferers. A total of 329 Red Cross nurses were used in this work in addition to other nurses working directly under the State boards of health.

This health work of the Red Cross, of course, was supplementary to that done by the State boards of health, and the resources of the Red Cross were applied mainly where State and local health resources were inadequate to meet the situation. Throughout the entire flood area there was no serious epidemic of disease; which, under the circumstances, was considered a decided victory for the agencies engaging in this preventive work. Fourteen States outside the flood area lent the Red Cross personnel and donated large quantities of supplies.

As the waters receded, first in Illinois, Missouri, and Kentucky, and then discouragingly slow in Arkansas, Tennessee, Mississippi, and Louisiana, the relief organization faced reconstruction and other post-disaster problems commensurate with, if not exceeding, those of the emergency period. An area of thousands of square miles had been under water. Crops had been destroyed over an agricultural acreage equal roughly to that of the New England States, if Vermont is omitted. Thousands of homes had been destroyed and other thousands damaged. Barns, farm implements, live-stock, and other equipment were gone. As the refugees returned to their destroyed or mud-coated homes, they had to be given substantial help of a permanent nature in order to become again self-supporting. Food was supplied them until they could take care of their own needs. They were given live-stock as well as feed for the animals. They were provided with household furnishings, including clothing, bed furnishing, stoves, kitchen utensils, and other essential articles. Their homes were repaired. Seed was furnished for replanting acreage laid waste by the flood. With the aid and advice of experts detailed to the Red Cross by the department of agriculture, farmers were given every possible assistance in planting wisely, especially in places where the water remained on the ground until it was too late in the season to plant the customary crops for the section.

As in all Red Cross disaster relief operations, this reconstruction aid was based on the actual needs of the families; the family in each instance bore as much of the burden as it was financially able to bear through the use of normal credit and other channels.

At the same time the disease-prevention program was prosecuted with unrelenting vigor. Large quantities of lime were distributed to cope with sanitary problems precipitated by the presence on the land of dead animals, which in one State alone numbered more than 25,000 head of live-stock. Emergency health units were established by the Red Cross and maintained for from thirty to sixty days in localities whose normal organization was inadequate to deal with the situation. Through these units the immunization and vaccination campaign was continued, and a campaign of education was carried on to enlist the coöperation of all residents in health and sanitary measures. Doctors, public health and sanitary experts, and Red Cross and other nurses gave the returning flood sufferers every possible protection until conditions approximating the normal were restored.

At the time this was written, the pressure of work had made it impossible for the Red Cross to make any careful compilations for statistical purposes. Also, the work was still in progress, and figures on relief operations in this book cannot be considered final. On July 27 the organization was still operating four refugee camps, in which it was caring for 2,000 persons whose homes were still inundated. The emergency work had been completed in all States except Louisiana, but there the water still covered a large section of the land. Over the entire area, approximately 170,000 agricultural acres were still flooded.

Although the rehabilitation program was by no means completed at that time, 80,000 families, or approximately 400,000 individuals, had been given reconstruction aid. Figures available at that time showed that more than 200,000 head of live-stock had been fed by the relief organization, many of which were rescued from levees, where they sought safety as the water flooded the land.

Adding materially to the problems of relief were the recurring floods in many sections. Rivers which had overflowed their banks, or whose waters had broken through the levees in April and May, again flooded the land later on in the season, washing away replanted crops, driving returning refugees once more into concentration camps, and materially slowing up the process of reconstruction.

BIBLIOGRAPHY FOR "FATHER MISSISSIPPI"

Publications of the Louisiana Historical Society.

Publications of the Mississippi Historical Society.

Publications of the Kentucky Historical Society.

"The Navigator," by Cramer and Spear, Pittsburgh, 1818.

James's Traveler's Companion, by S. L. Massey, Cincinnati, 1851.

"New Orleans: the Place and the People," by Grace King.

"Creole Families of New Orleans," by Grace King.

"De Soto in the Land of Florida," by Grace King.

"Life on the Mississippi," by Mark Twain.

"The Valley of the Mississippi," by J. W. Monette.

"Floods on the Mississippi," by J. W. Monette.

"Mississippi, the Heart of the South," by Dunbar Rowland.

"Exploration of the Red River of Louisiana in 1852," by Randolph Marcy.

"Standard History of New Orleans," by Henry Rightor.

"Lloyd's Steamboat Directory and Disasters on Western Waters."

"Social Life in Old New Orleans," by Eliza Ripley.

"Timothy Flint, 1780-1840," by Kirkpatrick.

"Flint's Geography."

"Historical Recollections of Louisiana," by B. F. French.

"Old Times on the Upper Mississippi," by Merrick.

"Mississippi Steamboatin'," by Herbert and Edward Quick.

"Beyond the Mississippi," by Albert D. Richardson.

"Mississippi Valley Beginnings," by Henry E. Chambers.

"The Mississippi and Its Wonderful Valley," by Julius Chambers.

"Down the Great River," by Willard Glazier.

Swain's "Red River Directory."

James's "River Guide for 1860."

"Gambling Unmasked," by J. H. Green.

"Curbing the Mississippi," an article by Walter Parker in "The Nation."

Scrapbooks compiled by James T. Flint of Alexandria, Louisiana.

Scrapbooks compiled by Mrs. Cammie Garrett Henry of Melrose, Louisiana.

The files of "The New Orleans Item-Tribune," "The New Orleans Daily States," and "The New Orleans Times-Picayune."

The files of "The Baton Rouge State-Times."

"The Influence of the Mississippi River upon the Early Settlement of Its Valley," an article by Richard Brownrigg Haughton in the publications of the Mississippi Historical Society for 1901.

Numerous other books, magazines, and newspapers cited in the text.

INDEX

A

Acadians,
  driven out by flood, 331
  in St. Bernard Parish, Louisiana, 327
  refugees, 333
  their country flooded, 357
Allouez, Father,
  Jesuit, 69, 83
America,
  steamboat, 34
American Red Cross,
  report of all activities 1927 flood, 411
  reports for May 10, 1927, 345
  vaccinates refugees, 316
animals,
  deer crowd on levee, 298
  driven out by flood, 297
  prehistoric, 64
"Annie Christmas,"
  river tramp, 138
Arkansas River,
  discovery of mouth, 83
Associated Press,
  describes rescue work, 347
  describes Stops Landing crevasse, 296
  pictures distress in Greenville, Mississippi, 318
  reports approach of flood toward New Orleans, 295
  reports exodus from Poydras, 325
  reports reconstruction 1927 flood, 377

B

Baton Rouge,
  establishment of refugee camps, 348
Baton Rouge State-Times,
  gives report April floods, 294
Bayou des Glaises,
  completely inundated, 359
  description of country, 358
  levee breaks, 341
Bayou Goula,
  founded, 126
Bayou Sara, 40
Bayou St. John, 104
Belle Key,
  sets record, 217
Beyer, Professor George E., 63
blue laws,
  early, 129
Boone, Daniel, 134
Bostona,
  sets record, 217

C

Caernarvon, Louisiana,
  cost of artificial crevasse, 370
  levee is dynamited, 335
  plans for cutting levee, 330
Cahokia,
  founded, 128
Canon, Capt. John W.,
  commands *Robert E. Lee*, 219
Cape Girardeau,
  founded, 129
  subject to overflow, 253

419

Frost, Meigs O.,
reports blasting of levee, 335
Fulton, Robert,
experiments in steam navigation, 211

G

gamblers,
some methods of, 225
gambling houses,
New Orleans, description of,
226
Garcillasso, 69
"Gentleman of Elvas," 76
German settlers in Louisiana,
111
Green, J. H.,
steamboat gambler, 224
Greenville Democratic-Times,
issued in flooded city, 349
Greenville, Mississippi,
distress reported by Associated
Press, 318
life in a flooded city, 319
prepares for flood, 284
refugee camp established, 296
Grey Eagle,
finest steamboat, 222

H

Hart, Albert Bushnell,
corrects error about Mississippi, 256
Helena, Arkansas,
disaster in, 320
prepares for flood, 284
Helen MacGregor,
explosion of, 228
Hennepin, Father Louis, 85
diary of, 92
Hoover, Herbert,
arrives New Orleans, 330
broadcasts appeal from Memphis, April 30, 345
discusses reconstruction, 372

Hoover, Herbert, *continued*
estimates flood, 385
gives final figures on 1927
disaster, 383
tells plight of refugees, 374
Hulls, Jonathan,
inventor of steam vessel, 210
Humphreys and Abbott's Physics
and Hydraulics of the
Mississippi cited, 256

I

Iberville, founder of New
Orleans, 102
Illinois massacre, 121
Independent,
editorial in, on reservoirs, 402
India Company, 110
Indian dances,
description of, 169
Indian mounds, 61
1927 flood, 66
places of refuge, 298
refugees on, 65
refugees taken from 1927, 346
Indians,
Algonquin, 68
ancient worship of, 65
visit French King, 114
Istrouma,
early name for Baton Rouge,
125

J

Jackson, General Andrew, 174
Jadwin, Major-General Edgar,
discusses reservoirs, 403
in New Orleans, 328
Jesuit relations, 69
jetties,
constructed by Capt. Eads,
1879, 248
Joliet, 83
Julian Poydras,
steamboat, 34

Mississippi, *continued*
discovery of, 71
in dispute among nations,
132
U. S. gains jurisdiction of,
132
"Mississippi Bubble," 102
Mississippi River,
area of overflow, 253
causes of overflow, 255
delta, 253
depth of, 268
drainage area of, 253
drainage basins, 254
errors concerning, 255
flat boat trip in 1810, 160
increase in flood levels, 255
mileage, 254
rainfall in valley, 254
squabbles over, 140
subject to overflow, 253
Mississippi River Commission,
Col. C. McD. Townsend states
his case, 267
criticized by Lyman E. Cooley
1916, 275
criticized by Owen P. White
in Collier's Weekly, 274
discussed by Gifford Pinchot,
408
divided on remedy against
floods, 266
formed 1879, 266
members of, 275
policy criticized by engineer,
308
policy outlined, 267
Mississippi Valley,
actual drainage area, 383
early commerce, 135
settlement of, 135
Monget, John W.,
levee engineer predicts flood,
342
Moscoso, Luis de, 80
murder trial,
court procedure in 1780,
142

Murphree, Dennis, Governor of
Mississippi,
appeals for boats, 319
appeals to President for
troops, 315
asks flood aid, 287

N

Natchez, Mississippi,
founded, 106
life in refugee camp, 351
refugee camp, 343
Natchez,
steamboat, 34
Natchez Trace, 65
Natchez-Under-the-Hill,
caves into river, 226
gambling houses, 226
Natchipoches,
founded, 103
navigation,
difficulties of, 136
difficulties of, 139
difficulties of, 177
difficulties of upstream, 128
variety of craft on river, 137
negroes,
babies born on levee, 302
funeral routed by flood, 390
give away food, 350
in refugee camps, 348
sing spirituals on levee, 310
tragic-comic episode in flood,
306
tragic figures in flood, 301
New Madrid, Missouri,
earthquake of, 212
New Orleans,
arrives in Natchez, 1811, 212
arrives in New Orleans, 1811,
212
description of, 198
goes down Mississippi,1811,211
New Orleans,
commercial importance of, 240
description of early city, 107
destruction by hurricane, 112

reservoirs,
  as a method of flood control,
    387
  suggested by the Independent,
    402
Review of Reviews,
  suggests reservoirs, 403
Rhine,
  compared to Mississippi, 268
Rio del Spiritu Sancto,
  early name of Mississippi, 68
Rio Grande,
  early name of Mississippi, 68
Ripley, Eliza,
  gives description of steamboat
    in 1840, 222
River,
  prehistoric, 62
Robert E. Lee,
  sets record, 216
Robert Mitchell,
  record trip to Cincinnati, 216
Rock-in-Cave,
  rendezvous of criminals, 224
Roosevelt, Nicholas, J., 211

S

showboat, 21
Simpson, O. H., Governor of
    Louisiana,
  asks federal permission to
    dynamite levee, 328
  inspects flooded country, 371
slaves,
  introduction of, 106
  methods of buying and prices,
    111
songs,
  Roustabout, 39
Shelly,
  sets record, 216
spillways,
  as flood solution, 404
  objections to, 405
St. ernard Parish, Louisiana,
  description of trappers, 326
  evacuation begins, 330

Ste. Genevieve, Missouri,
  founded, 128
St. Louis,
  city of, 128
  fur-reproducing post, 129
steamboat,
  explosion of boiler, 203
  first Mississippi, 210
  passenger and freight rates in
    1817, 201
  romance of, 209
  rules for passengers' behavior
    in 1817, 201
  wages paid in 1817, 200
steamboat disasters, 228
steamboating,
  reaches zenith, 213
steamboat racing, 215
  dangers of, 217
  famous race between the
    Natchez and *Robt. E.
    Lee,* 218
  famous wagers, 221
  New Orleans to Natchez, 218
  records of, 216
steamboats,
  cost of construction, 214
  descriptions of early, 197
steamboat travel,
  difficulties of, 222
  dining on board, 223
sugar bowl,
  sugar lands flooded, 341
Sultana,
  sets record, 217
  superstitions, 26

T

Tecumseh,
  sets record, 217
Thompson Dean,
  makes record, 216
Times-Picayune, New Orleans,
  issues flood warning, 287
  reports Clarendon, Arkansas,
    flood, 296
  reports federal appeal, 328